THINKING THE U

RICHARD COCKETT teaches his
Bedford New College, University
author of the much-acclaimed *Tw*
Appeasement and the Manipulation of the Press (1989; 'both scholarly and acerbic' – CHRISTOPHER HILL, *Observer*).

from the reviews:

'Absorbing, lively and stimulating . . . this excellent book will further enhance Richard Cockett's growing reputation for original scholarship already firmly established by his highly acclaimed studies of both press promotion of 1930s appeasement and David Astor's *Observer*. In *Thinking the Unthinkable* he traces the origin, painfully slow development, political triumph and ultimate decline of free-market classical liberal think-tanks over a fifty-year period. Cockett argues that an intellectual counter-revolution to collectivist and Keynesian notions paved the way for Thatcherism – and free-market political economy elsewhere in the world – by the sheer power of ideas that captured the intellectual high ground . . . This book traces the history of an idea, not the history of a political party. The enterprise is fascinating, not least in its originality. But it is the author's scholarly methodology that makes this a brilliant book. Indeed it is a pleasure to read . . . Occasional flashes of dry humour are impishly inserted to lighten the text. Cockett's research is painstaking and meticulous. The command of the archival sources is awesome; the bibliography is extensive but not indiscriminate; primary documentation illuminates every chapter; the appendices are a mini-archive of historical gold nuggets; and scholarly objectivity is scrupulously observed despite the ideologically controversial subject matter.'

MARTIN HOLMES, *Times Higher Educational Supplement*

'A sparkling and meticulously researched account of the manner in which the free-market creed came to dominate British politics. The book tingles with intellectual enjoyment.'

MAURICE WOODS, *Eastern Daily Press*

'An exciting story because it deals, at one level, with the most important intellectual conflict of the twentieth century – between the forces for centralized planning and socialist government controls, against the old liberal tradition of individual freedom, unfettered markets and minimum government interference.'

MAX WILKINSON, *Financial Times*

'Richard Cockett does sort out which set of initials was which, and this is useful. It is mildly thrilling to read about men like Hayek and Sherman and Joseph as noble champions. It's a bit like seeing *Star Trek* with the Klingons as the good guys.'

TIM HAIGH, *New Statesman & Society*

'Cockett is good on the institutions behind economic liberalism's success.' DAVID WILLETTS, *Times Literary Supplement*

'Richard Cockett recounts this tangled tale well ... His book has the great merit of striking a balance between the achievements and limitations of the think-tanks.'

ANTHONY HARTLEY, *Tablet*

by the same author

Twilight of Truth: Chamberlain, Appeasement and the Manipulation of the Press

My Dear Max: The Letters of Lord Beaverbrook to Brendan Bracken, 1928–1958 (ed.)

David Astor and the Observer

THINKING THE UNTHINKABLE

*

Think-Tanks and the Economic Counter-Revolution 1931–1983

RICHARD COCKETT

HarperCollins*Publishers*

Fontana Press
An Imprint of HarperCollins*Publishers*
77–85 Fulham Palace Road,
Hammersmith, London W6 8JB

Published, with revisions, by Fontana Press 1995
1 3 5 7 9 8 6 4 2

First published in Great Britain by
HarperCollins*Publishers* 1994

ISBN 0 00 637586 3

Set in Linotron Ehrhardt

Printed in Great Britain by
HarperCollinsManufacturing Glasgow

for my parents

CONTENTS

ILLUSTRATIONS

ACKNOWLEDGEMENTS

My primary debt is to the British Academy, as the research and writing of this book was made possible by a British Academy Research Fellowship at Royal Holloway and Bedford New College from 1989 to 1992. I have benefited greatly from the support over the last few years of the History Department at Royal Holloway, to say nothing of the financial munificence of the Research Committee of the department. Professor Francis Robinson has always been a generous sponsor of my academic career, and I am also grateful to the department for the opportunity of discussing some of the ideas in this book in the departmental seminar in 1991. My other institutional debt is to the Institute of Contemporary British History which has always cultivated a convivial atmosphere in which to discuss and learn about modern British history – most of which is due to the work of Drs Brian Brivati, Harriet Jones and Peter Catterall.

During the course of the research for this book I enjoyed the hospitality and guidance of several people in Britain and America. My primary debt is to Linda Whetstone, the daughter of Sir Antony Fisher, and her family, who gave me first access to the archive of the Institute of Economic Affairs (IEA) at their home and then put up with me for several weeks while I went through it. Dominic Ziegler was a patient and entertaining host in Washington, as was Sarah Teale, as ever, in New York. My thanks also to Lords Coleraine and Clitheroe for letting me see the papers of their respective fathers in the comfort of their own homes. I owe a special debt of gratitude to Dr Laurence and Mrs Eska Hayek for letting me see private papers and family photographs, and to John Raybould, Special Projects Consultant, for picture and historical documents research. My thanks also to Milton Friedman, Charles Smedley, Simon Webley, Lionel Bloch, Norman Strauss and Sir Leonard Neal for putting their private papers at my disposal, usually in their own homes. Nigel Morgan was equally helpful in giving me the remaining papers of the Centre for Policy Studies.

I owe several important intellectual debts, but first and foremost to Dr Harriet Jones and John Barnes who took an interest in this book at an early stage and who both gave generously of their time and knowledge about the history of the Conservative Party on several occasions; Harriet Jones' recent Ph.D. thesis on 'The Conservative Party and the Welfare State, 1942–1955' was of particular value to my work. I would also like to thank Peter Clarke for an important conversation in Cambridge on the dispute between the

Keynesians and Hayek during the 1930s which helped to clarify my thinking on the subject. John Barnes together with John Blundell of the IEA read the manuscript with their customary attention to detail and they helped me to avoid many errors of fact and interpretation; although, needless to say, the opinions and conclusions contained in this book remain mine entirely. Professor Geoffrey Alderman also commented on the manuscript, and my thanks are due to Linda Whetstone, Arthur Seldon, Lord Harris and Sir Alfred Sherman for their comments on the chapters relating to their parts in the story of the revival of economic liberalism. Arthur Seldon, in particular, was always helpful, sceptical and iconoclastic, as all good think-tankers should be. I also owe an important debt to Ken Smith, the librarian at the IEA, whose comprehensive knowledge of the literature of economic liberalism saved me a great deal of time. I remain grateful to Dr John Campbell who showed me an early draft of his excellent biography of Edward Heath, and to Professor Max Hartwell, who let me use the draft of his own history of the Mont Pèlerin Society and who gave me access to several vital documents in his possession. My thanks also to Professor John Turner for his continuing support. I don't think that my two intellectual mentors, Peter Hennessy and David Astor, would necessarily approve of economic liberalism, but I hope that at least they could appreciate the spirit in which I have set about the subject.

The author would like to express his gratitude to the following who have very kindly given their permission for the use of copyright materials: Lord Howe of Aberavon for his permission to quote from his letters to Arthur Seldon; Norman Strauss for his memos from the Downing Street Policy Unit and 'Stepping Stones'; Routledge and Kegan Paul for their archive and *The Road to Serfdom*; Professor Karl Popper for his letters to Hayek and Routledge; John Blundell for the IEA archive; Dr Carl John for the archives of the Mont Pèlerin Society; Lord Joseph for his letters to the IEA; Sir Alfred Sherman for his archive at Royal Holloway College; Sir Samuel Brittan for his letter to Arthur Seldon; and Arthur Seldon and Lord Harris for their correspondence.

Lastly, and most importantly, I must record my debt to a brace of Warners – to Rachel, for inadvertently giving me the idea for this book during a walk across a field in Norfolk in 1987, and to Jonathan who, by pure coincidence, suggested in 1989 that HarperCollins publish a book on think-tanks. It is a shame that Jonathan could not see this book through to the end, but I have been lucky in having Philip Gwyn Jones as my editor instead. Karmani Ward has surpassed herself in her ability to read my spidery handwriting and my agent, Araminta Whitley, has always stood by when my spirits have flagged. I just hope I recover in time for the next book.

RICHARD COCKETT
September 1993, London

Introduction

L'INTERNATIONALE – REVISED VERSION

Arise, ye starveling Statisticians!
Arise, ye Bureaucratic Clerks!
Arise, Economists, Technicians,
And Synthesists of Ford and Marx!
Arise, all ye Government Inspectors,
Ye Co-Ordinators every man,
Trade Union Leaders and Directors,
For see, the World is yours to Plan!

World-Planners, come rally;
The last Fight let us face!
L'Internationalé
Controls the Human Race!

At last Imperfect Competition
Shall yield to Super-State Cartels,
Research, Collation, and Prevision
By hand-picked Academic Swells.
United Nations' Rehabilitation
And Price-Wage Stabilizing Pegs,
Combined with Federalization,
Will set Old Europe on its legs!

Then, Experts, come rally;
The last Graph let us trace!
(etc.)

We'll brave the Free-Consumers' rancour,
And all men's purchases arrange
Through Unitas or Keynesitas (or Bancor)
And a Regulated World-Exchange.
Propensity to Maximum Consumption
Has been latent for a long time past
And with *our* Administrative Gumption
We'll make this Round Globe rich at last!

Then, Expansionists, come rally,
The last loan let us place!
(etc.)

Our scheduled Schemes of Reconstruction,
Our Quotas, Questionnaires, and Doles,
Shall tap Hot Springs of Wealth Production

Under Integrated World-Controls.
As in War we've evolved and fully tried rules
For mastering Monopolies and Mobs,
With our Logarithmic Charts and Slide-rules
We now can all get Cosmic jobs!

Then, Bureaucrats, come rally;
The last Chit let us chase!
L'Internationalé
Controls the Human Race!

by 'F. J. O.', collected by F.A. Hayek
from an unspecified newspaper, 10 March 1944

This book is a study of the revival of the doctrine of 'economic liberalism' in British intellectual life, and eventually political life, from 1931 to 1983. In the early 1930s, the ideas of economic liberalism and free-market economics were at their lowest ebb, superseded by the contemporary enthusiasms for various forms of collectivism – planning, protectionism and Keynesianism, for instance – and this book traces the story of a conscious revival of the ideas of economic liberalism from that low ebb to the point in the mid-1980s when economic liberalism had become not only the governing orthodoxy in Britain – accepted by all the mainstream political parties – but also the idea that helped precipitate the downfall of the Communist regimes in the Soviet Union and Eastern Europe in 1989–90 and elsewhere subsequently.

The revival of economic liberalism in Britain in the 1980s is often characterized as 'Thatcherism', for the policies of Mrs Thatcher's governments, as this book will show, were largely designed and often implemented by people who would have called themselves 'economic liberals'. However, it is equally true that there was a lot more to 'Thatcherism' than merely economic liberalism. Mrs Thatcher was, after all, a Conservative Party politician and her politics have been perhaps best defined as those of 'the free economy and the strong State'.[1] As the political scientist Andrew Gamble and others have frequently pointed out, 'economic liberalism' formed an important part of 'Thatcherism', but was by no means the whole of Thatcherism, for Mrs Thatcher combined her politics of promoting free-market economics with a strong element of traditional Conservative nationalism and an emphasis on the need to maintain a strong defence to 'deter' enemies such as the Soviet Union. There is no doubt that much of her programme would not have endeared itself to nineteenth-century economic liberals such as Cobden and Bright – they were opposed to even moderate governmental expenditure on defence and the military, and would not countenance Britain's overseas commitments and involvement in wars. Mrs Thatcher's brand of Conservative nationalism, however, was something that she shared with all her Conservative predecessors from Disraeli onwards, as well as with her 'opponents' within her own Party. Mrs Thatcher and her Tory adversaries never wavered in their shared belief that Britain should have Trident nuclear submarines or go to war over remote South Atlantic islands – the kernel of their ideological differences lay, instead, in her distinctive approach to the economy, her 'economic liberalism'. It was thus the doctrine of 'economic liberalism', I would argue, that made 'Thatcherism' distinct and enabled the Thatcher governments to embark on what many regarded as a revolution in the 'political economy' of the country itself.

In a celebrated essay on the origins of the 'New Right', originally published in *Encounter*, the Cambridge historian Maurice Cowling has described the almost schizophrenic range of political, religious and philosophical beliefs held by the pioneers and leaders of the economic liberal counter-revolution in Britain which was:

> conducted by about fifty people (mainly graduates and mostly men) who have come from no one type of social, sexual or intellectual background and who include among their number a smattering of atheists and agnostics, a few converted, a few practising and a few lapsed Catholics, a handful of Jews, observing or otherwise, some Dissenters and Evangelicals, a fair number of converted Anglicans, and a contingent for whom religion is of little significance . . . Many of those who have supported market economics have been authoritarian about moral and social questions, many who supported Mr. Powell economically did not support him about Europe, Ireland, Immigration or the Soviet Union. Cold Warriors and Anti-Cold Warriors, Europeans and Anti-Europeans, Americans and Anti-Americans, and both the friends and the enemies of Israel, have been distributed fairly randomly. Some of the economists – Mr. Samuel Brittan, for example – have come to be unenthusiastic about Mrs. Thatcher, among whose most enthusiastic supporters

> are ex-Socialists some of whom assume that Society can be reformed by legislation.[2]

This book is the story of those fifty people. Many of them embodied that intellectual contradiction in the politics of both the 'left' and the 'right' that, for instance, Samuel Brittan has observed: 'the non-Muscovite left favours freedom in everything but economics . . . the right is sympathetic to freedom only in the economic sphere.'[3] But while it is true that the intellectuals, economists, journalists and politicians who made the Thatcherite revolution might have disagreed on many issues – from immigration to Britain's role in Europe – they *were* united on the issue of economic liberalism.

This study is therefore *not* concerned with offering a comprehensive view of 'Thatcherism', much less a full description of the political history of her governments. I am, rather, concerned to trace the antecedents of the unique and galvanizing idea behind 'Thatcherism', namely 'economic liberalism'. Furthermore, this is a study of an intellectual counter-revolution, tracing the development of an idea, forged in the 1930s during the debates about countering the influence of Keynesianism, and the eventual translation of that idea into a coherent body of specific policy proposals and initiatives which governments could deploy in power as part of a wider political programme. As this book will, I hope, make plain, the counter-revolution in British economic and political thinking since the Second World War was very much the result of the work of individuals. It was a conscious and, in the end, successful attempt to turn the tide of political and economic thinking in a particular direction. Much of this book is focused on the work of several 'think-tanks', the Institute of Economic Affairs, the Centre for Policy Studies and the Adam Smith Institute, as well as that of more obscure organisations such as the Society of Individualists, Aims of Industry, the National Association for Freedom and the Selsdon Group. It is thus a study of the extent to which ideas can influence the political process.

In 1968, the Fabians dubbed the revival of economic liberalism the 'rise of the New Right' in a description of the work of the Institute of Economic Affairs. This unintentional tribute was well deserved, as the think-tanks did indeed do much to articulate and publicize the application of 'economic liberalism' to economic affairs and this book is, perforce, principally a study of the work and influence of the free-market think-tanks, which did as much intellectually to convert a generation of 'opinion-formers' and politicians to a new set of ideas as the Fabians had done with a former generation at the turn of the century. Indeed, the manifest aim of the IEA, in particular, was to reverse the intellectual trend started by the Fabians over a half-century earlier, by employing many of their methods.

How should one define economic liberalism? Economic liberalism is derived from the concept of 'classical liberalism', the political economy which governed Victorian Britain and which found its most consistent political expression in the policies of Gladstone's Liberal Party. Historically, liberalism was a reaction against the mercantilist, feudal and aristocratic societies of the *ancien régime*, and stressed a commitment to individual liberty against the coercive powers of the State. Its intellectual roots may be traced to John Locke and Adam Smith, who first described a free-market economy in *The Wealth of Nations* of 1776. Classical liberalism based the freedom of the individual on the twin institutions of private property and the free market; freedom and liberty could only be guaranteed by the wide dispersion of economic powers that could alone be brought about by the working of the free-market economic system and the freedom of the individual to dispose of his or her private money and assets as he or she saw fit. As John Gray, the historian of liberalism, has written, 'private property is the embodiment of individual liberty in its most primeval form and market freedoms are indivisible components of the basic liberties of the person.'[4] F. A. Hayek, the most powerful modern exponent of classical liberalism, has written that

> The central concept of liberalism is that under the enforcement of universal rules of just conduct, protecting a recognizable private domain of individuals, a spontaneous order of human activities of much greater complexity will form itself than could ever be produced by deliberate arrangement, and that in consequence the coercive activities of government should be limited to the enforcement of such rules . . .

Hayek went on to distinguish such a society based on the political economy of economic liberalism from a 'collectivist' society, which establishes certain common goals or purposes that 'society', governed and guided by the State, should strive for:

> The conception of the common welfare or the public good of a free society can . . . never be defined as a sum of known particular results to be achieved, but only as an abstract order which as a whole is not oriented on any particular concrete ends but provides merely the best chance for any members selected at random successfully to use his knowledge for his purposes. Adopting a term of Professor Michael Oakeshott, we may call such a free society a nomocratic (law-governed) as distinguished from an unfree teleocratic (purpose-governed) social order.[5]

This was the essence of classical liberalism, as opposed to the ideology of 'collectivism' which eclipsed economic liberalism in Britain in the late-nineteenth century. That intellectual revolution was led by the Fabian Society, founded in 1884, the subject of Chapter One. The counter-revolution against Fabianism, which is the subject of this book, sought a return to the 'political economy' of classical liberalism or, in Mrs Thatcher's memorable phrase, a return to 'Victorian Values'. One can see the history of the last two centuries in terms of ideological cycles of liberalism vs collectivism; the first cycle comprising the triumph of liberalism over feudalism and mercantilism and lasting from the 1760s to the 1880s, a period divisible into two halves – one prior to the 1820s, during which the ideological war was fought, and one thereafter, when economic liberalism became the 'economic orthodoxy' of all governments. The second cycle began in the 1880s and ended in the mid-1970s, and can be divided into the period 1880 to the 1930s when the ideological battle against liberalism was fought and won, and the period of the 1940s to the 1970s when collectivism, premised on Fabianism and Keynesianism, was the ruling orthodoxy of all parties and governments. The third cycle began in the 1930s and is still in progress. The first part of this cycle, the subject of this book, was the period of the 1930s to the 1970s when the ideological battle for liberalism against collectivism was, again, fought and won; the second part of the cycle, the period of the late 1970s to the early 1990s, when the new political economy became the ruling orthodoxy of all parties and governments, is still extant. Indeed, one can also interpret this process in Hegelian terms as these cycles bear a close resemblance to the dialectic of thesis/antithesis/synthesis. As with the previous cycles, the economic liberal challenge to the prevailing collectivist orthodoxy came when that orthodoxy was most prevalent, in the 1940s. The subsequent thirty years or so saw the exposition of the antithesis against collectivism, and when Mrs Thatcher finally began to put the ideas of the antithesis into practice in the 1980s, her governments only achieved a limited success in implementing these ideas, thus achieving a compromise, or synthesis, between the older concepts of state control and collectivism and the newer ideas of economic liberalism. This synthesis, presided over in Britain by Messrs Major and Blair, is the new orthodoxy. Much as it would have been difficult to find any substantive differences in economic policy between two such notorious political opponents as Messrs Gladstone and Disraeli in the 1870s, or between R. A. Butler and Hugh Gaitskell in the 1950s, so it is hard to discern any such differences between Messrs Major and Blair in the 1990s. However, the challenges to this new orthodoxy will be considered briefly in the epilogue.

For those who eschew such historical determinism, or merely dislike Hegel, and prefer more down-to-earth descriptions, this last cycle, the intellectual revolution of the 1940s to the 1970s, has been neatly summarized by Karl Popper, who lived through a microcosm of this cycle in inter-war Vienna and has described his ideological journey in his autobiography, *Unended Quest*. He remained a Socialist – a collectivist – for 'several years ... and if there could be such a thing as socialism combined with individual liberty, I would be a socialist still. For nothing could be better than living a modest, simple, and free life in an egalitarian society. It took some time before I recognised this as no more than a beautiful dream; that freedom is more important than equality; that the attempt to realise equality endangers freedom; and that, if freedom is lost, there will not even be equality among the unfree.'[6]

Lastly, classical or economic liberalism is not to be confused with the British Liberal Party, now led by Paddy Ashdown MP. Although the Liberal Party of Gladstone might have embodied the ideas and values of classical liberalism, under the impetus of the ideas of 'New Liberalism' the Liberal Party moved in an avowedly collectivist direction – laying the foundations of the Welfare State from the early 1900s onwards. The post-First World War Liberal Party upheld little of the old economic liberal agenda, much to the chagrin of the remaining economic liberals in the Party, as will be seen in Chapters Four and Five. To avoid confusion, I have therefore referred to the Liberal Party and Liberal Politics with a capital 'L' throughout, whereas the idea of 'liberalism', or economic 'liberals', is printed with a small 'l' throughout. This is by no means intended to reflect the relative importance of the ideas of 'liberalism' and the Liberal Party in British political life, but rather merely to avoid confusion.

1
Keynes and the Crisis of Liberalism, 1931–1939

*

From the 26th to the 30th of August 1938, but one month before the Munich conference which seemed to bring the triumph of totalitarianism in Europe an important step closer, an obscure conference took place in Paris to discuss what its participants called the 'crisis of liberalism' in Europe. The conference was convened and organized by a French academic, Professor Louis Rougier, Professor of Philosophy at the University of Besançon, and held at the Institut International de Coopération Intellectuelle. The twenty-six who attended the Conference were all academics, with one notable exception, the American columnist Walter Lippmann. Indeed, the gathering was named in his honour 'Le Colloque Walter Lippmann' in an attempt by Rougier to unite the disputatious academics around the central importance of Lippmann's book *The Good Society*, published in 1937. For Rougier, Lippmann's book was, simply, 'la meilleure explication des maux de notre temps'.[1] 'Le Colloque Walter Lippmann' was, naturally, dominated by Frenchmen; their number included the prominent political philosopher Raymond Aron, and the economist Jacques Rueff. Amongst the other Europeans were two Austrians of particular significance – Friedrich von Hayek, then a lecturer at the London School of Economics, and his mentor and teacher Ludwig von Mises, then resident in Geneva at the Graduate Institute of International Studies. Also from Geneva came another exiled central European economist, Wilhem Röpke, later architect of Germany's post-war Social Market Economy. They were all drawn to Paris by a shared concern at the apparently inexorable decline of liberalism in Europe. 'Le Colloque Walter Lippmann' represented the first coherent attempt to analyse the reasons for that decline and to suggest ways in which that decline might be reversed.

Lippmann's *The Good Society* was but one of a number of books published during the mid-1930s which warned of the seemingly unstoppable advance of 'collectivist' ideologies and governments throughout the world since the end of the First World War. Lippmann himself acknowledged the contributions of two of the academics at the Paris Conference – Hayek and von Mises – to the intellectual development of this theme at the beginning of his own book. The first chapter of *The Good Society* described the contemporary situation in stark terms, describing 'Collectivism' as 'the dominant dogma of the Age':

> Throughout the world, in the name of progress, men who call themselves Communists, Socialists, fascists, nationalists, progressives, and even liberals, are unanimous in holding that government with its instruments of coercion must, by commanding the people how they shall live, direct the course of civilization and fix the shape of things to come . . . [so] Universal is the dominion of this dogma over the minds of contemporary men that no one is taken seriously as a statesman or a theorist who does not come forward with proposals to magnify the power of public officials and to extend and to multiply their intervention in human affairs. Unless he is authoritarian and collectivist, he is a mossback, a reactionary, at best an amiable eccentric swimming hopelessly against the tide. It is a strong tide.[2]

In what was then a comparatively novel intellectual formulation, anticipating George Orwell by almost a decade, Lippmann identified the two most powerful ideologies of the age, Fascism and Communism, as being no more than similarly extreme versions of the same collectivist impulse. Furthermore, collectivism could also be seen as an increasingly important ideology in countries which were supposedly opposed to those very extremist collectivisms, such as the United States of America (then in the throes of the collectivist 'New Deal') and Great Britain (where the virtues of Keynesian ideas about governmental intervention in the economy were being proclaimed to an increasingly sympathetic audience). The philosophy of individual freedom – classical liberalism – was, according to Lippmann, all but dead, and had been supplanted by collectivism. For Lippmann, the 'liberal philosophy' had stagnated during the mid-nineteenth century, when it had become 'frozen in its own errors', a 'great tradition that [had] become softened by easy living . . .'[3] Only with the failure of liberalism as a coherent, progressive philosophy was it conceivable that men 'should be tempted to regard the primitive tyrannies in Russia, Italy or Germany as the beginnings of a better life for mankind . . .'[4] Lippmann, like his fellow participants at the Paris conference, might acknowledge that collectivism was indeed the new intellectual orthodoxy, but to him this was 'little short of a disaster in human affairs'.[5]

In his opening remarks to the published proceedings of *Le Colloque Walter Lippmann* on 26 August 1938 Professor Rougier spoke of the evils of Communism, which after the Stalinist purges of the army and bureaucracy from 1936 to 1938 were especially evident in the West, but also argued that those people who thought there was some 'middle way' between the extreme of Fascist/Communist collectivism and the pure theoretical individualism of classical liberalism were labouring under the most dangerous illusion of all:

> Le drame moral de notre époque, c'est, dès lors, l'aveuglement des hommes de gauche qui rêvent d'une démocratie politique et d'une planisme economique, sans comprendre que le planisme economique implique l'Etat totalitaire et qui un socialisme liberal est un contradition dans les termes. Le drame moral de notre époque, c'est l'aveuglement des hommes de droite qui soupirent d'admiration devant les gouvernements totalitaires, tout en revendiquant les avantages d'une économie capitaliste, sans se rendre compte que l'Etat totalitaire dévore la fortune privée, met au pas et bureaucratise toutes les formes de l'activité économique d'un pays.[6]

In a long paper on 'The Urgent Necessity of Re-orientation of Social Science' written for the Conference, Röpke and Rustow argued against thinking that there was any easy solution to the manifest economic dislocation and unemployment of the 1930s, and that any attempt to solve these problems by 'monetary tricks and public works will only end in disaster, or to be more specific, in the totalitarian state, where all policy of giving coherence to society without giving it inherent and spontaneous stability must inevitably end'.[7] All the participants in the conference agreed that liberalism as a coherent philosophy was at its lowest ebb, discredited and neglected, tarred with the brush of

Dickensian, Manchester School *laissez-faire*, just as they all agreed that the future of liberalism, as Rustow and Röpke understood it 'in the widest sense of anti-totalitarianism', depended on people like themselves. They wanted to develop a new, revitalized interpretation of liberalism: 'the combination of a working competition not only with the corresponding legal and institutional framework but also with a re-integrated Society of freely co-operating and *vitally satisfied* men is the only alternative to *laissez-faire* and to totalitarianism which we have to offer'.[8] In his closing address, Rougier outlined various areas where liberalism thus needed to be re-examined, and he proposed to set up the 'Centre International d'Etudes pour la renovation du Liberalisme' for this purpose. The proceedings of the conference were published as '*Le Compte-Rendu des séances du Colloque Walter Lippmann*', which Rougier rather grandly called the 'Magna Carta of Liberalism', and the twenty-six academics, intellectuals, journalists and others returned to their own countries at the beginning of September, with Lippmann, Hayek and Röpke charged with founding American, British and Swiss sections of the new organization.

However, it was, of course, an inauspicious moment to start founding new international organizations of ambitious intentions, and this was to remain the first and last time that 'Le Colloque Walter Lippmann' ever met, the war intervening only a year later. Rougier had, nonetheless, given an institutional focus to 'La Rénovation du Liberalisme', and had started an intellectual movement for the revival of economic liberalism that would come to fruition nearly half a century later. But to understand why economic liberalism had reached such a low ebb by the 1930s, and why these philosophers and economists found themselves gathering in Paris on the eve of war to launch their intellectual counter-revolution against collectivism, it is necessary to examine the decline of liberalism as an ideology and to reflect, in the British case in particular, on the impact made by the thinking of one man – John Maynard Keynes – who had done more than any other single individual to bring Hayek, Rougier, Röpke, Aron, von Mises and the others together in Paris to mourn the end of liberal, even civilized, society as they understood it.

The rise of collectivism in Britain has been chronicled by several historians, the first, and perhaps most famous, of them being A. V. Dicey. Indeed, it was Dicey who first identified the nineteenth century as an 'age of individualism', giving way towards the end of the century to an 'age of collectivism'.[9] More recently, and most exhaustively, W. H. Greenleaf has published his two large volumes on *The Rise of Collectivism* and *The Ideological Heritage*.[10] As Rougier and Lippmann had in Paris in 1938, Greenleaf identifies the two great currents of the British political tradition as the opposing ideological positions of 'libertarianism' and 'collectivism'. For Greenleaf, this represents the 'basic contrast' in British political thought and practice, between 'on the one hand, the growth of a natural harmony in society achieved without recourse to state intervention [what Hayek called the state of 'spontaneous order'] and, on the other, the idea of an artificial identification of human interests resulting from legislative or other political regulation'.[11] All the major 'Party' ideologies in Britain – Socialism, Conservatism and Liberalism – have reflected both strands of thought in their separate historical traditions; libertarianism and collectivism have been the two fixed poles on the compass by which, since the early nineteenth century, politicians have, in practice, navigated their way across the legislative map. Economic liberalism, of course, was very much an economic expression of the 'libertarian' tradition, and reached its peak as an ideological and practical economic concept in the 1870s and 1880s, tracing its ideological roots back to Adam Smith's *The Wealth of Nations*, which was published a century before, in 1776. Economic liberalism was the governing principle of both the Liberal Party, under Gladstone, and the Conservative Party, particularly under Disraeli, up to 1880. The point has often been made that for all Disraeli's purple prose about Young England and Tory Democracy, as Prime Minister from 1874 to 1880 he was as frugal in his conduct of the country's finances as Gladstone had always been.

However, at the same time as the liberal tradition seemed to reach the peak of its influence, 'collectivism' had gradually been making inroads on the liberal state, beginning with such legislation as factory reforms and public health reforms, which, to varying degrees, compelled people to carry out laws laid down by Westminster in the name of what came to be called 'social justice'. *The Times* was later to name this steady erosion of individual liberty, orchestrated by an ever more intrusive State, the 'Silent Revolution', which meant that even before anybody had formulated a coherent intellectual case for collectivism, Government had started to intervene in such matters as industrial relations and national education – areas where it had previously feared to tread.[12] Greenleaf has written of this general drift towards collectivism – or 'creeping collectivism' as some have called it – as a process which was

> not, at least initially, deliberately induced. Rather it rested for a long time on what Sidney Webb used to call the unconscious permeation of an overtly individualist society by a contrary principle . . . He said, the 'advocates of each particular change intend no further alteration, the result is nevertheless an increasing social momentum' in the collectivist direction. The cumulative, incremental effect of these piece-meal reforms was indeed considerable.[13]

However, if, by the end of the nineteenth century, the increase in State powers was only small, the result of pragmatism rather than ideology, this all changed with the foundation of the Fabian Society in 1884, the creation of Beatrice and Sidney Webb, and George Bernard Shaw. The Fabian Society was the first British organization to formulate and aggressively and successfully promote a coherent intellectual justification for the extension of the power of the State in pursuit of certain specific aims, such as the creation of a 'national minimum' standard of living. In Shaw's phrase, commending the original Fabian programme, the Fabian Society sought to replace the existing 'scramble for private gain' with 'the introduction of design, contrivance, and co-ordination' in the conscious pursuit of 'Collective Welfare'.[14] The Fabians, through their tactics of 'gradualism' and 'permeation', sought to persuade *all* political parties of the virtues of their programme, particularly the Liberal Party and, after 1900, the nascent Labour Party. The Fabians were sowing their seeds on extremely fertile ground, for, as the memory of the old century receded, the certainties of the Victorian, liberal free-traders seemed to slip away, too. The old shibboleth of 'free trade' came under vehement attack from the politician Joseph Chamberlain with the Tariff Reform Campaign, which, though it split the Conservative Party in the process, was eventually vindicated by the gradual erection of Tariff Barriers from 1915 onwards, culminating in the Ottawa agreements of 1932. In signing these, Britain, in protectionist mood, finally created the system of 'Imperial Preference' that the Tariff Reformers had been pressing for since the first years of the century. Furthermore, the Liberal Party, under the guidance of its economic mentors J. A. Hobson and L. T. Hobhouse, adapted the ex-German Chancellor Bismarck's social insurance system (which had created, for instance, the first modern state-financed pension system) and applied it to Britain during Asquith's great Liberal administrations of 1908 to 1915, thus ushering in the age of 'New Liberalism'. Asquith's governments embraced the new Fabian model of collectivism, and introduced old-age pensions, social insurance, school meals and other 'welfare' measures. For the first time, the State took it upon itself to tax its citizens in order to fulfil a specific collectivist, social aim, that of 'social welfare'. The 'National Efficiency' movement, which embraced politicians of all parties, also supported the Fabian arguments for the increase of State powers, in order to increase 'national' defence against the rising power of Bismarckian–Wilhelmine Germany. All the legislation passed in the fourteen years before the First World War, by politicians of both the Conservative and Liberal Parties – whether in the name of 'Social Welfare', 'National Efficiency' or 'Industrial Rationalization' – represented a distinct and accelerating step towards the Fabian collectivist State, and, as Shaw later put it, 'the Fabian policy was to support and take advantage of every legislative step towards Collectivism no matter what quarter it came from, nor how little its promoters dreamt that they were advocating an instalment of Socialism.'[15] The 'New Liberals' were in the vanguard of this movement, led by Lloyd George, whilst the old Liberals, loyal to the Party's Gladstonian roots of free-trade, *laissez-faire* and minimum governmental intervention, were, like the libertarian political philosopher Herbert Spencer, left to lament the withering of the Victorian liberal ideological tradition. It is ironic that Spencer's greatest exposition of the liberal creed, *Man Versus the State*, was published in 1884, the same year as the Fabian Society was founded. As early as 1894, a Fabian, William Clarke, could say of old 'classical liberals' like Spencer, with only a touch of hyperbole, that

> His political ideas are already as antiquated as Noah's ark. I do not know a single one of the younger men in England who is influenced by them in the slightest degree, though one hears of one occasionally, just as one hears of a freak in a dime museum.[16]

This steady march of collectivism was, of course, given a tremendous fillip by the First World War, when the demands of war saw the final buckling of the Victorian liberal State, giving way to an unprecedented degree of central control and central economic planning, measures which were, again, supported and carried through by politicians of all parties, barring the initial reservations of the Asquithian Liberals.[17] The coal industry was virtually nationalized in 1917, and the McKenna duties of 1915 saw the first break with the tradition of free-trade, a measure introduced by a Liberal Chancellor of the Exchequer. The war witnessed the proliferation of new Whitehall departments, such as the Ministry of Munitions and the Ministry of Foods. Moreover, the very success of Britain's 'collectivist' war effort seemed to many to vindicate the claims of the Fabians that 'collectivism' was not only the route to a more just and equitable society, but that it was also a more efficient way of running a modern economy. It was no coincidence that in 1918 the Fabians persuaded the Labour Party to accept a new, specifically Socialist constitution, with its commitment in Clause IV to the nationalization of what would later be termed the 'commanding heights' of the British economy.

It was thus not surprising that collectivist measures did not end with the War; the Conservative-dominated Lloyd George coalition government founded the Ministry of Health and passed the Housing Act of 1919, which for the first time committed the Government to subsidizing local authority housing so that rents could be fixed at below the market price, at a level those needing to be housed could afford. Furthermore, the government also intervened in the economy as never before, instituting formal machinery for arbitration in industrial disputes in the form of the Whitely Councils; and in the name of 'rationalization', substantial state assistance was given to certain industries, such as the railway companies, to amalgamate. With the creation of the Central Electricity Board in 1926, the first state industrial monopoly was established and in the early 1930s loans were given to ailing industries such as the ship building industry. When British broadcasting began in 1926, it was created, in unprecedented fashion, as a newly born state monopoly – the British Broadcasting Company. All this entailed a considerable increase in government expenditure; total government expenditure as a percentage of Gross National Product rose from a low of nine per cent in 1870–90, to twenty-six per cent by 1926, and to sixty per cent by 1940. As Greenleaf has pointed out, increasing governmental expenditure was common to all political parties. In terms of state spending, it became impossible to distinguish between a high-spending and a low-spending party.[18] As Greenleaf concludes,

> Taken together, then, these policies of national efficiency, tariff reform, and rationalization, as they emerged over the early decades of this century, invited substantial steps towards a collectivist economy. Their introduction was piecemeal but was none the less cumulatively significant. Moreover, they intimated, even if they did not overtly entail, the further notion of the planned economy itself, the idea of government intervention to attempt nothing less than the systematic management of life as a whole.[19]

Thus, by the time of the economic deluge of the 1930s, which effectively started with the Wall Street Crash in 1929, the ideological course towards collectivism was firmly set, not least by the Liberal Party of Lloyd George which was in the forefront of demanding an ever-increasing extension of governments' power and the spending of governmental money to alleviate Britain's economic problems. The famous Liberal 'Yellow Book' with which the Party launched its 1929 election campaign was but the culmination of decades of 'progressive' thinking, starting with Hobson and Hobhouse, that had produced a more collectivist vision. As early as 1903, Herbert Spencer had already noted how far the Liberal Party had strayed from its original principles:

> I do not desire to be classed among those who are in these days called Liberals. In the days when the name came into use, the Liberals were those who aimed to extend the freedom of the individual versus the power of the State, whereas now (prompted though they are by desire for popular welfare), Liberals as a body are continually extending the power of the State and restricting the freedom of the individual.[20]

Spencer's gloomy prognosis for the future of classical liberalism was famously echoed by Hilaire Belloc in his book *The Servile State*, published in 1912. Belloc predicted that 'Collectivism' would not lead to the fulfilment of the Socialists' dream of 'social justice' but to a new condition of slavery, in which the people would be completely subordinated to the demands of a central state authority. It was a prescient book, and an early rehearsal of the arguments that Hayek would deploy thirty-two years later in *The Road to Serfdom.* However eloquent Belloc and Spencer might have been in their warnings about the dangers of collectivism for individual liberty, they both, nonetheless, acknowledged that they were fighting against a current that was running strongly against them.

The defence of the 'liberal' tradition was, indeed, peculiarly ineffective and became focused on a number of groups which tried to unite multi-party opposition to the idea of collectivism. The most important of these groups was undoubtedly the Liberty and Property Defence League, founded in 1882 by Lord Elcho, later the Earl of Wemyss.[21] The LPDL took its inspiration from Herbert Spencer and his two disciples Wordsworth Denisthorpe and W. C. Crofts; the former had been instrumental in founding the Personal Rights Association in 1871, a body set up originally to campaign against the State's regulation of prostitution, a quixotic issue on which to start the fight-back against the growing encroachment of the State on personal liberty.[22] The LPDL was an active pressure group, and published a journal called the *Liberty Annual* which later became the *Liberty Review*. One of its leaders, Lord Brabourne, stated that the LPDL existed to 'uphold the principle of Liberty and guard the rights of Labour and property of all kind against undue interference by the State, and to encourage self-help vs. State help'.[23] One historian of the LPDL has described it as being

> composed of landed aristocrats, 'old liberals', new model employers, whigs, and other vested interests, many of whom had practised private paternalism. The league was founded in reaction to the growth of 'grand-motherly' legislation, 'trade unionism' and 'promising politicians'. An examination of its strategy and tactics reveals an 'Establishment' defending its position in a mass democracy with an ideology based on the doctrine of Liberty and property.[24]

The same could be said of other organizations founded at about the same time with the same aims, such as the British Constitutional Association and the Anti-Socialist Union, founded in 1907–8, which claimed to be as anti-Protectionist in the Conservative Party as it was anti-Socialist in the Labour movement.[25] It was founded by R. D. Blumenfield, editor of the *Daily Express*. None of these organizations had much contemporary impact, and the LPDL petered out in the 1920s, whilst the others failed to last much longer. Such groups were increasingly seen as 'reactionary' apologists for 'vested interest groups', rather than defenders of a relevant, broad and universal political philosophy. Indeed, groups such as the Anti-Socialist Union and the LPDL seemed in their very membership to embody the stagnation of liberalism (as Lippmann was to recognize in 1938) into little more than a pseudo-philosophical defence of those who had done well from the unbridled *laissez-faire* capitalism of Victorian times. Harold Laski, the most prominent Socialist academic of the inter-war years, was a perceptive critic of the decline of liberalism and he might have had exactly such organizations as the LPDL very much in mind when he summarized the decline of liberalism thus in a lecture at the LSE in 1940:

> Perhaps I may best put it by saying that the earlier liberals released the individual from a type of social organisation [feudalism] which restricted his capacity for growth. But the assumption which underlay that release made it in fact valid only for men who were in a position to surmount the conditions of a fiercely competitive industrial society, that is, broadly, the owners of property. The liberty predominantly secured was their liberty; the others came in as residuary legatees of their triumph. And when the war of property was won, they conceived that the campaign was over. You can still catch the confidence of their victory in the triumphant perorations of Macaulay. What they did not see was that the new social order their liberalism had built brought with it new problems as intense as any they had solved.

And, he might have added, problems which the LPDL did little to address.[26] A good example of the atrophy into which liberalism had sunk was the foundation in 1919 of the extremely secretive Economic League by coal and steel magnates. This organization, which still exists, was formed by Admiral 'Blinker' Hall, who had been Director of Naval Intelligence during the war, 'to fight Communism and other forms of subversion by a combination of exposure and constructive economic education'.[27] It mainly produced fairly crude anti-socialist propaganda, pamphlets and newsletters and organized meetings – most importantly during the General Strike of 1926. But the Economic League was essentially the creature of big business, dedicated to exposing left-wing influences in the work-place, perhaps the only capability that these self-anointed defenders of 'property and liberty' had to offer a 1920s electorate. It was small wonder perhaps that, by the 1920s, liberalism was no longer regarded as a mainstream ideology; and those businessmen and scholars who did try to defend liberalism in public, such as Ernest Benn and the liberal journalist F.W. Hirst, were, at best, regarded as merely eccentric. The work of Benn will be referred to in the next chapter; Hirst was still energetically preaching the gospel of liberalism during the 1930s, publishing two books, the titles of which clearly indicated his own philosophical preoccupations, *Liberty and Tyranny* (1935) and *Economic Freedom and Private Property* (1935). However, by the 1930s Hirst was regarded as an anachronism, and his books rapidly disappeared into well deserved obscurity.

In continental Europe, the Spanish writer, José Ortega y Gasset, echoed the warnings of his British fellow-liberals in his seminal work, *The Revolt of the Masses*, first published in English in 1932. Surveying a Europe in which Communism already held sway over Russia, while Fascism flourished in Italy and was about to sweep Germany – and would also come to do so in his own country before the end of the decade – Ortega wrote of the promise and perils of collectivism as it was being practised in Italy and Russia:

> The mass-man sees in the State an anonymous power and feeling himself, like it, anonymous, he believes that the State is something of his own. Suppose that in the public life of a country some difficulty, conflict, or problem presents itself, the mass-man will tend to demand that the State intervene immediately and undertake a solution directly with its immense and unassailable resources.
>
> This is the gravest danger that today threatens civilization; State intervention, the absorption of all spontaneous social effort by the State, that is to say, of spontaneous historical action, which in the long run sustains, nourishes, and impels human destinies . . . The mass-man does in fact believe that he is the state, and he will tend more and more to set its machinery working on whatsoever pretext, to crush

> beneath it any creative minority which disturbs it – disturbs it in any order of things, in politics, in ideas, in industry.
>
> The result of this tendency will be fatal. Spontaneous social action will be broken over and over again by State intervention . . . can we help feeling that under the rule of the masses the State will endeavour to crush the independence of the individual and the group, and thus definitely spoil the harvest of the future?[28]

* * *

However, it was at this low point of intellectual interest in liberalism that the few remaining liberals in Britain began to turn their interest to the continent, and in particular to Austria, where what became known as the 'Austrian School' of economics began to attract considerable attention, for it provided a trenchant critique of Socialism and an equally robust defence of economic liberalism. The traditional home of liberalism, Britain, turned to Austria to reinvigorate the philosophical position of liberalism at home, it having fallen into such disrepute in the land of its birth. The founder of the Austrian School was Carl Menger, who in 1871 published his *Grundsätze der Volkswirtschaftslehre.* He was soon joined by Eugen von Boehm-Bawerk and Friedrich von Wieser, who during the early years of the twentieth century, attracted a 'small but vigorous stream of adherents', among whom the most distinguished and certainly the most important for the revival of British economic liberalism were Ludwig von Mises and Friedrich A. von Hayek.[29] Von Mises, who launched the intellectual counter-attack on collectivism, was born in Lemberg in Austria-Hungary in 1881, and from 1892 to 1900 he attended the Akademische Gymnasium in Vienna. He studied law and economics at the University of Vienna under Boehm-Bawerk and from 1913 to 1938 he was Professor of Economics at the University of Vienna; from 1926 to 1938 he was also Vice-President of the Institute for Business Cycle Research in the Austrian capital. His first book, *Nation, Staat und Wirtschaft* was published in 1919; it amounted to a restatement of the principles of economic liberalism. His seminal work, and the most important contribution to the Austrian 'neo-classical' School of economics, appeared in 1922, and was entitled *Die Gemeinwirtschaft; Untersuchungen über der Sozialismus*, translated as *Socialism; An Economic and Sociological Analysis* when it was published in English in 1936. At that time, von Mises's book was the most powerful theoretical attack on Socialism as a theory ever written, and attacked socialism – which he directly equated with collectivism – at its weakest point, its economic theory.

Like his fellow English liberals and those that gathered together in Paris in 1938, von Mises began his book by acknowledging the undoubted fact that

> Socialism is the watchword and the catchword of our day. The Socialist idea dominates the modern spirit. The masses approve of it, it expresses the thoughts and feelings of all; it has set its seal upon our time. When history comes to tell our story it will be written above the chapter 'the epoch of Socialism'.

As Hayek was to point out in *The Road to Serfdom* in 1944, (a book addressed 'To the Socialists of All Parties') von Mises maintained that many who would not have called themselves Socialists but were 'supporters of the various "Social–political" and "social reform" movements', had, nonetheless 'fundamentally accepted the principle of the Socialist programme' by seeking greater collectivist state action. Thus, for von Mises,

> The supporters of Socialism therefore are not confined to the Bolshevists and their friends outside Russia or to the members of the numerous socialist parties; all are socialists who consider the socialist order of society economically and ethically superior to that based on private ownership of the means of production . . . If we define Socialism as broadly as this we see that the great majority of people are with socialism today. Those who confess to the principles of liberalism and who see the only possible form of economic Society in an order based on private ownership of the means of production are few indeed.[30]

Having identified his target, von Mises then delivered his famous economic critique of Socialism in the chapter on 'Economic Calculation', showing that without a price mechanism Socialist economic planning would be unscientific and ultimately chaotic. He concluded of a Socialist economy that 'All economic change, therefore, would involve operations the value of which could neither be predicted beforehand nor ascertained after they had taken place. Everything would be a leap in the dark.'[31] Von Mises argued that Socialism would decrease productivity and create widespread poverty. What was particularly pertinent to the British political situation was his attack on 'mixed' economies, the 'Middle Way' that many British politicians were beginning to accept as a necessary corollary of the increase in collectivism, a *via media* between the extremes of central planning *à la* Soviet Russia and the unbridled capitalism of Victorian economic liberalism. Von Mises wrote that

> All attempts to abolish by a compromise the contrast between common property and private ownership of the means of production are . . . mistaken. Ownership is always where the power to dispose resides. Therefore State Socialism and planned economies, which want to maintain private property in name and in law, but in fact, because they subordinate the power of disposing to state orders, want to socialize property, are Socialist systems in the full sense.
>
> . . . It is not possible to compromise, either, by putting part of the means of production at the disposal of Society and leaving the remainder to individuals. Such systems simply stand unconnected side by side, and operate fully only within the space they occupy. Such mixture of the social principles of organisation must be considered senseless by everyone.[32]

This argument against the apparently less extreme form of collectivism that became known as the 'mixed economy' was to acquire particular importance in Britain in the 1930s, as we shall see. Von Mises became the greatest theorist of the Austrian School, and an uncompromising enemy of all forms of state intervention and collectivism. He was therefore a vigorous opponent of Nazism (or 'National Socialism' – he and his fellow classical liberal critics were always careful to name it in full), and in 1934 he left the University of Vienna to take up a post at the Graduate Institute of International Studies in Geneva. He emigrated to the United States in 1940, where he published his *magnum opus* on classical liberalism, *Human Action – A Treatise in Economics*, in 1949, an enlarged version of a book he had already published in Geneva in May 1940. In America, von Mises was to become vitally important to the revival of classical liberalism in that country, paralleling the work that his colleague, F. A. Hayek, undertook in Britain in the 1930s and 1940s.[33]

For it was Hayek, von Mises's younger colleague at the University of Vienna, who was to prove the inspiration for the revival of economic liberalism in Britain. Hayek was born in Vienna on 8 May 1899, of an old Austrian family which had been ennobled by Franz Josef I in the early eighteenth century. His prosperous upper middle-class family were predominantly civil servants and academics. He was brought up in the twilight years of the Austro-Hungarian Empire, and his family enjoyed all the advantages of Viennese life at a time when that city was at the height of its creative and cultural powers. As Hayek later recalled, his family had 'this fantastic flat in Vienna, Kartnerstrasse 25 . . . it was the dancing centre of Vienna's upper academia. That, and my grandparents' villa in the Vienna Woods, is where I spent my youth.' He had two brothers, who became university professors in zoology and chemistry, and he was a second cousin of the philosopher Ludwig Wittgenstein. He gained two doctorates at the University of Vienna, in law and in political science, and worked for six years under von Mises at the Austrian Institute for Economic Research; from 1929 to 1931 he was a lecturer in economics at the University of Vienna. In 1925 his first paper on economics was published, and in 1929 his first book, *Monetary Theory and the Trade Cycle*, appeared. This was a direct result of his work with Mises, which was published in English in 1933.

It is difficult to account for the almost fanatical attachment to the main tenets of classical liberalism shared by von Mises and Hayek, and indeed by the rest of the Austrian School, at a time when many of their peers throughout Europe dreamt of one kind of socialism or another: in Britain young intellectuals were turning to the Fabian summer schools for their inspiration – this was after all the generation of Hugh Dalton, Rupert Brooke and Leonard Woolf. However, the Austrian intellectual interest in liberalism was probably a consequence of the fact that Austria had no effective liberal tradition of its own, something that was to become all too evident in the wake of the collapse of the Austro-Hungarian Empire at the end of the First World War. Politics tended to be dominated by the struggle between the Catholicism of the Christian Socialists and the Socialism of the Social Democrats, so for Hayek and von Mises liberalism was still very much a novel and exciting, as well as slightly radical, political doctrine, whereas in Britain familiarity had only bred contempt. The Austrian School also looked to Britain as the cradle of liberalism and as the model of a modern democracy of the sort that the liberal middle classes aspired to in Austria, so it was only natural that Hayek should have looked to the British liberal tradition, with its values of tolerance and fair-mindedness, as a beacon of political hope under the darkening skies of Central European politics during the first three decades of the twentieth century. In 1985 Hayek recalled that the Vienna of his youth was an 'extra-ordinarily exciting place, bursting with ideas and energy', but, 'except for the Tyrolean mountains all my emotional attachment is to England. I fell in love with England when I first went to Cambridge in January 1931. Emotionally and intellectually it was my climate and still is. It isn't really that the English are more intelligent than others, but they have great Social strength.'[34] It was thus with some excitement that he accepted an offer to come to the London School of Economics (LSE) in 1931 as Tooke Professor of Economic Science and Statistics. Hayek thus joined the exodus of the Austrian School to Britain and America; two others of his circle who had also been profoundly influenced by Mises, Gottfried Haberler and Fritz Machlup, followed von Mises to America before the outbreak of war, and, as one chronicler has written, 'the dispersal of the Austrian School to England and America was . . . one of the most significant chapters in the history of modern American Conservatism.'[35]

Hayek received his offer to come to the LSE from the Director, Sir William Beveridge, on the recommendation of Lionel Robbins, who, at the age of thirty, had become Professor of Economics at the LSE in 1929. The relationship between Hayek and Robbins was to become crucial to the development of a school of economic liberalism in Britain during the 1930s and 1940s, just as their work at the LSE was to make its economics department the outstanding centre of economic liberalism in Europe. The relationship between Robbins and Hayek had much in common with the equally fruitful relationship between Hayek's cousin Wittgenstein and another comparatively youthful English academic, Bertrand Russell; the Hayek–Robbins relationship was to have as much impact on British economics as the Wittgenstein–Russell relationship had on the development of philosophy in Britain during the first half of this century.[36] Robbins was born in 1898 into a non-conformist background; his father was a market gardener on the outskirts of London. Robbins fought in the First World War and was injured in the hand at the Ypres Salient. After the war, he continued his higher education at the LSE, where he was taught by Hugh Dalton, later Labour's post-war Chancellor of the Exchequer, who did much to advance the young Robbins' career. After a brief spell as a tutor at New College, Oxford, from 1927 to 1929 (where he taught, amongst others, Hugh Gaitskell, Evan Durbin and David Eccles), he returned to the LSE where a new ordinary professorial chair was created for him, and he never left, ending his career as Chairman of the Court of Governors during the years of student unrest in the late 1960s. Intellectually, like many of his generation, Robbins started as a Guild Socialist, attracted to the ideas of G. D. H. Cole, but after his initial period of study at the LSE, he became increasingly converted to the ideas of economic liberalism and capitalism, with the result that by 1929, when he took up his chair at the LSE, he was probably the outstanding liberal economist in Britain. He described his own intellectual conversion to economic liberalism in his autobiography, as well as the debt that he owed to von Mises in prompting him to reconsider his position. For Robbins, his conversion to economic liberalism came about not

> because I have come to regard free-enterprise systems, as they existed, as necessarily perfect, or, even in their ideal type, as free from all possible disharmony. It was rather because taking a broad view of the probabilities as I conceived them, I had come to the conclusion that both personal liberty and economic efficiency were likely to be more prevalent under the dispersed initiatives of a system of markets and private property. I thought I saw grave danger to freedom of individual thought and action under a completely socialised system . . .
>
> In reaching this conclusion I was considerably influenced by the examination by von Mises of the possibilities of economic calculation under total Collectivism.

Robbins found fault with some of von Mises's propositions,

> but his main contentions that without a price system of some sort, a complex collectivist society is without the necessary guidance and that, within the general framework of such a

> society, attempts to institute price systems which have meaning and incentive in a dynamic context are liable to conflict with the main intention of collectivism – these still seem to me to be true and to be borne out by the whole history of totalitarian societies since they were propounded.[37]

Robbins was rare for a British economist of the time in that he took a keen interest in European developments in economics, and his knowledge of German gave him access to the work of the Austrian School, as many of the works of von Mises, Hayek, Machlup et al. were only translated into English years after their immediate significance might have been lost. As one of his biographers has written, Mises and other Austrians, notably Hayek, 'exercised a pervasive influence on Robbins's early work. . . ', an influence which is particularly evident in his attack on tariff protection and planning, *Economic Planning and International Order*, published in 1937, and his account of *The Great Depression*, published in 1934.[38] For Robbins, Austrian economics in the late 1920s and 1930s was modern economics, however opposed to the supposedly 'revolutionary' theories of Keynes and his disciples von Mises and Hayek might have been. Robbins himself considered von Mises's influence to have been of paramount importance in the development of modern economics, and later wrote that 'as a thinker in his own right and as the teacher of such men as Haberler, Hayek, Machlup and Morgenstern, he [was] one of the significant figures in the history of economics in the first half of this century' and 'as a result of these various influences I had now moved to a position in which those who enjoy simple classifications would have described me as an economic liberal.'[39] Robbins himself, as he admitted in his autobiography, was not an original or creative thinker like von Mises or Hayek, but he was a superb expositor of other people's work and a brilliant collator of the different schools of economic theory, as the book on which his academic reputation rested, *The Nature and Significance of Economic Science*, showed. This book was a staple ingredient, alongside Frank Knight's *Risk, Uncertainty and Profit*, of the economics undergraduate's diet during the 1930s, and these two books, as one student remembered, were 'all you wanted to read as a young man on these theoretical matters'.[40]

It was thus perfectly natural that Robbins should have invited Hayek over to London in January 1931 to deliver the special University

Lectures in economics on his work, carried out under the guidance of von Mises, on the trade cycle. Robbins later wrote that:

> I can still see the door of my room opening to admit the tall, powerful, reserved figure which announced itself quietly and firmly as 'Hayek'. In the event, the lectures were a sensation, partly for their revaluation of an aspect of classic monetary theory which for many years had been forgotten . . .
>
> The lectures were at once difficult and exciting; and they conveyed such an impression of learning and analytical invention that when, greatly to my surprise, Beveridge asked if we would care to invite the lecturer to join us permanently as holder of a Tooke Chair of Economic Science and Statistics which had long been without a tenant, there was an unanimous vote in favour . . . and Hayek returned as a permanent member of the staff at the beginning of the next academic session.[41]

For Robbins, the advantages of having Hayek at the LSE were immense, as not only was he a powerful, if relatively untried, intellectual addition to the Department of Economics, but he also provided a direct link between the LSE and the Austrian School, and, as Robbins later acknowledged, he thus 'brought to the [LSE] a host of intellectual contacts from abroad which otherwise would not have existed'.[42] For Robbins himself, the importance of Hayek's presence at the LSE cannot be over-estimated, as he later admitted that 'Both in terms of intellectual companionship and academic collaboration I should find it difficult to overstate the stimulus and help which I derived from this relationship.'[43] For Hayek's part, Robbins, although only a year older than him, was his mentor and guide to the academic world of Britain. Robbins was Hayek's chief intellectual consultant during the formative years of the 1930s, and he was not exaggerating when he described Robbins in a letter to Karl Popper in 1943 as 'my closest friend whose opinion I value most highly'.[44] They lived near to each other in Hampstead Garden Suburb and their respective families also remained very close.

As it was, Hayek was joining an economics department which was already very sympathetic to his own views, quite apart from the immediate intellectual kinship he shared with Lionel Robbins. The LSE has acquired a reputation in popular mythology as a bastion of 'left-wing' agitation and socialist political action, crowned by the student '*événements*' at the School in the late 1960s and early 1970s. Much of this reputation was originally based on the presence of Harold Laski at the LSE, the celebrated Socialist political theorist who had been appointed Professor of Political Science in 1926.[45] Laski was a flamboyant and charismatic lecturer, who paid less attention to the demands of academic detachment than his colleagues usually tried to preserve. He was a prolific author, flirting with the idea of revolutionary Socialism in the 1930s,[46] and as a lecturer was described by one of his students as 'by far the most fascinating [at the LSE] and as a human being he had probably the softest heart . . . No wonder the lecture room was crowded and Laski's influence spread far beyond the shores of the British Isles . . .'[47] Indeed, by the late 1930s he was probably the most famous academic in the English-speaking world and played an influential role in Labour Party politics. There were socialist academics in other departments as well, especially after the Second World War, but the economics department, by contrast, was a haven of economic liberalism even by the time that Hayek arrived there in 1931. As such, the LSE was to be the most important centre of the revival of interest in economic liberal thinking from the early 1930s onwards. This was ironic, as the LSE had, of course, been founded by the Fabians in 1895 to advance the cause of academic research into social and economic problems. The Fabians probably felt that all 'disinterested' and 'objective' academic research would lead any intelligent person down the path of collectivism and socialism – which was certainly the case with many at the LSE – but this was not true of the economics department. Hayek himself in an essay on 'The Transmission of the Ideals of Economic Freedom' traced the economic liberal tradition at the LSE back to Edwin Cannan, the most prominent member of the department in its first years, and editor of a famous edition of Adam Smith's *The Wealth of Nations*. Like Robbins, Cannan was not an innovative thinker, but his importance lay in his teaching at the LSE. For Hayek,

> Cannan's greatest merit . . . was the training, over many years, of a group of pupils at the London School of Economics; it was they who later formed what probably became

> the most important Centre of economic liberalism – though, it is true, at a time when such a development had already got under way in Austria . . .'

Robbins overlapped with Cannan, and to Hayek it was then Robbins who 'became the real nucleus of younger economists all very nearly the same age, which emerged at the London School of Economics during the Thirties'.[48]

The most important member of this 'nucleus of younger economists' was Professor (later Sir) Arnold Plant, a fellow student of Robbins's at the LSE and his principal colleague in the department from 1930 onwards. Plant, too, was an excellent expositor and tutor, and his students included Arthur Seldon, who was his research assistant from 1937 to 1941 and later editorial director of the Institute of Economic Affairs, and Basil Yamey, one of the IEA's most important contributors. The most senior of the LSE group was T. E. Gregory; his younger colleagues included W. H. Hutt, F. W. Paish, S. H. Frankel, R. H. Coase and, after the war, Peter Bauer. All of these economists were to contribute to the revival of economic liberalism in various capacities, and most came to be closely associated with the IEA after it was founded in 1955.

Hayek thus found himself in congenial surroundings and became devoted to the small rabbit warren of buildings off Aldwych which housed the LSE. The affection that Hayek felt for the LSE was reciprocated, and it was a singular honour when Hayek was chosen to write the fiftieth anniversary article on the LSE in the school's own journal, *Economica*, in 1946.[49] The presence of Hayek in the economics department undoubtedly reinforced the economic liberal tradition at the school, and his British colleagues learnt much from the Austrian School, via Hayek, that refined and buttressed their own liberal positions. As one student of modern liberalism has observed, 'It was only with the work of the Austrian School that the conception of economics as the Science of catallaxy* or exchange, together with the subjective theory of economic value, allowed the shaky intellectual foundations of liberalism to be strengthened.'[50]

Hayek was not a charismatic, or even persuasive lecturer, unlike

* For Hayek's linguistic preferences on the subject, see page 53.

Laski or Robbins, and the same student quoted above who observed Laski in action wrote of Hayek that, by comparison, he 'wore a perpetually benevolent smile, a trait which did not belie his nature. But his English was thick and his thought appeared tangled. One had to sit near the front in order to try and follow.'[51] Hayek was not a proselytizer in the Laski style, and was more at home outside the lecture hall in small discussion groups or seminars, where his courtesy, respect for opposing views and good nature won over even those who did not agree with him. As one contemporary observed of him, he was essentially 'Aristocratic in temper and origins; physically, morally and intellectually fearless; clear and incisive in thought; the embodied principle itself of following the logic where it leads; the soul of scholarly generosity . . .'[52] Robbins was justifiably proud of the work of the economics department, under his own leadership, in defending and then developing the ideas of economic liberalism and resented the charges frequently levelled against the school that it was just a 'nest of reds', and little better than a surrogate think-tank for the Labour Party, especially when such accusations came from Conservative MPs sympathetic to the LSE's economic liberalism who he felt ought to have known better. On one such occasion he was provoked into delivering a blistering riposte to the Conservative MP, and son of the former Prime Minister Bonar Law, Richard Law, with whom he had worked closely during and just after the war. Robbins wrote to Law in 1946, only two years after the publication of Hayek's *Road to Serfdom* had put the debate over economic liberalism versus collectivism at the centre of the political stage, and at a time when Robbins was helping Law write his own, important work on Conservatism and the free-market, *Return from Utopia*. Robbins's letter is worth quoting at length, as it does show the contribution that he felt the LSE had made to a cause dear to his heart:

> I see to my grief from Hansard that you have adopted the habit – common I am sorry to say on your side of the House – of attributing political bias to the LSE . . .
>
> To get some concrete illustration of how wide of the mark your accusations are, I have just analyzed the record of the present professorate. There are seventeen of us holding Chairs. Of these, one is a prominent leftist; two have played a moderate part in Labour politics, the rest are entirely non

> political. Four . . . [including] myself indirectly . . . have been your own advisers.
>
> The real and bitter joke is that in fact in the last fifteen years the school has done more to create an intellectual apologia for the sort of policy you believe in than any other institution in the world. I'm not denying the existence of another political group; I don't think we should be political at all in the sense of giving support to any particular party – But it is a fact that as a by product of work done by some of us you have available at the present day a more formidable armoury of weapons against totalitarian tyranny than has ever existed before. The back-benchers who applaud your jokes about the school are only too pleased to take passages (often completely wrenched out of their context) from the works of Hayek or myself to justify positions which otherwise they would only be able to defend by an appeal to tradition and prejudice. And yet you think it appropriate to guy us all as a set of propagandists of the doctrinaire left.[53]

Law was suitably apologetic, recognizing the force of Robbins's argument.

It came as no surprise to his audience that Hayek's inaugural lecture as Tooke Professor, delivered at the LSE in 1933, should have been infused with a note of optimism about the future. Whilst admitting, as von Mises had done a decade earlier, that his own generation was bewitched by 'planning . . . and its older brother Socialism', and that economists, such as von Mises and himself, who had based their critique of planning and collectivism on a scientific basis, were nonetheless ignored by contemporary policy-makers, Hayek was still certain that despite these circumstances, 'an intellectual reaction was on the way . . .', as

> the people who call for a further extension of government controls of economic life have certainly ceased to be in any way intellectual path-breakers – they are most definitely the spirit of the age, the ultimate product of the revolutionary thinking of an earlier generation – the Fabian Generation.[54]

He admitted that the trend towards planning and socialism was so strong that it would be 'revised, if ever, only at the cost of bitter experience and grave disillusionment'; but he remained optimistic that 'in the course of time' the views of economists such as himself would prevail.[55] It was a bold, almost foolhardy assertion to make in 1933, but one that was to be fully justified, after many decades, in the course of events.

There was another passage in Hayek's inaugural lecture which was of more direct contemporary relevance, and hinted at the great debate in economics which would draw the disparate groups and schools of economic liberalism together. Towards the end of his lecture, Hayek returned to his main theme:

> The isolation of the contemporary economist and the refusal of modern progressivism to avail itself of the knowledge he can provide – a knowledge which is the product of the only persistent attempt systematically to explore the possibilities of change. The peculiar historical development [the rise of collectivism] which I have sketched has brought it about that the economist frequently finds himself in disagreement in regard to means with those with whom he is in agreement with regard to ends; and in agreement in regard to means with those whose views regarding ends are entirely antipathetic to him – men who have never felt the urge to reconstruct the world and who frequently support the forces of stability only for reasons of selfishness. In such a situation, it is perhaps inevitable that he should become the object of dislike and suspicion. But if he recognises the circumstances from which they spring, he will be able to bear them with patience and understanding, confident that he possesses, in his scientific knowledge a solvent for differences, which are really intellectual, and that although, at present, his activities have little effect, yet in the course of time they will come to be recognised as serving more consistently than the activities of those he opposes, the ends which they share in common.'[56]

This passage, although somewhat obscure to the modern eye, was in fact a thinly veiled description of the quickening debate between the

Austrian School and the LSE's economic liberals on the one hand and, on the other, a new generation of economists. This last grouping, in response to the great depression of the early 1930s, wanted to go further down the road of collectivism: they were led, of course, by the economics guru of his generation, John Maynard Keynes. The debate between Hayek, the economic liberals and Keynes during the 1930s was crucial in sharpening and crystallizing the thinking of the former school, and paved the way for the formulation of an international movement of economic liberals against Keynesian economics, of which the Paris meeting in 1938 was the first small rally. This movement ultimately led to the development of a coherent anti-Keynesian school of economics in post-war Britain, led by the Institute of Economic Affairs, and later to 'Thatcherism'. The academic debate between the 'Keynesians' and the economic liberals during the 1930s, sometimes referred to as the 'economic calculation' debate, was, it could be said, the crucial intellectual debate of the century in the democratic West. It clearly divided economists – and ultimately politicians – into two distinct camps; the borders set down between these two camps were to run through British politics, across Party boundaries, and out into the wider democratic world, as the century unravelled, and the debate that first negotiated this new politico-economic map must therefore be examined closely.

That Hayek arrived in Britain in 1931 was, of course, particularly significant, as that year saw the culmination of several years of economic depression and decline which climaxed in the fall of Ramsay MacDonald's second Labour government and the formation of a National government, together with Britain leaving the Gold Standard, which she had joined under Churchill's guidance as Chancellor of the Exchequer in 1925. In fact the momentous events of 1929, when the 'depression' is usually thought to have begun, had merely exacerbated an economic downturn – accompanied by historically high rates of unemployment – that had been plaguing Britain since the early 1920s. The 'great depression' that lasted from 1929 to the late 1930s was merely an accentuation of circumstances that had prevailed in Britain for much of the previous decade. The politicians seemed to be able only to react to events, rather than to guide them; a political generation – of MacDonald, Chamberlain, Baldwin and Herbert Samuel – schooled in the tenets of late Victorian *laissez-faire* economics waited for the economic upswing to begin again, as it always had done in the past, whilst all the time making this less likely by resorting to protectionism and spending growing amounts of public money on specific projects such as building ocean liners and on special regional assistance grants.[57] They were, as Hayek liked to point out, incremental collectivists without even realizing it. These were the men, in Hayek's phrase, who 'have never felt the urge to reconstruct the world and who frequently support the forces of stability only for reasons of selfishness'. They worked in concert with the captains of industry and trade union leaders, who all had a vested interest in securing government money to assist their uncompetitive and ailing industries. Against the Labour and National Governments were ranged that school of economists and politicians which came to be known as the 'Keynesians', who began to argue in the mid-1920s for a large programme of public works, and by implication planning, to solve the country's economic problem. As we have seen, it was the Liberal Party, led by Lloyd George, which put itself at the head of such a programme, advised by Keynes. As Hayek indicated in his lecture, he appreciated that what Keynes and his followers were trying to do was basically to preserve a liberal democracy in Britain from buckling under the enormous pressures of the depression, which is what Hayek and the economic liberals wanted to achieve. Thus, for Hayek, 'the economist', such as himself, found himself in 'disagreement in regards to means with those with whom he is in agreement with regards to ends', because the means by which the Keynesians and the economic liberals chose to achieve their agreed ends were very different – and in this difference lay the kernel of the debate between them.

The argument between the economic liberals and the Keynesians had already been exposed within the confines of Whitehall and academia a year before Hayek arrived in England, as the two sides had already locked horns on the government's own Economic Advisory Council. The EAC had been set up in 1929 by the MacDonald Government to advise it on the causes of the depression, and to suggest possible economic remedies. The Committee which had to carry out this work was led by Keynes, and included several of the country's leading economists: Sir Josiah Stamp, Henry Clay from Manchester University, Hubert Henderson and Dennis Robertson, both of whom had worked closely with Keynes in the past, Arthur Pigou, the doyen of the Cambridge Economics Department, and the young Lionel Robbins.[58] Keynes had already put himself at the head of a younger school of economists (particularly the Cambridge 'Circus' of Richard Kahn, one of the secretaries to the EAC, Austin Robinson, Joan Robinson and Piero Sraffa) which had been arguing for increased public expenditure and a programme of public works in order to alleviate unemployment and to provide a reflationary kick-start to the economy, a process which Richard Kahn was already defining as the employment 'multiplier'. Keynes had already declared '*The End of Laissez-Faire*' in a short book of that title published in November 1924, and instead proposed a mixed political economy; as he put it in 1939,

> The question is whether we are prepared to move out of the nineteenth-century *laissez-faire* state into an era of liberal socialism, by which I mean a system where we can act as an organised community for common purposes and to promote economic and social justice, whilst respecting and protecting the individual – his freedom of choice, his faith, his mind and its expression, his enterprise and his property.[59]

Keynes outlined such a course in the celebrated Liberal Party paper, 'We Can Conquer Unemployment', and in the pamphlet 'Can Lloyd George Do It?', written with Hubert Henderson. In economic terms, Keynes urged a programme of selected public expenditure, mainly on local works, to expedite a recovery. But he was resisted on the EAC by both Lionel Robbins and Hubert Henderson, who together mounted the first counter-attack against Keynesianism – for Robbins, at least, a counter-attack based largely on the work of the Austrian School. The charge against Keynes was that he was designing his new economic policies to surmount one outstanding problem, which was a political problem rather than an economic one – the fact that due to the existing power of the trade unions, real wages could not be reduced to make British industry more competitive in the international trading environment in which it had to survive. For Robbins, as he outlined at length in his book *The Great Depression*, published in 1934, the real cause of Britain's post-war economic problems lay in the country's failure to adapt to changing market conditions, caused by the development of rigidities on both sides of industry that had become increasingly entrenched since the war. According to Robbins, 'the cartelisation of industry, the growth of the strength of trade unions, the multiplication of State controls, have created an economic structure which, whatever its ethical or aesthetic superiority, is certainly much less capable of rapid adaptation to change than was the older more competitive system. This puts it very mildly.' For Robbins, 'the post-war rigidity of wages is a by-product of unemployment Insurance.' He concluded thus:

> In general it is true to say that a greater flexibility of wage rates would considerably reduce unemployment; in particular, that a greater flexibility of wage rates in the industries first affected by fluctuations would almost certainly diminish the spread and the violence of the repercussions of these movements. If it had not been for the prevalence of the view that wage rates must at all costs be maintained in order to maintain the purchasing power of the consumer, the violence of the present depression and the magnitude of the unemployment which has accompanied it would have been considerably less. If the obstacles to cost adjustment in Great Britain had been less formidable the whole history of the last ten years would have been different.[60]

For Robbins, what was required were not measures such as increased public spending to *circumvent* these rigidities in the economic system, but measures designed to *tackle those rigidities themselves*, chiefly fixed rates of wages, as spiralling labour costs were beginning to make Britain internationally uncompetitive. One of Keynes's most recent and sympathetic biographers, D. E. Moggridge, has, in a brief but telling passage, got to the heart of the argument when he has written of Robbins's critique of Keynes that for Robbins

> any reduction in the rate of interest [to make money cheaper to borrow] or increase in investment outside normal channels [government expenditure financed by borrowing, or deficit financing] would merely exacerbate the difficulties caused by the initial over-investment which had led to the collapse of the previous boom. What was required were measures that would decrease rigidities in the economic system and allow the necessary adjustments. Thus, whereas Keynes took the rigidity of money wages as almost a given and tried to adopt policy to this fact of economic life,

> Robbins took it as a source of so many of Britain's economic problems that the [EAC] report should highlight this rigidity and the roles of unemployment insurance, monopolies and restrictive practices in creating it.[61]

In other words, what Keynes was proposing was a *political* solution dictated by the apparently politically impossible task of *lowering* real wages in a recession and of tackling trade union restrictive practices and distortions in the market caused by governmental interference in the economy. To the economic liberals, Keynes was not solving the real problems of the economy, whose existence Keynes fully recognized, but was merely running away from them by proposing solutions that would be *politically* acceptable, but which would be, ultimately, economically disastrous. As a prominent Treasury official, Sir Frederick Leith-Ross, had said in 1929 of Keynes's proposals:

> The main trouble with our industrial situation at the present time is that our costs of production are not yet on a fully competitive level. This is admitted by all economists, however much they may differ in regard to remedies. Only last year Mr Keynes wrote that the fundamental blunder of the Treasury and the Bank of England has been due to their belief, that if they looked after the deflation of prices, the deflation of costs would look after itself. If this diagnosis is correct, what we have to do is to reduce costs by improving the organization of our industries, the efficiency of management and the output of Labour.'[62]

This has come to be known as 'The Treasury View'. To Leith-Ross and others, Keynes was inventing a whole new 'system' of economics, of 'macro-economics', to gloss over the real problems which lay at the micro-level, with the individual industries and businesses which created the real wealth. In Lionel Robbins's words, Keynesian economics ensured that 'We eschew the sharp purge ... we prefer the lingering disease.'[63] Leith-Ross, in a celebrated memorandum entitled 'The Assumptions of Mr. Keynes', set out a similar critique (that was to become a familiar refrain of the IEA during the 1960s and 1970s) as early as March 1930:

> The fact is that Keynes, like other economists, lives in a world of abstractions. He speaks of 'Industry', 'Profits', 'Losses', 'Price Level', as if they were realities. In fact we have no such thing as 'Industry'. What we have is a series of different industries – some prosperous, some depressed and a number carrying on normally. The position of each has to be examined separately.'[64]

To the Treasury, the remedy for mass unemployment was 'easy enough to find'; a 'reduction of ten per cent in' the wages of 'our workmen' or an 'increase in their efficiency by ten per cent'. But, as Leith-Ross continued,

> organised Labour is so attached to the maintenance of the present standard of wages and hours of labour that they would prefer that a million workers should remain in idleness and be maintained permanently out of the Employment Fund than accept any sacrifice. The result is to throw on to the capital and managerial side of Industry a far larger reorganization than would otherwise be necessary; and until Labour is prepared to contribute in large measure to the process of reconstruction, there will inevitably be unemployment.[65]

The most devastating critique of Keynes's economic solutions to the depression was made by Hubert Henderson, his former collaborator, who had become increasingly distrustful of the faith that Keynes was putting in his 'macro-economic' analyses. Henderson received Keynes's draft, proposing his own expansionist economic policies, for the EAC report in October 1930, and penned a blistering reply to Keynes's proposals – and indeed his entire economic thinking – which encapsulates the contemporary economic liberal case against Keynes. As Moggridge tactfully remarks, Henderson's memorandum 'produced considerable difficulties for the committee'. For Henderson, as Robbins and Leith-Ross had argued, Keynes's economic ideas seemed

> to run away, under cover of complex sophistication, from the plain moral of the situation it diagnoses; namely, that . . . we have no alternative now but to face up to the disagreeable

> reactionary necessity of cutting costs (including wages) in industry and cutting expenditure in public affairs . . .
>
> That is the plain moral of the situation, as plain as a pikestaff. It is of course highly disagreeable in itself. Furthermore, it is the moral drawn by the ordinary, conservative, unintellectual businessman; and some may find it still more disagreeable that the ordinary businessman may be right. But, if we allow ourselves to be swayed by such distaste we run a danger of making applicable the Duke of Wellington's description of another controversy: 'All the clever fellows were on the one side, and all the damned fools were on the other; and by God! all the damned fools were right.'
>
> [Keynes's] Draft Report, as it seems to me, after half-recognising the truth of the fore-going, runs right away from it, and proceeds to twist and wriggle and turn in a desperate attempt to evade the logic of the situation. Its practical drift is that we may with luck be able to evade the necessity for reducing costs by adopting a series of expedients of the most different kinds, which are all labelled 'Remedies for Unemployment', but some of which, whether they deserve that description or not, are in no sense remedies for but aggravations of the fundamental maladjustment that has got to be put right . . .'[66]

Instead, Henderson argued, as Robbins and the Treasury had before him, that wage cuts and public expenditure cuts were necessary, and that other remedies like devaluation would not succeed unless 'there was an earlier attempt to reduce costs'.[67] Both Robbins and Henderson also argued against Keynes's proposals for tariffs, plunging the work of the EAC into disarray. In the end, such were the disagreements that surfaced between the economists on the EAC that the eventual *Report of the Committee of Economists* presented to MacDonald in the autumn of 1930 was of little use to the government as it could propose few coherent courses of action. The economists had neither managed to agree on the cause of the depression, nor on Keynes's remedies for it. Robbins even submitted a separate report.[68] In 1929 and 1930, all these deliberations took place in private, sheltered from the gaze of an expectant world by the demands of Whitehall confidentiality, but the intellectual gulf which had opened up between different members of the committee of economists came into the open with a series of letters to *The Times* in 1932, in which both sides, for the first time, publicly formulated their opposing positions. On 5 July and 17 October the 'Keynesians' – in the case of the 5 July letter forty-one academic economists, mainly from Cambridge and Oxford, and in the case of the 17 October letter Keynes, Pigou, Stamp, Arthur Salter, Walter Layton and D. H. Macgregor – argued for both private investment and publicly funded expansionary measures. Their second letter was answered by a joint letter from Professors Hayek, T. E. Gregory, Plant and Robbins from the LSE, arguing against further public spending. For the first time, the battle-lines in economic policy had been drawn up in public, dividing the economic liberals of the LSE from the 'Keynesians' of Cambridge and increasingly Oxford, too; Keynes had crystallized the differences between them, and had moved those differences to the heart of the political debate about the causes of – and cures for – the depression.

Keynes's fully worked-out theory of 'deficit financing' and 'demand management' only appeared in 1936 with *The General Theory of Employment, Interest and Money*, in which he laid out his policy proposals for cheap money and government spending. In the *General Theory* Keynes presented in detail the arguments that he had been developing, in front of the EAC and elsewhere, since the mid-1920s. In particular he expounded a new 'political economy' of the 'liberal-Socialist' character that has already been referred to. He argued that the imposition of 'State Socialism' was unnecessary to cure unemployment in the new Keynesian System, as 'If the State is able to determine the aggregate amount of resources devoted to augmenting the instruments and the basic rate of reward to those who own them, it will have accomplished all that is necessary. Moreover the necessary measures of socialization can be introduced gradually and without a break in the general traditions of Society.' Keynes argued that he was not destroying liberal capitalism, but strengthening it instead. In his own words,

> the result of filling in the gaps in the classical theory is not to dispose of the 'Manchester system', but to indicate the nature of the environment which the free play of economic forces requires if it is to realise the full potentialities of production. The central controls necessary to ensure full employment will, of course, involve a large extension of the

> traditional functions of government . . . But then there will still remain a wide field for the exercise of private initiative and responsibility. Within this field the traditional advantages of individualism still hold good.[69]

To the economic liberals, however, *The General Theory*, far from being a coherent new theory of economics, merely compounded all the errors and evasions that had dogged Keynes's thinking since the EAC debates of 1930. The more perceptive economic liberal critics who reviewed Keynes's book, which was greeted with enormous acclaim in Britain, specifically focused on the consequences for inflation if the Keynesian system was introduced. For the economic liberals, the obvious point about what Keynes was proposing was that if real money wages could not be lowered, then the *value* of money could be lowered as an alternative by an expansion of the money supply – a process otherwise known as inflation. Frank Knight, the doyen of the Chicago School of economic liberalism, pointed this out forcefully in his review of Keynes's *General Theory* in 1937, stating 'that the direct contention of the work seems to be quite unsubstantiated . . . It seems to be reasonable to interpret the entire work as a new system of political economy, built around, and built to support, Mr. Keynes's conception of inflation as the cure for depression and unemployment.'[70] Jacob Viner, the Canadian economist, wrote of *The General Theory* that

> Keynes expresses sweeping dissent with the 'classical' doctrine that money wage rigidity is a major cause of cyclical and secular [structural] unemployment, although he freely grants that in general increased employment must mean lower real wages. He maintains that Labour strongly resists money wage-reductions but takes reductions in real wages much more calmly, and therefore, if money wage-reductions were logically a remedy for unemployment they would not be a practicable one. His view is that a lowering of money wage-rates, unless it proceeded simultaneously and uniformly all along the line, would chiefly alter the relative rates of wages of different Labour groups . . .

Viner ended with a prophetic flourish:

> In a world organised in accordance with Keynes's specifications there would be a constant race between the printing presses and the business agents of the trade unions.[71]

William Hutt, in his 1936 book *Economists and the Public*, repeated these charges, as did von Mises, who dubbed Keynes 'The new prophet of inflation'.[72] Wilhem Röpke, the prominent German economist, also argued to this effect, as did Jacques Rueff.* Much later Hayek summarized the case against Keynes in his *Constitution of Liberty*, published in 1960:

> The development of Lord Keynes's theories started from the correct insight that the regular cause of extensive unemployment is real wages that are too high. The next step consisted in the proposition that a direct lowering of money wages could be brought about only by a struggle so painful and prolonged that it could not be contemplated. Hence he concluded that real wages must be lowered by the process of lowering the value of money. This is really the reasoning underlying the whole 'full-employment' policy now so widely accepted. If Labour insists on a level of money wages too high to allow of full employment, the supply of money must be so increased as to raise prices to a level where the real value of the prevailing money wages is no longer greater than the productivity of the workers seeking employment. In practice, this necessarily means that each separate union, in its attempt to overtake the value of money, will never cease to insist on further increases in money wages and that the aggregate effort of the unions will thus bring about progressive inflation.'[74]

* Jacques Rueff, the prominent French economist, attacked the 'Fallacies of Lord Keynes's General Theory' in an article of 1947:

> In the situation foreseen by the Keynesian hypothesis – a depression caused by the refusal of certain workers to utilize the increment of income afforded them by an increment of employment – inflation can supply them with the increments of cash holdings which they want to obtain. In this way, so far as the offer of employment is accepted by the under-employed workers, whether it corresponds to their previous specialization or they accept the modifications in activity which it implies, an investment programme financed by inflation can bring about an increase in employment.'[73]

This was the real meaning of 'demand management'. Röpke, in an even clearer prediction of the Keynesian future argued in 1950 that

> A policy, therefore, which sees unemployment of whatever kind, and due to whatever cause, as sufficient reason for increasing 'effective demand' is necessarily tantamount to a policy of *constant inflationary pressure* . . . the social evil of partial employment will then be [replaced] by the even greater social evil of general inflation . . .[75]

But then Germans of Röpke's generation had lived through the devastating effects of 'general inflation', and the British had not. The German experience of rampant inflation in the 1920s was to have an important and enormously beneficial influence on Germany's post-war economic policies, of which Röpke was one of the main architects.

The central charge against Keynes was that he had constructed a new 'system' of economics which was based not on economic theory, but on a strictly political judgement that it was impossible to lower wages in Britain during the depression. As Hayek later wrote, although Keynes had 'called it a "general" theory, it was to me too obviously another tract for the times, conditioned by what he thought were the momentary needs of policy'.[76] Keynes was fully aware of the fact that governments could not afford to offend the unions in the political circumstances of the late 1920s and early 1930s by tackling the real problems of the economy, the rigidity of wages, the plethora of 'restrictive practices' and the concomitant uncompetitiveness of British industry – in this respect the 1926 General Strike was, indeed, a watershed in industrial relations, as the politicians were thereafter afraid that the body politic itself would not survive another attempt to drive down wages in a depressed industry as the coal-owners had eventually succeeded in doing after the General Strike itself had collapsed. It was the spectre of class war that haunted the deliberations of both politicians and economists as they grappled with the problems thrown up by the depression. Keynes's latest biographer, Robert Skidelsky, has argued that his solution to the problems of the depression represented a comprehensive answer to Karl Marx:

> What Marx had diagnosed as a distributional struggle to be settled by power, Keynes saw as a problem of insufficient

> demand to be remedied by expertise. If the leaders of capitalism insisted on treating problems of demand as though they were problems of supply, and on screwing down the wages of workers in order to restore profits, then a class war could easily arise which would vindicate Marx's prophecy. But such a result would be correctly attributable to error or stupidity; it was not necessary to the survival of the capitalist system that it should act in such a way as to precipitate its own downfall.[77]

In fact, by working from the premise that the coercive power of organized labour was such that it was *politically impractical* to reduce wages as part of a solution to the problem, Keynes had already conceded Marx's argument. The moment when economists and politicians accepted Keynes's alternative, mild inflation, to class war was the moment when the class war was effectively won by the industrial proletariat, because, as Jacob Viner had pointed out, only the massed battalions of organized labour stood to gain in the Keynesian system of demand-management, that 'mad race between the printing presses and the business agents of the trade Unions'. In the long run, Keynes was, in fact, running up the white flag on behalf of capitalism, and negotiating an honourable withdrawal. It was a very English revolution – virtually unnoticed at the time, and presided over by an old Etonian.

Equally, the trend of Keynesian thinking reinforced the politicians' confidence that they need not tackle the economy's underlying weaknesses. Although the National Governments of MacDonald and Baldwin implemented their own comparatively 'radical' policies to try to escape from the depression – erecting tariff barriers at Ottawa, leaving the Gold Standard and pursuing a policy of industrial rationalization – nonetheless, to many, these policies seemed, at best, to have been forced on the government by the pressure of events and, at worst, to be tangential to the real problems of the country. Despite the government's attempts to escape from the depression by pursuing collectivist policies in their external economic relations, Keynes was aware of the fact that governments were still searching for some alternative to the painful industrial restructuring that the economic liberals saw as both inevitable and necessary. He pointedly emphasized this fact (if anyone should have missed it) at the end of his *General Theory* when he wrote that 'At the present moment people are unusually expectant of a more fundamental diagnosis; more particularly ready to receive it; eager to try it out, if it should even be plausible.'[78] As the economic liberals feared and Keynes knew only too well, the attraction of his whole system of 'demand management' was its very plausibility – it offered the promise of curing unemployment without, apparently, resorting to complete collectivism as undertaken in the Soviet Union; just a little bit of planning and governmental intervention, which would not fundamentally affect society, and all would be well. For a political class faced with unemployment and economic stagnation, it is small wonder that Keynes's ideas were taken up with alacrity by many politicians in all parties from the mid-1930s onwards, from Young Conservatives like Bob Boothby and Harold Macmillan (the latter the author of the '*Middle Way*', the most important contemporary political expression of Keynesianism) to the rising young generation of Labour politicians such as Hugh Gaitskell, Anthony Crosland, Harold Wilson and Evan Durbin.

To the economic liberals, Keynes had betrayed his profession. Keynes's attraction to governments was that he had by the 1930s acquired an unrivalled reputation as an academic economist, and so, despite the fact that his whole system was based on *political*, not economic, foundations, the politicians could plausibly suggest that an economic system predicated on the imperatives of full-employment policy was based on sound economics. Hayek and Robbins, by contrast, hardly rated Keynes as an economist at all; Robbins referring to 'the dilettante economists of wealthy universities' in *The Great Depression*. Even Keynes's most recent and sympathetic biographer has written, with a remarkable degree of candour, that 'Keynes was not a political animal, but he was a political economist. He invented the theory to justify what he wanted to do. He understood that his theory had to be usable for politicians and administrators; easily applied, offering political dividends.'[79] Dennis Robertson, Keynes's collaborator at Cambridge for much of his career there, broke with him almost completely over the *General Theory* and what he saw as Keynes's craving for political influence at the expense of economic wisdom. In a brave lecture to the Royal Economic Society in 1949, called 'On Sticking to One's Last', delivered at a time when Keynesianism had hardened into an intellectual orthodoxy, Robertson pointedly warned his fellow economists not to be in

> too much of a hurry to pose as the complete man – too anxious to show that he is duly sensitive to the 'changed temper of the age' and has taken full account of what is 'politically' and 'psychologically possible' . . .

For if the economist followed this course, he '*will be in danger of betraying his calling*'.

Robertson continued that

> Twenty-five years ago it needed some spirit on [the economists'] part to develop the case for deficit financing as a remedy for trade depression without being prematurely silenced by the argument that it would scare the business-man and so do more harm than good. Now the boot is on the other foot, and it takes some spirit to state clearly and fairly the case for wage reductions as a cure for unemployment or an adverse balance of payments, or the case for the curtailment of subsidies . . . as a solvent of inflationary pressures, without being prematurely silenced by the argument that 'nowadays Trade Unions would never stand for such things'. Perhaps they wouldn't, but that is no reason for not following the argument withersoever it leads.[80]

It was Keynes who had abandoned economics for politics and political influence, and had completely disregarded his own injunction to readers of the Cambridge Economic Handbooks (instituted by Keynes himself in 1922) that economics 'does not furnish a body of settled conclusions immediately applicable to policy. It is a method rather than a doctrine, an apparatus of the mind, a technique of thinking, which helps its possessor to draw correct conclusions.' Robertson and some of his colleagues held to these modest and self-restraining principles, but Keynes had, by the early 1930s, 'completely disregarded his own cardinal principle'.[81] As Hutt observed in 1971, Keynes was always searching for a 'politically possible' solution because

> the economists who became influential and gained coveted reputations (Keynes and his early disciples in Britain and the 'New Deal' Economists in the United States) were those who could encourage governments to think there was a pol-

> itically easier way of maintaining sufficient popularity for re-election than that of eradicating by government action the privately contrived obstacles to the restoration of the wages-flow – not least monopolistic trade unions and industrial associations.[82]

The charge against Keynes that he had betrayed his profession by pandering to the political demands of the moment was a familiar one to inter-war liberals. The general malaise in European intellectual life was the subject of Julien Benda's celebrated work, *Le Trahison des Clercs*, published under the title *The Great Betrayal* in English by George Routledge in 1928. Benda's theme was the startling change in the role of 'les clercs' – the intellectuals – in the Europe of the twentieth century. In previous centuries, men like Kant and Erasmus had acted as true 'clercs', seeking after profound truths at a 'chiefly theoretical' level, without regard to the relevance of their work to modern society; indeed, for this very reason men such as Galileo had been condemned by their contemporaries for telling truths that they did not want to hear. But for Benda, at the end of the nineteenth century 'a fundamental change occurred, the "clerks" began to play the game of political passions. The men who had acted as a check on the realism of the people began to act as stimulators.' Surveying Europe during the 1920s, Benda lamented that

> First of all the 'clerks' have adopted political passions. No one will deny that throughout Europe to-day the immense majority of the men of letters and artists, a considerable number of scholars, philosophers and minister of the divine, share in the chorus of hatreds among races and political factions . . . the modern clerk is determined to have the soul of a citizen and to make vigorous use of it.

Benda could easily have had in mind that generation of British intellectuals, such as Laski, Beveridge and later the Auden generation, who would all succumb to the allure of exciting and guiding the 'political passions' of their own country, and who were honoured with political or other offices as a result. Benda called the true *clerc* 'an official of abstract justice . . . sullied with no passion for a worldly object'. On Benda's principal criteria of intellectual integrity, there can be no doubt that men like Keynes failed lamentably: 'there exists a certain criterion by which we may know whether the "clerk" who takes public action does so in conformity with his true functions; and that is, that he is immediately reviled by the layman, whose interests he thwarts. We may say beforehand that the "clerk" who is praised by the laymen is a traitor to his office.'[83] To many contemporary economic liberals, Keynes was the economist – if that – who sought the 'praise' of the laymen and was rewarded as a result, whilst Hayek, Robbins, von Mises et al. remained true to their calling and were largely ignored.

Keynes was also preaching to the converted in his avowed acceptance in *The General Theory* of the need for further encroachments by the State on the workings of the economy. Keynes was swimming with the tide of collectivism in British politics, and, indeed, his economic theory was used by many to justify further collectivist measures. To many economic liberals, and Hayek in particular, this was the most dangerous, and seductive, aspect of Keynesian economics, Keynes's claim that his economic theory of 'aggregate demand management' would allow the government to pursue an avowedly collectivist aim – 'full employment' – whilst still preserving all the essentials of individual freedom and liberty present in the old, pre-Keynesian capitalist countries. This is what Keynes called the political economy of 'liberal socialism', or the 'middle way'; in the Keynesian system, the government could pursue an economic policy 'for common purposes to promote economic and social justice' – mainly 'full employment' – whilst at the same time 'respecting and protecting the individual – his freedom of choice, his faith, his mind and its expression, his enterprise and his property'.[84] It offered politicians a path to recovery whilst avoiding the Scylla of central planning Communist-style and the Charybdis of *laissez-faire* individualism, which conjured up unpalatable visions of a return to the 'dark, satanic mills' of Victorian England. Keynes's 'liberal socialist' vision was, of course, the foundation of the Butskellite post-war consensus, but his ideas were already held in high regard by the mid- and late 1930s.[85] Indeed, such was the general enthusiasm for Keynes's ideas that as early as April 1936, only a few months after *The General Theory* was published, Hubert Henderson was complaining to a critic how exasperated he was by the 'assumption that prevails in certain circles that those who do not accept its general doctrines are to be regarded as intellectually inferior beings'. Henderson himself was one of the few British reviewers to be highly critical of the book, whilst he was positively scathing about Keynes's theories in an address to the Marshall Society at Cambridge in May 1936, arguing that Keynes's 'new theoretical system . . . asserts what is false and denies what is true, and is likely to cause an immense amount of intellectual confusion'.[86] But despite Henderson's strictures, by the late 1930s Keynes was already beginning to exert an almost mystical hold over his generation, as well as the generation after him. Keynes's standing in Britain ensured that within a decade 'Keynesianism' had become the new intellectual orthodoxy in Britain and its universities.

However, abroad, as we have seen, economists could look at Keynes's ideas in a light unclouded by excessive reverence. As a result, the economic liberal counter-revolution against Keynesianism was to be started and led mainly by overseas economists and intellectuals. Just as Halévy proved to be the best historian of Victorian England, so Austrians, Germans and Americans proved to be most objective and intellectually persuasive critics of the Keynesian orthodoxy. As several of them pointed out in the years after the publication of *The General Theory*, Keynes was, in fact, offering a fool's paradise, for to restrain the inflationary effects of the Keynesian system that even Keynes himself admitted to, governments would have to take progressively more and more micro-economic interventionist steps to restrain that inflation by statute or legislation, thus gradually curtailing the individual's freedom of economic action – a situation that was to arise, as predicted, in Britain from the early 1960s onwards with the interminable 'pay pauses', 'wage freezes' and 'prices and incomes policies' that characterized economic policy making during the 1960s and 1970s. A debate has raged amongst modern economists as to how far the 'Keynesian system' as it developed in Britain from 1950 onwards was, in fact, a true reflection of Keynes's ideas or a corruption of them.[87] Keynes died in 1946, before the full impact of his thinking was felt in government, so we shall never know whether he would have sanctioned what was done in his name after his death. But the economic liberals predicted from the start that Keynesianism would eventually lead to the sort of detailed government economic controls to contain inflation that the Keynesian system was designed to avoid. Thus it was flawed from the start; Keynesianism would not save liberal democracy, but over-burden it and eventually destroy it. This was the gist of Lionel Robbins's attack on Keynesian economics in his *Economic Planning and International Order*, published in 1937, in which he assailed the panacea of 'partial planning' as a dangerous illusion. As D. P. O'Brien has summarized Robbins's argument,

> Partial attempts at industrial planning had led to high prices and over-investment in particular industries, followed by their collapse, playing a part in the 1930s depression. When attempted in a basically free society industrial planning involved corruption, inter-governmental friction, political structures which threatened democracy. Such plans multiplied because their very failure seemed to lead to a need for more planning.[88]

Robbins was describing a 'collectivist spiral' that was to become familiar to readers of Hayek's *The Road to Serfdom*.

The whole point of the Keynesian system was to eschew politically painful change by manipulation of the currency – a system which would work, in the end, only by 'authoritative regulation'. Far from saving the liberal capitalist system, as Keynes claimed to be doing, he was in effect undermining it by debauching the currency – a tactic that, as Keynes himself acknowledged, had been recommended to his fellow Bolsheviks by Lenin himself.[89]

This was the aspect of Keynes's work that was most alarming to Hayek, and it was for his attack on Keynes's 'liberal Socialist' path of the 'mixed economy' that Hayek was to become most famous – or notorious. Hayek had already touched on this theme in his inaugural lecture at the LSE in 1933, which was delivered after he had already engaged in his first intellectual joust with Keynes in the columns of the academic journal *Economica*, in which he had attacked Keynes's book *Treatise on Money* in two articles in August 1931 and February 1932. Keynes replied to Hayek's first article in November 1931.[90] The exchange was highly technical, but in his reply to Hayek Keynes betrayed perhaps some of his irritation with those who doubted his own wisdom by turning on Hayek's book *Prices and Productions*, describing it as 'one of the most frightful muddles I have ever read, with scarcely a sound proposition in it . . . and yet it remains a book of some interest, which is likely to leave its mark on the mind of the reader'.[91] Hayek, as he was to recall later, felt that he had had the better of the exchange, which is one of the reasons why he, surprisingly, neglected to write a critique of *The General Theory* when it appeared five years later:

> I felt that I had largely demolished his theoretical scheme [of a *Treatise on Money*]. . . Great was my disappointment when all this effort seemed wasted because after the appearance of the second part of my article [in *Economica*] he told me that he had in the meantime changed his mind and no longer believed what he had said in that work
>
> This was one of the reasons why I did not return to the attack when he published his now famous *General Theory* – a fact for which I later blamed myself. But I feared that before I had completed my analysis he would again have changed his mind . . . My disagreement with that book did not refer so much to any detail of the analysis as to the general approach followed in the whole work. The real issue was the validity of what we now call macro-analysis, and I feel now that in a long-run perspective the chief significance of the *General Theory* will appear that more than any other single work it decisively furthered the ascendancy of macro-economics and the tapering decline of micro-economic theory.[92]

This is, perhaps, not an entirely convincing account, and Hayek's silence on *The General Theory* remains somewhat of a mystery. But Hayek contributed to the debate on planning and Keynesianism in another way, by editing a book called *Collectivist Economic Planning*, published in 1935, with contributions by Hayek himself, Professor N. G. Pearson, George Halm, and, most importantly, von Mises, who wrote the chapter on 'Economic Calculation in the Socialist Commonwealth', reiterating his original critique of 'planning' in *Socialism*. The whole book was a powerful attack on economic planning in a Socialist society, arguing that only the price system could ensure that rational production decisions could be made. As one historian has written

> For Hayek and the Austrians the point is not just that only a decentralised market system can handle the vast volume of information in a developed economy, but that this information is only *generated* in such an economy. It is not that there are millions of bits of objective data to be handled, but that knowledge of, for example, possible production techniques only arises because of competition and is

> inherently subjective, specific information available only to those who discover it.[93]

Indeed, Hayek himself was later to discard the word 'economy' altogether to describe the spontaneous financial interactions involved in the free-market system, preferring to use the word catallaxy.[94] Naturally, this argument was also deployed against those who advocated a 'mixed economy', combining public ownership with a market system. There is, indeed, some evidence to suggest that Hayek's arguments in *Collectivist Economic Planning* had some influence on the younger 'liberal-socialist' economists such as James Meade and Evan Durbin.[95] The debate between Hayek, von Mises and the younger Keynesians, the 'economic calculation' debate, was important for being Hayek's first practical contribution to the discussion.

In truth though, as Hayek was the first to admit, *Collectivist Economic Planning* did little to stem the tide of enthusiasm for Keynesian economics that swept through the universities and Westminster during the latter half of the 1930s. That the Keynesian economic system was 'politically' possible, and offered a painless solution to seemingly intractable problems, ensured its popularity; and all collectivists, Socialists, Liberals, and even many Conservatives, such as Macmillan, rushed to embrace it. Even before the 1930s were out, as Henderson had observed in 1936, to challenge Keynesianism was to cast oneself as a reactionary and, in a favourite phrase of the time, a 'die-hard'. This was especially true at Cambridge University, Keynes's intellectual home, where those who dissented from the new orthodoxy suffered both personally and professionally. One such was Dennis Robertson, Keynes's former intellectual collaborator, a self-torturing and meticulous scholar, who had split with Keynes over *The General Theory* after 1936. He had a torrid time at Cambridge after the war as the sole intellectual dissident in the economics faculty, despite succeeding Pigou as Professor of Economics in 1947.[96] The economist John Vaizey, a student at Cambridge in the early 1950s, befriended Robertson, but later admitted that under the veneer of cordiality 'I disapproved, sanctimoniously, of Robertson because he was politically a reactionary'. Vaizey wrote that Keynes was 'lately dead. Everybody was at sixes and sevens, war to the knife about the full significance of the General Theory . . .'[97]

Milton Friedman went to Cambridge on a Fulbright Scholarship in

1952–3 and also testified to the 'terrible atmosphere' there, Robertson and his few followers being excluded even from socializing with the Keynesians (led by the Robinsons, Sraffa and Kahn) at sherry parties.[98] Not that Robertson had many followers; indeed, there was only one of any significance, Stanley Dennison, the economics tutor at Gonville and Caius (home also to the conservative philosopher Michael Oakeshott), who was later to help Hayek lead the intellectual counter-attack against Keynes.

Such was the extraordinary and pervasive impact of Keynesianism on Britain that the arguments of the economic liberals against it hardly received a public hearing. Hayek was right in his inaugural lecture in 1933 in stating that there was an 'intellectual reaction' underway, led by the Austrians, against collectivism and planning, but the success and popularity of Keynesianism had swamped this 'intellectual' reaction in Britain, and completely overshadowed it. Whereas the economic and political ideas of Keynes received a wide audience and he was consulted by governments and politicians of all political colours – because he was telling them things that they wanted to hear – the arguments of the economic liberals were confined to the academic journals, the academic press, and in the case of the EAC debates, the Public Record Office. What Keynes had done was to divide the economics profession and the wider intellectual community into two camps, thus forcing the economic liberals to coalesce as a 'school of thought', based around Hayek and the LSE economics department, but including men such as Dennison at Cambridge and Polanyi and John Jewkes at Manchester, all of whom were later to play a role in reviving interest in economic liberalism under Hayek's leadership after the war. From 1935 onwards scholars out of the reach of Keynes's charismatic and beguiling personality launched their own counter-assault. The European intellectual opposition to planning and collectivism became focused on L'Institut Universitaire des Hautes Etudes Internationales at Geneva, founded in 1927 and supported by the Rockefeller Foundation, who were also the major financial backers of the LSE during the inter-war years. On the staff at the Institute during the 1930s were William Rappard, Ludwig von Mises and Wilhem Röpke, who was appointed Professor of International Studies in 1937. A Swiss businessman, Dr Hunold, who was later to assume a role of particular significance in the post-war revival of economic liberalism, was also involved with the work of the Institute. The Institute organized two conferences in the 1930s to discuss the implications of planning and Keynesianism for Europe's future. The first, held under the title of 'Les Mystiques économiques' ('Economic Myths') was held in June 1935, and the second, entitled 'Les Mystiques politiques', was held in June 1937. Professor Rougier wrote two books based on the work of these conferences, during the course of which he expounded two arguments that economic liberals were already familiar with; that Communism and Fascism, far from being polar opposites, were in fact two identical manifestations of the same collectivist mentality, and that 'Entre la Liberté et la constrainte, entre le libéralisme constructif dans le cadre de l'interdependence des peuples et l'étatisme oppressif dans le cadre de la nation on de la Race, il n'y a pas d'autre solution.' – There was no Keynesian 'middle way'.[99] The theme of the 1937 conference was familiar to readers of Julien Benda's work and Keynes's economic liberal critics, that economics had been hijacked by politics, and certain economists were now conjuring up economic 'myths' to solve 'political' problems. Rougier attacked the 'pseudo-demonstrations scientifiques' of the collectivists, and urged economists to revert to their own professional standards:

> Il n'y a pas une science economique liberale, Marxiste, dirigiste, corporatiste, planiste; la science economique se confine a decrire les lois auxelles obeissant les phenomenes economiques sous les regimes les plus variees . . .

Furthermore, he agreed with Robbins's and Hayek's analysis of the depression: that it was not caused by 'le désordre inherent au régime liberal', but by 'les directions et des contraintes imposées à l'organisme économique par l'intervention de l'Etat . . .'[100] It was thus at Geneva, under the guidance of Rappard, Röpke, Rougier and von Mises that the initial international efforts were made to develop an articulate and coherent critique of 'planning', collectivism and Keynesianism, efforts that paralleled the more modest efforts of Hayek, Robbins and others in Britain. The next step was to unite the anti-Keynesian critics in Europe and Britain and so, three years after the 'Mystiques Economique' Conference, Rougier, Röpke and Rappard came together for this purpose in Paris in 1938 at 'Le Colloque Walter Lippmann'. Although Hayek's principal allies at the LSE, Robbins and Plant, did not attend the 1938 Paris meeting, they were included on a list of members of 'Le Colloque' for the projected 1939 meeting, together with Michael Polanyi. Thus the Paris conference of 1938 represented a drawing together of the disparate threads of Western economic liberal thinking, and of those united by their opposition not just to totalitarian collectivism, but, more specifically and importantly, also their opposition to Keynesianism. The 1938 Conference acknowledged the work which had already been done to revive an interest in liberalism, whilst admitting that those ideas were at a peculiarly low ebb. There was a clear need for someone to captivate the public eye with a popular exposition of the case against collectivism and Keynesianism, a case largely ignored during the 1930s. The arguments were already at a highly developed stage by the beginning of war, but they still awaited an intellectual impresario to elucidate them and present them to the public in Keynes's very own polemical manner. It was now that several people urged upon Hayek his 'duty' to don that mantle, and he began to turn his mind to a book which would eventually become, just over five years later, *The Road to Serfdom.*

2

The Beveridge Report and *The Road to Serfdom*

*

The beginning of the Second World War effectively put a stop to any further intellectual gatherings such as the Colloque Walter Lippmann of 1938. The meeting planned by Rougier and his associates for September 1939 was cancelled, and Rougier's grand vision for a 'Centre Internationale d'Etudes pour la Rénovation du Liberalisme' was thus stillborn and the whole exercise achieved little in its own right. The real importance of the Rougier initiative was to emerge only later: without question, it prepared the ground for the more ambitious and successful liberal conference that Hayek was to found after the war. The Mont Pèlerin Society, as it came to be called, was modelled largely on Rougier's prototype; Hayek was to pick up where Rougier left off.

The coming of war not only brought Rougier's schemes to a hasty conclusion, but also dispersed those liberals in Britain who had been associated with it. In particular, the LSE was evacuated to Cambridge on the outbreak of hostilities and Hayek lived in lodgings arranged by Keynes at Peterhouse for much of the war, although he was occasionally entertained in King's College at weekends by Keynes, who from the summer of 1940 worked in the Treasury. Robbins was drafted into Whitehall, in the summer of 1940, to work as an economic assistant in the Office of the War Cabinet. Working with Robbins in what came to be known as the Economic Section of the War Cabinet were Stanley Dennison and John Jewkes, who were both to be closely associated with the revival of economic liberalism after 1945. John Jewkes, then at Manchester University, was initially head of the Economic Section, before moving to the Ministry of Aircraft Production. Both Jewkes and Robbins were to play a significant role in the formulation of one of the principal documents that was supposed to herald the arrival of the post-war era, the 1944 White Paper on Employment. Their roles in the formulation of this controversial White Paper will be examined later. Others in what Robbins called the 'distinguished group' of economists working in the Economic Section included Alec Cairncross, D. N. Chester, James Meade, Austin Robinson, Richard Stone and Harold Wilson.[1]

The 'Phoney War' that lasted from September 1939 to May 1940 saw little change in British politics or in British economic planning as Chamberlain continued to try and conduct affairs in a spirit of 'business as usual', much to the rising anger of those back-bench Tories and Ministers who hankered after more direct action against Germany and a greater sense of urgency in the production of armaments. Their feelings were shared by certain sections of the labour movement, represented by papers such as the *Daily Mirror*, who would never forgive Chamberlain and the 'Men of Munich' for their craven appeasement of Nazi Germany. The political situation was, however, transformed by the inept British campaign in Norway of April 1940, which, combined with Hitler's even more successful invasion of the Lowlands and France, swept away Chamberlain's dithering administration, to be replaced by Churchill's new Government on 10 May. The sudden and relentless victories of the German armed forces in France and Britain's isolation during the Battle of Britain transformed Britain's political and military situation, and, whereas Chamberlain had tried to fight the war while maintaining a high degree of peacetime economic activity, under Churchill's leadership the economy was, necessarily, transformed very quickly into a war economy, with all that that implied in terms of government controls, regulation, rationing and planning. By the end of 1940 Britain was the most rigorously planned and regimented society in Europe, fighting 'total war' to a degree that even the Germans never achieved.

It was, as several people observed at the time, Socialism by default. The political transformation which occurred during the years 1940–1 within the context of this forced collectivism has been chronicled before, most effectively by Paul Addison.[2] The Government's extension of its powers over property and labour during 1940 was mirrored by a determined groundswell of opinion outside Parliament for a new vision of society, based on a similar extension of governmental intervention in the lives of its citizens. The creation of a new and better Britain was 'vociferously taken up by the press and a multitude of pressure groups'[3] and also by the Labour ministers in Churchill's

Coalition Government. The political mood of the country seemed to be dominated by the demand to build a 'New Jerusalem' at the end of the War.[4] It was in this heady atmosphere that the Government's planning for post-war reconstruction started in 1941, most significantly in the appointment of Sir William Beveridge in July to chair a Committee 'to undertake, with special reference to the inter-relation of the Schemes, a survey of the existing national Schemes of social insurance and allied services, including workmen's compensation, and to make recommendations'. Out of this seemingly innocuous brief came the celebrated Beveridge Report of December 1942, which, more than anything else, crystallized the new collectivist mood abroad in wartime Britain. To add a further twist to the crisis of liberalism as identified by Hayek and his colleagues, Beveridge himself was, like Keynes, a prominent member of the Liberal Party – and, indeed, Hayek had helped to draft passages of Beveridge's speeches at the LSE before the Second World War.

The increasing rush towards collectivism in Britain that the war precipitated was analyzed, appropriately enough, by Harold Laski, in the Tenth Hobhouse Memorial Lecture, which he gave at the LSE on 24 May 1940, on the 'Decline of Liberalism'. Capturing the atmosphere of incipient political crisis and the forging of a new popular mood brilliantly, Laski pronounced liberalism dead: 'We must, if we are to be honest, admit that the liberalism for which Hobhouse battled so bravely has suffered an eclipse as startling and as complete as that which attended the doctrine of the divine right of Kings after the revolution of 1688.'

Laski's analysis of the liberal dilemma has already been referred to, and he finished his lecture by urging liberals to go further down the road to planning and 'Social control', ending: 'We must make of our society a co-operative and not a competitive adventure; it is now historically beyond discussion that the mere conflict of private interests can never produce a just Commonwealth.'[5]

This became the prevailing orthodoxy of the day, an intellectual orthodoxy which had been solidifying during the 1930s, as the pre-war debates over 'economic calculation' had shown, and which now became enshrined in the Beveridge Report, with its emotive prologue describing the combined attack on the 'five giants on the road to reconstruction', namely 'Want, Disease, Ignorance, Squalor and Idleness'.[6] As one historian of the period, Dr Harriet Jones, has written:

> This vision galvanised public opinion on Social reform at a time when the country was still in grave danger. Unquestioning acceptance of Beveridge became a sort of litmus test of decency, and soon there were few who dared to criticise the plan openly at the risk of appearing mean. On the day it was published a queue a mile long formed outside the Government bookshop in Central London. Within three hours 70,000 copies were sold. Two weeks later, a BIPO [British Institute of Public Opinion] Report determined that 95% of the public had heard of the Report, with 88% in favour, 6% against, and 6% undecided. Interest was marked particularly among the lower income groups . . .[7]

The Beveridge Report was extraordinarily popular amongst the British public, and was eagerly taken up by most of the Labour Party and the press. For the Coalition Government, however, it presented a major political and ideological problem, as, almost single-handedly, Beveridge had managed to expose the divisions within the Coalition that had always lain just below the surface.

The main problem lay with the Conservative Party, whose MPs were largely sceptical of, if not downright hostile to, the Beveridge Report. The divisions that now opened up were to reflect, in embryonic form, the ideological divisions which would dog the party for many decades thereafter. For it is clear that many Conservatives, those who can be called 'liberal Conservatives', were thoroughly opposed to the increasing trend towards economic collectivism that the Beveridge Report embodied. As the most recent historian of wartime politics has written, 'the absence of any major initiatives in the first two years of coalition clearly reflected the mood of the Conservative majority in Parliament . . . Tory back-benchers were resentful of what they saw as the socialistic trend of Wartime controls over the economy, and were determined to limit, where possible, the influence of Labour Ministers'.[8] Sensitive to the popular acclaim for Beveridge, the Party, instead of holding an open debate on the subject of his report, commissioned an *ad hoc* Committee appointed by the Party's Post-War Problems Central Committee (PWPCC) to prepare a confidential report on Beveridge's proposals for the Party leadership. The Committee was chaired by Ralph Assheton (later Lord Clitheroe, who became Party Chairman in 1944) as well as a number of the Party's more committed 'liberal Conservative' MPs – 'die-hards' to their opponents – such as Spencer Summers.[9] Assheton's chairmanship of this Committee was to prove of particular importance, as he quickly emerged as one of the more imaginative thinkers of that wing of the Conservative Party which found itself increasingly at odds with the collectivizing tendencies of the age. Making full use of the confidentiality afforded them by the Party leadership, Assheton and his colleagues attacked the Beveridge Report with a frankness which was sadly lacking in the public debate on the subject. The Committee took issue with Beveridge on two main points. In the first instance, they argued that Beveridge's proposals were just too expensive, that the country's priority after the war should be to revive her shrunken export trade rather than to embark on an expensive and apparently open-ended scheme of comprehensive social provision in what were bound to be straitened financial circumstances; 'The whole scheme is one for sharing prosperity and if there is no sufficient prosperity to share, it fails.' In the second instance the Committee heavily criticized the implicit 'universality' of Beveridge's Scheme, the idea behind the phrase 'social security' that *everyone* should contribute, via taxation, to the Scheme and that everyone should benefit from it, regardless of *want*. This lack of targeting on those in genuine need was seen not only as extravagant, but also as avowedly redistributionist in its effect; as the Committee pointed out, 'the Scheme becomes more and more one for distributing national income'. The Committee made its objections to both the economic and moral implications of the Beveridge Report very clear:

> it must be realised at once that a great part of the money required for putting his scheme into effect is not devoted to curing want. Sir William is in search of a comprehensive and unified Scheme of Social Security for the citizens of this country. Provision by the State of complete Social Security can only be achieved at the expense of personal freedom and by sacrificing the right of an individual to choose what life he wishes to lead and what occupation he should follow.[10]

In presenting their Report to the Party leadership on the eve of the debate on the Beveridge Report in the House of Commons, the Committee claimed to represent no less than ninety per cent of the Parliamentary Party, a figure authenticated by modern research on the subject.[11] Given this weight of feeling against the Report, which Churchill himself shared, it was hardly surprising that the Government's spokesmen in the House of Commons debate, Sir Kingsley Wood, the Chancellor of the Exchequer, and Sir John Anderson, were hard-pressed to give the Report anything more than a lukewarm endorsement. For, in the last analysis, Churchill and his Party were at one in the Prime Minister's assessment of Beveridge as 'an awful windbag and a dreamer'.[12] As a result of the Government's refusal to contemplate immediate legislation to implement the Beveridge Report, the vote on the Labour amendment against the Government produced the largest anti-Government vote of the war. In the end, the Government successfully stalled any legislation based on Beveridge for the remainder of the war, only producing a White Paper in 1944, with no binding commitments, which was also fiercely attacked by Labour.

The Beveridge Report was thus a searing experience for politicians of all sides, as it opened up the basic ideological divisions within the Conservative Party between those who wanted to advance, together with the Liberal and Labour Parties, further down the road towards the New Jerusalem of a Welfare State and greater collective economic controls, and those, the ninety per cent who opposed the Beveridge Report for instance, who saw no need for a brave new world, and who took a more pessimistic view of Britain's economic situation at war's end. Contrary to popular belief in the legend of wartime consensus, from 1942 onwards the ideological split opened up by Beveridge only deepened. These divisions were only obscured by the 'electoral truce', which ensured that candidates of the three main parties did not stand against each other in by-elections during the War, thus curtailing the range of open debate on politics – but the divisions were, nonetheless, real enough. Subsequent White Papers and plans for post-war reconstruction did not represent any sympathetic consensus between the two major parties, but rather the limits of agreement that could be reached. As Kevin Jefferys has written:

> Consensus ... did not ... embrace the opposing front-bench teams by 1945, still less party stalwarts on the back-benches and in the constituencies ... the maintenance of agreement between Tory and Labour leaders was contingent upon agreeing to disagree. The Government deliber-

> ately limited its areas of domestic activity, and on crucial issues where controversy threatened to erupt – such as over the future ownership of industry – conflict was avoided simply by postponing the matter under consideration. The Coalition programme for reconstruction, moreover, remained very much at the planning stage. In spite of all the sound and fury, the Beveridge Report was not acted upon before 1945, and, apart from the 1944 Education Act and the introduction of family allowances, no major items of social legislation reached the statute book before the end of the war. The reasons for this were clear-cut; it reflected, at base, intractable differences between the major coalition partners . . . The White Papers it produced were not intended as an inviolable guide to post-war policy, and were sufficiently ambiguous to allow of very different interpretations by opposing political leaders, as was evident in the run-up to the 1945 election.[13]

Nothing illustrates this point better than the fabled White Paper on Employment Policy of 1944, which has usually been seen, especially by Socialists, as the precursor of the post-war corporatist state of Keynesian demand management. In fact, as Jefferys has shown 'the White Paper represented the very limits of Coalition consensus; and the parties were able to support the document only by agreeing to disagree on future policy. The drafting of the White Paper required a series of compromises at every level, from civil servants and economic advisers through to ministers . . .'[14] The impetus for a White Paper on Employment originally came from James Meade, the young Keynesian economist at the Treasury who broached the subject in a memorandum of February 1941. However, the real push for a paper on post-war employment policies came with the publication of the Beveridge Report; Meade recognized, in a letter to Keynes of 8 January 1943, that

> the great support which the Beveridge Report has received has suggested to me that there ought really to be a similar publication on the subject of post-war unemployment. The enthusiastic public reception of the Social Security proposals shows that there is an exceedingly strong feeling in

> the country about post-war internal reconstruction and that people are in such a mood as they have never been before for the reception of imaginative ideas for social reform . . . it occurs to me, to be quite frank, that what we really require is a Keynes Report to follow up the Beveridge Report.[15]

In fact, Keynes was notably cool about the idea, preoccupied, as he was, with the tortuous problems of Britain's post-war external financial arrangements. However, spurred on by the looming threat of Beveridge publishing his own book on post-war employment policies, throughout 1943 the Economic Section of the War Cabinet worked with Treasury officials to produce a paper that the Government could show to the House of Commons. This proved a delicate business, as the entire subject of full employment was bound to highlight all those differences in economic policy making that had been so keenly felt in the 1930s. Sir Hubert Henderson, Lionel Robbins and John Jewkes were all closely involved in the drafting of the White Paper, and they were quick to criticize any exaggerated claims for economic management that their more Keynesian colleagues, such as Meade, might have wanted to include in the Report. Robbins was particularly keen that, whilst the White Paper should commit the Government to a 'high and stable level of employment', it should also encourage the Government to tackle restrictive practices in order to enhance a competitive economy. Only by encouraging such reforms at the micro-economic level could British industry be made competitive again and 'high and stable' levels of employment be achieved. Robbins 'parted company' with the rest of the drafting Committee on this point, and, as Alec Cairncross has recalled, 'produced a note of dissent which is a trumpet call for free competition'.[16] Henderson was equally critical of some of the proposals, and reiterated his argument of the 1930s that commitment to an employment policy which involved 'budgetary policy of an unorthodox type' would only 'result in external difficulties owing to the fact that unemployment in Britain normally came from a decline in demand for British exports and resulted in a deterioration in the balance of payments and that, in those circumstances, especially with the large sterling balances left behind by the war . . .' deficit financing 'would prove difficult to pursue'.[17] Keynes himself, whilst agreeing with Henderson's gloomy prognosis about 'our prospect in external financial position', argued, nonetheless, that full employment policies should be pursued *precisely because* unemployment 'could not be allowed' in a country trying to maximize its industrial production; besides, large-scale unemployment would not appeal to international financiers.[18] As Cairncross, who was in the Economic Section of the Cabinet at the time, has testified, the final shape of the White Paper, given these opposing views, was in doubt up to the very last minute, and the series of compromises needed to produce anything at all meant that the White Paper, published on 26 May 1944, was very cautious, demanding not 'full employment' as has often been alleged, but a 'high and stable level of employment', defined as an unemployment rate of less than 8.5 per cent of the population. Whilst more direct management of the economy was accepted than in the past, with a higher level of public investment, the White Paper envisaged that wartime controls over the economy were to be relaxed 'and was openly contradictory about the value of deficit finance as a means of countering cyclical depression'.[19] Thus the paper could, on the one hand, be openly praised by the Tories, who saw in it a continuing commitment to private enterprise and a very limited role for the State in economic management, whilst on the other hand the Keynesians in Whitehall could likewise see the White Paper as a great victory for Keynesianism. The historian Peter Clarke has written that both the Beveridge Report and the 1944 White Paper represented not a surrender by the Treasury to Keynesian ideas, but an 'incremental encroachment' of Keynesianism which was 'certainly gathering pace'.[20] Thus the White Paper of 1944 was, if nothing else, certainly Janus-faced.

However, for Robbins and Jewkes, the White Paper clearly contained all the significant warnings about trying to operate a Keynesian system of demand management that they could have hoped for. According to Jewkes, it was Robbins who insisted on the term 'high and stable' level of employment, rather than 'full employment', as the latter would have created 'over-ambitious expectations which might easily lead to frustration and disillusionment.' Whilst, however, looking back on the White Paper in 1976, Jewkes conceded that it had outlined 'a formula for maintaining stability of employment and prices through the manipulation of demand'; he insisted that, owing to his own, as well as Robbins's and Henderson's efforts, it had also 'embodied a set of clear warnings of the conditions to be satisfied if adverse reactions, and especially inflation, were to be avoided'.[21] These 'warnings' were largely ignored at the time, but brilliantly picked up by Peter Jay, economics editor of *The Times*, at an IEA Seminar in 1974, reprinted in the IEA paper 'Inflation: Causes, Consequences, Cures'. Jay quoted the White Paper's warnings:

> If we are to operate with success a policy for maintaining a high and stable level of employment, it will be essential that employers and workers should exercise moderation in wage matters . . . the principle of stability does mean . . . that increases in the general level of any rates must be related to increased productivity due to increased efficiency and effort. The stability of these two elements [wages and prices] is a condition vital to the success of employment policy; and that condition can be realised only by the joint efforts of the Government, employers and organised Labour . . .
>
> It would be a disaster if the intention of the Government to maintain total expenditure [and thereby full employment] were interpreted as exonerating the citizen from the duty of fending for himself and resulted in a weakening of personal enterprise. For, if an expansion of total expenditure were applied to cure unemployment of a type due, not to absence of jobs, but to failure of workers to move to places and occupations where they were needed, the policy of the Government would be frustrated and a dangerous rise in prices might follow.

This is a straight reiteration of the Robbins/Henderson critique of Keynesianism, expressed on many occasions during the 1930s, and contained in a White Paper supposedly committing the Government, for the first time, to a Keynesian system of demand management to secure full employment! In fact, as Jay pointed out in 1974, the passage quoted above: 'in a nutshell, is the history of Britain's post-war economy. The rhetoric being endlessly repeated while the warnings were ignored and the forebodings were fulfilled . . .'[22]

It is not clear why these warnings were made in vain; Jewkes certainly attributed this to the much more ambitious report published by Beveridge soon after the White Paper, *Full Employment in a Free Society*. This was, in Jewkes's view, a much more 'fundamentally collectivist book', but due to Beveridge's heroic reputation with the public at the time and his previously close relationship with the Government, this work was, perhaps, taken to be the summation of all contemporary wisdom on the subject in the White Paper's stead. Beveridge's was certainly a much more optimistic work, and the book's argument for 'a reduction of unemployment to no more than three per cent, as compared with the ten to twenty-two per cent experienced in Britain between the wars' was much better suited to the optimistic political mood of the period than the often gloomy forebodings of the White Paper. But equally important was the fact that Beveridge's low figure was urged on him by the trade unions, and then publicly endorsed by them. Given the popularity of Beveridge after his 1942 Report as well as his own vanity and vaulting ambition, it was perhaps inevitable that the warnings of the economic liberals in the White Paper should have been swamped by the sweeping tides of Beveridge-enthusiasm.

Just as the liberal Conservatives fought their corner in the House of Commons, so the economic liberals in Whitehall fought theirs. However, this meant that, especially in the Conservative Party, there was an uncomfortable outbreak of factionalism as the ideological divides deepened. As well as the majority of Tories who opposed Beveridge, there was a significant number of mainly younger MPs who were convinced of the need for a more 'progressive' policy approach, and who backed the Beveridge Report. They formed the Tory Reform Group, (the TRG) specifically to campaign for the Beveridge Report within the Party. The TRG consisted of about forty MPs, and was led by Viscount Hinchingbrooke, and included such young bloods as Quintin Hogg, Hugh Molson, and Peter Thorneycroft. They argued that it was essential for the Party to find its Disraelian roots, and to once again put the 'condition of the people' at the forefront of the agenda, to offer the electorate an alternative to Socialism. They looked to R. A. Butler for leadership, the one Minister responsible for the actual passing of a piece of wartime reconstruction legislation, the 1944 Education Act. They opened up the old cleavage between 'liberal Conservatives' and 'paternalists' with renewed enthusiasm. They supported most of the Government's limited plans for post-war reconstruction, and also issued a series of pamphlets, subsidized by Viscount Astor.[23]

As a reaction against the formation of the Tory Reform Group, the 'liberal Conservatives' within the Party who had opposed the Beveridge Report also began to form their own cabal, and in November 1943 they founded the 'Progress Trust', made up of about 20 MPs who 'believed that the primary aim of the Conservative Party should be to protect private enterprise and to safeguard the individual's liberties against the centralised power of the State, and who still hankered after *laissez-faire* individualism'.[24] The Progress Trust was a highly secretive, select group of MPs, dedicated to combating the influence of the TRG in the Party. Regular weekly dinner meetings were held, and Cabinet Ministers were invited to address them. The Trust managed to staff an office in Westminster and also did some fund-raising. Amongst those identified as members were some influential MPs; A. G. Erskine-Hill, the Chairman of the 1922 back-bench Committee, Spencer Summers, who had sat on Assheton's Committee on the Beveridge Report, and who was also a close friend of the Swedish classical liberal economist Gustav Cassel, Henry Willink, who served as Minister of Health when the White Paper on the National Health Service was being discussed in 1944, as well as the prominent back-benchers E. G. R. Lloyd, R. E. Manningham-Butler and Sir Douglas Thomson. The Progress Trust survives to this day (a recent chairman was Sir Peter Horden) but it is difficult to gauge its influence within the Party during the war. Other Tory MPs were also joining up with the equally obscure National League for Freedom, which at the end of the war was to merge with the Society of Individualists.

The launch of the Society of Individualists in November 1942 was probably the most constructive and influential of the wartime attempts to revive interest in the politics of classical liberalism. It was largely the creation of Ernest Benn, a scion of the Benn publishing family. By way of contrast to his own creed of militant individualism, Ernest's father, John, had been leader of the Progressive Party on the London County Council, his brother Wedgwood, after starting his political career with the Liberals, joined the Labour Party and (as Viscount Stansgate) served in Attlee's post-war Labour Government, whilst Ernest's nephew Tony Benn MP remains as fervent a believer in economic collectivism as was Ernest Benn in economic individualism. Ernest Benn joined the successful family publishing business in 1891, and during the First World War served in Whitehall at the Ministry of Reconstruction, where he was involved in the setting up of the Whitley Councils, the first attempt at Government-sponsored institutional arbitration between trade unions and management. Ernest Benn was, at first, an energetic advocate of such schemes, but his enthusiasm was tempered by his direct experience of working in Whitehall and trying to administer the Whitley Councils, which led him to a life-long 'impatience with the ways of bureaucracy'.[25] Disillusioned by Whitehall and inspired by a trip to America in 1921, he quickly developed a creed of social and political individualism based on unfettered capitalism. He outlined his new-found faith in *The Confessions of a Capitalist*, which he published in 1925, and which by the late 1940s had sold an extraordinary 250,000 copies. The book, written in an easy but combative style, was an overnight success and made him, at least in the public eye, the most famous exponent of Manchester School-style radical liberalism during the inter-war years. From 1925 onwards Benn devoted himself to the cause of individualism with admirable gusto and energy, penning a stream of pamphlets and books on the subject, as well as founding the Individualist Bookshop in 1926 and 'The Friends of Economy' in 1931, to campaign for cuts in public expenditure to lift the country out of the depression. The fact that Benn's views seemed increasingly antediluvian as the 1930s went on served only to redouble his commitment to his chosen cause. As *The Times* obituary remarked, 'It was easy to mock his views, for he knew no middle way and was often exaggerated in the emphasis of his warnings . . . He was the spokesman of no interest but of an idea – of one aspect of Liberalism which not even a collectivist society, if it wishes to remain free, dare ignore.'[26]

It was not surprising, therefore, that many people looked to Benn for a lead when the debate between economic liberals and the 'New Jerusalemers' sharpened during the early years of the war. Even before the publication of the Beveridge Report, on 20 May 1941 Benn and his allies met for the first time in the Reform Club to decide on a full-scale programme of pamphlet-publishing against what they conceived to be a direct attack on competitive capitalism, individualism and political liberty from the more collectivist-minded members of the Government. Benn was joined in his endeavours by, amongst others, Collin Brooks, the editor of the somewhat unsavoury Conservative magazine *Truth*,[27] Major Leonard Cripps, the shipowning brother of the leading Labour politician Sir Stafford Cripps, the Oxford academic Dr K. C. Allen, and Francis Hirst, who thus provided a link with the anti-collectivist organizations of the first years of the century. Another significant contributor was S. W. Alexander, a journalist specializing in economics and industry matters for the Beaverbrook-owned press, then with the *Evening Standard*. Alexander's belief in free trade was held with a passionate conviction matched only, perhaps, by his proprietor's equally unshakeable attachment to tariffs and Empire protectionism, and the two subsequently parted company in 1946. S. W. Alexander was forcefully reminded of the new 'spirit of the age' when he was invited to attend Archbishop Temple's famous Malvern Conference on social policy after clashing with the prelate on this subject in the correspondence columns of *The Times*. The Conference assembled in the autumn of 1941, and Alexander recorded his sense of isolation:

> Overwhelmingly those attending the Conference were on the left-wing of politics or sentimentalists with no experience of Commerce or understanding of the economic factors of earning a living. . . .
>
> I found a very deep prejudice amongst those present against anyone they believed represented 'City of London' opinion . . . to them Free Trade signified a 'free-for-all' with victory to the rich and the strong and the 'devil take the hindmost' . . . And there was a special hostility to private property, particularly to private ownership of productive resources . . .'.[28]

With the suspension of overt party politics for the duration of the war, Alexander and others like him looked to Ernest Benn to alert the public to the dangers that they saw in the Government's drift towards a more centralized society, a natural consequence, as they saw it, of much of the planning for post-war Britain. Soon after Beveridge had been commissioned to write his Report, on 3 July 1941 Benn and his followers issued the *Manifesto of British Liberty*, and in November 1942, a month before the Beveridge Report was actually published, they founded the Society of Individualists. The 'Liberty Manifesto', as it came to be known, was divided into several sections, under the headings, 'State and Individual', 'Government', 'Economics' and 'National Morale'. Under all these headings the manifesto vigorously rejected any further encroachment of State powers, and the final paragraph bleakly anticipated Hayek's central message in *The Road to Serfdom*:

> The assertion of individual right has been regarded as hopelessly reactionary, and its advocacy by any public man as equivalent to a political suicide. That sentiment persists and,

> despite the so-called political truce, innumerable efforts are being made to persuade our people that social salvation is only to be found in millennial plans which involve vast expansion of the functions of the State, and corresponding limitations of the rights of the individual. This spirit, unless it is fought promptly and resolutely, can only result in the country's lapsing into one or other of the forms of totalitarian Government.[29]

The Society published numerous pamphlets during the war and members defended the Manifesto at meetings up and down the country; S. W. Alexander, for instance, engaged Lord Longford in debate on the subject of the Beveridge Report at the Cambridge Union in January 1943. The Society was thus able to engage the 'New Jerusalemers' in debate in a way that the bulk of Conservative MPs, either hidebound by the electoral 'truce' or away at the front, could not. There was a good deal of interest shown by Conservative MPs in the activities of the Society of Individualists, and in 1944 some of those MPs who had formed the National League of Freedom (which included several members of the Progress Trust) amalgamated their organization with the Society of Individualists.[30] It is difficult to assess what influence the Society had on wartime politics. Their newsletter, *Freedom First*, did not sell well and Benn himself was considered by many to be too extreme to be taken very seriously. An article that he wrote in the *National Review* of July 1945, alleging, amongst other things, that the Labour Party had 'wanted' the war in order to lay their hands on the economic levers of power, was indicative of a style of political invective that often exposed him to ridicule.[31] However, the Society of Individualists was important as the only non-Party meeting-place for those concerned with the issues of classical liberalism in the 1940s and early 1950s, and as such it provided a forum for the expression of views that were not to be heard anywhere else. It thus attracted renegades from all the other political parties. Many of the men involved in the revival of economic liberalism in the post-war years first met through the Society of Individualists and it represented an important link between an older generation of economic liberals, through the likes of Francis Hirst, and younger adherents to the cause who were to do much to stimulate the revival of interest in the men such as of economic liberalism in the post-war era, including the likes of Oliver Smedley and Antony Fisher, the founders of the Institute of Economic Affairs, who first met at the Society of Individualists.

'Sure you've got the right war, blokes?' Cartoon by Sir David Low, from the *Evening Standard* of 20 August 1942. © Cartoon Study Centre, University of Kent, Canterbury/Solo.

The Progress Trust, the National League of Freedom and the Society of Individualists all represented an ideological reaction against the Government's plans for further post-war collectivism, and, also in 1942, these organizations were joined by 'Aims of Industry', which had a more direct interest in the political trend towards collectivism, as it sought to represent the views of that section of society that had most to lose from any further progress towards industrial and economic collectivism, the industrialists themselves. In 1942, worried by the increasing enthusiasm amongst Parliamentarians and the electorate for a higher level of governmental control over industry as well as demands for higher taxes on profits after the war, a group of industrialists met to, in their own words, 'anticipate the need to combat the false ideologies of the left, and to establish an understanding of the need for freedom and free enterprise'. Present at the first meeting were Garfield Weston, head of Associated British Foods and Conservative MP for Macclesfield, J. Arthur Rank, Sidney Askew, a business partner of the

Ranks, Sir Felix Pole, Chairman of Associated Electrical Industries, and the ubiquitous Collin Brooks of *Truth*. It was decided to start an organization to represent the case of free enterprise to the public, and Hubert Starling, an industrialist then working for Lord Beaverbrook in Whitehall, was drafted in to become the first Director of Aims of Industry. In fact, it was Collin Brooks who did most of the work and who also edited the pamphlets that Aims began to publish towards the end of the war. Founded by the owners of industry to represent their views to the public, Aims of Industry was essentially a special-interest pressure group, and devoted most of its energies, especially in the late 1940s, to fighting the Labour Government's nationalization programme. Despite early reverses, Aims of Industry came to national prominence in 1949 with its famous campaign on behalf of Tate and Lyle against the Government's plan to nationalize the sugar industry. The 'Mr Cube' Campaign (in which every sugar packet was used for a propaganda cartoon featuring a worried 'Mr Cube') was outstandingly successful. Aims of Industry had little effect on the course of politics during the war, but from 1950 to 1970 it certainly played a very important role as almost the only pressure group working on behalf of free-enterprise industrialists. Michael Ivens, who joined Aims of Industry in 1962 and has been Director of Aims from 1972 to the present day, was closely involved in the work of other free-market think-tanks in the 1970s and 1980s. Aims of Industry also cultivated close links with the Conservative Party right from its foundation, not only through Collin Brooks, but with the help of MPs such as Commander Galbraith, Tom Margesson and W. S. ('Shakes') Morrison, who were all, in the studiously obscure words of the organization's own literature, 'brought in to help'.[32] A similar organization was British United Industrialists (BUI), founded towards the end of the war in order to raise money from industrialists for 'free enterprise parties'. Founded by Robert Renwick (later Lord Renwick, an early investor in the Institute of Economic Affairs) and Sir William Goodenough, the Chairman of Barclays, it came into existence through the merger of the Home Counties Industrialists Association and the British Industrialists Association. Amongst other organizations that benefited from the largesse of BUI were Aims of Industry, the Progress Trust and the Conservative Party itself. The history of BUI, as it preferred, is suitably vague, but, once again, it was to make occasional but vital contributions to the work of later free-market think-tanks in the 1970s and 1980s.[33]

Except for BUI, which was closed down by John Major in March 1992, all these groups survive, in varying degrees of health, to the present day. Although the Progress Trust, the Society of Individualists, Aims of Industry and BUI were all founded by different people to represent separate sectional interests, whether it be amongst Conservative MPs or the captains of industry, they shared common cause – resisting the encroachment of further governmental control upon all aspects of the nation's life. Each organization embodied one particular aspect of this general phenomenon; the Progress Trust was founded as a response to the general enthusiasm for the Beveridge Report, whereas Aims of Industry was founded to present the case against Labour's plans for the nationalization of industry. The Society of Individualists was primarily concerned with the Government's encroachment on the civil liberties of the citizen, and Ernest Benn was to retain his greatest wrath for the successive Defence of the Realm Acts passed during the war and the 1950 Census, which he campaigned vigorously against on the grounds that it was not only an extravagant waste of public money, but also a gross intrusion on the privacy of the individual. Nonetheless, they all shared a broad philosophy of anti-collectivism, and were all founded within a year or two of each other. The foundation and work of the Society of Individualists and Aims of Industry in particular was symptomatic of the despair felt by many at the so-called 'electoral truce' between the major political parties, as it was believed that the free-market cause was thus going by default in Parliament. This is why so many Conservative MPs, representing that majority of the Parliamentary Party who were sceptical of the Beveridge Report, became involved in groups such as the Progress Trust, Aims of Industry or the National League of Freedom/Society of Individualists; they felt that they were being ignored by the Party Leadership.

The Conservative Party's difficulties were compounded by the fact that its leader, Churchill, was relatively uninterested in the debate about post-war economic, employment and social policy, and insisted that all decisions on these issues should be postponed until after the cessation of hostilities. In this he was only partially successful, being himself forced into making a reluctant pledge to a 'four-year' plan in a radio broadcast to satisfy public expectations in the wake of the Government's refusal immediately to implement the recommendations of the Beveridge Report in 1943.[34] Churchill's interest in these issues was only rekindled in the weeks leading up to the general election of

1945, by which time he had forfeited the opportunity to give a lead to the economic liberal wing of the Party, a lead which they desperately needed. Not only was the Party leadership unwilling to become involved in the debate on post-war policy and the free-market enterprise/planning debate, but the Party itself abdicated responsibility in this field by closing down its own Research Department for the duration of the war, which is why Ralph Assheton's Committee had to be specially convened to formulate a Party view on the Beveridge Report. Butler's ineffective Post-War Problems Central Committee was hardly a substitute for the CRD, and was unable, and unwilling, given the degree of difference of opinion in Conservative ranks, to formulate a coherent Party policy. The Committee's *Signpost* pamphlets were a useful exercise, with contributions from MPs such as Kenneth Pickthorn and Erskine-Hill, for instance, but made little public impact, by comparison with the volumes of lucid propaganda flowing from the other side of the political divide, let alone with the combative pamphleteering of the Tory Reform Group. These problems were exacerbated by the poor quality of the Parliamentary Party during the war. As Harriet Jones has written, 'Backbench leadership . . . was unimaginative and even openly hostile to the leftward swing of opinion in the country.' The leaders of the liberal-conservative wing of the Party were, indeed, unimaginative and inarticulate representatives of what looked to many like an outdated parliamentary generation. Butler wrote of A. G. Erskine-Hill, Chairman of the 1922 Committee, leading light in the Progress Trust and author of the woefully simplistic *Signpost* pamphlet *The Future of the Small Trader*, that he was 'too stupid to do anything but intrigue'.[35] Such men were easily dismissed as unashamed reactionaries, the 'Colonel Blimps' of Low's famous cartoons.

One of the more thoughtful liberal Conservatives was the Marquess of Salisbury, who wrote to a colleague to explain the Conservative dilemma in June 1941:

> The foundation stones are at home *not* nationalization (with certain exceptions) and *laissez-faire*, but private enterprise controlled and guided and in some cases assisted by the State . . . I expect you may say that in these days of anxiety it is impossible to give our minds effectively to post-war policy. If others would behave on those lines I should

> perhaps be content, but there are lots of Committees and Congresses and Conferences hammering away at post-war policy and it seems that unless we do something moderate Conservatives will be left high and dry.[36]

This was indeed, the dilemma for the liberal Conservatives and the Conservative Party as a whole. The transformation in public opinion that had taken place between May 1940 and 1942 had taken them completely by surprise; as people like James Meade remarked at the time, the war, with its radicalizing effect on the civilian population, had made possible the popular public reception of such collectivist Government proposals as the Beveridge Report that would have been unthinkable only a few years before. Hayek's erstwhile colleague at the LSE, Harold Laski, was constantly badgering Attlee during the war about Labour's supposedly slow advance towards the Socialist millennium, but Attlee was perfectly aware of the astonishing change of public opinion in his favour during the early years of the war, writing to Laski on 1 May 1944:

> Take the whole conception of State planning and the control of the financial machine by the Government . . . Here again I see the change since the days of 1931.
>
> In my time in our movement, now getting quite long, I have seen a lot of useful legislation, but I count our progress much more by the extent to which what we cried in the wilderness five and thirty years ago has now become part of the assumptions of the ordinary man and woman. The acceptance of these assumptions has its effects both in legislation and administration, but its gradualness tends to hide our appreciation of the facts . . .[37]

The foundation of those organizations dedicated to the survival of the pre-war economic liberal status quo in 1942 was symptomatic of the bewildered confusion in the ranks of the economic liberals of whatever Party, as the tide of popular acclaim for schemes such as the Beveridge Report threatened to make political and ideological dinosaurs of them. With no time to develop a consistent critique of the Government's White Papers and Reports on post-war policy, they could do little but cling to a pre-war status quo that was already discredited in the popular imagination by appeasement and unemployment. Despite a definite political reaction against the collectivist trend of wartime governmental planning and legislation, the economic liberal case was neither articulated nor consistently stated by any of those Conservative politicians involved in the debate; indeed, most of them seemed completely unaware of the academic 'economic calculation' debate that had been raging in the 1920s and 1930s. The case for economic liberalism thus threatened to go unheard, leaving liberal Conservatives, as well as those gathered in the Society of Individualists and other non-Party organizations campaigning for the preservation of a free economic system, truly 'high and dry'. It was at this time of considerable confusion and perturbation for the classical liberals and individualists that F. A. Hayek entered the debate with *The Road to Serfdom*, published, with adept timing, on 10 March, 1944.

Hayek had been observing the rather confused and muffled debate on the question of post-war planning and the Beveridge Report from his temporary eyrie at Peterhouse, Cambridge. He made no public contribution to that debate during the first few years of the war. However, it was clear to him, as it was to others involved in the 'economic calculation' debate of the 1930s, that the rarefied discourse on the virtues of planning and Keynesian economics that had occupied intellectuals such as Hayek since his arrival at the LSE in 1931 had now reached the arena of public debate with a vengeance. Furthermore, with the increasing acceptance of the Beveridge Report and of the need for a Keynesian demand-management employment policy, amongst politicians and public alike, it was clear that the tide was running even more strongly in favour of the collectivists than it had done before the war. Despite the rearguard action being fought by Conservative back-benchers, the Society of Individualists and Aims of Industry, no-one seemed able to express the coherent critique of collectivism that Hayek and like-minded colleagues had been developing before the war.

Nor was Hayek alone in his concern that the case against collectivism was not being put. Given the renewed interest in the planning–private enterprise debate, many economists rushed into print on the subject towards the end of the war. Von Mises published two books in 1944, *Omnipotent Government* and *Bureaucracy*, both of which attacked planning and Keynesian economics. In the preface to *Bureaucracy*, he rounded up the usual suspects with his customary zeal:

> The main issue in present-day social and political conflicts is whether or not man should give away freedom, private initiative, and individual responsibility and surrender to the guardianship of a gigantic apparatus of compulsion and coercion, the socialist State. Should authoritarian totalitarianism be substituted for individualism and democracy? . . . Should the Citizen be deprived of his most precious privilege to choose means and ends and shape his own life?
>
> Our age has witnessed a triumphal advance of the Socialist cause. As much as half a century ago an eminent British Statesman, Sir William Harcourt, asserted: 'We are all Socialists now.' At that time this statement was premature as far as Great Britain was concerned, but today it is almost literally true for that country, once the cradle of modern liberty.[38]

George Schwartz, the LSE economist, wrote a *Signpost* pamphlet *Why Planning?* in 1944 attacking the economic fallacies of planning, whilst Francis Hirst returned to the attack with his *Principles of Property*, a particularly limp defence of free enterprise, also published in 1944.[39] Colin Clark warned of the inflationary consequences of the high taxation and full employment policies proposed by certain members of the Government in an article in the *Economic Journal* in 1945, whilst Jacques Rueff similarly warned of the temptation to debauch the currency in the promised Keynesian utopia in his *L'Ordre social*, published in 1945.[40] Michael Oakeshott, the political philosopher, was to tackle similar themes in his celebrated essay on 'Rationalism in Politics', published in the *Cambridge Journal* in 1947.[41] However, none of these works made any impact on the public mind, which is why Hayek termed it his 'important duty'[42] to write his own contribution to the debate, the difference being that Hayek's book was calculated to make as much impact on the public debate on planning as possible.

Hayek must have started writing his book at the end of 1942, just before the widely leaked Beveridge Report was published at the beginning of December. On 30 May 1943 he wrote to his publisher, Routledge, to inform them that he had completed a 'semi-popular' book,[43] and, on settlement of a £50 advance to Hayek, they received a copy of the manuscript of *The Road to Serfdom* on 9 August. In his covering letter to the publishers, Hayek urged them to get the book out quickly, given the political circumstances of the time:

> I have made a special effort to get it ready rather earlier than I expected as I believe that there are many signs that the time is becoming rather favourable for the reception of a book of this kind, and I am especially anxious not to miss the opportune moment. I believe you will find it worth-while making an effort to get it out before the winter.[44]

The Road to Serfdom was thus written in some haste. Hayek's main purpose was to provoke a measure of public awareness and critical scrutiny of the main principles of 'planning' that were by now largely taken for granted behind the closed doors of Whitehall. However, his self-imposed deadline can have been of little inconvenience to Hayek, as the book was essentially a recapitulation, in more accessible language, of the arguments in common circulation amongst those intellectuals who had attended the 'Colloque Walter Lippmann' in 1938. Indeed, as Hayek admitted in the preface, the central argument of the book, that there was no 'middle way' between totalitarianism and a liberal, competitive economic system, had already been outlined by Hayek himself in an article entitled 'Freedom and the Economic System', which appeared in the *Contemporary Review* of April 1938, just as Professor Rougier had already written a detailed exposition of this theme in his *Les Mystiques Economiques* of 1938 (which was not, however, translated into English). Hayek referred to Rougier's work in the bibliographical note at the end of *The Road to Serfdom*. The central thesis of Hayek's book was, therefore, by no means original; the originality of *The Road to Serfdom* lay in its polemical political style, transferring the more abstruse academic debate on planning of the 1930s to the centre of political discussion. As he confessed in the preface, *The Road to Serfdom* 'is a political book', and he also wrote that he was fully aware that such a political book would doubtless 'prejudice the reception of the results of the more strictly academic work to which all my inclinations lead me – a prediction that proved all too true'.[45] Hayek wrote to Routledge that he had been encouraged to write such a popular, polemical book 'at the suggestion of an American friend',[46] the economist H. D. Gideonse, the President of Brooklyn College, New York. Much to some people's surprise, Hayek proved to be perfectly capable of writing the populist book that the economic liberals needed and, indeed, he surpassed even his own expectations. Moreover, Hayek wrote that the writing of *The Road to Serfdom* was 'a duty which I must not evade', as he alone among the liberal economists who had argued against Keynes in the 1930s was in a position of sufficient leisure to guide 'public opinion' on 'these problems', as the debate on planning was now being 'guided by amateurs and cranks, by people who have an axe to grind or a pet panacea to sell'. Hayek was consciously writing the book on behalf of Robbins, Jewkes and others who, being in Whitehall, were 'silenced by their official positions'[47]; Hayek was continuing in public the debate which Robbins, Henderson and Jewkes had necessarily to confine to the corridors of Whitehall.

Having set out to make as big an impact as possible on 'public opinion', Hayek was assiduous in making his message as clear as possible, even to the point of distilling its contents into the twelve 'Points from the Book' he wrote and had printed on the back of the yellow dust-cover (see opposite). As Hayek wrote to his editor in November 1943, enclosing the 'Points': 'I don't know whether you will think the enclosed too highly coloured, but after giving the book such a title I might as well be hanged for stealing sheep as for stealing a lamb. After all, I believe what I say is the truth.'[48] Because of the speed with which the book was sent to the publisher, Hayek had time to elicit the comments of only one person, Stanley Dennison, on the proofs of the book, but he was nonetheless confident of the impression that it would make and wrote to the publisher to urge them to print as many copies of the first edition as possible; as it turned out, the print-run of two thousand, although perfectly respectable by wartime standards, proved woefully inadequate. There is no doubt that Hayek had a much keener sense of the book's potential than his publisher. Moreover, Hayek was encouraged in his work by a fellow Austrian who he discovered was working on a very similar book at exactly the same time. Karl Popper, born in Vienna in 1902, was then Senior Lecturer in Philosophy at Canterbury College, Christchurch, New Zealand. Hayek had met Popper before the war, when Popper had addressed the Hayek-Robbins Seminar at the LSE in 1936.[49] Despite the brevity of their personal contact, Hayek and Popper had recognized a mutual interest

POINTS FROM THE BOOK

★ Is there a greater tragedy imaginable than that in our endeavour consciously to shape our future in accordance with high ideals we should in fact unwittingly produce the very opposite of what we have been striving for?

★ The contention that only the peculiar wickedness of the Germans has produced the Nazi system is likely to become the excuse for forcing on us the very institutions which have produced that wickedness.

★ Totalitarianism is the new word we have adopted to describe the unexpected but nevertheless inseparable manifestations of what in theory we call socialism.

★ In a planned system we cannot confine collective action to the tasks on which we agree, but are forced to produce agreement on everything in order that any action can be taken at all.

★ The more the State "plans" the more difficult planning becomes for the individual.

★ The economic freedom which is the prerequisite of any other freedom cannot be the freedom from economic care which the socialists promise us and which can be obtained only by relieving the individual at the same time of the necessity and of the power of choice: it must be the freedom of economic activity which, with the right of choice, inevitably also carries the risk and the responsibility of that right.

★ What our generation has forgotten is that the system of private property is the most important guarantee of freedom, not only for those who own property, but scarcely less for those who do not.

★ We shall never prevent the abuse of power if we are not prepared to limit power in a way which occasionally may prevent its use for desirable purposes.

★ We shall all be the gainers if we can create a world fit for small states to live in.

★ The first need is to free ourselves of that worst form of contemporary obscurantism which tries to persuade us that what we have done in the recent past was all either wise or unavoidable. We shall not grow wiser before we learn that much that we have done was very foolish.

in each other's work, and corresponded. At the start of the war, Popper was working on the long essay *The Poverty of Historicism* which was published in *Economica* in 1944 and 1945. However, much more intriguingly for Hayek, he discovered that Popper was also working on a book that was very similar to his own *Road to Serfdom*. On 12 July 1943, Hayek wrote to Popper in New Zealand after receiving news of his work: 'I have been particularly interested in what you say about your work, as it seems to be extraordinarily close to what I have been doing myself at present.'[50] Popper was equally excited that Hayek was, as he called it, 'fighting parallel actions on different frontiers'. As Popper explained:

> To be more explicit. You are fighting 'scientism'; I fight rather 'philosophism'. But we both fight collectivism. That collectivism in our own age appears in a 'scientistic' cloak is undeniable, and I have, by implication, admitted it when making Marx . . . the main hero of my modern part [of the book].[51]

The book Popper was writing was of course, *The Open Society and Its Enemies,* which in 1943 Popper was calling *The Flight from Freedom.* Popper was fully aware of the topical implications of his own book, and, like Hayek, he was anxious to secure an early publication date, as he felt the 'urgency' to make his own 'contribution to the internal unity in the "Camp of Freedom"'.[52] Popper was undoubtedly inspired by Hayek's work, and it was also extremely reassuring to find a scholar engaged on the same sort of work on the other side of the world, as Popper confessed that 'When I wrote my book, I felt that I was morally at one with the great majority of civilized men; but at the same time I felt that I was intellectually quite alone.'[53] Moreover, Popper, as a fellow Austrian, was motivated by that same fear of the intellectual allure of totalitarian ideology that motivated Hayek.[54]

When Popper finally received a copy of *The Road to Serfdom* in May 1944 – 'a most exciting event' – he wrote to Hayek that: 'When I came to the passage in the Preface in which you described the writing of the book as "a duty which I must not evade", I felt that you were driven by fundamentally the same experience which made me write my book and which made me describe it . . . as a War effort.'[55]

Popper's book was, in fact, very different from Hayek's; it was longer, a scholarly critique of collectivist thinking, as exemplified by three of its most famous exponents, Plato, Marx and Hegel. As Popper wrote in his own Preface, 'the final decision to write it was made in March 1938, on the day I received the news of the invasion of Austria.'[56] Despite the fact that, as Popper acknowledged to Hayek, *The Open Society* was not (given its length and scholarship) going to make as much of an immediate contribution to the 'Camp of Freedom' as *The Road to Serfdom*, Hayek was in no doubt as to its long-term importance, nor as to the book's usefulness as a more scholarly accompaniment to his own. At the same time as Hayek was putting the finishing touches to *The Road to Serfdom*, he was therefore also trying to find *The Open Society* a publisher in London. He had no joy with Nelson's, Macmillan or Jonathan Cape, but eventually persuaded Routledge to take the book on 17 March 1944, just three weeks before the publication of his own work. This decision represented a considerable risk to Routledge, as *The Open Society* was a forbiddingly complex book, and Popper was unknown in Britain, with only one obscure book to his name, *Die Logik der Forschung*, published in 1927. But Mr Ragg of Routledge was doubtless persuaded by Hayek's letter of recommendation of 4 February 1944. Admitting that he had admired Popper's work 'for a long time', Hayek recommended Popper's book

> most strongly . . . the only new work of this kind the reading of which in recent years has given one a real thrill. One of the remarkable things about it is that in this view of its quality I am for once in complete agreement with my colleague Laski, who has also read it and who, on the particular problems involved, is more competent to judge. Professor Robbins also . . . agrees with us on the quite exceptional merits of the book.[57]

As this was probably the only matter on which Hayek, Laski and Robbins ever agreed, the case for publication was surely irresistible.

Popper, like Hayek, wanted his book to be published as soon as possible, in order to influence the political debate. Popper pleaded for an early publication with Mr Read of Routledge, writing in March 1945 that

> The possible success of the book is endangered by its late

> publication. It is a War book . . . Although it never mentions the war, it was written as a War effort, and it openly bears the Stamp of the time in which it was written *sub specie eterni*, though in a definite historical moment. Now it is likely to lose this appeal more and more with every day, since the tension of this conflict begins to subside.[58]

Despite Popper's pleadings, *The Open Society*, which Routledge had initially hoped to publish by December 1944, was not published until 2 November 1945. However, in another attempt to hasten publication, Popper wrote a very revealing letter to Mr Read of Routledge in July 1944, explaining his exact intentions in the book:

> I feel that nothing is so important at the present time as an attempt to get over the fateful desertion within the camp of the friends of the 'Open Society', i.e. the camp of humanitarianism,; or, if I may say so, within the camp of the 'Left', if this term is used to include liberals who appreciate the need for social reform. The ultimate humanitarian aims of this 'Left', and the sincerity of the vast majority of its members, seems to me beyond doubt; and yet, within this 'left', there is perhaps more internal quarrel, more suspicion, and more reluctance to co-operate than between the 'Left' and the 'Right'. My book was written in an attempt to emphasize the unity of the humanitarian camp and to criticize its mistakes in a form of self-criticism.
>
> Now it appears from the first reactions of which I have heard that from the point of view of this particular aim, my arguments are more successful than I ever dared to hope. The approval of the book by some prominent members of the extreme 'left' as well as by some really Conservative Liberals [Hayek], was indeed a nearly surprise to me, and a proof that a book which is certainly outspoken enough and does not gloss over difficulties can be approved by people who are very far indeed from agreeing among themselves . . .
>
> The agreement expressed by people of such diverse opinions makes me hope that the book may contribute to the consolidation of the 'Left' and to clearing the air within the camp of humanitarianism. But what could be a more

> urgent and more important task for a political book at the present moment?[59]

Although *The Open Society* was published too late to effect the immediate wartime political debate, despite Hayek's hopes, the book was to become as important in the long term as his own *Road to Serfdom*. As Anthony Quinton has written, 'Until the publication of Karl Popper's *Open Society* there has been no large scale reformulation of liberal doctrine that has presented it in a significantly novel way.'[60] Just as Hayek in his own work was concerned with the rise of collectivist thinking amongst 'liberals' and Conservatives, so Popper was equally concerned with the same phenomenon amongst the 'Left'. It was an intellectual assault on both flanks, conceived of by two men writing with similar intellectual interests born of their own unhappy experiences in Central Europe, from which they were both exiled. It is remarkable that at the same time as publishing his own seminal contribution to the 'Camp of Freedom', Hayek was also responsible for the publication of Popper's book, which was to become as important a contribution to the post-war revival of liberalism as his own. It was also Hayek who secured a post for Popper at the LSE in 1945, where Popper was to spend the rest of his academic career.

As Hayek had predicted, the publication of *The Road to Serfdom* on 10 March 1944 caused an immediate stir, and the initial print-run of two thousand was sold out within a few days. Routledge ordered an immediate reprint of a thousand copies, and in the following two years they were to be engaged in a losing race to satisfy the huge public demand for the book. As Routledge wrote to Hayek on April 11: 'We all unanimously came to the conclusion over the Easter holidays that paper has to be found for a reprint of your book, no matter what other book had to be postponed . . .'[61]

Owing to the constraints of wartime paper rationing, however, Routledge could never satisfy demand, despite another five-thousand-copy reprint in December 1944. Hayek wrote irritatedly during the summer that it had earned the reputation as 'that unobtainable book', and Routledge had to resort to putting out a cheap edition of five thousand in February 1945. News of *The Road to Serfdom* even reached Christchurch, New Zealand, from where Popper wrote admiringly in May 1944:

> This morning I find in our Christchurch newspaper an article saying that your 'Road to Serfdom' has 'caused a stir' in England . . . I write to congratulate you most heartily to your success [sic] . . . I mean, especially, the great success of the cause you are serving. If news like this comes to our remote little corner of the globe . . . then it is big news. I must say I expected all sorts of things, and possibly your participation in very high councils, but I did not expect to find (so soon) an article about your book in the Christchurch Press – especially since my copy must be the only one in town, if not in New Zealand.

The reason for the success of the book is not hard to find; as Popper noted (albeit in his rather stilted English), it was 'the right word said in the right moment'.[62] As we have seen, Hayek planned the publication of the book specifically to catch the high tide of debate over planning and post-war policy, and he wrote it in such a way that it was easily accessible to a wider public who were ignorant of the work of Rougier, von Mises, Lippmann and others published during the 1930s. His central thesis, therefore, that the supposed 'Middle-way' of what Keynes had earlier described as the 'liberal-socialists' would inevitably lead to totalitarianism and 'Serfdom', was new to most people in 1944. However, the most controversial aspect of the book was his comparison with Germany, that 'Socialism' would lead to 'National Socialism' in Britain as assuredly as it had in inter-war Germany. As he wrote:

> Students of the current of ideas can hardly fail to see that there is more than a superficial similarity between the trend of thought in Germany during and after the last war and the present current of ideas in this country. There exists now in this country certainly the determination that the organization of the nation we have achieved for purposes of defence shall be retained for the purposes of creation. There is the same contempt for nineteenth-century liberalism, the same spurious 'realism' and cynicism, the same fatalistic acceptance of 'inevitable trends'.[63]

This was, perhaps, the least convincing of his arguments in the context of wartime Britain, and attracted the most criticism. However, in choosing Germany as his main ideological comparison, he was acting under constraints not entirely of his own making, as he admitted later that 'in order to get a hearing I had somewhat to restrain myself in my comments on the regime of our wartime ally [the Soviet Union] and to choose my illustrations mainly from developments in Germany.'[64] The comparison with the Soviet Union was, of course, much more appropriate, but at a moment in time when admiration for that country's war effort was at its height, Hayek had to ignore Soviet Communism, thereby considerably reducing the force of his argument. It was a handicap that he shared with Orwell, who was also having great difficulty making similar comparisons in his own work, eventually resorting to the metaphor of a farmyard in *Animal Farm*, published in 1945.

Facetiously dedicating his book 'To the Socialists of all Parties', Hayek's strength was that he was writing from a detached, non-Party position; his strictures were aimed as much at the aspiring collectivists in the Conservative Party (such as the Tory Reform Group), the Liberal Party (such as Beveridge and Keynes) as at the Labour Party. Hayek's central criticism was that all Parties were now suffering from the same delusions, that collectivism, defined as 'the deliberate organization of the labour of society for a definite social goal', would decrease freedom and was inherently undemocratic. Furthermore, and most importantly for those in the Conservative and Liberal Parties who were enthusiasts for Beveridge and the Macmillanesque Middle Way (which sought to combine central industrial planning with a large measure of free enterprise), Hayek argued that this was an illusion, for

> Both competition and central direction become poor and inefficient tools if they are incomplete; they are alternative principles used to solve the same problem, and a mixture of the two means that neither will really work and that the result will be worse than if either system had been consistently relied upon. Or, to express it differently, planning and competition can be combined only by planning for competition, but not by planning against competition.[65]

By arguing that democracy and the freedoms enjoyed by modern Britain were only possible under a liberal, free-market system, Hayek was effectively demolishing the ideological edifice carefully built up by the Keynesian 'liberal-Socialists' between 1931 and 1944. It was this that gave the book its vitality, as it re-sited the political divide along collectivist–individualist lines, cutting across the traditional Party borders; and, in still more heretical fashion, it identified Socialism, not just Soviet Communism or German Nazism, as not a harbinger but an *enemy* of freedom. Until *The Road to Serfdom* appeared, few had really questioned the efficacy of the Keynesian 'Middle-Way', assuming, pragmatically, that as it combined what was taken to be the best of the two opposing systems of communism and free-market capitalism, so it represented a happy and workable synthesis of the two.

Not surprisingly, given the manner in which Hayek had sought to polarize the debate between the opposite extremes of collectivism and competitive free-enterprise, the reviewers also took up equally unequivocal positions. Michael Polanyi, for instance, in his review in the *Spectator* of 31 March 1944, agreed with Hayek that 'National Socialism was not a reaction against Socialism, but an outcome of it'. By contrast, Thomas Balogh, the Hungarian-born economist who was to be one of Harold Wilson's key economic advisers during the 1960s, savaged it in the *Political Quarterly*. For Balogh,

> There is not a single old economic fallacy . . . which Professor von Hayek does not serve up once more. The barrel-load of red herrings which he now offers on the political and sociological terrain will provide gargantuan feast for those reactionaries whose 'freedom-loving' policies brought Britain to Dunkirk and Singapore. On the next occasion, if their influence once more prevails, there may be no Stalingrad to retrieve the issue.[66]

Two of the most perceptive reviews were those by George Orwell and Evan Durbin, a young economist who had trained at the LSE under Hayek, and who was prominent amongst those trying to reconcile classical economics with Socialism. Orwell, at that time searching vainly for a publisher for *Animal Farm*, recognized the force of what he termed 'the negative part' of Hayek's thesis, that 'Collectivism is not inherently democratic, but, on the contrary, gives to a tyrannical minority such powers as the Spanish inquisition never dreamed of.'

However, he refused to accept that people would rather have 'slump and unemployment' than 'State regimentation'.[67] Durbin also sympathized with much of what Hayek had to say, but argued that Hayek had been unfair in his characterization of Central Planning British-style, and asserted that in fact the growth of State interference during the twentieth century had gone hand-in-hand with an extension of liberalism and democracy.[68]

However, for the future course of the intellectual debate in the post-war years, much the most interesting response was that of J. M. Keynes himself; he read the book on his way by ocean liner to the Bretton Woods Conference in June 1944. Keynes wrote privately to Hayek that he thought it 'a grand book', and, perhaps surprisingly, found himself 'in agreement with virtually the whole of it, and not only in agreement with it, but in a deeply moved agreement' -although he did not accept 'quite all the economic dicta in it'. The above has often been quoted, but the concluding passages of his letter come to the hub of the argument between Hayek and Keynes and deserve to be quoted at length:

> I come finally to what is really my only serious criticism of the book. You admit here and there that it is a question of knowing where to draw the line. You agree that the line has to be drawn somewhere [between free-enterprise and planning], and that the logical extreme is not possible. But you give us no guidance whatever as to where to draw it. In a sense this is shirking the practical issue. It is true that you and I would probably draw it in different places. I should guess that according to my ideas you greatly under-estimate the practicability of the middle course. But as soon as you admit that the extreme is not possible, and that a line has to be drawn, you are, on your own argument, done for since you are trying to persuade us that as soon as one moves an inch in the planned direction you are necessarily launched on the slippery path which will lead you in due course over the precipice.
>
> I should therefore conclude your theme rather differently. I should say that what we want is not no planning, or even less planning, indeed I should say that we almost certainly want more. But the planning should take place in a com-

> munity in which as many people as possible, both leaders and followers, *wholly share your moral position. Moderate planning will be safe if those carrying it out are rightly orientated in their own minds and hearts to the moral issue.** This is in fact already true of some of them. But the curse is that there is also an important section who could almost be said to want planning not in order to enjoy its fruits but because morally they hold ideas exactly the opposite of yours, and wish to serve not God but the devil . . . What we need is the restoration of right moral thinking – a return to proper moral values in our social philosophy. If only you could turn your crusade in that direction you would not feel quite so much like Don Quixote.[69]

Keynes was thus looking to Plato's 'Philosopher-kings' to administer the 'New Jerusalem' – disinterested, public-spirited men working wholly for the public good – whilst admitting that this was an unlikely eventuality. Balogh, in his review, was even more brazen in his assertion of the duty of the 'rightly-orientated' leaders to run society on behalf of those who could not cope for themselves: '[Hayek] refers . . . to the perfect foresight, willingness and ability of individuals to plan their lives for themselves. Such general statements were, perhaps, permissible in the last century, when social science had no realistic studies at its disposal to demonstrate their adequacy. Who is that individual ?'

The innate arrogance of Balogh's conviction that the individual was simply incapable of running his own life was neatly encapsulated in Douglas Jay's unintentionally accurate phrase, 'the man in Whitehall knows best'. The intellectual and moral arrogance of Balogh and Keynes, as expressed in their reactions to *The Road to Serfdom*, was, of course, to prove their undoing in the long run, as the Thatcherites were able to harness the resentment felt by many ordinary people at their exclusion from the politics of the cabal of 'rightly-orientated' Keynesians that was perceived as running Britain in the 1960s and 1970s, and turn that resentment into something akin to a moral crusade against bureaucracy and government. The responses of Balogh and

* Author's italics.

Keynes demonstrated that Hayek had touched a raw nerve in the moral system of the mid-century British collectivist.

The Road to Serfdom earned the unusual distinction of being reviewed at length in almost every national British newspaper as well as the academic journals. So seriously was its attack taken by those on the left that, within a year, two political writers had devoted entire books to the task of rebutting Hayek's arguments – Barbara Wooton in *Freedom under Planning* and Herman Finer in *Road to Reaction*. However, just as *The Road to Serfdom* caused a great popular sensation, nowhere was it greeted with more interest than in the serried ranks of the Conservative Parliamentary Party. For the liberal Conservatives, that majority of the Party who had objected to the Beveridge Report, *The Road to Serfdom* appeared as manna from heaven. Adrift on a sea of Socialism, they immediately sensed the importance of Hayek's book, for it gave them, at one blow, the intellectual apparatus to assail the gathering political enthusiasm for the post-war planning which they had, up to then, only managed to postpone. Their spirits revived, and they eagerly embraced Hayek's thesis as the articulation of their own worst fears about the post-war world. In August 1944, several Conservative MPs, including some members of the Progress Trust, wrote to Churchill urging him to set up a 'fighting fund for freedom'. In so doing, they tried to give the Prime Minister his theme for the forthcoming election campaign, referring him to the 'epoch-making' *Road to Serfdom*.

> We are fighting this war for eternal values, for Christian principles, for liberty and freedom of the soul of man . . . and for freedom from the continuance of state control after the war. We have *lent* our personal freedom to the Government for the duration – it is vital that the loan be repaid . . . Today the trend of post-war legislation is in the opposite direction. Bill after Bill is being introduced, or encouraged, which involves compulsion and loss of personal freedom.

They urged Churchill to halt 'the race down the road to totalitarian State', and ended, rhetorically, 'Have we fought this war to preserve our Freedom from foreign tyranny in order to lose our liberties to the Bureaucrats at home?'[70] Hayek had given them the unifying theme that they had been groping towards since 1940, for, despite the work of the Society of Individualists, the Progress Trust, Aims of Industry and the National League of Freedom, no-one had been able to catch the popular imagination with a critique of collectivism. This was Hayek's achievement, and, just as he had hoped, *The Road to Serfdom*, having given the Conservatives a theme, quickly got sucked into the political 'phoney war' before the general election, which was presumed to be less than a year away by most parliamentarians.

Of course, not every Conservative MP was cognizant of Hayek's arguments, and some, such as the members of the Tory Reform Group, were actively opposed to his denunciation of the 'Middle Way', but there were enough Conservatives who recognized the immediate relevance of Hayek's message to ensure that it became the central focus of the 1945 general election. Churchill's admission to his doctor that 'I am worried about this damned election, I have no message for them now', was symptomatic of a great deal of unease in the Party,[71] and the more imaginative Conservatives realized that Hayek's ideas could fill this ideological vacuum, and give them a chance to fight the election on their own terms. The key figure in bringing *The Road to Serfdom* to the centre of the election campaign was Ralph Assheton, now Conservative Party Chairman. He was one of the more thoughtful, reflective liberal conservatives and virtually cornered the market in the 'unobtainable book' in the Spring of 1944, buying fifty copies and distributing it not only to his Conservative Party colleagues, but also to Herbert Morrison and Clement Attlee, who wrote back to Assheton that he would 'read it as soon as I have time'.[72] As First Secretary to the Treasury from 1941 to 1943 Assheton had been assiduous in drawing the Treasury's attentions to Britain's post-war industrial problems, warning against any excessive public spending.[73]

Assheton readily grasped the usefulness of Hayek's warnings about the consequences of abandoning economic liberalism, and began to incorporate Hayek into his speeches. One of these, given at a meeting in the north of England in April 1945, is of particular interest, because he sent it to Churchill, who minuted in reply: 'I read your speech and think it very good. I ventured to make a few comments on it.'

Assheton's speech, essentially an election speech, defended the free-enterprise system, and argued for a lifting of restrictive burdens on industry after the war. He ended on a very Hayekian note:

> But there are even more fundamental reasons which should make us hesitate to adopt Socialist doctrines. We in this country have been fighting against totalitarianism in Germany and we do not wish to adopt as our creed the German-made doctrines of Karl Marx. I do not think that most of those who toy with Socialist theories and doctrines in this country realise sufficiently that Socialism, which means the ownership of the means of production, distribution and exchange, inevitably leads to a totalitarian State. When the State owns everything, the State is the only master and every man must work for the State or starve. In such a condition of affairs, we should indeed be slaves, for what is a slave but a man who has only the opportunity of working for one master?[74]

There is no evidence that Churchill ever read *The Road to Serfdom* before the 1945 election, but he was certainly familiar with the central thesis of the book, learnt at second-hand from Assheton, if no-one else. Like many in his Party, it provided Churchill with his missing theme for the forthcoming election.

The prospects of a general election had been in the air at Westminster since the summer of 1944, which is why for many Tories the publication of *The Road to Serfdom* in the spring of that year was so fortuitous. By June 1945, the arguments of *The Road to Serfdom* had percolated through to all sides involved in the election campaign, and Labour, confident of the popular appeal of their own brand of collectivism, were more than willing to fight the election campaign on 'the basic, clear cut [principle] of Public versus Private Enterprise'.[75] The Conservatives, for their part, also tried to make this issue the central one of the campaign, and as they had no better propaganda on this issue than *The Road to Serfdom*, Conservative Central Office, prompted no doubt, by Assheton, offered to expedite the publication of a further edition of the book (which in the early summer of 1945 had once again become unobtainable) by surrendering 1½ tons of its precious paper assignment for the general election campaign to Routledge so that they could publish an abridged version of the book before the end of the campaign. That tonnage of paper would have enabled twelve thousand copies of a thirty-thousand-word abridged version of the book to be produced. This was an extraordinary sacrifice by Central Office, and is ample testimony to the value they now attached to Hayek's work. The abridgement was written for Central Office by Geoffrey Rippon, later a Cabinet Minister in Edward Heath's government. In the end, however, their efforts were to no avail, as due to printing delays, this abridged edition was not actually published until March 1946, too late to influence the 1945 electorate.[76]

However, *The Road to Serfdom* was, nonetheless, never very far from most people's minds after Churchill opened the election campaign of June 4, 1945 with his notorious 'Gestapo' election broadcast. This broadcast has often been dismissed as an aberration, or, especially by Churchill's Labour opponents, as the work of 'evil political advisers who know how to trade on fear'.[77] In fact, Churchill worked on the speech on his own, with no help from Beaverbrook, Brendan Bracken or his son, and it was no more than an exaggerated version of the Hayekian thesis, as recycled to him via Assheton and others. His criticism of Socialism was a direct echo of Assheton's speech:

> My friends, I must tell you that a Socialist policy is abhorrent to the British idea of freedom. Although it is now put forward in the main by people who have a good grounding in the Liberalism and Radicalism of the early part of this century, there can be no doubt that Socialism is inseparably interwoven with Totalitarianism and the abject worship of the State . . . liberty, in all its forms, is challenged by the fundamental conceptions of Socialism.

Churchill's references to Labour's need for 'some form of Gestapo, no doubt very humanely directed in the first instance' to stifle 'few, sharp, or violently-worded expressions of public discontent' and his warning that Labour would try and control 'the entire life and industry of the country' were nothing more than a colourful and clumsily phrased extension of Hayek's critique of Socialism in *The Road to Serfdom*. Interestingly, Churchill never regretted the speech, and, reminiscing with David Clarke of the Conservative Research Department in 1950, he told Clarke that the only thing wrong with the speech was that he had been obliged to refer to the Gestapo instead of the NKVD, the Soviet equivalent.[78] Attlee, who had, perhaps, read the copy of *The Road to Serfdom* sent to him by Assheton, referred directly to the 'Austrian Professor Friedrich August von Hayek' in his own broadcast of the following night, dismissing Hayek's charges that socialism would lead to a loss of liberty, whilst subtly stressing Hayek's foreign origins to persuade his listeners that Hayek was nothing more than a mad foreign professor who did not understand the English way of doing things. Churchill had put Hayek's thesis at the centre of the election debate, and Attlee, backed by his own Party Chairman Harold Laski, was quite content to fight Churchill on the ground laid out by Hayek. Indeed, there is a great deal of truth in Lance Beale's contemporary observation in the *Leader* magazine of June 1945 that 'the rival doctrines of the 1945 general election were derived from the London School of Economics'.[79]

The 1945 election campaign is sometimes portrayed as a mere rubber-stamping of the political consensus which had evolved during the war; in fact, there was precious little consensus and the campaign was 'marked by profound and often bitterly expressed disagreements. And in spite of the artificial posturing that characterises all elections, the divisions on the issue of public versus private provision, above all, reflected a recognition that the outcome would be vital in determining the shape of post-war society.'[80] Far from the rest of the Tory Party disowning Churchill's 'Gestapo' speech, the authors of the first Nuffield election study observed that Churchill

> had set a fashion which was followed throughout the country. Henceforth many of his leading supporters attacked 'Socialism' in the abstract . . . In so doing they nearly always went on to blacken Socialists as anti-democrats and friends of Fascism. Mr W. S. Morrison, speaking on 11 June, reminded his hearers that Hitler and Mussolini began as Socialists. He then said that although the Socialists objected to the Conservatives calling themselves 'National', yet the Conservative Party had no objection to their opponents calling themselves National Socialists.[81]

Whatever else one can say about the 1945 election, it was certainly not devoid of serious ideological debate.

Hayek himself had returned from a lecture tour of North America to observe the campaign, and lunched with John Wood and Stanley Dennison at the Reform Club on the day after Churchill's broadcast, and was evidently pleased that his ideas had been taken up with such gusto by the Conservatives.[82] When Attlee mentioned Hayek by name in his own broadcast, the press descended on Hayek, and he now found himself sharing star-status in the campaign with Laski. However, much as he was thrilled by the success of the book and much as he enjoyed the subsequent media attention, in private he was less sanguine, and even disappointed by the nature of the support for his book. He wrote to Popper in July 1944:

> I fear you somewhat overrate the importance and probable effect of my book, though I cannot deny that I have been very pleased by all the kind and flattering things you say about it. The success is in a way much greater than I had ever hoped for – but not altogether of the right kind; not, so far, among the liberals but almost exclusively amongst the Conservatives, at least if one is to judge by the discussion in the press. The liberal press was rather sniffy about it and the definitely left (included some so-called liberals) try on the whole to pass it over by silence, even, in one scandalous instance, by deliberate suppression of a review already set up in type!
>
> All this is very gratifying and gives one some hope about *long run* developments; but in so far as the immediate future is concerned, I am very far from hopeful i.e. for the next ten or twenty years, during which the present collectivist trend is bound to continue.[83]

Hayek's assessment of the mood of the electorate proved to be rather more shrewd than that shared by many in the Conservative Party. Hayek might have given the Tories a target to attack, but by merely stressing the perils of Socialism their Party propaganda 'therefore seemed negative and pessimistic', whereas the Labour Party was confident and forward-looking.[84] When the election results came through, the Labour Party won their famous landslide victory, capturing 393 seats to the Conservatives' 213. The Liberal Party was all but wiped out. As he had written to Popper, the Liberal Party was a particular disappointment to Hayek, as he saw it, rightly, as the natural repository of his ideas – the Party most closely associated with his own creed of liberalism. However, not only had Beveridge and Keynes taken 'New Liberalism' to the point where it was virtually indistinguishable from Labour Party Socialism, but the Party had now become a terminally ineffective political force. It was the Conservatives, by contrast, who were most active in rediscovering their own liberal roots.

The end of the Second World War thus saw a decisive victory for collectivism in Britain, and the advent, for the first time, of a majority Labour Government dedicated to building the 'New Jerusalem' using all those economic and industrial policies which Hayek had been arguing against since his arrival in Britain in 1931. As he had written to Popper, Hayek was fully aware of the fact that the classical liberals of all Parties were fighting a rearguard action, and that the trend towards collectivism was, in the short term, irreversible.

On the other hand, although the 1940s witnessed, in Hugh Dalton's apt phrase, the 'high tide' of Socialism in Britain, with Attlee's government passing into legislation much of what had first been conceived of by the Fabians nearly fifty years earlier, it is also clear that at that very moment of greatest Socialist advance, Hayek and Popper had, within a year of each other, laid the intellectual foundations for the critique of that Socialist society which was to prove so persuasive for many people over the course of the next thirty years. *The Road to Serfdom* and *The Open Society and Its Enemies* were like two landmines lying dormant under the post-war collectivist Society which the electorate had embraced with such alacrity in 1945; with long fuses they lay, waiting to detonate while their grim warnings appeared to come true.

The Road to Serfdom, in particular, succeeded, as Hayek had intended, in redefining the political debate in Britain in a way that no single book or statement of belief has done since. Hayek's arguments were not novel, he was merely popularizing the arguments of the 'economic calculation' debate of the 1930s, but he made people think about such matters who had never given any thought to political philosophy or economics before. Politically, *The Road to Serfdom* was vitally important as it transformed the nature of the political debate not, as Hayek had vainly hoped, in the Liberal Party but in the Conservative Party. Hayek articulated the feelings of most of those in the Party who felt bewildered and leaderless in the face of the wartime collectivist advance, and reorientated the political discourse within the Party along an individualist–collectivist axis, thus laying down the parameters for the post-war debate within the Party, as it came to grips with its election defeat. As Beaverbrook caustically observed in October 1945: 'The battle within the party is fought between the Tory individualists who follow, ironically enough, the creed of nineteenth-century liberalism and the Tory reformers who raise the banner, or rather the pocket handkerchief of Disraeli's Young England. Their ideas may be described as Socialism without Socialists.'[85]

There can be little doubt that, given the swell of support for Hayek's attack on collectivism within the higher echelons of the Party, most of the reforms of the so-called 'post-war settlement' implemented by Attlee's Governments from 1945 to 1950 would *not* have been carried out by any Conservative Government led by Churchill, Assheton, or Oliver Lyttleton, let alone Brendan Bracken and Lord Beaverbrook! In the historiography of the Conservative Party of the post-war period, much stress has been laid on Butler's historic compromise with collectivist economic planning and nationalization embodied in the Industrial Charter of 1947. While this may be true, equal stress should also be laid on the Party's search for a road *from* serfdom, to find policies which would free industry and the economy from the burdens of collectivist controls and high governmental spending. Churchill discovered the positive message which he wished to convey to the electorate at a speech in Edinburgh just after the end of the war – the creation of a 'property-owning democracy', a phrase which he picked up from the Chief Scottish Agent.[86] The tensions between the liberal wing of the Party and the more collectivist-minded were never far beneath the surface in the post-war years, and the record of Churchill's government in power, 1951–5, is, in essence, the record of an ideological drive to reduce the role of the Welfare State and the nationalized industries running up against cold political logic.[87]

What did bode well for the future, from the liberal point of view, was that Hayek's work had stimulated an interest in economic liberalism as an alternative to socialism amongst some of the younger Conservative MPs and activists, in whose hands lay the future of the Party. One of the most prominent of these MPs was Richard Law, the son of Bonar Law, and one such party worker was Diana Spearman, a member of the Conservative Research Department from 1934 to 1939, and then from 1949 to 1965, and the wife of a Tory MP, Alec Spearman. With considerable help from Diana Spearman, Lionel Robbins and John Wood, Law published *The Return from Utopia* in 1950, which became the gospel of post-war liberal Conservatism. As well as being the first politician to outline the framework of a social market economy, Law also urged the Party to turn its back on the Keynesian-Beveridgean

Utopia, and 'to hold out once again the prospect of a Society in which man is free to be good because he is free to choose'.[88] Diana Spearman was instrumental in introducing the Hayekian concept of the 'spontaneous order' into the thinking of men like Law, and, indeed, her young colleague at the Research Department, Brigadier Enoch Powell. Law, like other young Conservative MPs, revelled in the intellectual discovery that there was an *alternative* to the Collectivist State, and that it was worth courting unpopularity to write books about it. As Law wrote to Spearman in October 1945, 'I had lunch with Lionel [Robbins] before he went off to Washington. I told him that under your influence and Alec's I had become a diehard, and he thought that this was a move in the proper, as well as the right direction . . .'[89]

During the 1940s, Hayek had thus made as much impact on the political scene as an intellectual had any right to expect in Britain, not only through his own work but through his sponsorship of Karl Popper's work as well.[90] When Aims of Industry invited a cross-section of those most concerned with the Thatcherite revolution during the 1980s to choose the two books which had most influenced them, *The Road to Serfdom* and *The Open Society* were the two most popular choices. Indeed, an early reader of Hayek's book was Margaret Roberts, then an Oxford chemistry student. By articulating the anti-collectivist argument, Hayek had redefined the post-war political and economic debate in Britain, and had planted the seed for the future blossoming of economic liberalism. It was the start of what he knew was a long haul, and his next task was to take the war of ideas to those people who had been largely responsible for bringing about the collectivist revolution in the first place, the intellectuals.

3
The Mont Pèlerin Society

*

The publication of *The Road to Serfdom* by Routledge brought Hayek the kind of intellectual celebrity that his rival Laski had been used to for a decade or more. Invitations to lecture before guest audiences, both lay and academic, began to flood in. In April 1945, he embarked on a lecture tour of North America, after publication of *The Road to Serfdom* by the University of Chicago Press had created the same sort of intellectual ferment in the USA as it had in Britain. The book was actually turned down – on political grounds – by three American publishers, before the Chicago economist Aaron Director secured a contract with his University Press.[1] The book sold out within a day of publication, and the University of Chicago Press had to fight a similar battle with the paper-rationing authorities in the United States as Routledge had done in Britain to satisfy public demand for the book. The connection with the University of Chicago was to be an important one in Hayek's life, as the economics faculty there, under the direction of Frank Knight, was already fertile ground for the Hayekian view. The University sponsored and organized his tour of America in 1945, and created a special chair for him as Professor of Social and Moral Sciences in 1950 when he left the LSE.

However, the publicity that his ideas received in printed form courtesy of Routledge and Chicago was dwarfed by the condensed version of *The Road to Serfdom* published in the *Reader's Digest* of April 1945. Their editions sold in the hundreds of thousands. The publication of a condensed version of the book in the *Reader's Digest* was arranged by Henry Hazlitt, and gave Hayek an exposure to a far larger audience than he had expected. Propitiously, it was published on the eve of his American visit, thus altering his schedule considerably. As he later recalled:

> While I was on the ship, the Reader's Digest published a condensation and when we docked in New York I was told all our plans were changed; I would be going on a nationwide

> lecture tour beginning at NY Town Hall . . . Imagine my surprise when they drove me there the next day and there were 3,000 people in the hall, plus a few score more in adjoining rooms with loudspeakers. There I was, with this battery of microphones and a veritable sea of expectant faces.[2]

During the course of his lecture tour, he found that *The Road to Serfdom* had divided opinion in America much as it had done in Britain, with the Rooseveltian New Dealers attacking it with as much venom as Balogh and his colleagues had in Britain. One such 'New Dealer' was the academic Charles Merrian of the University of Chicago, and the round-table discussion with Hayek on a normally staid University radio programme of April 1945 was typical of some of the hostility which Hayek encountered. As Merrian's biographer relates,

> Listeners must have been puzzled at the speed with which hostilities began, without prior introduction of the dispute and initially without explanation throughout. What they did not know is that the six-hour warm-up session the evening before had been considerably more heated than was normally the case and that Merrian and Hayek were scarcely on speaking terms as the programme opened . . . Merrian accused Hayek of doubting the efficacy of democracy and Hayek's efforts at a gentlemanly response cracked. 'I am saying that people like you, Merrian, are inclined to burden democracy with tasks which it cannot achieve, and therefore are likely to destroy democracy.'[3]

However, amidst the hostility, Hayek also found a more benign reception – many academics, especially at Chicago, were very sympathetic to his ideas. This persuaded Hayek to proceed with his long-standing interest in picking up from where the 'Colloque Walter Lippmann' had left off in September 1938, and to revive the concept of an international forum for liberal scholars and economists. Hayek had first publicly broached the idea of an international society of liberal scholars in a paper read to the Political Society of King's College Cambridge (Keynes's intellectual home) on 28 February 1944, just over a week before the publication of *The Road to Serfdom*. With the historian Sir

John Clapham in the chair, Hayek proposed the idea of an 'Acton Society', in honour of the British historian whom Hayek revered as the greatest exponent of the principles of a liberal society. Hayek suggested that such a society could be a forum allowing British, German and other European intellectuals to meet and to publish,

> for the cultivation of certain common standards of moral judgement. Collaboration across frontiers could contribute a great deal – particularly where we have to deal with a country where traditions have been so disrupted and standards so lowered as in Germany of recent years. Even more important, however, is that collaboration will be possible only with those . . . [in] agreement, that the ordinary rules of moral decency must apply to political action, and beyond that also certain minimum agreement on the most general ideals. The latter need be no more than a common belief in the value of individual freedom . . . and, finally, an equal opposition to all forms of totalitarianism, whether it be from the Right or from the Left.[4]

Quite independently, and at the same time, another economist who had been at the 'Colloque Walter Lippmann' was also suggesting a revival of Rougier's original idea of an international liberal forum. In a paper written at L'Institut Universitaire des Hautes Etudes Internationales in Geneva dated August 1945, Wilhem Röpke, the German economist, suggested that such a forum was urgently needed to challenge the reigning intellectual fallacies of Western Europe.[5] Röpke suggested that an international meeting of liberal scholars should be convened at regular intervals; it should publish an international periodical, appealing to the 'upper intellectual classes'. Röpke circulated his paper amongst his colleagues and to members of the 'Colloque Walter Lippmann', and raised a small amount of money for the projected periodical.

It was a Swiss businessman, involved in the work of the Institut d'Etudes Internationales at Geneva, Dr Hunold, who brought the ideas of Röpke and Hayek together. Hunold invited Hayek to address the students of the University of Zürich in November 1945 and afterwards Hunold dined with Hayek and a group of Swiss industrialists and bankers, at which point Hayek told them of his own plans for a gathering of those intellectuals who shared his views to discuss and redefine liberalism. Hayek proposed that it would be 'an enormous help' if these people 'could come together and meet for about a week somewhere in a Swiss Hotel in order to discuss basic ideas'.[6] Hunold pledged his financial support and that of his fellow businessmen to support the project, promising to divert the funds which they had raised for Röpke's periodical to Hayek, as Röpke's idea had proved too costly and difficult to organize.

During 1946, Hayek took soundings in both Europe and America, and, with Hunold's financial and moral backing, decided to go ahead with the idea of a meeting in Switzerland in the spring of 1947. On 28 December 1946, he sent a circular letter to all those he wanted to invite to the meeting, outlining his own thinking on the matter, and defining the meeting's purpose. Writing from the LSE, he wrote that:

> In conversations I have had during the last two years with friends in a number of countries I have found a strong desire for closer contacts between all those who have become gravely concerned about the chances of preserving a free civilization, and who feel that not only the whole relation between governmental coercion and individual freedom requires re-examination, but also that current views of recent history will have to be revised if the dominant beliefs and misconceptions are not to drive us ever further in a totalitarian direction. While in each country those who think actively on these questions are comparatively few, combined they represent a considerable force and I have been struck by the similarity of the aims and of the conclusions reached by many of the isolated men in different parts of the world. It seems certain that by closer co-operation their work would benefit and gain greatly in effectiveness. . . .
>
> While the philosophy of freedom which would have to form the common basis for such a joint effort is not easily defined in a few sentences, I have found the suggestion widely acceptable that the ideals underlying the works of Lord Acton and Alexis de Tocqueville might serve as the agreed foundation from which such a common effort might start.'[7]

Hayek conceived of the society he was founding as a focus for scholars to carry out the long-term task of converting the next generation of intellectuals to a creed of liberalism that was then largely discredited. In a further note circulated to those invited to the conference, Hayek defined their purpose as

> not to spread a given doctrine, but to work out in continuous effort, a philosophy of freedom which can claim to provide an alternative to the political views now widely held. Our goal, in other words, must be the solution not of the practical task of gaining mass support for a given programme, but to enlist the support of the best minds in formulating a programme which has a chance of gaining general support. Our effort therefore differs from any political task in that it must be essentially a long-run effort, concerned not so much with what would be immediately practicable, but with the beliefs which must regain ascendance if the dangers are to be averted which at the moment threaten individual freedom.[8]

If Europe was not to move blindly into a 'new kind of serfdom', Hayek wrote,

> an intense intellectual effort is needed. We must kindle an interest in – and an understanding of – the great principles of Social organization and of the conditions of individual liberty as we have not known it in our life-time . . . We must raise and train an army of fighters for freedom . . . If we do not flinch at this task, if we do not throw up our hands in the face of overwhelming public opinion but work to shape and guide that opinion, our cause is by no means hopeless. But it is late in the day and we have not too much time to spare.[9]

In a paper on 'The Intellectuals and Socialism', circulated to Members of the Society after its first meeting, he explicitly compared their task to that of the early Socialist and 'New Liberal' intellectuals of the late nineteenth and early-twentieth century, who had, in Hayek's opinion, 'regularly and successfully acted as if they fully understood the key position of the intellectuals and have directed their main efforts towards gaining the support of the "elite"', which was certainly true of the Fabians and Keynes in Britain. For Hayek, 'what to the contemporary observer appears as a battle of conflicting interests decided by the vote of the masses, has usually been decided long before in a battle of ideas confined to narrow circles.'[10] It was this battleground which Hayek was mustering his troops to fight on, with a view to a twenty-year campaign before the battle was won.

Hayek's summons to his proposed 'Acton-Tocqueville' conference was greeted with pledges of support from many liberals. From England, he invited Robbins, as well as Arnold Plant, Karl Popper and A. G. B. Fisher. He also invited the remaining anti-Keynesian economists, John Jewkes, appointed Professor of Economics at Oxford in 1947, and Stanley Dennison. He also invited the historians G. M. Young and E. L. Woodward, and the scientist-turned-philosopher Michael Polanyi from Manchester. The journalist and historian C. V. Wedgwood was also invited. Of these, only Robbins, Popper, Dennison, Jewkes, Polanyi and C. V. Wedgwood attended the 1947 meeting, and all of those, except Robbins, were to become regular attendees at later meetings, as was Arnold Plant. The LSE, as befitted its role in the intellectual resistance to Keynesian economics during the 1930s, thus formed the English core of Hayek's liberal crusade.

Liberated from Whitehall, Robbins and Jewkes left the economic section of the War Cabinet with all their fears about central planning amply confirmed by their wartime experience. As a direct result of this, as well as his own observation of the Labour Government's nationalization programme, Jewkes wrote *Ordeal by Planning*, published in 1948. It was to become the most celebrated dissection of the shortcomings of planning published in post-war Britain, much admired by both Hayek and Mrs Thatcher. In his introduction, Jewkes, like Popper and Hayek in the prefaces to their own two 'war-books', apologizes in advance for the fact that his book would 'offend' a lot of people, but declares it his duty to put his views on record:

> For I believe that the recent melancholy decline of Great Britain is largely of our own making. The fall in our standards of living to a level which excites the pity and evokes the charity of many other countries, the progressive restrictions of individual liberties, the ever-widening destruction of respect for law, the steady sapping of our instinct for

> tolerance and compromise, the sharpening of class distinctions, our growing incapacity to play a rightful part in world affairs . . . At the root of our troubles lies the fallacy that the best way of ordering economic affairs is to place the responsibility for all crucial decisions in the hands of the State.[11]

At a time when the myth of Britain's wartime industrial and technical achievements was still intact, Jewkes exposed, with ruthless logic and considerable wit, the realities of Britain's war planning, describing, for instance, from his own experience, 'the history of the appalling delays in British tank development, even during the war, [which] is another excellent illustration of what a technical bureaucracy is capable'.[12] Robbins drew on a similar experience of wartime Whitehall to issue his own warnings about planning when he entered the lion's den and delivered the Marshall Lectures in front of an audience of Keynes's disciples at Cambridge in 1947. Robbins gave his own account of 'collective planning' as he had observed it:

> Our theories of State action usually imply, not merely infinite wisdom on the part of administrators, but also infinite time in which to use it. It is not until you have sat in the smoke-filled Committee rooms working against time to snap decisions from Ministers who, through no fault of their own, are otherwise preoccupied, that you realise sufficiently the limitations of these assumptions. Nor are the more fundamental of these limitations removable by improvements of organization. You may reform your system of ministerial Committees. You may augment the number of their advisers. You may employ troops of investigators to ascertain the reactions of consumers. You may stretch the sympathetic imagination to the utmost to seek to provide, within the limits of your plan, the kind of variety which you consider to be desirable. You may sincerely believe that the process as you work it is, in some sense, good for the people. But I cannot think that, if you are honest with yourself, you can believe that such a system involves, or can involve, such degree of freedom for the consumer to get what he wishes,

> such an active participation in the daily moulding of social life, as a system which is based upon demand prices . . .[13]

In the introduction to his Marshall Lectures, Robbins conceded that this was a message which would be very unpalatable to his audience, but, like Jewkes, he was doing little more than putting the lessons of his own experience at the disposal of his audience. Stanley Dennison, who had returned to Cambridge at the end of the war after his own stint in the Economic Section, shared the misgivings of Robbins and Jewkes. Michael Polanyi, in many ways the most interesting of those who attended Hayek's gathering in 1947, had just been appointed to a new Chair in Philosophy by Manchester University in 1946, and was busy working out his ideas on the philosophy of science in the Gifford Lectures, which would form the core of his most influential work, *Personal Knowledge*. During the 1940s, Polanyi was much concerned with the freedom of science under the State, and in particular the threat to that freedom posed by collectivism. As he wrote to a friend in 1940: 'If the continuity acting through the power of the State is to be the sole judge of what is bad for men living in society, then it has to claim also supremacy over what is to be considered true and what untrue. Science cannot be free in a State formed as sovereign master of the community's fate . . .'[14] Polanyi was a co-founder, with Dr John Barber of Oxford University, of the Society for Freedom in Science, which, between 1945 and 1949, produced nine pamphlets on the threat to science from collectivism, and from Soviet Russia in particular. Polanyi wrote three of them himself.[15] Polanyi, Robbins, Jewkes and Dennison, as well as Popper, were all concerned with the basic philosophical implications of collectivism in their respective areas of expertise, and were thus natural allies of Hayek in 1947.

As it was, another Englishman had already tried to start an international liberal forum of the kind which Hayek proposed to found in 1947, Sir Alfred Suenson-Taylor, later Lord Grantchester. Born in 1893, Taylor (whose Swedish wife's surname was Suenson) was a prominent City figure, and Chairman of London and Manchester Assurance from 1953 to 1961. His brother was a Conservative MP. Although by no means an intellectual, he was equally concerned with the decline of liberalism and can lay claim to have founded the first liberal think-tank with a coherent organizational structure, the 'International Liberal Exchange'. Taylor was a friend of Dr Hunold's and his organization had an office in Geneva, in addition to its main office in London at his own home at 54 Prince's Gate. The International Liberal Exchange had been operating before the war, but the war had abruptly terminated its activities. As Taylor was at pains to point out to Hunold, his organization had nothing to do with the British Liberal Party, but existed to 'Provide a clearing house for the ideas of the World's leading *liberal* philosophers, economists, and writers' and to 'produce a journal that will combat collectivism in the realm of ideas'.[16] Taylor also wanted to start a book club, a research centre and an international liberal library. In fact, Taylor achieved few of his ambitions, although most of those involved in Hayek's undertaking were also aware of Taylor's efforts. Indeed, it is evident that Hayek proceeded with his own meeting in 1947 because of the failure of Taylor's rather more grandiose plans. Nonetheless, Taylor was important to Hayek and economic liberalism, as he co-operated with Hunold to fund the early meetings of Hayek's Society and he also negotiated with the Bank of England to release funds for the British delegates to travel to the second of Hayek's meetings; he himself attended many meetings during the 1950s. The magazine of the International Liberal Exchange, the *Journal of International Liberal Exchange*, did not sell well, even – or perhaps unsurprisingly – after it changed its name to *The Owl* in 1950. Despite this, it proved an important public forum for several younger people who were interested in Taylor's ideas in the early 1950s, including Oliver Smedley, the co-founder of the Institute of Economic Affairs, and Arthur Seldon, a regular contributor to *The Owl*, who was to become editorial director of the IEA.

So, it was Hayek's international liberal society which now became the focal point of international efforts, and the delegates invited by Hayek to his inaugural Conference assembled at the Hotel du Parc on the slopes of Mont Pèlerin overlooking Lac Léman on 1 April 1947. The Conference lasted until 10 April. As well as the funding secured for the Conference by Dr Hunold's Swiss backers, the participation of a large American contingent was ensured by the financial contribution of the William Volker Charities Trust. Apart from the British academics such as G. M. Young and E. L. Woodward who could not attend the meeting, other prominent absentees included Walter Lippmann and Jacques Rueff. The former never became involved with what became known as the Mont Pèlerin Society (MPS), whilst the latter became a regular attendee from the second meeting onwards. These absentees, added to the fact that Hayek's natural contacts lay within the field of academic economics, ensured that from the start the membership of the Mont Pèlerin Society was composed largely of economists. Hayek himself regretted that he could not have included more historians and political philosophers at the inaugural meeting.[17]

This first meeting of the MPS was attended by thirty-eight people, and amongst their number were almost all those academics and intellectuals who were to be most important in the revival of economic liberalism in the post-war era. As has already been mentioned, Hayek himself identified three main intellectual centres of the revival of contemporary liberal thought, and the composition of the MPS reflected the intellectual influences of those three centres – London (the LSE), Chicago and Vienna.[18] The LSE contingent has already been mentioned, and at later meetings of the MPS the founding LSE fathers of the MPS were to be joined by other LSE economists, including Sir Arnold Plant, F. W. Paish, Peter Bauer and W. H. Hutt. The American contingent from Chicago included the doyen of American economists, Frank Knight, Aaron Director, George Stigler and the young Professor Milton Friedman. There were also three economists from the Foundation of Economic Education in New York, F. A. Harper (Professor of Economics at Cornell University, 1928–46), Leonard Read and V. O. Watts. Another important American was Henry Hazlitt, the financial journalist, who had spent most of his life on the *New York Times* before switching to *Newsweek* in 1946, for which he wrote an influential business column. He was a prolific and fluent author and an unforgiving and relentless critic of Keynes.[19] He was a very important publicist for economic liberalism and, for instance, had much to do with putting the Institute of Economic Affairs on the map by referring to their first publication in his *Newsweek* Column.

The most prominent Austrians were, naturally, Hayek, von Mises and Popper, but they were also joined by Fritz Machlup, then a Professor at the State University of New York at Buffalo and later at Johns Hopkins, Dr Karl Brandt, then a Professor at the Food Research Institute at Stanford University, and at subsequent meetings their numbers were swelled by the presence of Gottfried Haberler, also based in America. One of the main aims for Hayek at this conference was to reintegrate the German liberal tradition into the mainstream of European thought, and so he was careful to complement the Austrian contingent with several members of what was later to be called the

'Freiburg' School of Economics, the pioneers of the '*Soziale Marktwirtschaft*', the 'Social Market economy'. Present at the first meeting of the MPS was Walter Eucken, the leader of the 'Freiburg School', who died in 1950 in the middle of five lectures in London on the subject of the bitter lessons which Europe still had to learn from the collectivist economic policies of the Nazis. Wilhem Röpke was also a founder-member; born in 1899, he had taught in both Germany and Austria before the Nazis had come to power, and from 1948 onwards he was an economic adviser to the Adenauer administration in Bonn. The man most closely identified with this school, Ludwig Erhard, joined the MPS at the second meeting; which meant that the most constructive and celebrated school of post-war economic thought was well represented at the MPS.[20]

There was also an important French contingent. Jacques Rueff, born in 1896 and head of the French Treasury in the inter-war years, occupied several official positions in the French Government after 1945 and became the most famous exponent of liberal economics in France, and author of the 'Rueff Plan' of economic and fiscal reform which he was asked to draw up by General de Gaulle in 1958 on the General's return from political exile. Professor Maurice Allais, another prominent French economist, attended the first meeting, as did the French journalist-cum-political philosopher Bertrand de Jouvenel, who was later accused of collaboration during the war in a famous court case in 1985, but who in 1947 was in the midst of finishing one of the most thoughtful and persuasive critiques of Attlee's Labour Government, *Problems of Socialist England*.[21] Professor Rappard of the Institut Universitaire des Hautes Etudes Internationales of Geneva was also present, as were single representatives from some other European countries such as Italy (Carlo Antoni) and Norway.* The founding fathers of the Mont Pèlerin Society thus included most of the world's foremost liberal economists, many of whom were to have considerable influence in their own countries, especially in Germany, America, France and Britain. It was a remarkable gathering, from which much of the intellectual revival of economic liberalism would flow.

The meeting at the Hotel du Parc, reached by funicular from Vevey several hundred metres below on the shore of Lac Léman, opened on

* For the full list of those attending the first meeting of the Mont Pelerin Society see Appendix I.

Tuesday 1 April. Proceedings started with an address by Professor Rappard, who acknowledged the pre-eminent roles of Hayek and Dr Hunold in bringing them all together. He appropriately dedicated the meeting to the spirit of Adam Smith: 'Modern economic liberalism, as I see it, is the legitimate off-spring of the union between two first cousins: Adam Smith's penetrating and essentially sound scientific analysis of the economic world of his day, and Adam Smith's inborn love of freedom, constructive effort and wealth.' He called European Socialism 'the policy of a tired race', and urged his colleagues to work for an 'intellectual, economic and political renaissance' of economic liberalism.[22] The first working session was entitled *'Free' Enterprise or Competitive Order*, chaired by Rappard, with opening papers by Hayek, Director and Walter Eucken. Hayek's paper was much the longest and most important, as during the course of his remarks he not only defined the task of his fellow liberals assembled at the Hotel du Parc, but suggested the course that they should take if they were to resurrect liberalism as a living, relevant political philosophy. However, he started with an analysis of the situation as it stood in 1947, quoting in aid Lord Keynes (as he had become in 1942):

> If during the next few years, i.e. during the period in which practical politicians are alone interested, a continued movement towards more government control is almost certain in the greater part of the world, this is due, more than to anything else, to the lack of a real programme, or perhaps I had better say, a consistent philosophy of the opposition groups. The position is even worse than mere lack of programme would imply: the fact is that almost everywhere the groups which pretend to oppose socialism at the same time support policies which, if the principles on which they are based were generalised, would no less lead to socialism than the avowedly socialist policies. There is some justification at least in the taunt that many of the pretending defenders of 'free enterprise' are in fact defenders of privileges and advocates of government activity in their favour rather than opponents of all privilege . . . There is no hope of a return to a freer system until the leaders of the movement against state control are prepared first to impose upon themselves that discipline of a competitive market which they ask the

masses to accept. The hopelessness of the prospect for the near future indeed is due mainly to the fact that no organized political group anywhere is in favour of a truly free system.

It is more than likely that from their point of view the practical politicians are right and that in the existing state of public opinion nothing else would be practicable. But what to the politicians are fixed limits of practicability imposed *by public opinion must not be similar limits to us. Public opinion on these matters is the work of men like ourselves, the economists and political philosophers of the last few generations, who have created the political climate in which the politicians of our time** must move. I do not find myself often agreeing with the late Lord Keynes, but he has never said a truer thing than when he wrote, on a subject on which his own experience has singularly qualified him to speak, that 'the ideas of economists and political philosophers, both when they are right and when they are wrong, are more powerful than is commonly understood. Indeed the world is ruled by little else. Madmen in authority, who hear voices in the air, are distilling their frenzy from some academic scribbler of a few years back. I am sure that the power of vested interests is vastly exaggerated compared with the gradual encroachment of ideas. Not, indeed, immediately, but after a certain interval; for in the field of economic and political philosophy there are not many who are influenced by new theories after they are twenty-five or thirty years of age, so that the ideas which civil servants and politicians and even agitators apply are not likely to be the newest. But, soon or late, it is ideas, not vested interests, which are dangerous for good and evil.'

It is, as I suggested this morning, from this long run point of view, that we must look at our task. It is the beliefs which must spread, if a free society is to be preserved, or restored, not what is practicable at the moment which must be our concern.

The passage from Keynes is the concluding paragraph of *The General Theory*, and was to become the motto of the Institute of Economic

* Author's italics.

Affairs, framed and hung in a prominent position in their front office. For Hayek, as well as Keynes, it was an intellectual battle, 'for good and evil', and they were playing a long-term game. Hayek outlined the failure of liberalism in the same spirit, attributing the intellectual corruption of liberalism, as did many others, to J. S. Mill, since whose time it had passed into popular imagination as a political philosophy which gave the misguided impression that 'the abandonment of all harmful or unnecessary State activity was the consummation of all political wisdom'. Instead, Hayek invoked the State as necessary to stimulate competition by creating the necessary legal framework and anti-monopolistic environment in which free competition could work. For Hayek, liberalism was thus 'a policy which deliberately adopts competition, markets and prices as its ordering principles and uses the legal framework enforced by the State in order to make competition as effective and beneficial as possible – and to supplement it where, and only where, it cannot be made effective . . .' This, of course, was very different from a state of *laissez-faire*, and Hayek described his type of positive liberalism as 'competitive order', the purpose of which was to make 'competition work'. 'Thus understood this description of our subject at once distinguishes our approach as much from that of the Conservative planners as from that of the socialists.' Hayek's liberalism was thus a vigorous, radical creed designed to promote and maintain the conditions for free enterprise using the legal framework of the State. Hayek divided the areas of activity in which competition had to be made effective into those concerning employers and employees. As regards employers, he wanted to develop better policies to deal with monopolistic or quasi-monopolistic positions (cartels, protectionism, etc.), but it was on the subject of trade unions that his comments were most relevant and direct, because they reflected the frustrations shared by many economic liberals about the debates with Keynes in the 1930s, and were a very prescient warning about the future direction of politics if anything near a liberal, competitive economy were to be restored again to Europe:

> We must not delude ourselves that in many ways the most crucial, the most difficult and delicate part of our task consists in formulating an appropriate programme of Labour or trade union policy. In no other respect, I believe, was the development of liberal opinion more inconsistent or more

unfortunate or is there more vagueness even among the true liberals of today. Historically liberalism first for too long maintained an unjustified opposition against trade unions as such, only to collapse completely by the beginning of this century and to grant to trade unions in many respects exemption from the ordinary law and even, to all intents and purposes, to legalise violence, coercion and intimidation. That if there is to be any hope of a return to a free economy the question how the powers of trade unions can be appropriately delimited in law as well as in fact is one of the most important of all the questions to which we must give our attention.

Hand-in-hand with the thorny question of trade unions went the issues of 'monetary policy' and 'exchange controls'; the former was needed to prevent the inflationary consequences of Keynesian full employment policies, and the latter was needed to facilitate foreign trade.

In this paper, Hayek thus outlined not only the long-term aim of an intellectual revival of interest in economic liberalism, but also anticipated all the major areas of concern for British Governments of the 1970s and the 1980s which sought to move towards a market economy. In Britain, as Hayek had predicted, trade-union reform was to become the crunch issue. For Hayek, most important initially, in an era when almost all western European countries were at the height of their infatuation with planning and Socialism, was for the liberal intellectuals to make 'these question of a policy for a competitive order . . . once again live issues which are being discussed publicly . . .'[23]

The discussion that followed Hayek's paper elaborated on Hayek's central thesis that these were the principles of liberalism which had to be most closely scrutinized, but it also showed the range of intellectual disagreement which often characterized the early meetings of the MPS. On one occasion at a later MPS meeting, in a session chaired by Friedman, von Mises became so enraged by what he heard that he stormed out, shouting 'You're all a bunch of Socialists!' Tempers could, and did, become frayed with such combative and opinionated intellectuals as von Mises and his like competing for attention. In between excursions to local tourist spots the Society discussed such perennial subjects as 'The Problems and Chances of European Federation' (with an opening paper by de Jouvenel), 'Contra-Cyclical

Measures, Full Employment and Monetary Reform' (with a paper by Stigler) and 'Wage Policy and Trade Unions', opened by Fritz Machlup.* On Thursday 10 April, the last day of the Conference, it was unanimously agreed that they should reconvene two years hence, but there was still much disagreement about what the Conference should be called, with only a few supporting Hayek's original proposal of the 'Acton-Tocqueville Society', others favouring the names Burke and Smith. With the hour of departure drawing near, it was Karl Brandt who suggested that they agree to disagree, and simply call the Society after the location of their meeting – hence the Mont Pèlerin Society.[24] The final act of formally setting up the MPS on a proper legal basis was to register it as a corporation on 6 November 1947, in Illinois. The President was named as Hayek, and the Vice-Presidents were Eucken, Jewkes, Knight, Rappard and Rueff.

There is no doubt that those who attended this first meeting of the MPS found it extremely valuable and helpful. After eight years of travel restrictions brought about by war and then by exchange controls, it was the first time that most of those who gathered at the Hotel du Parc had met each other. Friedman, for instance, had never been to Europe before, and as Polanyi wrote to Dr Hunold: 'The Conference was most enlightening to me in many ways as it gave me my first glimpse of the Continent after these disastrous years and revealed to me at the same time an important section of American opinion; I feel sure that, quite apart from several additions to my knowledge and understanding of contemporary affairs, I have received a new background for my thoughts.'[25] Jewkes was similarly impressed and urged Hunold to hold another such conference in 1949;

> I have always felt that the first Conference was of very great importance in enabling the liberal social scientists to exchange views and establish personal relations. Since that Conference there has been most fruitful collaboration among many of the members . . . a further meeting would result in a further clarification of our aims and the strengthening of the links between us. This is all the more important since as I see it, the anti-liberal economic forces in the Western European countries are now very much on the

* A full list of the sessions and their participants is printed as Appendix B.

> defensive and what is badly required is the formulation of a set of liberal doctrines which might constitute a centre of gravity for the intellectuals of Europe.[26]

So encouraged, Hunold and Hayek invited the members of the Mont Pèlerin Society to a second meeting at Seelisburg, held from 3 July to 10 July 1949. Amongst the British delegates invited to Seelisburg, as well as the original participants of two years previously, were Arnold Plant and Michael Oakeshott. Diana Spearman was incorporated as one of the original sixty-four members of the MPS and attended the Conference, and another important LSE economist, Peter Bauer, attended the third meeting in Holland in August 1950. A second list of proposed members drawn up at the 1948 Conference included, from Britain, another healthy contingent from the LSE, T. S. Ashton, R. H. Coase, R. S. Edwards and W. H. Hutt (then at the University of Cape Town) as well as Dennis Robertson, the historian R. C. K. Ensor and the financial journalist Oscar Hobson.

The Mont Pèlerin Society was thus drawing together those liberal intellectuals in Britain who had no such opportunity for a similar gathering in Britain. However, useful and stimulating as this may have been for those concerned, many of those attending the first Conference began to question the aims of the MPS, and particularly the extent to which the MPS should remain just an academic talking-shop, rather than a more active and public organization, or even a more formal pressure group. The 'Statement of Aims' of the MPS was drafted at the end of the first Conference by Robbins, who was generally regarded as the 'major figure' at the Conference,[27] and who was already demonstrating his silky skills as a chairman and moderator; these were to stand him in such good stead when he became virtually a full-time public 'Committee-man' and leading member of the 'Great and the Good' during the 1960s. The 'Statement of Aims' outlined the general philosophy of those attending MPS meetings, which was as vague as might be expected of a document seeking to satisfy forty or more intellectuals from widely different cultural and national backgrounds. The document concluded that:

> The group does not aspire to conduct propaganda. It seeks to establish no meticulous and hampering orthodoxy, it

> aligns itself with no particular party. It's object is solely, by facilitating the exchange of views among minds inspired by certain ideals and broad conceptions held in common, to contribute to the preservation and improvement of the free society.[28]

Karl Brandt was one of those who argued that this very restricted definition of the MPS's activities would be detrimental to the 'cause' for which they were all fighting, and just before the 1949 Conference he wrote to Hunold complaining that 'The Statement of Aims' was

> wanting in the sense that it goes far beyond circumscribing our aims. It specifically defines the means in pursuing this aim, namely 'facilitating the exchange of views' among members, and by the word 'solely', confines the activity of the Society exclusively to this exchange of views between ourselves . . . This precludes any publication of a journal or even of proceedings of our conference. I feel certain that this was not the intention of the signers . . .
>
> If this statement is not amended or revised in the near future, adherence to it will tend to frustrate our Society in the pursuit of its avowed major aim.[29]

Specifically, Brandt urged the MPS to publish a journal and its Conference proceedings, as well as to hold regional conferences, working parties and to set up a Finance Committee. As Brandt and others pointed out, money was also going to be a problem, because if the MPS was to insist on conducting its affairs in privacy then they could not expect financial support from those sections of the business community which normally expected to see at least a small visible return on their money. On receiving yet another begging letter from Dr Hunold for funds for the MPS in 1954, Sir A. Suenson-Taylor pointed out that business people took rather a 'short-term view of judging such matters . . . The work done at the conferences does not gain the publicity it sometimes deserves. One of the complaints I hear often is that the views of our members [of the MPS] are not expressed in time to be of practicable value in dealing with current problems.' For the business community, Hayek's conception of a twenty-year battle of ideas was simply 'too much of a long-term policy for them to . . . support'.[30]

Despite the protestations of Karl Brandt and others, after a debate on strategy and aims at the Seelisburg Conference, the 'Hayekian' view prevailed and, in the words of the Mont Pèlerin Society's historian, Max Hartwell, 'the Society became an academy, a learned Society and not a pressure group'.[31] Hunold himself tried to develop the work of the MPS by setting up his own Institute for Economic Studies in Geneva – where his first two guest lecturers were Jewkes and Dennison – but the MPS remained solely an academic discussion conference, with no magazine or other publication. It thus remained an obscure and somewhat secretive organization, attracting scorn and ridicule from its intellectual opponents in equal measure. Max Hartwell has listed six ways in which the MPS contributed to the revival of liberalism, having chosen its own very low profile. 'It enlarged the corpus of knowledge about liberalism when serious discussion of liberalism was at its lowest ebb'; it bestowed authority on liberal ideas through the academic distinction of its membership, which included five Nobel Laureates by the mid-1980s; most importantly, it gave 'reassurance, comfort and camaraderie to individual liberals at a time when they were few in number and geographically isolated'; it disseminated liberal ideas to an international audience; it spawned liberal institutions all over the world [of which more later]; and it contributed indirectly to changing governments' policies through members' roles as advisers or policy-makers.[32] Amongst British politicians who attended MPS meetings in the 1960s and 1970s were Geoffrey Howe, Enoch Powell, John Biffen, Keith Joseph and Rhodes Boyson as well as a clutch of journalists (such as William Rees-Mogg of *The Times*) and members of free-market 'think-tanks' in Britain. With the international revival of economic liberalism in the period 1960 to 1980 the membership of the MPS ballooned, so that by 1980 six hundred members and guests attended a Conference at the Hoover Institute, Stanford University. Indeed, so popular had it become by that time that in his capacity as President of the MPS in 1972, Milton Friedman argued that the Society should end because its original function, as a mutual support organization for like-minded people in an intellectually hostile world, had long since been fulfilled. However, Friedman was thwarted and the MPS survives to this day.

After the second meeting at Seelisburg in 1949, a third was held in Holland in 1950, and thereafter meetings were held every one or two years. Hayek attended every meeting until a few years before his death in 1992. Regional Meetings were also held at regular intervals by European or American members in the years when general meetings did not take place. The first general meeting to take place in Britain was at Christ Church, Oxford, in 1959, but during the 1950s Jewkes and Dennison held a number of 'Regional Meetings', at Merton College, Oxford in 1952 and 1953, and at Gonville and Caius, Cambridge, in 1958. The ever-present Dr Hunold was also involved in organizing these 'Regional Meetings', which were conducted very much along Mont Pèlerin lines, with papers followed by a discussion. Amongst the speakers were regular Mont Pèlerin members, such as Robbins, Polanyi, Jewkes, Peter Bauer and Arnold Plant, as well as those somewhat younger economists who joined the MPS later and who were to be closely associated with the IEA, such as Graham Hutton, Alan Peacock, A. A. Shenfield and F. W. Paish. The interest of these meetings lies in the invitation lists, for Jewkes and Dennison made a conscious effort to try and usher the ideas of the Mont Pèlerin Society into the outside world by inviting a mixed gathering of politicians, Party officials, civil servants and journalists, as well as the usual sprinkling of academics. Thus, for instance, at the 1953 Merton College meeting several Conservative politicians associated with the more free-market wing of the Party were present, including Edward Heath and Ormsby Gore, as well as Angus Maude who gave a paper on 'Liberal and Conservative Economic Policies' with Arthur Shenfield.[33]

However, despite the best efforts of Jewkes and Dennison, these British 'Regional Meetings' did not create as much interest as they might have done, due partly to the prevailing ethos of the Mont Pèlerin Society that theirs was a long-term campaign to formulate, or restate, the principles of liberalism, and so they could have little to offer men like Maude and Heath in the way of practical economic advice on matters of 'political' urgency. Such purely intellectual cross-fertilization and discussion at MPS meetings was eventually to bear fruit in books like Hayek's own *Constitution of Liberty*, or Friedman's *Free to Choose* but in the context of the late 1940s, with the tides of Socialism and collectivism showing few signs of ebbing, there were some who felt that the MPS was choosing to proceed at too leisurely a pace, breathing the oxygen of pure thought which more ordinary mortals found difficult to inhale. One dissatisfied member of the MPS, Professor Griffin of the School of Business, University of Michigan, wrote in such a vein to Hunold after the 1949 Conference. Admitting that 'We did not very effectively come to grips with some of the important aspects of a positive programme of liberalism . . .', Griffin blamed this partly on 'the fact that the members of the group are so absorbed in the general philosophy of liberalism that they rather shun the tough job of considering in detail the knotty problems that must be met alike by adherence to that philosophy or any other'.[34]

If the meetings of the MPS were too abstract or remote for policy-makers grappling to formulate positive, practical alternatives to Socialism, the cause of economic liberalism in Britain also suffered a setback in 1950 when Hayek moved to Chicago to take up his Chair as Professor of Social and Moral Sciences. His departure was at least partly dictated by his own personal tragedy of the break-up of his first marriage; this might not have mattered had it not been for the fact that during his last few painful years in Britain he had, during the process of splitting up with his first wife, managed to alienate Lionel Robbins, to such an extent that the two rarely conversed for the next ten years or so. Furthermore, Robbins was so scandalized by Hayek's shoddy treatment of his first wife that he refused to attend any more Mont Pèlerin meetings. In explaining his decision 'not . . . to see' Hayek any more to Dr Hunold in June 1950, Robbins wrote, simply, that Hayek had 'behaved in such a way which I find impossible to reconcile with the conception of his character and his standards which I have cherished through twenty years of friendship . . . as far as I am concerned, the man I knew is dead and I should find it almost intolerably painful to have to meet his successor.'[35] Robbins was as good as his word, and the two were only reconciled in the early 1960s.

The breach in their friendship, as well as being personally distressing for both of them, also had very important intellectual consequences, as it meant the break-up of a closely knit partnership which, as we have seen, had been very important in the defence and advance of economic liberalism from 1931 onwards. Robbins had helped Hayek's career, whilst Robbins had leant heavily on Hayek as a source of ideas and as a conduit to European economic thought. Hayek's emigration to America in 1950 meant that Britain lost its most prominent liberal intellectual, whilst Robbins's breach with Hayek meant that Robbins had nothing to do with the MPS until the 1960s, nor was he as constructive a figure within the economic liberal movement after 1950 as he had been in the 1930s. Just as Hayek was quickly forgotten in 1950s Britain, so Robbins ploughed his own furrow which would eventually lead to him chairing the Royal Commission on Higher Education in 1961–3, producing a Report which would have been anathema to most of his former Mont Pèlerin colleagues.

For all the promise of *The Road to Serfdom* and the Mont Pèlerin Society, therefore, the early 1950s in Britain found intellectual interest in economic liberalism at a low ebb, with no-one prepared, seemingly, to utilize the grand theorizing of the MPS for more practical, immediate purposes. What economic liberalism now needed was an 'entrepreneur' of ideas, to bring the thinking of the Mont Pèlerins to a wider audience – and it was at this point that a chicken-farmer called Antony Fisher entered the story.

4

The Vision of a Chicken-Farmer

The Institute of Economic Affairs

*

It is, perhaps, wholly in keeping with the behind-the-scenes image which 'think-tanks' have traditionally cultivated that the man whom Professor Milton Friedman has described (with a touch of hyperbole) as the 'single most important person in the development of Thatcherism' should remain almost totally unknown in Britain.[1] Indeed, the only public recognition of his services to his country was the knighthood he received only five weeks before his death in July 1988. Antony Fisher, however, would not have minded the lack of publicity. It is his legacy which matters, as it was he who harnessed the intellectual efforts of Hayek and his fellow Mont Pèlerins to avowedly practical ends by founding the Institute of Economic Affairs – as well as many of the world's other free-market 'think-tanks'. For whereas Hayek and his fellow Mont Pèlerins might have appreciated the seminal importance of ideas, it was Fisher, by nature an entrepreneur, who saw the need and supplied the means to spread and popularize those ideas amongst a wider audience. Like so many, he was inspired by Hayek's ideas, but his own practical and entrepreneurial instincts were a perfect foil to Hayek's intellectualism. In later years, Fisher liked to recount his first meeting with Hayek at the LSE in 1947 which inspired his life's work, but there is an interesting, and partly tragic, prelude to that pivotal meeting.

Antony Fisher was born in June 1915, two years before his father was killed at Gallipoli. Antony and his younger brother Basil both went to Eton, after which Antony went up to Trinity College, Cambridge, where he studied engineering. He left in 1936, and showed the first signs of his commercial talents by founding one of the first hire-car companies in the country. The two brothers had learnt to fly at Cambridge, and so they both joined 111 Hurricane Squadron on the outbreak of war in 1939. 111 Squadron was one of the most heavily engaged in the Battle of Britain, and on 15 August 1940 Basil was killed in action. This was a 'shattering blow' for Antony, so much so that he was taken off active service, and thereafter invented the gunnery training machine for RAF pilots, for which he was subsequently awarded the Air Force Cross. At the end of the war he worked briefly for a merchant bank in the City of London, before buying, in 1947, a four hundred-acre farm in Sussex, where he started dairy farming. This might have seemed a fairly ordinary progression for an old Etonian, except that Fisher had, during the course of the war, become unusually concerned about the advance of Socialism and collectivism in British politics. His feelings of political unease were reinforced by his own personal experience, for, as his daughter Linda has written, 'After the war, he had recognised that both his father and his brother, among many others, had given up their lives for the freedom of their fellow countrymen, yet he saw freedom diminishing, not increasing.'[2] During the war, he had joined Ernest Benn's Society of Individualists and had started reading political literature, including the Communist Manifesto. However, his great moment of personal revelation came when he read the *Reader's Digest* version of *The Road to Serfdom* in 1945. This seemed to articulate all his own fears for the future, and he thus determined to seek out the author, which led to his meeting with Hayek at the LSE in 1947. Hayek was in the midst of preparations for the first Mont Pèlerin Society meeting when Fisher called, and so was in a peculiarly receptive frame of mind when Fisher came to seek his advice. Fisher later liked to recount how he had found Hayek's office opposite Laski's in the LSE (although, in fact, this is unlikely as Hayek and Laski were in different departments), and went on to describe his 'fateful meeting':

> My central question was what, if anything, could he advise me to do to help get discussion and policy on the right lines . . . Hayek first warned against wasting time – as I was then tempted – by taking up a political career. He explained his view that the decisive influence in the battle of ideas and policy was wielded by intellectuals whom he characterised as the 'second-hand dealers in ideas'. It was the dominant intellectuals from the Fabians onwards who had tilted the political debate in favour of growing government intervention with all that followed. If I shared the view that better ideas were not getting a fair hearing, his counsel was that

> I should join with others in forming a scholarly research organisation to supply intellectuals in universities, schools, journalism and broadcasting with authoritative studies of the economic theory of markets and its application to practical affairs.[3]

It was thus Hayek who provided Fisher with the intellectual formula for the IEA, his advice going beyond the bounds of what he was to recommend to the Mont Pèlerin Society. Fisher himself recognized that he was not an intellectual, but he was prepared to learn from Hayek and his fellow Mont Pèlerins, and he attended his first meeting of the MPS in 1951. A by-product of Fisher's interest in Hayek was his first book, *The Case for Freedom*, published in 1947, which was a comparatively simplistic but robust exposition of the free-market economy, laced with home-spun wisdom about politics and democracy. He also devoted considerable space to an attack on fixed exchange rates and the Bretton Woods agreement – the evils of fixed exchange rates would become a particular obsession throughout his life. *The Case for Freedom* also demonstrated that single-mindedness and inflexibility which were to become Fisher's hallmark; he summarized his economic philosophy as 'the Community which comes nearest to keeping its markets entirely free will be the most prosperous.'[4] But it needed someone as unwavering and determined as Fisher to act on Hayek's advice, and to keep Hayek's idea alive until a time when money was available. Fisher was obsessed by his cause, and struck everyone he met with his 'real conviction'.[5] He was a staunch Christian Scientist and an accomplished amateur painter, with little small talk. Ralph Harris said of him at his memorial service that 'he was touched by a goad of divine discontent . . . If things were out of order, he could not turn his back but must do whatever he could to get them right . . . he was always a perfectionist.' His favourite saying was 'For evil to succeed, it is only enough for good men to do nothing.'

In the years after his meeting with Hayek at the LSE, Fisher not only built up his farming business, but also began his early political campaigning against the bastions of agricultural subsidies, the British Egg Marketing Board and the Milk Marketing Board, and joined his local Conservative Party association. His farming business in Sussex met with mixed success, his cattle being wiped out by foot-and-mouth disease in 1951, but his fortunes were then transformed by a visit to

America in 1952, where he discovered broiler chicken-farming, which was then unknown in Britain. F. A. Harper, who had invited him to America to look at the Foundation for Economic Education (FEE), showed him the new farming method at Ithaca, and Fisher subsequently introduced this new form of production to his farm in Sussex, with spectacular success. Fisher was equally impressed by the work of the FEE in popularizing the ideas of the free market through a vigorous education programme and he thus returned to London with not only the commercial idea that would make his fortune, but also the model for his 'think-tank'. In 1953 Fisher founded his broiler chicken-farming business, Buxted Chickens, which within five years commanded sales of £5,000,000 and employed 200 people, handling 17,500 chickens a day. He eventually sold the business (which had become Allied Farm Foods) in 1968 for £21 million, although this profit was shared between him and his business partners. The phenomenal success of Buxted Chickens not only transformed the eating patterns of the British public, but it also gave Fisher the wealth to finally create the research institute which he had discussed with Hayek almost a decade previously. He was further encouraged in his endeavours by his warm reception at the 1954 MPS meeting in Venice where he read a paper on 'Government and Agriculture'.

However, Fisher was a novice in the world of pressure-groups and 'think-tanks', and so for advice and an institutional base for his proposed research institute he turned to a person whom he had met through the Society of Individualists, Oliver Smedley, who was, if anything, even more fervent and obsessive in his belief in the beneficence of the free market. Born in 1911, Smedley had been a paratrooper during the war and had won the Military Cross at Arnhem. He described himself as an 'uncompromising free-trader and libertarian', and after the war resigned from his 'lucrative' partnership with a firm of Chartered Accountants and set up his own 'little flag in defence of human liberty' at 24 Austin Friars, London EC2. This was in 1952, and by 1955, when Fisher proposed the idea of a new research institute to him, Smedley was already running a bewildering variety of free-trade campaigns out of his tiny office in Austin Friars. He was aided in his activities by John Heffernan and, in particular, by S. W. Alexander, who had earlier been instrumental in founding the Society of Individualists. S. W. Alexander had left Beaverbrook's employ at the end of the war, and from 1948 was editor of the *City Press* newspaper, owned by the City financier Harley Drayton, 'an old-fashioned free-trader who had come up from the bottom'.[6] The circulation of the *City Press* was comparatively small, but Drayton and Alexander used it to propagandize for free trade, and gave support to many of Smedley's campaigns. Smedley liked to describe himself and S. W. Alexander as 'the only active free-traders left in England in the 1950s'.[7] Smedley's main campaigning body was the Cheap Food League which denounced all forms of subsidy and protection in agriculture, particularly the marketing boards. Smedley also helped to found, and became organizing Secretary of, the Farmer's and Smallholder's Association, founded in 1947 to campaign against the Attlee Government's Agriculture Act of the same year. The first President of the Farmers and Smallholders Association was Waldron Smithers, the Conservative MP who had been a founder-member of the Progress Trust. In 1954, Smedley founded the Council for the Reduction of Taxation to campaign against high taxation. He also took over the running of the Free Trade League (founded in 1903) and the moribund Cobden Club in 1958, S. W. Alexander becoming editor of the Club's magazine, the *Free Trader*. He was also a highly committed anti-European, and when Britain began to move cautiously towards negotiating entry into the EEC in the early 1960s Smedley founded the 'Keep Britain Out' campaign in 1962, and later formed the Free Trade Liberal Party in 1979 to campaign against continued British membership of the EEC. All these were causes which were also very close to Antony Fisher's heart; he was, for instance, Joint Honorary Treasurer of the Farmer's and Smallholder's Association throughout the 1950s. Smedley also acquired a measure of popular acclaim as the man who broke the monopoly of the state-run BBC over the airwaves when he founded Radio Caroline in 1964. Less well known was the fact that he regarded the offshore transmitter as the last bastion of freedom if the country finally went Communist.

Where Smedley did differ markedly from Fisher was in his politics. Fisher was a passive member of his local Conservative Association, but believed in Hayek's central aim of long-term intellectual persuasion. Smedley and Alexander by contrast, were heavily involved in Liberal Party politics, and believed in the efficacy of direct political action. Both contested numerous elections, Smedley alone standing in eighteen Parliamentary elections by the time of his death in 1989, often against R. A. Butler at Saffron Walden. Together with Sir Arnold Suenson-

Taylor, another active Liberal, they sought to keep the flames of Gladstonian Liberalism burning within the Party, and to counter the influence of the two most celebrated modern 'Liberals', Beveridge and Keynes. S. W. Alexander was chairman of the London Liberal Party, and Smedley was a frequent speaker at Liberal assemblies during the 1950s. Smedley was a trenchant critic of the Liberal Party leadership during the early 1950s for what he regarded as their intellectual timidity and their gradual desertion of the Party's true principles of free trade and self-improvement. In a series of prescient speeches he warned of the dangers of inflation and the need for improved competitiveness in industry, but he went largely ignored by his audiences. He saw a historic opportunity for the Liberals to reassert their old authority by taking up a new political position, distinct from the two main parties locked into their Butskellite consensus. In a speech to a Liberal audience on 8 November 1952 at Church House, Westminster, he argued that:

> It surely becomes clearer every day that no significant issue really divides the front benches of the House of Commons ... A tremendous responsibility therefore rests on Liberals inside the House and out, to tell the people the truth. Members of the other two parties cannot bring themselves to do so ... We must warn the people that there can be no hope of survival in an intensely competitive world if our energies, enterprise and adaptability continue to be fettered by the outmoded trappings and controls of the centrally planned economy.

Smedley never set out to endear himself to the Party leadership by moderating his criticism of them or the other parties. However, in his disillusion with the Liberal Party he was by no means alone. The leading individualists within the Party, those who considered themselves to be the true heirs of the Gladstonian School of liberalism, led by Edward Martell, split from the Party in September 1956. Martell formed 'The People's League for the Defence of Freedom', with its own newspaper, the *News Daily*, which in 1964 claimed a circulation of ninety thousand.[8] Smedley and Alexander both split with the Liberal Party in 1962 over the Party's position on Europe, and they went on to found the Free Trade Liberal Party. Symptomatic of this intellectual unease within the party was the founding of the 'Unservile State Group' in 1953, with the object of developing and propagating Liberal ideas. The 'Unservile State Group' was formed in Oxford under the Chairmanship of Elliott Dodds, the Vice-President of the Liberal Party and the editor of the *Huddersfield Examiner*, whilst the editor of their papers was a Cambridge don, George Watson. The group's first book, *The Unservile State: Essays in Liberty and Welfare*, was published in 1957 and gently tried to nudge the Party in a more individualistic direction, as did their next collective work, *The Radical Alternative*, published under the auspices of the Oxford Liberal Group in 1962. To W. H. Greenleaf, 'all this constituted the first full-scale exploration of Liberal attitudes since the Yellow Book of 1928'.[9] In truth, however, the Unservile State Group had little impact on the Liberal Party, let alone the world beyond. The Group contained people of too diverse political and economic views to make a coherent political impact, and the fact that it contained amongst its number such stalwarts of the Party establishment as Jo Grimond MP and Nancy Seear meant that the Group could not afford to be openly hostile to the Party. However, the Unservile State Group did bring together a number of Liberal economists who shared Smedley's and Alexander's reservations about the direction of the Liberal Party's economic policy, notably Alan Peacock, Jack Wiseman and Graham Hutton, all of whom were to be closely associated with the IEA. Peacock was an undergraduate at St Andrews University, and met Wiseman at the LSE when he moved there in the early 1950s. Hutton was also a product of the LSE, and they were all guided in their economics at the LSE by the economic liberals there, particularly Robbins, Paish and Plant. Peacock and Wiseman, in particular, grew increasingly disenchanted with the Liberal Party's refusal to countenance more radical critiques of the Welfare State and Keynesian economics, and Alan Peacock used the opportunity of a seminal 'Unservile State' paper of 1961 entitled 'The Welfare Society' to accuse the Liberal establishment of accepting collectivism uncritically, and thus ignoring the opportunities for a re-evaluation of the whole Welfare System. Peacock's concluding paragraph of the pamphlet gives the flavour of his argument:

> I find that some members of the Liberal Party accept the Collectivist position, and I am disturbed by it. It implies a pronounced lack of faith, not only in free enterprise subject

> to anti-monopoly controls but also in the 'Middle way', i.e. the encouragement of non-profit making institutions such as educational trusts, housing and hospital associations. It is probably too late now to do much about re-organising the health service to allow for more voluntary action; but it is not too late to evolve a new policy for education and housing. I do not suggest, and have never suggested, that education and housing should be simply turned over to free enterprise. What I would like to see is greater diversity in the provision of these services, whether public or private, so that there is a genuine possibility of choice for ordinary citizens.[10]

However, the Liberal Party leadership refused to contemplate even this comparatively small step in the direction of economic liberalism, which meant that the economic liberals of the Liberal Party, spurned by the Party which they thought was their natural and historical home, eventually turned to the IEA instead. A recent historian of the Liberal Party has written that had the Liberals listened to Smedley, Grantchester, Peacock, Wiseman et al., the Party 'would certainly have acquired a distinctive position and would have been recognised as forerunners of the New Right in the 1970s'. This meant, as Andrew Gamble has written, that

> One major feature of recent British politics is that when the revival of liberal political economy did come about it was the Conservative Party with which it was associated and not the Liberal Party. So economic liberalism and Liberal economics diverged to add to the confusion of political terminology. The Liberals on the whole chose to remain with Keynesianism and the perspectives of social Liberalism. That they did so was partly because the radical individualists [such as Smedley] of the 1950s who would have purged the party of its Social liberalism never made much headway. They were resisted by the party establishment who did not want to see the Liberals staking out political ground too distant from the consensus policies which the two main parties were pursuing. They were resisted also by the Radical Reform Group, which believed the task of the Liberals was not to retreat from Social Liberalism but to

> propose ways in which the institutions and policies of the Welfare State and the managed economy could be improved and strengthened. This meant state action to redistribute wealth and decentralize power. In 1956 the party acquired a leader who inclined to the views of the Radical Reform Group, Jo Grimond.[11]

When Fisher approached Smedley with the idea of setting up a new research institute specifically to concentrate on the doctrine of economic liberalism, Smedley and other similarly disillusioned Liberals were thus in a very receptive frame of mind, and many Liberals were to become involved in the work of the new Institute. By going to Smedley, Fisher acquired the services of his existing umbrella organization at 24 Austin Friars, Investment and General Management Services Limited (IGMS), and the new Institute was called, at Smedley's suggestion, the Institute of Economic Affairs. Fisher was quite clear about the aims and rationale of the IEA from the beginning, wanting to follow Hayek's path of long-term intellectual persuasion, rather than more immediate political work – although even Fisher was occasionally tempted, out of sheer frustration, to try and have a more direct influence on the political process. He modelled the IEA very much on the Fabians and the early Socialists, as he outlined in a letter to Smedley in 1956:

> Money spent on politics has very little effect on the actions of the average grown person. Most people are far too busy with their own affairs to get involved with the dreary subject of politics. It is of course necessary to have political machinery but if we are going to increase the number of people who are prepared to vote intelligently, we much start putting the right ideas in front of them at an early age.
>
> The Socialists got round this problem by getting a rich man to support the London School of Economics and they put Lhaski [sic] and Dalton in there. Lhaski [sic] and Dalton between them must have done incalculable damage to sound thinking the world over. They teach young people at a time when they are actually exercising themselves in an effort to find out things. They are still at a formative age. Once young

> College and University students have got the right idea into economically [sic] they will never lose it and will spread these ideas as they grow up. In particular, those carrying on intellectual work must have a considerable impact through newspapers, television, radio and so on, on the thinking of the average individual. *Socialism was spread in this way and it is time we started to reverse the process.** It is probably impossible to do it in any other way but in any case with limited funds this method is the only way open to us.
>
> Therefore the Institute of Economic Affairs has been formed to propagate sound economic thought in the universities and all other educational establishments where we find it possible to do so. There are obviously many ways open to us, all depending on the amount of money available. The Institute is a charitable and educational organisation and therefore funds subscribed by businesses are not subject to tax. Where tax has been paid it can be recovered.[12]

Fisher was thus pitching the IEA at those whom Hayek had called the 'second-hand dealers' in ideas, the journalists, academics, writers, broadcasters and teachers who dictate the long-term intellectual thinking of the nation. He constantly stressed the non-Party political work of the IEA, as the Institute worked to propagate and revive interest in a particular set of ideas; this meant that it could claim charitable status, and thus receive tax-free donations. Both Smedley and Fisher were very sensitive on this issue, as Smedley wrote to Fisher in 1955 that it was

> imperative that we should give no indication in our literature that we are working to educate the Public along certain lines which might be interpreted as having a political bias. In other words, if we said openly that we were re-teaching the economics of the free-market, it might enable our enemies to question the charitableness of our motives. That is why this first draft [of the Institute's aims] is written in rather cagey terms.[13]

* Author's italics.

The aims of the IEA, as printed in their publications, were, indeed, excessively cagey, stating merely that the Institute was formed as 'a research and educational trust that specialises in the study of markets and pricing systems as technical devices for registering preferences and apportioning resources. Micro-economic analysis forms the kernel of economics and is relevant and illuminating in the public and private sectors in collectivist and individualist societies.' Nonetheless, the IEA pledged itself to be 'independent of any political party' and Fisher and the Institute's staff were scrupulous in observing this rule, partly because Hayek had laid this down as a pre-condition for their success, but also so as not to endanger their charitable status. It was an issue over which Fisher was to fall out very quickly with Smedley, and which came back to haunt the IEA in 1991.

The IEA was formally created on 9 November 1955, when the three founding trustees of the Institute, Fisher, Smedley and a colleague of Smedley's called J. S. Harding, met to sign the Trust Deed and the Rules of the Institute. Each of the Trustees contributed £100 each to give the Institute its first capital. The exact financial basis of the Institute in its early years is in some doubt as it was the subject of a highly acrimonious correspondence between Fisher and Smedley in 1982, long after the two had ceased to be on speaking terms, but Fisher's claim, which is probably right, is that he and Sir Robert Renwick, the industrialist, both contributed £500 each to form the IEA's first working capital and thereafter Fisher paid in £250 a year from the profits of Buxted Chickens to the Institute throughout the late 1950s and early 1960s. As well as the three Trustees, an Advisory Council was set up consisting of Lord Grantchester (formerly Sir Arnold Suenson-Taylor), three LSE economists – George Schwartz, Graham Hutton and Colin Clark – the celebrated financial correspondent of the *News Chronicle* Sir Oscar Hobson, and Professor Eric Nash. In June 1956, Fisher wrote in a buoyant mood to the only MP to take an interest in the birth of the IEA, Major Gough, that:

> After what I can honestly say is now many years of studying socialism, Communism, bad government, tyranny, whatever else you call it, I have come to the conclusion that possibly one of the only ways of defending the civilised community against completely false and wishful thinking is through an organization such as this. Even if it isn't the only way, I do

> believe it is the cheapest. I therefore intend to give up all my other 'social' activities so that I can give as much constructive thought to the work of the institute as it is possible for me to do . . .[14]

In July 1955, the IEA produced the first in a long and illustrious line of publications, *The Free Convertibility of Sterling* by George Winder. Fisher commissioned the economist Winder to write about his pet subject, floating exchange rates, and paid Batchworth Press £200 to publish the book. One of Fisher's first acts was to send a copy of the book to Henry Hazlitt, his fellow Mont Pèlerin member, who promptly devoted one of his 'Business Tides' columns in *Newsweek* entirely to the book. Hazlitt was, of course, a natural supporter of floating exchange rates, but was nonetheless genuinely impressed by Winder's 'most lucid, thorough, and uncompromising protest against continuation of British exchange control . . . Winder has published something more effective than a mere polemic. He has written a sort of elementary textbook.'[15] Hazlitt's coverage of the book in *Newsweek* ensured that it sold out within three months, although the IEA were unable to make any profit on the book because Batchworth Press went bankrupt soon after the book's publication. Nonetheless, it was a promising start. As Fisher later recalled, 'More orders came in than we had books for. I can remember that we got an order for 125 copies . . . from the Philippines. Professor Murray Rothbard actually recommended the book for reading in a magazine at the time . . .'[16]

The next task was to find the staff to run the new Institute, as Fisher was engaged full-time running Buxted Chickens, whilst Smedley, always a highly strung character, admitted to Fisher in June 1956 that he was 'extremely tired and for the past three and a half years have been doing more than I can maintain any longer'.[17] As it was, Fisher had always been clear in his own mind about whom he wanted to appoint as the first director of the IEA – Ralph Harris, whom he had first met in 1949. Harris, born in working-class north London, had left school in 1943 and had trained as Air Crew before going up to Queens' College, Cambridge, to read economics. At Cambridge he was farmed out to be taught at Gonville and Caius by Stanley Dennison. Dennison was also tutor to John B. Wood, who worked for the IEA, too. Dennison introduced Harris to the work of Hayek, especially the latter's paper on 'Socialism and the intellectuals', which he had given at one of the early Mont Pèlerin Society meetings. Another staple was the *Lloyd's Bank Review* then edited by Manning Dacey, the *Financial News* journalist. Unlike others involved in the founding of the IEA, Harris was politically a Conservative from a Liberal household; his hero at the time was Winston Churchill, and he campaigned for Beverley Baxter in London during the 1945 general election. Harris left Cambridge in 1948 and went to work in Conservative Central Office, first as education officer to the newly formed Conservative Political Centre (CPC) and then, briefly, for the Conservative Research Department. In 1949, Harris, a relaxed and engaging public speaker, addressed a CPC weekend meeting in Sussex. His subject was economics, and in the audience was Antony Fisher, who came up to Harris at the end to pay the speaker his compliments on an excellent speech. During the course of the ensuing conversation, Fisher recounted his conversation with Hayek in 1947 and his plans to found what he then called an 'anti-Fabian Society'. Harris was enthusiastic about the idea and Fisher promised that he would one day raise the money for such an institute. It was not until the summer of 1956 that Fisher wrote to Harris officially offering him the job of Director of the IEA, but during the intervening eight years it seems that Fisher never wavered from his initial choice of Harris as director of the new Institute, despite the fact that in the interim Harris might have been justified in despairing of Fisher's slowness at ever getting the IEA off the ground. During that period Harris had been a lecturer in economics at St Andrews University, a connection which was to prove very fruitful later on, and when Fisher finally wrote to Harris offering him the job of Director he was a leader writer for the *Glasgow Herald.* Fisher's letter to Harris of 7 June 1956 sought to persuade Harris that the IEA was finally up and running and that its first publication had been a success – in other words, that Harris was not being dragged all the way from Scotland to head an organization that only existed on paper. Fisher stressed that 'Our [the IEA's] strength lies in the fact that we are not beholden to politics, that we are out to seek and spread the truth. We are not beholden therefore to any past political history or any particular business gimmick. Everything we do must be of the very topmost quality and carry the stamp of complete sincerity and integrity.'[18] Although Fisher was certain that Harris was the kind of intellectual salesman that he was looking for, he was also concerned that Harris, who had not only worked for the Conservative Party but who had stood twice as a Parliamentary candidate for the Party, should now abandon politics and embrace the purely intellectual work of the IEA. Having re-assured Fisher on this point, and having had a satisfactory interview with Smedley, Harris was officially appointed Director of the IEA at a meeting of the Trustees at the National Farmer's Club in Whitehall on 5 July 1956. Harris started on a part-time salary of £50 a month, although he was soon on a full-time salary and gave up his regular journalism to devote himself to over a decade of full-time work for the IEA.

To complement Harris's work as Director, the IEA also needed an editorial director to oversee their main activity of publishing books and pamphlets. It was Lord Grantchester who recommended Arthur Seldon for this job in 1956, and he started work at the IEA in 1957. Seldon, too, was of working-class origin, having been born in the East End of London in 1916. He was educated at Sir Henry Raine's Grammar School off Commercial Road and then at the LSE from 1934 to 1937. Like most of those of his contemporaries who grew up in the East End during the worst years of the depression, he was an ardent Socialist before going to the LSE, where he absorbed the economic liberalism of his economics lecturers there, who included Hayek, Robbins and Plant, as well as Evan Durbin and Nicholas Kaldor. Seldon was particularly influenced by Hayek's *Collectivist Economic Planning* of 1935. Seldon has given a good account of his own conversion to economic liberalism at the LSE in his partly autobiographical book on *Capitalism*, so there is no need to repeat his own account of his life here, other than to note that as the Conservative Society at the LSE were 'too Socialist' – by which he meant corporatist and collectivist – Seldon joined the Liberal Society, which at least sounded right.[19] From 1937 to 1939 Seldon was Arnold Plant's Research Assistant at the LSE, during which time he was also becoming more involved with Liberal Party politics, and in 1940 produced a paper on 'The Corporate State' for the Party. He was also involved in the Liberal Party's attempt to define its position on the distribution of property. The Party instituted a Committee of enquiry on this subject chaired by Elliott Dodds, later Chairman of the 'Unservile State Group', and Dodds asked Seldon, then aged twenty-one, to draft the Committee's report. In 1938 the Committee's proposals were published under the title *Ownership for All*. As Seldon has written of this report,

> their proposals in 1938 for the diffusion of private property rather than its replacement by public (socialized) property raised the flag of classical liberalism for the last time in the Liberal Party. After the War it was seduced by socialism. The Conservatives under Anthony Eden stole the powerless Liberals' clothes in their advocacy of a property-owning democracy.[20]

Seldon himself made some attempt to redress the balance of ideology towards classical liberalism within the Party by joining a group of five LSE economics post-graduates to 'discuss ways of refuting collectivist economic heresies'. Seldon liked to see this group, which included the prominent economists A. A. Shenfield and Professor L. M. Lachmann, later associated with the IEA, as an 'embryo IEA-type organisation of liberals', but their hopes were frustrated by the outbreak of war. Nonetheless, Seldon's experience at the LSE had equipped him admirably for his work for the IEA, and as he later wrote, becoming editorial director of the IEA in 1957 was 'the fulfilment of my post-graduate hopes of 1938–39'.[21] Like Smedley and many others, he was partly attracted to the IEA because of the failure of the Liberal Party to, as he saw it, stay true to its principles. Lord Grantchester, for his part, hoped that Seldon's arrival at the IEA would provide a 'good infusion of Liberal thought into the IEA'.[22] Seldon started work part-time for the IEA in 1957, and became a full-time employee in 1958. Another important member of the IEA's staff was John Wood. Born in 1924, he was educated at the public school Oundle and took a degree in PPE at Oxford. He joined the Economic Section of the War Cabinet Secretariat in 1944, and there became a protégé of Stanley Dennison. It was Dennison who suggested that he go to Cambridge to take an abbreviated degree in economics, where he 'absorbed the classical liberal teaching of Dennison, Robertson and others'.[23] After Cambridge he joined the Conservative Research Department where he fell under the influence of Diana Spearman, and through her of Enoch Powell. Wood worked for Lazard's in the City, before working as an Economic Adviser to Lord Chandos of Associated Electrical Industries. Throughout this time he was closely associated with the IEA through Ralph Harris, whom he had met at Cambridge. Wood's contacts in the City were very useful for Harris and the IEA, and possible donors to the IEA were lunched by Wood and Harris at Queen's

Restaurant off Sloane Square. In 1969, Wood officially joined the IEA as Deputy Director. He also wrote or contributed to seven IEA publications.

The duo of Harris and Seldon effectively ran the IEA from 1957 until the mid-1980s. Antony Fisher was content to let Harris and Seldon run it themselves, and he left all matters of intellectual importance and publishing strategy to them. The running of the IEA was streamlined by the break with Oliver Smedley, which happened soon after the IEA was founded. The break came about because of Fisher and Harris's concern over Smedley's and Lord Grantchester's continuing links with the Liberal Party, which they felt might compromise the political independence of the IEA. It is clear that there was also a character clash between Smedley and Harris. As Fisher recalled to Smedley in 1982:

> I can remember that you were very unhappy with Ralph and that he wasn't a believer in the free market. It was probably for that reason that he was unhappy about you and then we began to find that in trying to raise money from others, because of the association of yourself and Lord Grantchester so firmly with the Liberal Party, people started to say that they didn't want to fund the Liberal Party.[24]

The IEA was only disentangled from Smedley's IGMS when Harris moved out of 24 Austin Friars in 1959 to a new office in Hobart Place. By the same token Lord Grantchester was removed from the Advisory Council. Smedley, in his own words, was 'naturally bitterly disappointed to be ejected from something that I had so much to do with inaugurating'. His cup of sorrow was filled to overflowing by the news that he was also *persona non grata* at the Mont Pèlerin Society on the rather spurious grounds that he was 'not an academic economist',[25] which was equally true of Antony Fisher. His lasting bitterness at the way in which he was treated manifested itself in a series of aggrieved letters to the press about the history of the founding of the IEA in the mid-1980s.

The IEA thus blended, in its personnel, the economic liberal renegades from both political parties: Harris and Fisher from the Tories, and Seldon, Smedley and Lord Grantchester from the Liberals. It was a blend that ultimately proved to be the essence of 'Thatcherism', or a new kind of Conservatism based on classical (not Liberal Party) liberalism. It was a new intellectual movement that grew out of a discontent with all the major parties, which were, at least for Fisher, Harris and Seldon, wedded to the damaging policies of collectivism and Keynesianism. The central partnership within the IEA was that between Harris and Seldon, and they also represented another important strand of Thatcherism in that they were both working-class in origin fighting against the intellectual creed, collectivism, which was supposed to have done the most to improve the conditions of their class. Both Harris and Seldon could call on their own experience when arguing with high-minded middle-class defenders of Keynesian orthodoxy who claimed to be acting on behalf of the less well-off in society. They represented the first stirrings of the Thatcherite revolt against paternalists and middle-class socialists that would prove to be one of the most radicalizing features of Thatcherism in the 1980s. Typical of this was Seldon's riposte to a speech by Lord Balniel on Conservative Welfare policy in 1967, when the Conservative peer had argued for a policy on welfare integrating 'cash and care'. Seldon wrote to Balniel:

> You have never been poor. I have. The poor do not thank those who bring them gifts in kind which question their capacity and affront their dignity. Cash gives the power of choice; care, service in kind, denies choice. But much more than that; the poor who are given care or kind will never *learn* choice, judgement, discrimination, responsibility. To give cash is to take risks but they are the risks the child takes when he learns to walk. Only the mentally or otherwise incapable of learning choice by using cash should be given care or kind.[26]

Harris and Seldon could thus attack Keynesianism and the Welfare State from the bottom up, giving their comments an authority which many Conservative Parliamentary critics of the Welfare State could never muster. Seldon and Harris formed such an effective partnership because they were very different people, and so complemented each other perfectly. Harris was the convivial, witty and extrovert 'front-man' of the IEA, combining, in Seldon's words, 'the knowledge of the case for Capitalism with good humoured wit to become the archetypal persuader of capitalists to support the study, and where academically necessary the criticism, of capitalism. It was a task that combined the arts of advocate, adviser, candid friend and salesman.'[27] Seldon, by contrast, was the more scholastic and thoughtful of the two, with none of Harris's flair as a genial and persuasive public speaker; he concentrated on maintaining the IEA's scholastic reputation and publishing output through a meticulous attention to detail as the editorial director. Seldon once said that the IEA had to fight the intellectual battle against collectivism 'in the footnotes . . .', and it was he who fought the trench warfare of the footnotes. Seldon described the team as 'The Gilbert and Sullivan combination of producer and projector respectively of the case for liberal capitalism . . .'[28] Even those who did not agree with their views had to concede their charm; as Jo Grimond testified, the duo were 'exceptionally good expositors . . . and exceptionally agreeable people'.[29] This was a vital ingredient of the success of the IEA. Harris's talents as a fund-raiser were particularly important, as, after the early 1960s, when he was giving the IEA £12,000 a year, Fisher's financial support subsequently fell away, and Harris and Seldon were increasingly left to fend for themselves. A measure of their success is that the IEA managed to preserve its independence by dispersing its financial support amongst 350 different sources.

The *modus operandum* of the IEA, as directed by Harris and Seldon, was clearly based on Hayek's original guiding principle, that they had to fight and win the intellectual battle over the course of twenty or more years without regard to the short-term political situation. Once the intellectual climate had changed, then the politicians would come round as well. Keynes's passage about politicians being guided by the 'academic scribblers' was always given pride of place on the walls of the IEA's office. The IEA was not a traditional 'think-tank' like the Royal Institute for International Affairs in Britain or the Brookings Institute in America, in the sense that they were searching for policies and ideas; as Antony Fisher had written in 1956, the IEA knew 'the truth', their task was to evangelize.

Harris and Seldon outlined what they termed 'The Tactics and Strategy of the Advance to a Free Economy' in a long paper delivered to the 1959 Mont Pèlerin Society meeting at Christ Church, Oxford. This gathering of the MPS was hosted by the IEA, and proved invaluable as an institutional introduction to the world community of economic liberal scholars. In their paper, Harris and Seldon stated that some progress had been made since the war:

'Before the War and up to about 1950, the warnings of liberal economists went largely unheeded, and only the short-sighted, stop-gap ideas of interventionists had the ear of the politician and the public. But for some years now, it has been possible to preach the free economy with some hope of being understood and without the automatic accusation of acting as lackeys of capitalists.' They could point to the speeches of Enoch Powell, who was already gaining a reputation as a powerful advocate of the free market. However, they also conceded that such gains for economic liberalism which had been made since the war 'are attributable fundamentally less to the power of ideas than to the evidence of experience'. They thus admitted that the positive acceptance of free-market ideas had not taken place, and that this was the next step, to be undertaken by the IEA. They continued:

> There are three basic requirements for the establishment and maintenance of a free society:
>
> 1. The philosophy of the market economy must be widely accepted; this requires a large programme of education and much thought about how to finance it;
> 2. The transformation from a controlled economy must be eased by compensating those interests whose expectations will be disturbed;
> 3. Policies must be designed to make otiose all pleas for protection from the consequences of change that democratic politicians would have difficulty in resisting.
>
> 1. Education at varying levels must be directed first at the influencers of opinion: i.e. at intellectuals, politicians, business men, and all (not least journalists) who help to form public opinion.
>
> It must first teach the virtues of free economy,
>
> secondly, show that they do not conflict with accepted ethical and political codes,
>
> thirdly, remove particular misapprehensions as they arise and perplex the public conscience; in Britain examples would include inheritance, inequality, industrial obsolescence, employee redundancy, bigness in industry, the 'func-

tionless' investor, institutional investment, capital gains, take-over bids.

It was the first of these 'basic requirements' with which the IEA was to be mainly concerned, the transformation of the intellectual climate through education. Most of the IEA's efforts were thus to be devoted towards its publishing programme, much like the Fabians. Already, by 1959, Harris and Seldon could tell the assembled Mont Pèlerins, from experience, that

> we have discovered that plainly written, well-informed and constructive efforts to relate the classical doctrine to present-day problems command attention . . . Undoubtedly, this has been helped by our frank criticism of many practices that masquerade as part and parcel of a free enterprise system. In other words, we have avoided appearing as apologetic defenders of established interests, although we do not lean over backwards to find fault where there is none.[30]

Under the direction of Arthur Seldon, the IEA thus tried to apply the principles of economic liberalism to as wide a range of areas of economic activity as possible, and to bear topical relevance in mind as well. Some of the subjects chosen were thus pointedly provocative, to stimulate interest in the Institute and its ideas; one of the memorable examples being Harris and Seldon's 1959 *Advertising in a Free Society*, a defence of advertising at a time when the industry was under attack for allegedly misleading consumers. The very first IEA pamphlet by Seldon, *Pensions in a Free Society* (1957), picked on an equally sensitive subject, and at a time when the Labour Party was planning an extension of the State pension scheme, this pamphlet argued for a gradual winding up of that scheme and its replacement by private saving for retirement. All the IEA's publications, although written by academic economists for the most part, had to be written as 'student texts' accessible to undergraduates, or even intelligent sixth-formers, as well as fellow academics, journalists, politicians and the like. Like the Fabian Tracts, the IEA pamphlets were cheap and quite short – about ten–fifteen thousand words on average – thus making the IEA's work available to as wide a market as possible. It was a testimony to Arthur Seldon's skills as an editor that the IEA achieved its aim of reaching a wide audience, as, apart from Friedman and Hayek, there were few IEA economists who made natural writers. It was Seldon who, more often than not, made them intelligible to a non-academic readership. Above all, true to Hayek's guiding principle, the IEA's authors were to pay no regard to the political practicability of their ideas. As Harris told the assembled guests at the IEA's thirtieth anniversary dinner: 'It was one of Arthur Seldon's most seminal principles that IEA authors must pursue their analysis fearlessly and indicate conclusions for policy without regard to what may be thought, *in the short run*, to be politically impossible.'

IEA authors were thus given licence to, in a later phrase of Alfred Sherman's, 'think the unthinkable', and as a result the IEA ploughed its own, initially very lonely, furrow. It was for politicians to come to them to learn about the free market, not the other way round. Seldon must have taken much pleasure in the following admonition from the Liberal MP John Pardoe in 1971, when he wrote to Seldon of the IEA's work that 'You are of course a confounded nuisance to any politician who wishes to be left alone in his unresearched ambitions . . .'[31]

Throughout the 1960s and through to the 1980s the IEA set out to be just that, a 'confounded nuisance' challenging the conventional wisdom with a cavalier disregard for its own popularity, armed with little more than an unequivocal belief in the justice of the cause.

The IEA thus sought, through its publications programme, to demonstrate the efficacy of economic liberalism and to apply the principles of the free market to all areas of economic activity, from the telephone service to the Welfare State, areas where the governing Butskellite consensus of the 'mixed' economy assumed that there was no alternative to the overwhelming state involvement of the day. Seldon was careful with his choice of authors for IEA publications, and the IEA's almost exclusive reliance on academic economists ensured that it acquired the reputation for academic excellence which Fisher had been so concerned about. Seldon tried to be catholic in his choice of authors, although there was unquestionably a hard core which was closely associated with Harris and Seldon: most of these had trained under the economic liberals (normally Robbins, Plant or Hayek) at the LSE, and most came from the same background and travelled the same political path as Arthur Seldon. The most important among them was probably Graham Hutton, who served on the Advisory Council of the

IEA from its early days. Hutton, like many others, was a disenchanted ex-Fabian who had worked on the *Economist* before the war and who then worked as an economic consultant to the Shell oil company – it was Hutton who secured the IEA's first corporate subscription, £500, from Shell. George Schwartz, Arthur Shenfield, Peter Bauer, William Hutt and later Alan Walters, all of whom trained or taught at the LSE, wrote for the IEA. Alan Peacock, founder of the Institute of Social and Economic Research at the University of York, and John Wiseman, were also closely involved with the IEA and were joint authors of one of the most famous IEA publications, *Education for Democrats* (Hobart Paper 25, 1964). This was the first public suggestion in Britain that education might be paid for by what was later to become known as the 'voucher system'. Colin Clark, the prominent welfare economist and lecturer at Cambridge (and ex-Fabian) was also a frequent contributor to the IEA, as was Brian Griffiths of the London Business School, later head of Mrs Thatcher's Policy Unit at Downing Street. As well as using these largely domestically based economists, Seldon was also adept at using his membership of the Mont Pèlerin Society to recruit writers, and so the IEA publications list included several economic liberals of international renown, including F. A. Hayek, Gottfried Haberler, Harry Johnson, James Buchanan and Milton Friedman, who was a frequent contributor to the IEA during the 1970s. The British Mont Pèlerins also wrote for the IEA, and Stanley Dennison, John Jewkes, Lionel Robbins and Frank Paish were all authors of some of the most persuasive IEA papers. Another favourite tactic of Seldon's was to find authors who were not automatically identified with the views of the IEA; as Seldon explained to the 1959 Mont Pèlerin Conference,

> we are seeking authors with Fabian or similar origins but whose basic love of liberty enables them to come most of the way with us on particular subjects (e.g. B. C. Roberts and J. Wiseman of the LSE and Desmond Donnelly, a Labour MP). This infiltration in reverse can prove most effective as was shown by the reception given to *Trade Unions in a Free Society* whose author went to Oxford on a Trade Union Scholarship. His criticisms were accepted as those of a 'frank friend' by the journal of the National Union of Railwaymen which concluded that his advice that unions

should come to terms with the market economy instead of obstructing its workings 'makes the book a major contribution to the literature on trade unionism.[32]

The most celebrated example of this 'infiltration in reverse' was the IEA occasional Paper No. 16 of 1967, *Paying for Social Services*, by Douglas Houghton, who until six months previously had been the Minister in Harold Wilson's Labour Government responsible for co-ordinating social policy in pensions, health and education. Seldon had met Houghton quite by chance at a conference on health expenditure in London, and had found, during the course of a brief conversation, that they shared much the same view on financing the Welfare State and Houghton, much to his credit, agreed to write the IEA paper based on his own experience of the problems in government. Flying in the face of all the contemporary political wisdom on the subject, let alone party policy, Houghton concluded that the country could no longer afford to go on spending more on ever-increasing social expenditure with only minimal increases in economic growth, and so he concluded that individuals *should be encouraged* to spend more on social expenditure themselves. That this came from the Chairman of the Parliamentary Labour Party, a man who had only recently been a minister in the Labour Government, attracted widespread press interest, which can be summarized by a leader in the then Labour-supporting *Sun* newspaper of 30 June 1967:

> The Labour Party's leading exponent on the Social Services today recommends that people should pay something for hospital treatment and prescriptions if they can afford to. This is a decisive departure from party principles. Labour have favoured a universal free health service and opposed any forms of means test . . . Nobody knows more than Mr Houghton about the outlook for the Social Services, their cost or their failings.
>
> So when he concludes that there must be some form of payment by those who can afford it, the evidence must be overwhelming.
>
> The only conclusion is that sooner or later any British Government will be compelled to adopt the principle.

A second edition of Houghton's pamphlet was rushed out in 1968.

From 1957 onwards, the IEA authors espoused courses of actions which seemed politically impossible at the time, but which were accepted as the conventional wisdom across the political spectrum by the 1980s. The IEA has itself given an excellent and detailed account of the content of its most influential publications in its own *festschrift*, *Not from Benevolence . . .*,[33] so I do not propose to do anything more here than point to some of the most important general areas of the IEA's work, and highlight its most important contributions to the economic debate. Above all, the IEA's interest lay in resurrecting an interest in micro-economics, as it was Hayek's prime complaint of Keynesian economics that the study of macro-economics which Keynes had encouraged had all but swamped the study of micro-economics, that area of the economy where wealth creation actually took place – or not, as was increasingly the case in Britain after 1960. As Harris and Seldon wrote in 1977,

> In the later 1950s it seemed to us that 'Keynesian' (not necessarily Keynes's) macro-economic analysis had dominated economics long enough and that it was time to correct the imbalance because macro-economics could not offer solutions to problems that required micro-economic analysis and micro-economic treatment. The 'economic system' has no impulse of its own apart from the personal impulses of the individuals who comprise it.[34]

The only IEA pamphlet which had a direct and immediate political impact was its first Hobart Paper, Basil Yamey's *Resale Price Maintenance and Shoppers' Choice*, published in 1960. Yamey, a South African-born Professor at the LSE (a student of Plant's) argued for the abolition of Resale Price Maintenance (RPM), which by fixing prices in shops prevented large stores from necessarily under-cutting smaller, so called 'corner shops'. Yamey argued that a free market in shop prices would save the shopper £180,000,000 a year, and prices would fall by five per cent. What really caught the headlines was Yamey's estimate that the abolition of RPM would save every person in the country £3.10*s.* a year. Yamey's paper was widely reviewed not only in the national press but in the trade magazines as well. *Marketing Trends* magazine was typical of many which managed to be very sniffy about Yamey's argument but was forced to concede, nonetheless, that he had 'produced what must surely be the definitive statement of the opinions and the facts (such as they are) relating to this thorny question. Hobart Paper No. 1 is an admirable first – a new publishing venture. It is the very best type of controversial pamphlet; urbane, polite, fair (it describes both the pros and cons of the question) and informed by a strong belief that the subject under review is entirely wrong.' Like the earlier *Pensions in a Free Society* and *Advertising in a Free Society*, Yamey's paper was timed to coincide with a period of public debate on the subject to ensure maximum impact, and Yamey's suggestions were taken up by the incumbent Conservative Government. Like all these questions of intellectual influence, as will be discussed later, it is impossible to attribute the abolition of RPM by Edward Heath in 1964 solely to Yamey's paper, but if Antony Fisher's story of Heath telling him at an IEA lunch in 1964 that the troubled passage of the legislation to abolish RPM was all Yamey's fault is to be believed, then Yamey could at least claim some credit for this small step towards a free market.[35]

In keeping with the IEA's promise to apply the laws of the free market on a micro-economic basis to areas of economic activity which had previously been off-bounds, the IEA published a series of pamphlets in the 1960s and early 1970s suggesting the application of market forces to a number of industries. The most famous of these was probably Michael Cane's *Telephones – Public or Private?* (Hobart Paper 36, 1966) a comparison of the British ('public') and American ('private') telephone systems. Cane, who was then a young postgraduate student at the LSE, provoked a storm in the press by gently concluding that 'the weight of quantitative evidence plus the impediments virtually inevitable to government-owned enterprise suggest strongly that the telephone service would be better off divorced from the public sector'. This started the long debate on the telephone system, and British Telecom was, of course, the first of Mrs Thatcher's major privatizations in 1984. Another Hobart Paper which attracted a lot of press attention was Georg Tugendhat's *Freedom for Fuel* (Hobart Paper 21, 1963). Tugendhat, an LSE industrial economist, argued that the coal industry was uneconomic, and that fuel prices were too high; he advocated the closure of about 350 pits, which would lead to 'a policy of lower fuel prices, increased competition, and thus the restoration of a vigorous free market both between alternative domestic supplies and imports'.

Seldon's special area of interest and expertise lay in the financial structure of the Welfare State in its broadest sense, and he remained a strenuous advocate of applying the laws of the free market to health care, housing, education and pensions, in order to cut the cost to the State of financing the Welfare State and to give people more choice over their own health care and education. He taunted the 'kindly rich' for over-compensating their 'bad consciences in making or inheriting money' by abrogating the responsibilities of the individual to a self-interested army of

> arrogant Social workers, sociologists and socializers . . . Not least, since British upper-class politicians have neglected to develop British working-class independence the Government must radically reverse the intellectual confusion of a century; instead of taxing people for 'free' services it must pump money into their pockets so that they can pay with dignity, and learn through choice the knowledge and self-confidence of the middle classes. That is the way to abolish social divisiveness without constricting freedom by State Welfare.[36]

The IEA thus published a stream of Hobart Papers and other publications on the alternative means for financing education, housing and medicine. As early as 1960 Professor Prest of Manchester University argued, in *Financing University Education* (IEA, 1960), for a system of student loans from the State to reduce the cost of the expansion of higher education to the State, and to 'provide an acid test of the genuine interest of potential undergraduates in taking a University Course'. On the economics of the Welfare State, Douglas Houghton's 1967 contribution has already been referred to, but Seldon himself wrote several IEA publications pursuing the same subject, including *Universal or Selective Social Benefits* (IEA, 1967), *Taxation and Welfare* (IEA, 1967), and *After the NHS* (IEA, 1969). Brian Walden, then a Labour MP becoming much attracted to the economic liberalism of the IEA, reviewed the latter in the *British Hospital Journal and Social Service Review* of 21 February 1969:

> It was not long ago that all right-thinking citizens agreed

> that Britain had the finest Welfare State in the World . . . All this has now changed . . .
>
> The current debate about the future of Welfare can do nothing but good. For too long every major problem in Welfare has been the victim of that kind of evasion that arises from intellectual sloth. Humanity is only too ready to believe that it has 'solved' a problem, if only the problem can be hidden away and a decent silence maintained about it. It is a matter for rejoicing that the silence over Welfare has ended.
>
> Arthur Seldon would not agree that there has been total quiet in the Welfare field, since he has been a critic of the present system for many years. Once a lonely captain with a pea-shooter, he finds himself now a general in the army of the new radicals. These new radicals are Jacobin inegalitarians, the sea-green incorruptibles of the Institute of Economic Affairs, who combine irreverence and the power of analysis with a certain political naivety. They reflect the more precise and lucid ruminations of Mr. Enoch Powell.

The IEA also devoted several pamphlets to the general state of the ailing British economy, such as Graham Hutton's *Politics and Economic Growth* (IEA, 1968), a searching analysis of the 'British Disease', diagnosing the size of the public sector and the weight of the tax burden as the two major causes of Britain's economic ills. The IEA also vigorously promoted the role of the businessman and the entrepreneur as the creator of wealth in the market economy, publishing the proceedings of a colloquium on *The Role of the Entrepreneur*, for instance, as an IEA Reading pamphlet (No. 23) in 1980. However, the IEA's most important and controversial contribution to the economic debate that dominated British politics from the mid-1960s to the mid-1980s was in the two areas which Hayek had originally pointed to as of special importance in his opening paper to the first Mont Pèlerin Society meeting in 1947 – trade unions and monetary stability. For it was clear to the economic liberals that a return to a market economy was only possible in Britain if the labour market was made more fluid through a great reduction in trade-union power, and if the Government pursued a policy of monetary stability, as opposed to the rampant inflation that increasingly disfigured the British economy from the mid-1960s onwards. Just as Hayek himself became the IEA's most persuasive critic of trade-union power, so Milton Friedman became the Institute's most celebrated exponent of monetary stability, or what came to be called 'monetarism'. The trade unions were, perhaps, the greatest sacred cow in British politics during the 1960s and early 1970s, while the discourse amongst economists over the effects of their power dated back to the early 1930s and the debate over Keynes's *General Theory*. The liberals argued that the power of the trade unions, as it existed in Britain through their privileged legal position, was in practice detrimental to their members' interests because it prevented the mobility of labour and lowered productivity to the point where heavily unionized industries (such as British Coal or British Leyland) could no longer compete in world markets – and thus everyone, managers and unionists, would eventually be out of a job. Harris and Seldon were well aware that this argument was extremely radical in the political climate of the time, and they thus took great care over the IEA's publications on union issues. One of the best IEA publications on the subject was *The Theory of Collective Bargaining* (Hobart Paperback, 1976) by William Hutt, the LSE-trained Professor of Commerce at Cape Town University, 1951–68. As Harris wrote to Hutt before the book's publication, the IEA wished 'to make a special effort to launch your latest Hobart paperback so as to make the maximum impact on an astonished world. Needless to say we both agree that all you have written deserves to be heeded and acted upon by our . . . politicians. However, we must face the difficulty that many on a first reading may be at least a little resistant and we have wondered how best we can bridge the gulf'.[37] Hutt's book, a critique of the argument that trade unions enhanced Labour's remuneration by the strike threat, was therefore accompanied by a commentary from Sir Leonard Neal, himself a prominent trade unionist and later a leading light at the Centre for Policy Studies. Hutt's other important IEA book, *Politically Impossible . . . ?* (Hobart Paperback 1, 1971), was a wider attack on economists and politicians for avoiding the truth in dealing with Britain's economy, including the trade union issue.[38]

However, the two most effective and widely discussed contributions on the trade union issue came from Hayek himself, in *A Tiger by the Tail* (IEA, 1972) and *1980s Unemployment and the Unions* (IEA, 1980). The first was particularly apt, as, in a collection of Hayek's writings compiled by Sudha R. Shenoy, the book put the trade union problem in its wider economic context. The book was of particular interest in that it took issue with Friedman's 'monetarist' doctrine that inflation was always a monetary phenomenon, and instead argued that monetary policy was only one source of inflation and that the vital task was to allow the economy to operate freely at a micro-level. Hayek wrote that:

> If we want to preserve the market economy our aim must be to restore the effectiveness of the price mechanism. The Chief obstacle to its functioning is trade union Monopoly . . . an exaggerated expectation of what can be achieved by monetary policy has diverted our attention from the chief causes. Though money may be one of them if it is mismanaged, monetary policy can do no more than prevent disturbances by *monetary* causes; it cannot remove those which come from other sources.[39]

Hayek's strictures lay at the heart of the economic debate that would rage over monetarism throughout the 1970s, and which would consume much scholastic ink at the IEA. For if there is one central idea that the IEA can be credited with placing at the centre of British politics, it is the doctrine of monetarism, which started life in the late 1960s as a highly technical economic technique for achieving monetary stability, but which later became the highly politicized motivating principle of Mrs Thatcher's economic reforms of the early 1980s. The process by which monetarism became so politicized – mainly by the Centre for Policy Studies – will be examined later on, but there is no doubt that the IEA is to be credited with importing the economic doctrine of monetarism into Britain and publicizing it in the first place, and thus handing politicians the 'big idea' that was to dominate political debate during the mid-1970s and early 1980s.

This is not the place to repeat either a history of the full development of Monetary Theory, or discuss the finer nuances of that theory – both of which have been done many times before – but it is illuminating to trace the role of the IEA in importing monetarism into Britain.[40] The IEA had always been interested in the role of money in the economy, and had started to try and focus popular attention on monetary discipline with their attack on the Radcliffe Committee's Report on Monetary Policy in 1959. In 1957, the Chancellor of the Exchequer, Peter Thorneycroft, had commissioned the eminent lawyer Lord Radcliffe to investigate the prominence that should be given to monetary factors for the avoidance of inflation. The Radcliffe Committee's Report relegated monetary policy to a relatively minor role in governmental economic management. The IEA took issue with this verdict, and commissioned three economists to look at Radcliffe again. Their publication was called *Not Unanimous: A Rival Verdict to Radcliffe's on Money* (IEA, 1960), and was a critique of Radcliffe's approach to monetary policy. One of the problems diagnosed in *Not Unanimous* . . . was that the Government's policy of securing full employment was in itself inflationary, so monetary policy – or monetary stability – was subordinated to the maintenance of full employment. The inflationary effects of full-employment policies based on Keynesian demand management were, as many of the Mont Pèlerin economists had predicted in the 1930s, already fully in evidence by the late 1950s; Hayek, in particular, kept returning to this point in a series of publications during the 1950s and 1960s.[41] The IEA published its first explicit attack on full-employment targets in 1964, with Frank Paish's *Policy for Incomes*, together with Professor Victor Morgan's *Monetary Policy for Stable Growth* (Hobart Paper 27, 1964). However, it was not until 1967 that the role of Monetary Policy was given international prominence within the economic community with Professor Friedman's famous address to the eightieth annual meeting of the American Economic Association on 29 December 1967, an address published in the *American Economic Review* in March 1968. Friedman argued that inflation was always a monetary phenomenon, and thus to maintain monetary stability he argued for strict control of the growth of the money supply, of three to five per cent a year. He argued that the problem with monetary policy in the past was that it had been too precipitous in effect, either in contracting or expanding the money supply, because Governments had tailored their policies to the present, rather than to what would happen in fifteen–eighteen months' time – 'Too late and too much has been the general practice'. Friedman was not, of course, the first American economist to develop monetary theory. Professor Irving Fisher had popularized the quantity equation MV = PT, the starting-point of all monetarist thinking, while Henry Simons, Professor of Economics at Chicago, had published the first and most influential article on the implications of monetary policy as early as 1936, 'Rules versus Authorities in Monetary Policy' in the *Journal of Political Economy*. However, it was Friedman who had done the empirical work linking the history of inflation to the money supply in the United States, and who became the monetarists' most energetic and enthusiastic spokesman. He was also addressing the American Economics Association at a time when inflation had come to be seen as the most serious threat to the economies of the West, and so his arguments were peculiarly relevant to the circumstances of the time. Friedman had, of course, been a founder-member of the Mont Pèlerin Society and so his views were well known to the British economic liberals of the MPS, such as Harris and Seldon. Friedman was thus willingly enrolled in the IEA's campaign for monetary stability during the 1970s, and he was a frequent contributor to IEA forums and debates, and published numerous papers for the IEA during the 1970s.[42] Robustly self-confident and unusually articulate for an academic, Friedman became the most famous exponent of the free-market economy during the 1970s, and a keen supporter of the IEA, which did much to secure him his high public profile in Britain. The IEA, for instance, helped in preparing his TV programme *Free to Choose* shown in six episodes in 1980, which had an enormous impact on British public opinion.

However, the honours for the first British publication of the monetarist case goes to Professor Alan Walters, then the young Sir Ernest Cassel Professor of Economics at the LSE. Walters was to be a key figure in the revolution in economic thinking during the 1970s, and as such shared much of the same social and intellectual background as Harris and Seldon and the other working-class pioneers of the Thatcherite revolution. His own personal history was familiar to many others in the 'free-market' think-tanks, such as Arthur Seldon, Alfred Sherman, Sir Leonard Neal and others:

> Born in 1926 of working-class parents in a Leicester slum, I was unpromising material. My father was then a clerk in a grocery chain store. He had left school at the age of 13, but he was, as we would say nowadays, both numerate and literate. From 1917 until 1937 or 1938 he was a Communist, but unlike many others, he was revolted by Spain's terror, in particular the massacre of the POUM in Spain. He remained a staunch ultra left-wing Socialist until the end. My early intellectual domestic diet was one of romanticized revolutions righting the capitalist exploitation of the working class, etc.[43]

Walters went to a local school, and was then accepted, 'almost as an act of local charity' by University College, Leicester as an external student for the London B.Sc. degree. He then spent a year at Nuffield College, Oxford, before going on to the University of Birmingham in 1952. It was here that, during the 1960s, he developed an interest in monetary policy, partly out of an interest, shared with the IEA, in the Radcliffe Report on Money, and partly out of his peripheral contact with, and great admiration for, Milton Friedman; he had first heard Friedman lecture at Cambridge in 1955 when Friedman was on a year's sabbatical at Gonville and Caius College. He was later to claim that 'the empirical and in particular the statistical analysis of money was substantially pioneered in the University of Birmingham in the first half of the 1960s. We challenged the conventional wisdom of the primacy of fiscal policy and the need for accommodating monetary stance ... Thus I was a natural candidate for the vanguard of the monetarist revolution in Britain.'[44] Mention should also be made of Professor David Laidler and his colleagues at the Manchester University Inflation Workshop which also did much of the empirical work on inflation and the money supply. Walters was, by now, an ardent economic liberal and on moving to the LSE in 1967 he was introduced to the IEA by Peter Bauer. Walters's initial training was as a transport economist, and it was on this subject that he wrote his first IEA paper, *Integration in Freight Transport* (Research Monograph 15), in 1968. But in 1969, the IEA invited him to write *Money in Boom and Slump* (Hobart Paper 44, 1969), which for the first time made accessible to a wider public the academic developments in monetary theory which had taken place over the previous years, while popularizing the work of Friedman. In his preface Arthur Seldon wrote that Walters

> concludes that, until at least the great depression of 1929, there was a clear relationship between the quantity of money and the state of activity in the economy, and less conclusively but still significantly for the period since 1945. For most of this period the effect of the supply of money on prices and incomes was significant, and it was in the direction predicted by the quantity theory. He concludes that the Stock of Money cannot be ignored in government monetary policy in managing the long-run stability of the economy.[45]

Money in Boom and Slump attracted widespread press comment, and went through an unprecedented three editions in two years. The IEA followed up Walters's paper with probably their most famous publication of all, Friedman's *The Counter-Revolution in Monetary Theory* (IEA Occasional Paper 33, 1970), originally given as a paper at the first Wincott Lecture in 1970, hosted by the IEA in memory of the financial journalist Harold Wincott who had been one of their staunchest supporters during the 1950s and 1960s. Friedman's lecture was listened to by an invited audience of politicians and economists, which included, amongst others, James Callaghan, the former Labour Chancellor and the politician who, as Prime Minister, would put the control of the money supply at the top of the political agenda in 1976. *The Counter-Revolution in Monetary Theory* explicitly heralded the counter-revolution against Keynesian economics, and argued, famously, that 'Inflation is always and everywhere a monetary phenomenon in the sense that it is and can be produced only by a more rapid increase in the quantity of money than in output.' The day after delivering the Wincott Lecture Friedman was discreetly ushered in to see the new Conservative Prime Minister, Edward Heath, for an hour's talk, but this did not seem to leave much of an impression on either party.[46]

During the 1970s Friedman was to be central to the IEA's campaign for monetarism, as was Alan Walters. The 1970 Wincott Lecture was very important in the dissemination of monetarism to a wider audience, as were Friedman's frequent subsequent IEA publications, such as his 1976 Nobel Laureate Lecture published as *Inflation and Unemployment* (Occasional Paper, No. 51) and his *Monetary Correction* (Occasional Paper, 1974). Alan Walters also wrote frequently for the IEA, and gave the 1977 Wincott Lecture on the subject of *Economists and the British Economy* (published as IEA Occasional Paper 54). In this he not only gave an account of his own conversion to monetarism but also sought to put his and Friedman's ideas in the micro-economic context which the IEA had tried to stress from its foundation. They were no Keynesians, trying to perfect the running of economic management, but rather deconstructuralists trying to allow the free market to operate quite independently. As Walters remarked:

> I have considerable sympathy with what I take to be the real thrust of the counter-revolution [in Monetary Theory], that is to say, that we know little about the forces that determine

> detailed economic conditions, such as prices and employment, exports and imports, output and productivity, savings and investment. True, the monetarists' results showed that the rate of inflation was ultimately determined by the excess of the rate of growth of the money stock over the rate of growth of real national income. True, also, the variations in the growth of the money supply had some transitory effects on employment and output; but all were highly uncertain both in timing and in magnitude. A government could do no good and on the average, would probably inflict much more harm by trying to fine-tune the economy – *and this holds true whatever the instrument used, whether monetary or Keynesian** . . . thus the best that can be done is to pursue a moderate and stable growth rate of the money stock – Friedman's famous rule.[47]

The IEA publication *Is Monetarism Enough?* (IEA Readings 24) of 1980 discussed much the same issue, with Patrick Minford, a student of Walters's at the LSE, arguing that the Government had to reduce the PSBR by at least four per cent as well as controlling the money supply, to reduce inflation. Thus the IEA presented in stark terms the dilemma facing Britain in the mid-1970s. On the Keynesian model full-employment policies only produced inflation, which made Britain uncompetitive and so would reduce the availability of jobs in the long term; the only alternative was an anti-inflation policy based on control of the money supply through a reduction of the PSBR and the curtailment of the power of the trade unions to demand wage rises unlinked to productivity.

The increasing acceptance of the IEA's argument for monetarism and the abandonment of full-employment policies in the 1970s, was based, as Friedman and Walters were the first to acknowledge, not so much on the force of their own intellectual arguments, but on a natural response by policy makers to new ideas at a time when the old economic policies of the Keynesian post-war consensus seemed to bring only more inflation and less economic growth – that baleful condition known as stagflation. As Walters wrote in 1977: 'The World is demanding some new economic messiah (such as some latter-day Keynes) who

* Author's italics.

will persuade us all that he has the key to understanding much that is now shrouded in mystery, and where there is demand supply will not be far behind.'[48] The IEA simply supplied the ideas, which they had been consistently analyzing for the previous twenty years. Furthermore, the encouragement that the IEA got from Government and political circles during the early 1970s strengthened them in their conviction that they were right, and that they were soon to be pushing at an open door. In July 1975, for instance, Alan Peacock, the Chief Economic Adviser to the Department of Industry, wrote to Arthur Seldon on receipt of the Friedman-Laidler pamphlet *Unemployment versus Inflation*: 'Not surprisingly, the Friedman/Laidler pamphlet excited considerable interest in Government circles and you will have received acknowledgement from some of our Ministers that it will receive attention'.[49]

This would have been unimaginable only a few years before, as the IEA had endured almost twenty years of being ignored by government. Undoubtedly one of the IEA's most important achievements was to create a public platform in Britain for the two most powerful academic dissenters of all, Hayek and Friedman, who, as we have seen, were not only instrumental in creating the Mont Pèlerin Society and then the IEA, but who also remained the two most eloquent advocates of the free market into the 1980s. The IEA kept Hayek's name alive when his international reputation was at a low ebb during the 1960s, despite the completion of his most significant book on liberalism in 1960, *The Constitution of Liberty*. One of the IEA's most devoted followers, Jock Bruce-Gardyne noted in 1978 that 'it was not until the IEA placed Hayek in their pantheon at the end of the 1960s that his works began to enjoy a wider audience in this country.'[50] Hayek was finally rehabilitated in 1974 when he was the joint winner of that year's Nobel Prize for Economics, which not only confirmed his academic stature, but also gave much publicity to his ideas when they were at their most relevant. Friedman won the Nobel Prize in 1976. Both these awards helped to cement the academic and intellectual credibility of the IEA's work, which, all along, had been its greatest asset.

By the mid-1970s, therefore, the IEA had, over the course of twenty years, developed a coherent body of free-market ideas, applicable to all areas of the economy. They had articulated a coherent set of principles, the principles of economic liberalism, applicable to a modern economy, thus fulfilling Hayek's 1947 hope that the economic liberals would refine and develop liberalism into a modern, vibrant philosophy. The exact nature of the IEA's influence in Britain, and the important limitations of its influence, will be discussed in more detail in the next chapter, against the political background of the 1960s and 1970s. Suffice it to say for now that the IEA's greatest achievement was to develop and publicize – 250,000 Hobart Papers had been sold in several countries by 1970 – a modern programme of economic liberalism, unrivalled in its intellectual eminence by any other comparable institute in the world. Perhaps the highest and most memorable accolade was conferred on the IEA by its alter ego, the Fabian Society, in 1968. In October of that year, whilst much of Europe *seemed* to be in a state of perpetual student-led, left-wing revolution, the Fabian Society perceptively published tract 387, *The New Right: A Critique*, by David Collard. Collard characterized the 'coherently expressed' philosophy of the IEA as a school of thought which he labelled 'New Right' – a label that, although somewhat misleading, was to stick. Collard, no intellectual sympathizer of the IEA, nonetheless argued that

> the New Right must be respected for the quality, consistency and rigour of its approach to the treatment of private industry. In this sense it is rather unfair to lump it together with organisations such as Aims of Industry. The economic vision of the New Right is the economists' model of perfect competition in which rational consumers indicate their preferences to profit-seeking producers by means of prices under conditions of perfect information. This is very far removed from a crude approach based on the vested interests of Capitalists.

Collard warned the 'left' that 'the majority of academic economists have not taken the New Right seriously', and so the economic case against them had gone by default. The sound, powerfully argued economic case of the 'New Right' was met only by 'instinct, sentiment and a vague distaste for the profit motive'. Collard warned that the IEA was, already, 'influential', and that the lack of coherent criticism of the 'New Right' only exposed the bankruptcy of thinking on the left. As 1968, the year of revolutions – the apogee of many left-wing lives – reached its climax, Collard was prescient enough to warn that whilst the rest of the left busied themselves with abstract debates about how much further nationalization and economic controls should go, his own worry was that 'the left is being successfully out-flanked by the New Right'.[51] He was more accurate than he knew, and even by the late 1960s, as Collard vainly attempted to alert his colleagues on the left to the growing influence of the 'New Right', the IEA had already, perhaps, done enough to justify Milton Friedman's later assertion that 'Without the IEA, I doubt very much whether there would have been a Thatcherite revolution.'[52]

5

'A Confounded Nuisance'

The IEA at Work

*

The influence of the IEA during the 1960s and 1970s can be seen working at a number of different levels, amongst those whom Hayek had described as the 'second-hand dealers in ideas' – politicians, journalists and academe. However, the success of the IEA at converting or shaping opinion at these different levels can only be understood in the political context of the era, for, as Alan Walters was to suggest in 1976, the IEA was responding to a new *demand* for ideas that reflected the wider socio-economic predicament of Britain during the 1960s. At the political level, as we have seen, the Liberal Party proved unresponsive to the message of the economic liberals during the 1950s, and it was in the Conservative Party that the IEA found its most responsive audience, much to some people's surprise.

Given the impact of *The Road to Serfdom* on the 1945 general election, there is no doubt that Hayek's philosophy of freedom had a lasting impact on the Conservative Party: as was noted in Chapter Two, people like Richard Law and Diana Spearman began to seek to articulate his ideas within a Conservative context. Other Conservatives, such as Ralph Harris and Antony Fisher, were instrumental in founding the IEA. The Churchill Government of 1951 to 1955 tried, with little success, to go some way towards fulfilling its pledge to 'set the people free', but political constraints acted against the Government's undoubted desire to cut public expenditure, especially the sum spent on the Welfare State, and to transfer some of the industrial base which had been nationalized by Labour back into the private sector – although the iron and steel industry was denationalized in 1952.[1] For the economic liberals, the nadir of post-war Conservatism came with Harold Macmillan's Government of 1957 to 1963. The latest in a long line of 'Thatcherite' critics of Macmillan's government is David Willetts, a former member of Mrs Thatcher's Downing Street Policy Unit, the head of the Centre for Policy Studies who became MP for Havant in 1992. In his book *Modern Conservatism*, he describes 1950s economic policy-making as a 'dry/wet' cycle, employing the nomenclature of the 1980s to summarize the 'looser' financial policies and increasing governmental intervention in the economy of the Macmillan years, following the Churchill government's attempts to keep the role of the State in check. As Willetts has it,

> The turning point in economic policy came when Macmillan became Prime Minister in 1957 and in 1958 the economy entered a recession. Grants to industry, which had declined in every year, from 1951 to 1958, began to rise again. This was part of a general trend for public expenditure to increase as a proportion of total national output – having fallen steadily for the previous seven years. Peter Thorneycroft, Nigel Birch and Enoch Powell resigned from the Treasury over public expenditure in January 1958 – that date marks the change in political direction . . . By the end of the 1950s, the fashionable model of modernization was . . . France, with its *dirigiste* 'indicative planning'. This seemed to require a much greater government role in directing the economy and helping industry . . . In July 1961 the government introduced a pay pause in an attempt to reduce inflation by controlling wages. In August 1961 the National Economic Development Council was established to bring together trade unions, industrialists and government to try to improve the growth rate of the British economy. In February 1962 the government set out a 4 per cent indicative growth target. This was a long way from the Conservatism of ten years earlier. These sorts of interventions also marked the abandonment of the original interpretation of Keynes's ideas. Instead of being a mechanism for demand management enabling the government to stay clear of detailed economic interference, the assumption now was that demand management could only be made to work if it was supported by detailed economic intervention. This was the difference between the economics of Keynes and what became Keynesian economics.

Conservatives therefore left office in 1964 having taken

> their first full spin round the dry/wet cycle of economic management.[2]

Ralph Harris launched a similar attack on the Macmillan years and the Prime Minister's embrace of corporatism in a 1980 lecture at the Centre for Policy Studies. Whilst praising Churchill – 'a Liberal-Tory of the better kind' – for doing such things as introducing commercial television, Harris castigated the Macmillan governments for congealing into a 'Keynesian-collectivist mould'. For Harris, as for many other economic liberals, 'the last brave stand – until Mrs Thatcher came to power in 1979 – was in 1958, when Peter Thorneycroft and his two Treasury colleagues tried to stop the remorseless subordination of taxpayer and private economy to the insatiable demands of State spending – and were driven by failure to resign from Mr Macmillan's government.' It was at this point, so Harris told his audience, that he deliberately chose the path of 'radical reaction' and 'started up' the IEA.[3]

With the defeat of Douglas-Home at the 1964 election, the Conservative catastrophe seemed to be complete. Many economic liberals were momentarily impressed by the Labour leader Harold Wilson's pledge to modernize *both* sides of industry, management and unions, with the 'white heat of technology', and some even voted for Labour in 1964, hoping that Wilson would demonstrate a more secure grasp of the country's economic problems than had Macmillan or Douglas-Home. However, such hopes were not to be fulfilled as Wilson's Government quickly became bedevilled by recurring balance-of-payment crises, and showed as little awareness of how to combat the country's real economic problems as their Conservative predecessors. For those Conservative politicians who were prepared to think about their party's policies, the Macmillan and early Wilson years represented a depressing time in British politics, because not only had the 'Keynesian' policies of Macmillan merely led to the 'stagflation' of the early 1960s, but they had not even been able to win the election of 1964 – let alone that of 1966 – for the Party. Moreover, despite Macmillan's claim before the 1959 election that the country had 'never had it so good', it was already obvious by the early 1960s that Britain was falling seriously behind her European competitors in economic terms, and that the recurring balance-of-payments and sterling crises only seemed to get worse, as both political parties tried to run the same economic system based on demand management to create full employment. To the more reflective – or even ambitious – politician, it was obvious that the economic travails of the early 1960s had deep-seated causes, and for Conservatives, the trauma of the lost election of 1964 only added to the need of some to re-examine their policies. It was perfectly natural that politicians should turn to the IEA for answers to the country's economic woes, as by 1964 the Institute had been publicizing a coherent analysis of Britain's economic problems for almost a decade, and proposing workable solutions to those problems. It was the economic and political failure of the Conservatives in the early 1960s which created the demand for the IEA's ideas. Sir Keith Joseph, the most thoughtful of those Conservative politicians who turned to the IEA for help in the 1960s was to write in another, similar context in 1974 that he and his fellow politicians were, in the end, 'practical people who judge ideas and policies by results'.[4]

Indeed, ever since philosophical debate had raged within the Conservative Party in the wake of the 1945 election defeat, there were many, especially amongst the younger MPs, who had been concerned to develop a distinctly anti-Socialist philosophy for the Conservatives. These efforts were concentrated in two 'ginger-groups' within the Party, the One Nation Group and the Bow Group, founded in 1950 and 1951 respectively. The One Nation Group's first pamphlet was published by the Conservative Political Centre in 1950, entitled *One Nation* in tribute to the Disraelian tradition of Conservative social reform, with which they were mostly concerned. *One Nation* argued against further indiscriminate expenditure on the NHS and for selective charges within the NHS which would produce a saving of £35 million. The pamphlet also argued for a 'financial policy' which anticipated much of the rhetoric of the 1980s; 'Its long term aim is to encourage, through the financial system, those qualities in which Conservatives particularly believe – energy, initiative, thrift, and individual responsibility.'[5] In 1954, the One Nation Group published a second pamphlet entitled *Change is our Ally*, which argued for a 'Return to the Free Economy' and for a programme of 'denationalization'. The authors also argued, rather over-optimistically, as it turned out, that 'the formation of a Conservative Government in October 1951, marked a reaction in opinion against the trend not merely of the years of Socialism since 1945 but in many respects of the whole period since the First World War.'[6] The One Nation Group were a fairly heterodox group of MPs, united more by their age than by anything else, and included Enoch Powell, Edward Heath, Angus Maude, Iain Macleod, Robert Carr and Gilbert Longdon. 'One Nation' did not represent a consistent reaction against the prevailing Keynesian orthodoxies, merely an exploration of how the Conservative Party could develop a distinct approach to the problems of the Welfare State, so that Sir Keith Joseph, who joined it soon after he entered Parliament in 1956, later claimed that 'One Nation' was 'compatible with Statism but did assert a Conservative emphasis upon private enterprise and voluntary services as essential for prosperity, vitality and welfare'.[7] For the later Thatcherites, therefore, the One Nation Group could be seen as one of the more significant developments in the 'development of modern Conservatism'.[8] The Bow Group, founded in 1950, was even more heterodox than 'One Nation', and grew largely out of the student politics of the Cambridge University Conservative Association.

The Bow Group self-consciously set out to demonstrate that intelligent Conservatism was not a contradiction in terms 'and that [not] all original and worthwhile political thinking came from the Socialist Party or further left'. It claimed to have no 'Corporate view', an assertion borne out by its wide range of contributors and publications. However, amongst the early Bow Groupers were the young barrister Geoffrey Howe and Russell Lewis, contemporaries at Cambridge. Lewis, who had read a lot of Hayek, Popper and Robbins at Cambridge, was a convinced economic liberal from an early stage, and, as head of the Conservative Political Centre, a semi-autonomous publishing and policy outfit at Central Office, from 1965 to 1974, was to exert a considerable degree of influence in that direction within the Party at a crucial time and was later to be appointed temporary Director of the IEA in 1992. Many of his fellow 'Bow Groupers' did not share Lewis's convictions, as it was designed merely as a forum for ideas, but as with the One Nation Group, the very existence of the Bow Group was symptomatic of an intellectual discontent with the Conservative compromise with Socialism which began to surface in the Party during the early 1950s onwards. Howe was one of the first Conservative MPs to call on the IEA in 1960–1, and his own ideas began increasingly to shadow much of the IEA's thinking.

Of course, the most prominent economic liberal amongst this new, post-war generation of Conservative MPs was undoubtedly Enoch Powell, the austere self-styled people's tribune from Wolverhampton.

Powell had become a hero to economic liberals such as Ralph Harris when he resigned, together with Chancellor Thorneycroft and the rest of the Treasury team, in January 1958 in protest against what they regarded as excessive public expenditure by Macmillan's Government. The team resigned when Macmillan refused to support a £50 million cut in public spending, and famously dismissed their departures as 'little local difficulties'.[9] Powell, always one who fought his own battles, very much came to his own conclusions in economics, although he was influenced by Dennis Robertson, whom he had met at Cambridge, and who was invited by Thorneycroft to speak to the Treasury team on the eve of their resignation. After his resignation, Powell became a natural ally of the IEA, and John Wood helped to edit several books of his speeches. There was what Powell described as a 'common sympathy' between him and the IEA, and Powell quickly began to espouse the whole range of the IEA's economic liberalism, from floating exchange-rates to trade union reform.[10] Powell was also a close friend and colleague of Diana Spearman, formerly of the Conservative Research Department, from which she had resigned after the 1964 election out of exasperation with Macmillan's and Douglas-Home's economic policies. 'Winning an election', she urged, was 'not a matter of angling for this or that packet of votes, changing the fly as appropriate, but rather of putting forward a consistent and coherent political philosophy.' Neither was she in any doubt as to what this coherent political philosophy should be; she wrote in the *Daily Telegraph* in February 1965: 'There is only one line of approach which holds any promise of success. It is to establish again a free and competitive economic system which, in spite of its imperfections (or perhaps because of them), works for social and moral as well as for economic good.' From the mid-1950s onwards, her house in Lord North Street, Westminster, became a Mecca for all those economic liberals and Conservatives interested in free-market ideas, and, by chance, in 1969 the IEA moved to 2 Lord North Street, but a few doors down from her. Diana Spearman co-operated closely with Powell on his speeches during these years, and would have agreed with Powell's ringing, but possibly unique, interpretation of the 1964 election as one which 'will principally turn [on the supreme issue] of the free society versus the Socialist State'.[11] Diana Spearman was also close to Lionel Robbins and Michael Oakeshott, and thus provided an extremely important bridge between intellectual Conservatism and the Party. In the wake of thc 1964 election defeat, she launched her own attempt at formulating a coherent Conservative philosophy of the free market by starting what she punningly entitled the 'Longbow Group', which met for the first time in February 1965. Amongst others at 7 Lord North Street at the inaugural meeting of the Longbow Group were G. E. Blundell, John Wood of the IEA, the IEA economist Arthur Shenfield, T. E. Utley, the distinguished Conservative journalist, and Peter Cropper, later special adviser to Sir Geoffrey Howe at the Treasury, 1979–82. The Group drafted a 'Manifesto for Freedom', which included vigorous pledges to a 'Free Economic System', which were distinctly Hayekian in tone: 'There is indeed a strong argument for economic freedom, valid even for those who do not accept the primacy of individual over state interests. This is the superiority of the spontaneous order, created by the uncoordinated efforts of individuals, over the imposed order of authoritarian direction.'[12] The manifesto argued against incomes policy and for trade union reform, and, most directly, the authors argued that 'Stable prices should be chosen instead of "growth" as the first objective of economic policy.'[13] The document was very much a distillation of Hayek's political philosophy, and anticipated much of Conservative Party policy in the 1980s, although it was far ahead of official Party thinking in 1965. Richard Law, who was also involved in the project, wrote to John Jewkes seeking to enlist his aid in 1967, and during the course of his letter expressed the mood of those Conservatives, like Spearman, Powell and himself, who wanted economic liberalism to play a greater role in Party policy:

> I know that you are allergic to the Conservative Party. So am I. It is just because I have been so disillusioned by its performance (and I am still disillusioned) that I think the kind of work which we are projecting may be of value.
>
> Ever since the days of Macmillan, at any rate, Conservative Party policy has been based on market research and on the attempt to appeal to the floating vote. Iain Macleod has summed up the official Party attitude well in the aphorism 'Politics is about the Centre'.
>
> It is this attitude of mind which, I think, has alienated people like you and me, and I hold, and I suspect that you do too, that ultimately politics is about faith and a view of life. The floating vote is important in a sense, but you attract

> it not by angling for it, and changing your fly from pool to pool, but by convincing it that you yourself are convinced.
>
> In other words, it is necessary to re-formulate Conservative philosophy. I don't mean that the Party should be ridden by dogma, only that it should have some base of principle from which it should carry out its operations.
>
> . . . It is important that the Conservative Party should command support in intellectual circles, for I believe that the intellectual has much more influence on events than is generally supposed. Although the Conservative Central Office is beginning to realize this, it is still adopting the market research technique and travelling round the academic groves to try to discover what people want and then to give it to them . . .[14]

Little became of the Longbow Group or their putative manifesto, but their efforts did not go entirely to waste as out of their deliberations emerged, by 1970, Lord Coleraine's (as Richard Law had by then become) second book, *For Conservatives Only*. It was a confident and lucid attack on the Conservative Party leadership for allowing itself to be seduced by the false god of electoral expediency from its historic mission of checking the power of the State. In a chapter entitled 'The Myth of the Middle Ground', Coleraine condemned the Party for pursuing the middle ground in politics at the expense of principles – 'when all is said, the floating vote lives up to its name. It floats with the tide; and whoever would influence it must first influence the tide.'[15] This warning was not only reminiscent of Hayek's opening talk to the Mont Pèlerin Society about the need to influence the opinion-formers and intellectuals ('the tide'), but also, perhaps more directly, of Disraeli's *Coningsby*, which had asked much the same questions of another Conservative Party leadership a little over a century before. The dust-jacket blurb was also unusually prescient, employing a phrase that was to become well known in the early 1980s: 'Politics is not an exercise in market research. Nor is politics about the centre; it is about convictions.'[16]

Coleraine's book was well received in certain Conservative Party circles, and became as much a rallying cry for a more free-market Conservatism as *Return from Utopia* had been for an earlier generation. Nonetheless, during the 1960s it was Enoch Powell who remained the

A studio photograph of Friedrich von Hayek, taken at the time of publication of *The Road to Serfdom* in 1944.

Hayek: (*above*) in uniform, 16 May 1918; (*right*) at St Jakob in his beloved Tyrol in 1933;
(*below*) with Professor Lionel Robbins at the wedding of Hayek's son Laurence, 15 July 1961.

The first gathering of the Mont Pèlerin Society, 1947; delegates leaving their hotel on the shores of Lake Geneva for a sightseeing tour (*left*); taking in the local scenery (*below*), with, from left to right, Lionel Robbins, Fritz Machlup, Stanley Dennison, T.J.B. Hoff, an unidentified woman, John Jewkes, H.D. Gideonse, Aaron Director (at the back), Popper (?), Henry Hazlitt and Miss Röpke; and, in the seminar, being addressed by Hayek (*bottom*).

The first session of the Mont Pèlerin Society, with delegates listening to Hayek's opening paper: (*above, left to right*) William Rappard, Karl Popper, Ludwig von Mises; (*right*) Wilhelm Röpke; (*below, left to right*) Michael Polanyi, F.A. Harper, Henry Hazlitt, Felix Morley, Karl Brandt, John Jewkes, Dr Eyck.

Antony Fisher, in front of the Buxted chickens that laid the golden eggs.

The twin pillars of the IEA: (*left*) Arthur Seldon, in the mid-1970s; and (*below, on the right*) Ralph Harris, seen here presenting Professor Milton Friedman with an Adam Smith tie.

Left: Sir Leonard Neal, chairman of the Trade Union Reform Committee at the Centre for Policy Studies.
Below: Stanley Dennison, economic mentor of the IEA.

Above: Alfred Sherman, as Director of the CPS, in 1980.
Right: John Hoskyns, at the Institute of Directors, 1989.
Below: Keith Joseph, in full flow.

most articulate and vocal exponent of the IEA's brand of economic liberalism within the political parties, and he drew on the IEA for intellectual sustenance and support.[17] Powell however, proved a mixed blessing for the cause of economic liberalism, as, after his notorious 'Rivers of Blood' speech against immigration in 1968, he was not only sacked from the Shadow Cabinet but was henceforth regarded by most Conservatives as a dangerous maverick, and his views, on all issues, were considered extreme. This was unfortunate, as the Conservative Party leadership, especially Heath, subsequently turned their backs on Powell's thinking, and struggled to ignore his economic thinking as much as his views on immigration. 'Powellism' became a dirty word among the Conservative Party leadership, and his brand of economic liberalism was irredeemably besmirched.[18]

However, after the election defeat of 1964 a stream of new, younger Conservative politicians were to beat a path for the IEA door. Dismayed by electoral defeat, they came in search of economic education. The most notable of these was Sir Keith Joseph, the Old Harrovian son of a prosperous businessman who ran Bovis, the construction company, and who had been Lord Mayor of London during the Second World War. Sir Keith – a hereditary baronet – had entered Parliament in 1956, and served as Minister of Housing from 1962 to 1964. Unlike many Conservative politicians, he positively thrived on the opportunities that a period of opposition offered to re-think and explore party policies and strategy without the responsibilities of government; indeed, the periods of opposition 1964–70 and 1974–9 were to prove the most constructive years of his long political career. As his biographer has noted,

> Joseph's special kind of energy actually seemed to leave him with extra resources of energy when he moved from Ministerial office into opposition. His distaste for the conspiratorial side of politics saved him from some of the jealousies and point-making of opposition politics. A word constantly applied to Joseph was *anguish*; and, indeed, he devoted immense quantities of nervous energy to decision-making and squaring his conscience.[19]

The story is often told of how Joseph arrived at the IEA soon after the 1964 election defeat, to be greeted by Harris and Seldon who had laid the IEA's publications on a table. Joseph studied them all earnestly, and then went off with a bunch of them. Joseph was an avid and serious reader, and was to become one of the most discerning and inquisitive consumers of the IEA's literature. He leaned heavily on it for intellectual support and economic data and arguments as he developed his own philosophy of economic liberalism during the late 1960s. He also attended the Mont Pèlerin Society meetings, as did Enoch Powell. Joseph used the IEA as an intellectual back-up system and as a sounding-board. Typical of his exchanges with the IEA during this period was this letter to Arthur Seldon in 1965, concerning the prospects for introducing health charges, as well as the preoccupations of the anxious politician:

> Any shift in health from public to private or partly private finance is going to be greeted with allegations that we are robbing the large pre-dominantly less well-off public clientele of irreplaceable doctor and medical man hours in favour of private and generally better-off clientele. The essence of the case as I see it is of course that in fact private demand at market rate will draw back into practice extra doctors who are now giving up either medicine or this country. But that would take a little time to prove and the first year of any such scheme would be bound in fact to reduce the amount of medical attention available to the public. I want to put into your head *the political difficulty of the short term and say** how helpful it would be if in some way we could establish that in fact more doctors would be available both to public and to private practice if we opened up health to a limited extent to the market.

The vital political point was underlined by Seldon, who annotated in the margin: 'Is this a plea for painless change? Isn't it the politician's job (paid) to educate and lead?'[20]

This was indeed the crux of the matter and was to be the source of much friction between Joseph and his unofficial advisers. Seldon and Joseph corresponded on all aspects of the Welfare State during the 1960s, and by 1969, when Joseph wrote a series of articles for *The*

* Author's italics.

Times outlining the case for the invigorating effect on industry of the free-market economy, he was regarded as the main exponent of economic liberalism in Heath's Shadow Cabinet. Seldon and Harris came to regard Joseph as their principal political hope, and in a letter to Joseph when he had returned to Office in 1970, Seldon wrote:

> I must not burden you but since I was turned away from the Conservatives by Lionel Robbins who taught me that they were doing more damage than Labour in the 1930s by socialising in the name of Capitalism, I have waited for the day when Conservatives like you would redeem their sins. I really do think that you could break Labour's hold on the working class and destroy Socialism for all time.[21]

Closely following Joseph was the young MP John Biffen, a grammar school-educated Cambridge graduate who entered the House of Commons in 1961. He became one of Powell's few disciples in the lower House, and, like Powell, learnt his free-market economics through independent study. As he told the author, 'If I had a mentor, it was probably Harold Wincott' (the *Financial Times* journalist who was an IEA author).[20] Once in Parliament, Biffen quickly made contact with the IEA and joined the Mont Pèlerin Society. Biffen was not directly influenced by the IEA, but he found it 'very reassuring' to know that there was a respectable body of opinion outside Parliament which held much the same views as he. A much more important recruit to the cause during the 1960s was the Winchester and Cambridge-educated MP and Bow Grouper Geoffrey Howe, who, even before Joseph, had become an avid reader of the IEA's publications. During the 1960s Howe was particularly interested in health and welfare spending, Seldon's special area of interest, and so the two corresponded frequently. Howe was an early and articulate critic of universal welfare services, and as early as 1964, in one of the first of a number of articles for the *Daily Telegraph*, he asked:

> Is it not time for Conservatives to consider once again the politically difficult business of reducing the area over which the State collects and spends our money for us and increasing the area within which we are free to spend it for ourselves? . . .

> Must it, therefore, be considered 'politically impossible' to suggest that people should be free to insure privately against ill-health without having to pay for the whole State Service as well?[23]

This was exactly the question that the IEA was asking, and which Douglas Houghton, the Labour Minister, posed in his 1967 IEA pamphlet. A typical exchange survives between Howe and the IEA from 1969 at the time when the Labour Minister for Health and Social Security, Richard Crossman, was trying to steer a new State pension scheme through Parliament. The memo is from Joan Culverwell, Harris's long-time secretary, to Seldon and Harris:

> Geoffrey Howe rang up re: the Crossman pension Scheme. There are many people in the City who are not aware of what is happening. Geoffrey is writing a pamphlet with Norman Lamont about the pension Scheme, and he thinks it may not be too late to start some front and popular movement against it.
>
> *A.S.* [Arthur Seldon] Have you any information, articles, publications, etc. you could send him which would help to throw his pamphlet together? When the time comes he wants to tell H.M. Opposition to vote against it and why. He would like this information *urgently* please.
>
> *R.H.* [Ralph Harris] Geoffrey suggests that perhaps half a dozen of you (us) could start up some organisation (i.e. like Wincott, I.U. [Independent University of Buckingham] etc.) into which you could get your teeth and call it something like *STOP* – Save the Occupational Pension. He would like to discuss this seriously with you . . . would you ring him please.[24]

Like Joseph, Howe thus used the IEA as a kind of research facility-cum-scholastic centre, an unrivalled source of expertise on the workings of the free market, providing the sort of information to politicians that the Conservative Research Department was not equipped to give. In 1987, when Foreign Secretary, Howe wrote to Antony Fisher to support a fund-raising exercise:

> I am always delighted to sing the praises of the IEA, with which my associations go back many years. It has had a profound effect on economic thinking in the UK and more widely, and made a major contribution to creating a climate of intellectual opinion which paved the way for the first Thatcher victory in 1979 and the subsequent transformation of Britain's economic fortunes. The IEA has demonstrated once again the power of an idea whose time has come, and the value of that kind of pamphleteering and intellectual stimulus in the wider world.[25]

Another rising star of the Conservative Party who called at the IEA, led there probably by Sir Keith Joseph and Howe, was Margaret Thatcher, who had occupied a junior ministerial post at the Ministry of Pensions from 1961 to 1964. Mrs Thatcher was introduced to Harris and Seldon in the early 1960s, and, as her main interest at the time also lay in the field of welfare economics, she too drew on the expertise of Seldon and Harris to refine her own arguments on the need for an increase in private funding in social provision. Seldon, by the late 1960s, already had great hopes for Mrs Thatcher; he wrote to Howe about her on 24 October 1969: 'May we hope for something better from Margaret. She said one day here (or rather at Eaton Square*) that she was one of a small group of Tory politicians like Enoch, Keith and you who saw the value of the market in economic affairs.'

Howe, however, was not so certain, and perceptively replied a few days later:

> I am not at all sure about Margaret. Many of her economic prejudices are certainly sound. But she is inclined to be rather too dogmatic for my liking on sensitive matters like education and might actually retard the case by over-simplification. We should certainly be able to hope for something better from her – but I suspect that she will need to be exposed to the humanising side of your character as much as to the pure welfare market monger. There is much scope for her to be influenced between triumph and disaster![26]

* Then the home of the IEA.

Mrs Thatcher, like Howe and Joseph, relied on the IEA for detailed economic analysis of the Welfare State that could not be got anywhere else. By 1968, the year of her address to the Conservative Political Centre at the Conservative Party Conference at Blackpool, she was clearly identified as one of the leading exponents of market economics within the Party. In that 1968 speech, she not only attacked the sacred cow of incomes policy but also argued against the temptations of 'consensus' politics: 'it could be an attempt to satisfy people holding no particular views about anything.'[27] In an article entitled 'Consensus – or Choice' in the *Daily Telegraph* of 28 March 1969 she made her new-found radicalism even clearer, arguing that whereas

> The left-wing believes that State ownership coupled with central government control enables its government to plan the production of each product in relation to the other . . . The Conservative approach is different. We dislike monopoly and seek to break it up, we believe that competition is the best and the only test of efficiency, that decisions should be made where the experience and knowledge are to be found, and that the test of their correctness is the market-place and that the consequences of wrong decisions should not be borne by the taxpayer.

She also advocated extensive 'denationalization', thus 'saving the taxpayer's money and giving greater consumer choice'. Arthur Seldon wrote enthusiastically to her a few days later: 'I have been trying to find time to say how much I enjoyed the article in the *Telegraph* the other day. It was unambiguous and courageous. I am especially glad you did not say that so-and-so policy was eminently desirable but "politically impossible". The last refuge of the unprincipled politician.'[28] Mrs Thatcher was particularly grateful to the IEA for the intellectual credibility that it gave to her own radical assault on the post-war consensus during the extremely difficult years of the mid-1970s when she was the newly elected leader of a divided Party, and thus to a certain extent restrained in the expression of her views. In January 1977, for instance, she wrote to Ralph Harris on finishing the IEA's anniversary publication *Not from Benevolence* at a time when the intellectual current seemed to be running very much in her direction:

> Just a line to say how much I enjoyed reading 'Not from Benevolence . . .' over the Christmas recess. The contribution which you and your staff have made at the IEA to economic thinking over the past 20 years is now becoming apparent to all and sundry . . .
>
> I notice from the advertisement that appeared in *The Times* [of 6 January] that even the *Labour Weekly* was admitting the vast contribution which you were making at the present time. Please accept my heartiest congratulations on your 20th birthday and above all my gratitude for everything that you have done. At times it must have seemed like bashing your head against a brick wall but political historians will, I believe, judge you in proper perspective.[29]

On her coming to power in 1979, Ralph Harris was among her first nominees to go to the House of Lords, and he accepted as a cross-bencher. A few days after her victorious election in May 1979, she wrote to the IEA and, in the first flush of victory, was fulsome in her praise. She thanked him and his two colleagues for their telegram of congratulations adding:

> but above all let me thank you all for what you have done for the cause of free enterprise over the course of so many years. It was primarily your foundation work which enabled us to rebuild the philosophy upon which our Party succeeded in the past. The debt we owe to you is immense and I am very grateful.
>
> With best wishes,
>
> Margaret[30]

The IEA was also helpful in keeping Mrs Thatcher abreast of the latest monetarist thinking during the mid-1970s, when the Conservative Party was forming its new economic policies. In 1978, Ralph Harris arranged for Milton Friedman to dine privately with Mrs Thatcher at the Stafford Hotel in London. The dinner was attended by just Friedman and his wife Rose, together with Mrs Thatcher and Harris. Friedman, who was meeting her for the first time, formed 'an extremely high opinion of her'. Unlike his meeting (also arranged by the IEA) with Heath in 1970, Friedman remembered this as a 'very productive meeting', and Mrs Thatcher listened intently to his advice that, in monetary terms, the first six–twelve months of the government that she was hoping soon to form would be crucial.[31] Hayek's IEA Papers also encouraged her to read his longer works, which she did with enthusiasm and admiration. She had been greatly influenced by *The Road to Serfdom* and Jewkes's *Ordeal by Planning*, and later by Hayek's *Constitution of Liberty*, probably Hayek's most comprehensive and highly developed theoretical work on the politics and constitution of a liberal state.

If anyone was in any doubt about her intellectual influences, they were often in for a sharp reminder. John Ranelagh, an officer in the Conservative Research Department during the mid-1970s, witnessed one such occasion:

> On the occasion of Thatcher's only visit to the Research Department, in the summer of 1975, a friend and colleague, Michael Jones, and I prepared a paper for her meeting with us. We proposed that the Party should adopt a 'Family Policy' – addressing benefits and taxation as they affected the family unit, rather than as they affected an individual – at the 1975 Party Conference. We took the idea from the German Christian Democrats, and in fits and starts such a policy entered the Conservative framework under Thatcher. Another colleague had also prepared a paper arguing that the 'middle way' was the pragmatic path for the Conservative Party to take, avoiding the extremes of Left and Right. Before he had finished speaking to his paper, the new Party leader reached into her briefcase and took out a book. It was Friedrich von Hayek's *The Constitution of Liberty*. Interrupting our pragmatist, she held the book up for all of us to see. 'This', she said sternly, 'is what we believe', and banged Hayek down on the table. 'She slammed it down', remembered Stephen Probyn, who was then responsible for energy matters at the Department. 'Then she delivered a monologue about the British economy.'[32]

Soon after she had become Leader of the Opposition in 1975, the IEA arranged for Mrs Thatcher to meet Hayek for the first time at Lord North Street. Mrs Thatcher arrived in her chauffeur-driven limousine in the early evening *en route* to a dinner, and was ushered

10 DOWNING STREET

LONDON SW1A 2AA

THE PRIME MINISTER

5 May 1989

Dear Professor Hayek,

It is with the greatest pleasure that I send you my warm congratulations on the occasion of your 90th Birthday. It is a tremendous milestone, especially for someone who has achieved so much.

It is ten years this week since I was privileged to become Prime Minister. Many people have been most kind in their comments on what the Government has been able to achieve in that time. There is of course still so much to do. But none of it would have been possible without the values and beliefs to set us on the right road and provide the right sense of direction. The leadership and inspiration that your work and thinking gave us were absolutely crucial; and we owe you a great debt.

With every good wish

Yours sincerely

Margaret Thatcher

Professor Friedrich August Hayek, C.H.

The letter Margaret Thatcher sent to Hayek on his ninetieth birthday.[33]

into the boardroom for a private audience with Hayek, which lasted for about thirty minutes. At the end of the half-hour, Mrs Thatcher left and the staff of the IEA gathered around an unusually pensive Hayek, seeking his reaction to the meeting. After a long pause, all he said, with obvious feeling, was 'She's so beautiful'.[34]

Others who were later to be closely involved with Mrs Thatcher's term as leader of the Conservative Party were also very influenced by the IEA, such as John Hoskyns, the first head of her Downing Street Policy Unit, a 'self-taught economist through reading their publications'.[35] Adam Ridley, an economic adviser and a director of the Centre for Policy Studies considered that the IEA deserved 'tremendous credit' as the 'seed-bed of liberalism'.[36] Nonetheless, it was the attention that Mrs Thatcher, Sir Keith Joseph and Sir Geoffrey Howe paid to the IEA that gave the Institute its critical political influence, as they became, of course, the three leaders of the 'counter-revolution' in the economic management of Britain that the IEA had been urging on all who would listen since 1955. Other Conservative politicians of a free-market inclination also sought intellectual support and encouragement from the IEA during the 1960s, most notably Sir Richard Body, a friend of Antony Fisher's, Patrick Jenkin, Jock Bruce-Gardyne and Peter Horden. Ralph Harris, who from the late 1960s onwards, with the agreement of Seldon, became involved in more overtly 'political' campaigns separate from the IEA, also participated in a project directed by the headmaster of Highbury Grove Comprehensive School in North London and future Conservative MP Dr Rhodes Boyson, who became as famous for his elaborate whiskers as for his Thatcherite views during the early 1980s. Like many connected with the IEA, Rhodes Boyson started in politics as a Labour activist, serving as a local councillor, but grew disillusioned with Labour politics during the mid-1960s and became a radical free-market Conservative. In 1970, Rhodes Boyson, Ralph Harris and Ross McWhirter (another aspiring Conservative MP but more famous as one half of the Guinness Book of Records brotherhood) set up the Constitutional Book Club, which published a series of important pamphlets under the imprint of the Churchill Press. The first, and probably most famous of the Churchill Press pamphlets was published in 1970, soon after Edward Heath's election victory, and was aptly called *Right Turn*. The book described itself as a 'symposium on the need to end the "progressive" consensus in British thinking and policy', and contained essays by a number of authors who were closely associated with the IEA, including Ralph Harris on 'The Morality of Capitalism', Russell Lewis declaring 'A Plague on Nationalization' and Arthur Shenfield on 'Trial by Taxation'. In his editorial prologue to *Right Turn* Rhodes Boyson described the mood of many on the burgeoning free-market wing of the Conservative Party as Heath took office after six years of opposition: 'We believe the Conservative Party . . . [has] . . . a duty to govern our people in such a way that they will so consciously enjoy the benefits of the free-market in a free society that the only chance for Labour to return to power will be when that party ceases to be Socialist in its aims.'

It took a little under twenty years for Dr Rhodes Boyson's aspirations to be fulfilled. The Churchill Press was responsible for some very influential, polemical publications including 'Goodbye to Nationalization' (1971) by the young journalist John O'Sullivan and Patricia Hodgson, 'Must History Repeat Itself?' (1974) by Antony Fisher, and most controversially of all, 'Rape of Reason' (1975) by John Marks and Caroline Cox.[37] It was wound up in 1979, but was re-started in 1993 by John Raybould. The Constitutional Book Club itself grew out of a similar publishing venture called the Black Papers, also inspired by Rhodes Boyson, together with the academic Anthony Dyson and Brian Cox; this was specifically concerned with the politics of education at a time when the Labour Government was destroying the grammar schools in favour of the comprehensive system. The first Black Paper, published in 1969, was called *Crisis in Education*. The second, against comprehensivization, included an essay by Harris, who was involved at the time with other parents in a legal action against the comprehensivization of his own daughters' school in Enfield – with Geoffrey Howe as the QC chosen to fight this action in court. Other contributors to the Black Papers included Kingsley Amis, who penned a famous piece attacking the proliferation of universities in the 1960s, Max Beloff, the prominent Oxford historian, Caroline Cox and Professor Antony Flew.[38] The Constitutional Book Club, the Churchill Press and, to a lesser extent, the Black Papers were all symptoms of a new anti-collectivist radicalism, drawing people from different backgrounds and parties together, which was already well organized and influential by 1970. Ralph Harris played a key role in pulling these disparate forces together, and giving them not only intellectual support, but a coherent political and economic outlook.

Although the IEA's influence was most pronounced within the ranks of the Conservative Party, it also had an impact on the thinking of a number of Labour MPs during the 1960s. The Institute was a non-party organization, and so was eager to persuade politicians of *all* parties of the virtues of the free market. As Seldon explained to Lord Balniel in 1967, 'To maintain the Institute's non-party posture, we prefer politicians to come to us . . .'[39] Amongst the Labour MPs who were most interested in the work of the IEA were Douglas Houghton, whose pamphlet on Health spending of 1967 has already been mentioned, Brian Walden, Desmond Donnelly and Ray Gunter; Seldon also welcomed the developing political contributions of Dr David Owen and David Marquand. Most of these were to break with the Labour Party completely by the early 1980s. Brian Walden was a frequent correspondent with Arthur Seldon on the subject of welfare policy, and in 1967 Seldon could already write to Walden to say that 'Ralph and I were delighted to have you here [at the IEA] and to be able to talk at leisure on matters of common interest – and substantially of common agreement.'[40] The Liberal Party, much to Seldon's disappointment, proved the least receptive to the IEA's ideas, and the only MP to show much enthusiasm was John Pardoe – although Jo Grimond also displayed a modicum of interest. Seldon wrote optimistically to Pardoe in August 1967 that 'what with Houghton and Gunter for Labour and Geoffrey Howe among the Conservatives, I am especially glad that you are not letting the other parties get away with what should be liberal (capital as well as small letter) policy.'[41] In truth, however, the Liberals as a Party remained steadfastly uninterested in the IEA's thinking, let alone anyone else's.

Indeed, although the Conservative Party proved the most fertile ground for the IEA's ideas during the 1960s and early 1970s, it fell to one of the Labour MPs who was most interested in the IEA's thinking, Desmond Donnelly, to be the first politician to get up in the House of Commons and comprehensively denounce the record of post-war economic management, as the IEA had been encouraging politicians to do since it was founded. In doing so, Donnelly also anticipated Sir Keith Joseph's famous series of speeches on the same theme in 1974 by six years. Donnelly had sought advice on his speeches from the IEA for a number of years, and on 26 November 1968, he made a speech on social services that included a comprehensive indictment of his own Party's handling of the economy in government since 1964. At a time when the Wilson Government was still reeling from the forced devaluation of 1967 and another balance-of-payments crisis, Donnelly observed that nonetheless: 'the government's expenditure has continued to increase and it has not been matched by comparable expansion in industrial production. There is a simple equation. If we expand government expenditure by, for example, ten per cent per annum, and it is not matched by a comparable amount of goods, there are two alternatives; either that expansion has to be cut back or we have to print more money.'

If this precise explanation of the causes of the growing rates of inflation was not enough, he went on to complete his party political immolation by praising Enoch Powell and Sir Keith Joseph for at least thinking about the country's straitened economic circumstances, and, as a final fillip, dismissed the Labour Party's favourite totem, the 'Social Wage', as 'a lot of hogwash'.[42] Donnelly had already resigned the Labour Whip in January of the same year, and after this he was expelled from the Party. To the IEA, Donnelly had uttered the economic truth that dared not speak its name during the heady era of Wilsonian demand-management, and the Institute did its best to publicize Donnelly's speech and his ideas. In a circular letter about Donnelly, Seldon recounted a political tale that was to become increasingly familiar during the next decade:

> [Donnelly] is a very interesting case of a man of high integrity, who started life on the extreme left (he was a Bevanite) and has gradually changed his mind as he has come to understand how private enterprise works . . . He now wants to learn more about domestic affairs, especially on the economic front, and I can testify that he is learning rapidly and also seeing the essence very clearly indeed.
>
> It is not surprising that he retains some relics of his original thinking, but he is abandoning them with astonishing rapidity. We are more interested in the direction in which he is going and in the goal he hopes to reach.[43]

In an effort to rally support around Donnelly, Harris and Seldon were instrumental in arranging a meeting at Donnelly's flat at 88 Portland Place in November 1968 to discuss his political prospects. Also present at the meeting were the historian Robert Skidelsky (Keynes's biographer), the Oxford political scientist Vernon Bogdanor, the economist John Vaizey and the historian of Soviet Russia Robert Conquest. Most of these had been 'intellectuals' of the left, and men such as Vaizey and Conquest shared Donnelly's discovery of the market as a mechanism for greater opportunity and freedom, following him into Mrs Thatcher's camp of radical, economically liberal Conservatives during the 1970s. Skidelsky was a moving spirit in the foundation of the Social Democratic Party in 1981; but already in 1968 this haemorrhaging of the left was well under way. Those gathered at Donnelly's flat decided to found a new political movement to express Donnelly's revolt against the political mainstream; they called it The Democratic Party. Donnelly fought under the colours of the Democratic Party at the 1970 election, but he lost his seat. In a broadsheet published by the new Party entitled *Opportunity*, Donnelly and his colleagues outlined a political programme which derived much of its inspiration from the IEA school of economic thinking, and anticipated much of what would be commonplace in Conservative manifestos of the 1980s, including plans for a single flat rate of income tax, a higher tax threshold, the introduction of an 'Added Value Tax' and the abolition of Corporation Tax. Speaking to the electorate of Grimsby in November 1969 Donnelly spelt out the stark truth that most politicians could not afford to articulate:

> There was a time – in the memory of everyone here – when we were a first division power. Now we are at the bottom of the second division and into the relegation zone. And we are moving into the third division in the 1970s.
>
> The basic problems are manifold . . . we are suffering from excessive centralization, excessive bureaucracy, weak leadership, grinding taxation at all times and the permissive society.[44]

After Donnelly's defeat in the 1970 election he also sent the following diagnosis of the future of British politics to the IEA, entitled 'Some Just Talk; Others Act'. It offered a remarkably accurate forecast of the immediate political future:

> The question arises; what is the future of the Labour Party? Its future is bleak and will be brief . . . for the reason that the concept of a politically cohesive working class which has

> been Labour's electoral base since the 1920s is disintegrating fast. Whilst there is always a time lag in this being felt in voting patterns, this process began in the 1950s. *I foresee that it will be completed in the 1980s if not before, by which time there will be no significant group in existence that thinks of itself as 'Labour' or 'Socialist'**. The whole mass trend of thought is for greater economic freedom and against state intervention . . . All this foresees a new power vacuum in British politics. It poses the requirement of a new political party to fill it which is for radical change and whose ethos is greater economic freedom and the national interest regardless of compromise and party advantage . . .[45]

The only error in Donnelly's forecast was that it would be Sir Keith Joseph who was the first to acknowledge the 'vacuum' in British politics, and it was the economic liberals, coached by the IEA, within the Conservative Party who captured their own Party for a programme of 'radical change' and 'greater economic freedom'. Donnelly's brief campaign fizzled out after the 1970 election, and he himself committed suicide in 1972. However, the Donnelly campaign was another small step in alerting the political parties and the public as a whole to the dangers, as many IEA authors saw them, facing the British economy by the late 1960s.

If the IEA thus had considerable success in its effort to win over political opinion to its ideas, in its direct dealings with politicians the Institute also had to acknowledge the limitations that its non-party, charitable status imposed upon it. As Seldon had written to Lord Balniel, the IEA's determination to maintain its independence meant that politicians had to come to them; it could not get too actively involved as a campaigning body with political parties. Sometimes it was a thin line – but it was one that had to be drawn somewhere. The difficulty is illustrated well by a suggestion of John Biffen's in July 1970, soon after the Conservative Party's election victory, that the IEA should organize a one-day seminar on 'Welfare in the Seventies' for the new intake of Tory MPs. The IEA was initially enthusiastic about the idea, but in September Seldon replied to Biffen:

* Author's italics.

> I have been having some changes of mind about the idea I first mooted with you . . . Ralph [Harris] has reminded me of something which I often tell him, that we must not seem to be too near one party. And I think the one day Conference is therefore not for the IEA to organise . . . so it looks as if we are back to informal talks. We are also rather anxious not to appear to be approaching individuals of one party rather than another. Therefore we rotate our invitations to gatherings of various sorts.
>
> Ideally, of course, to maintain pristine purity, we should not approach politicians at all but wait for them to come to us. This is not our intellectual arrogance; but desirable if we are to maintain our status as an institution concerned with research rather than advocacy.[46]

This need for political neutrality did, of course, effectively curtail the IEA's direct input into the Conservative Party, as even when that Party emerged as the one taking the IEA's ideas most seriously, the IEA could still not afford to get too close to it, especially after the Conservative Party formed the new Government in 1979. The IEA thus maintained its strategy of concerning itself with the broad principles of the free-market case, rather than trying to place those principles within a Party political context – that, after all, was the job of the 'paid' politicians. Arthur Seldon sometimes liked to use a military analogy to illustrate this argument:

> The IEA would be the artillery firing the shells (ideas). Some would land on target (the intellectuals), while others might miss. But the Institute would never be the infantry engaged in short-term, face-to-face grappling with the enemy. Rather, its artillery barrage would clear the way for others to do the work of the infantry later on. The IEA would show why matters had gone wrong and set out broad principles, while others would argue precisely how matters should be put right.[47]

This obviously left a clear vacuum for a more political organization to fight for economic liberalism *within* a political Party, which was the *raison d'être* of the Centre for Policy Studies when it was founded in

1974. Sometimes, for those involved in the IEA this lack of political involvement could be maddeningly frustrating. During the worst months of the 1976 economic crisis, when the very survival of the body politic seemed to be at stake, Antony Fisher wrote impatiently to Ralph Harris after an IEA meeting that he found himself 'ever more bothered, bewildered and perhaps I could say frightened at the inability of the I.E.A. to come up with economic solutions to the country's problems . . . I do not believe for one moment that it is not within the, should I say, remit of the I.E.A. to develop a policy prescription from the analyses published so regularly.'[48] Despite Fisher's frustration, the IEA maintained its academic purity and refused to publish detailed policy recommendations, as its whole reputation beyond the narrow confines of Westminster rested on its non-party, authoritative scholarly publishing programme. The rewards for sticking to its guns lay elsewhere for the IEA.

In Hayek's original prescription to Fisher of the free-market think-tank, he had specifically targeted those to whom the IEA should make its strongest appeal; the journalists, academics and students who went into the media and the other professions which created the intellectual environment in which the politicians operated. Harris had worked as a professional journalist and Seldon had written for a variety of news media, so they both had a finely attuned sense of what would interest the press. Like the politicians, once the failure of contemporary policies during the 1950s and early 1960s became apparent, Fleet Street also began to turn to the IEA in search of new ideas and new copy.

The most important paper in this respect was the *Daily Telegraph*, the guardian of the Tory conscience and the biggest selling 'quality' newspaper. It was merely a coincidence that in the summer of 1964, just before the Conservative Party was forced into its long period of collective introspection by the election defeat of that year, the *Daily Telegraph* acquired a new editor, Maurice Green, who had trained as an economist and who wanted to 'intellectualize' a paper which had justifiably earned a reputation for serving up a brand of anodyne Conservatism for those who didn't want to think too much about politics. He was also described by one of those who worked under him as a 'very firm economic liberal',[49] and took a keen interest in the ideas of the IEA. Until he retired from the editorial chair in 1974, Green did much to recruit a swathe of journalists and leader-writers who were to become closely associated with economic liberalism and the work of thc IEA and the Centre for Policy Studies, including T. E. Utley, Alfred Sherman, Andrew Alexander, John O'Sullivan, Frank Johnson and, later, Jock Bruce-Gardyne. Green was ably supported by Colin Welch, the deputy editor, who continued to argue on the paper for economic liberalism after Green's replacement by Bill Deedes as editor in 1974. Both Green and Welch benefited from the IEA's flow of economic analyses, and Green not only recruited a new generation of economic liberal journalists to the paper, but also allowed the staff of the IEA generous access to the centre pages of the *Daily Telegraph*; Arthur Seldon alone wrote over sixty leader-page articles for the paper during the 1960s. Green also gave a substantial amount of space to those other Conservative MPs who were interested in the ideas of economic liberalism, such as Geoffrey Howe and Margaret Thatcher. The former wrote for the paper frequently. The *Daily Telegraph* was a stern critic of Edward Heath's government when the Prime Minister performed his famous U-turn in 1972, and Green and Welch were turned on by Heath for letting him down.[50] Although much has been written of *The Times* and the *Financial Times* in this context, the *Daily Telegraph* was really the key paper as it did much to introduce the philosophy of the IEA to precisely that constituency of people which would later make that philosophy such a radical motivating force within the Conservative Party. The IEA was as important to the *Daily Telegraph* as the *Daily Telegraph* was to the IEA.

The Times and the *Financial Times*, both with a much smaller, more specialized readership than the *Daily Telegraph*, were also important in introducing the economic thinking of the IEA to a wider audience. There were three journalists on these two papers who were instrumental in this process, Samuel Brittan of the *Financial Times*, and Peter Jay and William Rees-Mogg of *The Times*. Brittan, the brother of Leon, had studied economics at Cambridge (where he had been taught briefly by Milton Friedman), and had then gone into the Treasury before becoming the main economics commentator on the *Financial Times*. Up to the late 1960s, Brittan was, like most of his contemporaries, a Keynesian by upbringing if not by conviction, and he explained his own conversion to Arthur Seldon in a letter of 21 January 1975, after attending an IEA lecture given by Friedman:

> I very much enjoyed the Friedman lecture . . . The subject has a personal aspect about which you may be interested to

> know. It was his earlier version of the argument for a vertical Philips curve in his 1968 [sic, 1967] Presidential Lecture which converted me from being a demand expansionist and thus away from policies such as indicative planning and the growth targets, designed to secure demand expansion through the back door. It was my conversion to this particular point and basically on nothing else, which caused my public identification to change from that of a fashionable growth man to that of an IEA sympathizer . . . In a sentence the message simply is that conventional full-employment policies are futile and that an arbitrarily chosen unemployment target is likely to lead not merely to inflation but to accelerating inflation.[51]

Brittan's conversion to a broadly monetarist position was very important, as his position as the doyen of economic commentators in the British press gave the IEA fort a powerful buttress. Brittan wrote several long and critical articles in the *Financial Times* in the early 1970s which crystallized much of the monetarist thinking of the period, and also helped to stimulate renewed interest in the thought of Hayek and Friedman.[52] Brittan remained independent of much of what IEA authors were saying at the time, but he did contribute to several of its pamphlets, as well as writing the first Centre for Policy Studies pamphlet in 1975.[53] To a certain extent, Brittan was doing no more than continuing an honourable tradition in this respect: Harold Wincott, the distinguished *Financial Times* columnist, who had been at his peak in the 1950s, had also given the IEA much encouragement and support in the early days. Wincott 'had an enormous influence on City thinking'; it was he who invented the character Solomon Binding in his column, a skit on the endless 'solemn and binding' promises and pledges made at TUC Conferences.[54]

Peter Jay, economics editor of *The Times* from 1967 to 1977, was equally influential, and must be credited as the first financial journalist to cover the new school of monetarism in the British press in the 1960s. Like Brittan, Jay had been a standard Keynesian economist whilst serving at the Treasury from 1961 to 1967, and he was also at the heart of the Labour Party establishment; his father was the Labour Minister Douglas Jay and he married the daughter, Margaret, of another eminent Labourite, James Callaghan. He was unusual in being one of the very few converts to monetarism who did not embrace Thatcherism or Conservatism, but instead tried to fit monetarism into a specifically Labour political context. Jay became acquainted with the new school of monetarism on his frequent visits to the United States for *The Times* in 1967–8. In particular a former colleague at the Treasury, Geoffrey Bell, who was then stationed at the British Embassy in Washington, showed Jay the work of the Federal Reserve Bank of St Louis, Missouri, which was an important compiler of statistical data on money. An article by Leonall Andersen and Jerry Jordan in the *St Louis Fed Review* of November 1968, stating the monetarist thesis boldly, as well as Friedman's 1967 AAE Presidential address, both helped to convert him to monetarism.[55] Jay was also the recipient of several letters from his American monetarist friends criticizing his attacks on Enoch Powell's economic ideas. One article in particular, of 31 May 1968, 'Inflation: is the Money Supply Crucial?', attacking Friedman, drew a number of letters from the American monetarists, convincing Jay that monetarism was important and should be discussed. As a result of his rethink, Jay led the *Business News* section of the newspaper on 24 September 1968 with a warning of the 9.9 per cent growth of the money supply in the second quarter of that year. This was followed by a further article on 15 October 1968, 'Understanding the role of the Money Supply'. From 1970 onwards, under Jay's direction, *The Times* became a leading advocate of monetarism, and, like the *Daily Telegraph*, was very critical of Edward Heath for his handling of the economy during 1972–4. Jay, like other monetarist economists such as Alan Walters, predicted that the Chancellor Tony Barber's 'boom' of 1973 based on old-fashioned Keynesian demand-led expansion policies, could only end in tears as the money supply was thus set to rise at over twenty per cent a year.[56] Jay, although he did not learn his monetarism directly from the IEA, also became closely associated with them and participated in several IEA-organized symposia on monetary policy during the 1970s, as well as co-authoring several IEA pamphlets. In 1975 he gave the Wincott Lecture, 'A General Hypothesis of Employment, Inflation and Politics', a gloomy analysis of mid-1970s Britain, in which he argued that the post-war political economy was disintegrating before their eyes.[57] Jay's importance to monetarism was that he was aggressively *not* a Conservative, and thus seemed to reflect the objective, non-party, technical economic approach that characterized the early advocates of monetarism such as the IEA. Jay, because of his unique position on *The Times* and in the Labour Party, was thus listened to attentively by elements in the Labour Party establishment, particularly Denis Healey, the beleaguered Chancellor of the Exchequer from 1974 to 1979, and Callaghan himself. Jay can be claimed to have been at least partly responsible for the Party's public repudiation of Keynesian full-employment policies in 1976. Indeed, it was Jay who wrote Callaghan's Party Conference speech of 1976, which finally spelt out publicly the collapse of the post-war consensus, and proclaimed the death of economic policies which all the economic liberals – Hayek, Robbins, von Mises, the Mont Pèlerin Society and the IEA – had been arguing against since the publication of Keynes's *General Theory* in 1936. It is worth quoting Jay's words in Callaghan's Conference Speech again as they echoed forty years' worth of prediction by the economic liberals:

> For too long, perhaps ever since the war, we postponed facing up to fundamental choices and fundamental changes in our society and in our economy. That is what I mean when I say we have been living on borrowed time. For too long this country – all of us, yes, this Conference too – has been ready to settle for borrowing money abroad to maintain our standards of life, instead of grappling with the fundamental problems of British industry . . . The cosy world we were told would go on forever, where full employment would be guaranteed at the stroke of the Chancellor's pen, cutting taxes, deficit spending – that cosy world is gone . . . we used to think that you could just spend your way out of a recession to increase employment by cutting taxes and boosting Government spending. I tell you in all candour that that option no longer exists and that insofar as it ever did it worked by injecting inflation into the economy.[58]

Remarkably, Callaghan's speech of 1976 amounted to little more than a rather eerie recapitulation of Hubert Henderson's memorandum criticizing Keynes's initial proposals for demand-management presented to the Economic Advisory Council in 1930, quoted in Chapter One (see p. 39). The economic liberals had argued from the start that Keynes's schemes were no more than an attempt to run away from the 'fundamental problems of British industry'. Forty-six years later, the chickens had come home to roost!

Jay received great encouragement and support from the editor of *The Times*, William Rees-Mogg, whose conversion to monetarism and economic liberalism was rather slower than Jay's; he only finally changed direction in 1972–3, even becoming an advocate of a return to the Gold Standard. Rees-Mogg became a highly sophisticated economic liberal, and attended the Mont Pèlerin Society gatherings. In his long leader-page articles he became a fluent and trenchant critic of Britain's post-war economic record, reflecting much of the work of the IEA in the same field. His most famous article was 'One Dutch man-hour = two British man-hours', printed in *The Times* on 28 September 1977, an attack on restrictive practices and the subsequent lack of productivity in British industry. Rees-Mogg described his paper's rapprochement with the monetarists as 'the most important development on *The Times* during my period there'. Indeed, in the wider context, there is probably nothing of equal importance in post-war British newspaper history than the role played by the *Daily Telegraph*, *The Times* and *Financial Times* in converting a wider public to monetarism.[59] When Sir Keith Joseph delivered his celebrated Upminster speech in 1974, Jay and Rees-Mogg thus instantly recognized the significance of what Joseph was saying – indeed they had been *waiting* for someone to say it – and cleared the features page to reproduce the speech almost in full. It was the *Sunday Times*, however, which made the most memorable contribution to the economic debate of the mid-1970s when in the autumn of 1975 it invited two economists, Walter Eltis and Robert Bacon, to write three articles of six thousand words each on the subject of British industry's chronic over-manning and lack of productivity. The articles were later reproduced as a book, *Too Few Producers* (1977), which became probably the most famous exposition of the economic liberal critique of Britain's post-war industrial and economic performance.

The contribution of the press was crucial to the transformation in the intellectual climate during the mid-1970s, but just as important was the IEA's influence at the universities during the 1960s, for, as Hayek had observed to the founder members of the Mont Pèlerin Society, if liberalism was to prosper, they had to 'raise and train an army of fighters for freedom . . .'[60] The IEA consciously set about doing this, and one of the principal objects of the IEA's publishing programme was to make the fairly complex concepts of economic liberalism and monetarism available to a student or sixth-form audience. The work that the IEA did in this field reaped a rich harvest during the 1970s and 1980s, as many of the younger political activists who staffed the various free-market think-tanks, such as the Centre for Policy Studies, the Adam Smith Institute, the Freedom Association and the Selsdon Group, received their economic education from the IEA at a time when the ideas of the political economy of the free market were at an all-time low in British universities. IEA papers normally reached the hands of students through the university Conservative Associations, and during the 1960s, the IEA's central message of economic freedom chimed well with the 1960s mood of personal and moral freedom. As a result the younger Conservative students who began to exert an influence in the late 1970s were mainly 'libertarian' in character, and many owed as much to the writings of the American 'anarcho-capitalists' Ayn Rand and Murray Rothbard as they did to the IEA.

The IEA had a particular impact on those universities which already had strong Conservative Associations, and of nowhere was this more true than that university where Ralph Harris had been a lecturer, St Andrews. Because of its distance from metropolitan political culture and its purposeful rejection of Oxbridge intellectual influences, St Andrews University had always had an unusually strong Conservative association. The economic liberal influence was strengthened by the presence of economics Professor Nisbet, author of *The Case for Laissez-Faire* (1932), who encouraged his students to read IEA papers. John Marshall, later an economics lecturer at Glasgow and Aberdeen Universities and subsequently a Conservative MP, 'used to read all the IEA's pamphlets' at St Andrews while an undergraduate there, and Eamonn Butler, later a co-founder of the Adam Smith Institute, used IEA pamphlets for essays and political debate, describing the IEA as 'very influential' at St Andrews.[61] Quite apart from their pamphlets, the IEA had a separate connection with St Andrews through Ralph Harris, who was a frequent speaker at the University's Political Economy Club, especially during the 1960s and 1970s. Alan Peacock, another economist closely associated with the IEA, was at St Andrews just after the war. The tradition of Conservatism at St Andrews was thus of the vigorous, iconoclastic free-market variety and the new generation of mainly grammar school-educated students expressed their own youthful radicalism in the exposition of a full blooded free-market assault on the prevailing economic and political wisdom – at a time when most of their contemporaries were cheering on *les événements* in Paris. Chief amongst the St Andrews students of that era, those that became politically active in the early or mid-1970s, were the brothers Stuart and Eamonn Butler and Madsen Pirie, who went on to set up the Adam Smith Institute (ASI) in London in 1976. Eamonn Butler was a very active consumer of IEA literature, whilst Madsen Pirie described the role of the IEA at the universities in a letter that he wrote to Antony Fisher from America in 1975:

> The point which I always try to make about the Institute of Economic Affairs is that it has its most far-reaching effect on the up-coming generation in the Universities and Colleges. I, as thousands of others must have done, first encountered the work of the Institute when I was at University and was just in the process of developing my own ideas. The fact that the IEA has such academic prestige, and publishes research of such a wide range of topics, acts as a considerable reinforcement to those who are groping their own way towards a commitment to free-market and liberal ideas.
>
> The IEA's success in the academic world has meant that it is impossible for a British student not to be aware of its work and its ideas. The situation has been created in which no student of economics can be taught a one-sided collectivist view of the discipline. Whatever he is taught, he will inevitably encounter the IEA's publications and research documents, and will realise that there is a solid body of academically-respectable opinion oriented towards the consumer rather than the central planner.
>
> Since the IEA has concentrated much of its work on empirical studies, they have forced into the academic study of economics an emphasis on the practical effect of policy. It has become impossible for abstract reasoners to speculate about 'ideal' economic systems without having the IEA's evidence from the real world thrust under their noses. I think that this, more than any other factor, has brought about its academic triumph. IEA views do not dominate everywhere, but they do dominate in more than a few insti-

> tutions, and, more importantly, they are represented everywhere. When you reflect what the influence of the IEA had on my ideas, and remember that I am a philosopher, you can gather how much more dramatic its effect has been on Economists. One generation of students is the next generation of teachers; which is why the IEA is so well represented among the younger economists now working their way through University departments.
>
> . . . The IEA not only alters the background intellectual climate of the debate; it puts arguments directly into the mouths of interested parties. You must take great satisfaction in seeing how many times it is that IEA work finds its way immediately into debate in the House of Commons, as well as in the media.
>
> Such are my views on the IEA as an outsider, a non-economist.[62]

As well as economic liberals such as the Butlers and Pirie, Stephen Eyres, Douglas Mason and Richard Henderson – all of whom went on to play roles in either the Conservative Party itself or the various free-market groups and 'think-tanks' which proliferated in the mid-1970s – St Andrews also produced a generation of free-market Conservative MPs who were to become very much the praetorian guard of Mrs Thatcher's economic reforms during the 1980s. This tradition extended as far back as John MacGregor, who was at St Andrews in the mid-1950s, up to the Adam Smith Institute generation of MPs, which included John Marshall and Allan Stewart, both professional economists by training, Robert Jones, Chris Chope, Michael Forsyth and Michael Fallon. All of these MPs except MacGregor were founding members of the No Turning Back Group of Conservatives dedicated to preserving the revolutionary momentum of Mrs Thatcher's Governments of the 1980s. The Mont Pèlerin Society held its general meeting at St Andrews in 1976, which was important in introducing many of those younger economic liberals to the wider liberal intellectual community, especially the Americans.

Other students who were also influenced by the IEA were later to play key roles in the intellectual revolution of the 1970s and 1980s. John Blundell, for instance, read economics at the LSE from 1971 to 1974 and was introduced to the IEA at the LSE; he was later a founder, in 1975, of the Carl Menger Society for the study of Austrian political and economic ideas, before becoming Vice-President of the American Institute of Humane Studies, founded in 1961 by the Mont Pèlerin member F. A. Harper to nurture the remnants of classical liberalism in America. Blundell later became President of the Atlas Economic Research Foundation, Fisher's international 'think-tank' organization (see Chapter Seven), before returning to Britain to become the new General Director of the IEA in 1993. Chris Tame, from a working-class background, discovered the IEA and Ayn Rand at the University of Hull, and went on to work for the National Association for Freedom and the IEA, before founding the Libertarian Alliance in the late 1970s. He is now the Director of FOREST, the anti-anti-smoking lobby. Philip Vander Elst was at Oxford in the early 1970s, where he first encountered free-market economics through reading IEA literature. He was a founder member of the anti-Heath Selsdon Group and became a research officer at the IEA in 1978, and later editor of *Freedom Today*, the journal of the Freedom Association, and National Branch Officer of the Freedom Association. Graham Mather similarly started out in the Freedom Association, before moving to the IEA as its General Director, 1987–92. All these young economic liberals formed a new generation of 'political activists', with ready access to a network of think-tanks, institutions and literature produced by the MPS, the IEA and similar bodies which not only gave them intellectual guidance but could, in the case of the IEA and the CPS, actually employ them. The very idea of a 'political activist' of anything other than a far-left persuasion was a novelty in the 1970s, but these were Hayek's 'fighters for freedom' who were essential troops in the campaign for the ideas of economic freedom.

Many of these young economic liberals became involved in Conservative politics through the Federation of Conservative Students, which, under their guidance, became a force for radical change within the Party even before the Thatcher era. The influence of the IEA was brought into the mainstream of the Conservative Party's intellectual life by the presence at the Party's training school and conference centre, Swinton College, of several of the IEA's staunchest younger supporters within the Party. In the late 1960s and early 1970s Swinton College, housed in a wing of Lord Swinton's country house in Yorkshire, was home to Stephen Eyres, the St Andrews graduate who welcomed each new IEA Hobart paper 'as though it were a fresh

Chapter of the Bible',[63] as well as David Alexander, a graduate of Cambridge and later the moving spirit behind the Selsdon Group, and John O'Sullivan, a graduate of London University who became interested in the ideas of economic liberalism whilst he was at Swinton. Alexander started as a tutor at Swinton in January 1964, and stayed until 1970; Stephen Eyres was a tutor for a few years and John O'Sullivan was a tutor, at first part-time, from 1965 to 1969. David Alexander and John O'Sullivan were also co-editors of the *Swinton Journal*, a quarterly which circulated widely in Conservative circles. They were encouraged in their efforts and supported within the Party by Russell Lewis, who as head of the Conservative Political Centre from 1965 to 1974 was responsible for maintaining links between Swinton College and the rest of the Party. Alexander, Eyres and O'Sullivan used to invite a stream of similarly minded Conservative MPs, most notably Enoch Powell, to Swinton to talk to the students and others who gathered there for courses and conferences; Ralph Harris and others from the IEA also came to address the assembled initiates.

The thinking of the economic liberals at Swinton can be followed in the *Swinton Journal*, and the best example of the new radical free-market fervour at this younger end of the Conservative Party can be found in the Summer 1968 issue of the journal. As *les événements* in Paris reached their climax, and the very existence of liberal democracy seemed to be under siege from a generation of militant left-wing student activists, the youthful editors of the *Swinton Journal* were blithely proclaiming 'The Liberal Hour', with a symposium on the role of economic liberalism in modern Conservatism, opened by John Biffen, entitled 'Intellectuals and Conservatism'. In his editorial summary of the symposium, John O'Sullivan felt confident enough of what he had heard to write that:

> Despite the lively expressions of disagreements and the polemical exchanges, a consistent theme links almost all of the contributors – namely, a belief in a liberal society in which people exercise control over their own lives . . . it is obvious that most contributors support the general approach recommended by Arthur Seldon; personal liberty . . . individual and corporate initiative, decentralised authority, and government limited to services that cannot be organised by spontaneous contract in the market.

O'Sullivan concluded his editorial by remarking on the new-found 'vitality of economic liberalism', inspired largely by the IEA.

> It is scarcely an exaggeration to say that liberalism claims to cure more ills than patent medicine. Are you worried about the world monetary crisis? Flexible exchange rates will ease your mind. Is urban congestion a problem in your town? Enquire about road pricing today. Have you lain awake at nights, praying for choice in education? The voucher scheme is meant for you. Do high prices make you feel faint? Abolition of RPM will soon do the trick. Naturally it is easy to mock at this out-pouring of ideas – and probably some of them will not work – but it is the mark of a dynamic philosophy that it provides clear, consistent and above all, simple solutions to the problems thrown up by society and the economy. Nor should we forget that it is precisely these qualities which intellectuals, if they are true to their vocation, will particularly value.
>
> For all the reasons outlined above, Conservatives should find the intellectual audience attentive and receptive when they present a view of society derived from the tradition of liberal conservatism. This tradition was responsible for important achievements during the thirteen years [of Conservative Governments, 1951–64] – The dismantling of controls and the abolition of RPM in particular. It is the inspiration behind much of present Tory policy, like the move towards occupational pension schemes. Now is the time for the Conservative Party to commit itself to this liberal tradition in clear and unequivocal terms.[64]

As John O'Sullivan indicated, it was just such an all-embracing 'world-view' that the fully developed theory of economic liberalism offered to the young which made it so attractive, just as that equally comprehensive ideology, Marxism, had seemed so alluring to the students of the 1930s, for exactly the same reasons – it offered compellingly simple solutions to complex problems. To those youthful minds, economic liberalism offered a complete replacement for Marxism, a straightforward meta-narrative that would explain almost anything. Amongst those taking part in the symposium were Biffen, Geoffrey Howe, Quintin Hogg, David Howell (a former head of the CPC and later a prominent MP), Russell Lewis, Arthur Seldon, Michael Spicer, T. E. Utley and Timothy Raison, later a Minister in Mrs Thatcher's governments. In fact, John O'Sullivan was being somewhat disingenuous in his editorial summary, as most of those participants, especially Raison, Howell and Spicer, argued, with varying degrees of intensity, *against* an overemphasis on dogma and ideology in the Conservative Party, especially that of economic liberalism, and stressed instead the Conservative tradition of pragmatism. It was a debate that was to become all too familiar in the early 1980s, but one which was already being addressed by Conservatives in 1968 as economic liberalism began to exert an undoubted hold over certain sections of the Party. Arthur Seldon's contribution to this symposium was an excellent *tour d'horizon* of the relationship between economic liberals like himself and the Conservative Party and is reproduced in Appendix III below.

In the Spring 1970 issue of the *Swinton Journal* John O'Sullivan returned to this theme, and, on the eve of Edward Heath's election victory, wrote an article on 'The Direction of Conservatism' arguing, convincingly, that the old 'paternalistic' Conservatism of Baldwin and Macmillan was now irrelevant to Britain's changed political and economic position in the world:

> The Empire has gone, but the tariffs remain, like the visible masts of a sunken ship. Economic interventionism, introduced to deal with the problems of a slump, is out of place in a world where oil is fast replacing coal, where manufacturing capacity is largely devoted to the exploitation of new inventions, and where international trade shows a steady annual increase. And, finally, when typists spend their holidays in Yugoslavia or when average industrial earnings are over £1,000 p.a. and certainly rising, it is nonsense to argue that security is attainable only through State-run, universalist, tax-financed social services. In short, the problems, to which Tory paternalism provided answers, either have been solved or have simply faded away leaving the heirs to this tradition and a significant section of the Conservative Party floundering as helplessly as whales stranded by a receding tide . . .[65]

The battle-lines were thus being drawn in the Conservative Party between those who wanted to rediscover the Party's economically liberal, 'Peelite' past, and those who wanted to continue the paternalistic, collectivist and '*dirigiste*' policy of Macmillan and Butler.

The influence of the IEA in these different areas – at Westminster, in the press and at the universities – was vital in creating the intellectual climate in which economic liberalism could challenge successfully for ideological hegemony as Keynesianism broke down under the pressures of runaway inflation, sinking industrial productivity and rising unemployment, culminating in the IMF crisis of 1976. The precise nature of this 'intellectual' breakdown of Keynesian economics will be discussed in more detail in the next chapter. The IEA reached the peak of its influence during that period, when all the economic liberal predictions of the previous thirty or forty years came to pass. If politicians needed reminding of those predictions, they had only to read the IEA's collection of writings by Hayek, *A Tiger by the Tail*, published in 1972, which quoted from Hayek's warnings about the dangers of inflation and industrial decline inherent in the Keynesian system, some of them dating back as far as 1947. This fact, that the IEA's economic warnings seemed to have been vindicated, gave it the intellectual credibility and authority to press home the arguments for monetarism and economic reforms in the early and mid-1970s. As Alan Walters pointed out, it was a question of demand and supply; as the Keynesian system broke down after the 'Barber Boom' of 1973–4, the most credible alternative on offer was the economic liberalism of the IEA, and so it was to the IEA's policies that the politicians looked. Ronald Butt of *The Times* observed in January 1976 that:

> Ten years ago, the IEA, with its devotion to Adam Smith, free market economics and the guidance of the economy by strict control of the money supply rather than by Collectivist intervention was still regarded as a bit of a joke by most economic writers.
>
> Today, helped by the pressures of real life, it has shifted some of the best known economic writers in its direction and a good deal of the most influential economic thinking comes from economists published by the IEA. To most economists, the analysis of Hayek, Friedman and other IEA authors has taken on a new relevance – as it has to Chancellors and Shadow-Chancellors . . .[66]

Even the Left, having invented the term 'New Right', was obliged to recognize the contribution of the IEA to the changed intellectual climate of the mid-1970s. Robert Taylor wrote in *New Society* in 1979 that

> from being a collection of cranks, the IEA has come of age, with its serious but entertaining pamphlets, which are now required reading in Whitehall, especially for Sir Keith Joseph's mandarins at the Department of Industry . . . The IEA loves to provoke, tilting at windmills and questioning current assumptions. Harris and Seldon are enthusiastic innocents, believing their opponents misguided but redeemable. With no State help of any kind on principle, the IEA has pushed a way through a hostile world, to a kind of vindication. Keynes and Beveridge no longer attract reverence, while the Left offers an unpleasant mixture of economic nationalism and State control for its own sake.[67]

The *New Statesman* joined the general chorus of praise in 1975, conceding that 'It is the IEA which has to take most of the credit for years of patient work . . .' in bringing economic liberalism to its contemporary pre-eminence.[68] Sir Douglas Allen, head of the Home Civil Service and a contemporary of Arthur Seldon's at the LSE, wrote to Ralph Harris in 1977 on receipt of the IEA's *Not from Benevolence . . .* that he found himself 'much more in sympathy with its main theses than I would have thought likely in the early 1960s. Indeed, on many basic issues the general tide of opinion has turned much more in your direction . . .'[69]

At the same time as emphasizing the role of the IEA in this intellectual revolution, it must also be stressed that the IEA was not working in a vacuum; other, often more immediate pressures were forcing British governments to take measures which the IEA recommended. For instance, well before the IEA had persuaded the press and politicians as a whole to take monetarism seriously, monetary targets, which were finally officially embraced as part of the Government's long-term economic strategy in 1980, had already been forced on the Labour Chancellor of the Exchequer, Roy Jenkins, when in 1968 he went to the International Monetary Fund to negotiate drawing rights to support sterling following the devaluation of 1967. The letter of intent signed by the Chancellor to the IMF stated that the growth of the money supply in 1968 would be limited to its estimated rate of growth in 1967. In his second letter of intent of May 1969, the Chancellor set a target for the growth of Domestic Credit Expansion (DCE) of £400 million for 1969–70. The result of Jenkins's deflationary squeeze was a cut in the rate of the money supply measured as £M3 from 10.5 per cent in 1967 to 1.8 per cent in 1969. This led to a much healthier external trade balance and domestic financial position by 1970, which is why, after all the trials and tribulations of devaluation after 1960, the Labour Party went to the polls in 1970 expecting to win. Although the position had improved so much by 1971 that the new Conservative Chancellor did not feel obliged to set a new target for DCE after April 1971, nonetheless those monetary targets 'introduced in 1969–70 and 1970–1 were the first examples of the use of monetary aggregates as intermediate variables'.[70] Thus the Treasury and the Bank of England were all aware of the new school of monetarism before it was being discussed, prompted by the IEA, in the press and elsewhere. Similarly, the Callaghan Government of 1976 was forced by the IMF to accept monetary targets in 1976, without showing any evidence that the Government believed in the intellectual efficacy of what they were doing. Milton Friedman, for one, was perfectly happy to accept that the intellectual 'vindication' of the IEA and monetarism came not necessarily from the powers of argument and persuasion, but from the force of events. He ended his 1976 Nobel Prize Lecture with the thought that:

> Government policy about inflation and unemployment has been at the centre of political controversy. Ideological war has ranged over these matters. Yet the drastic change that has occurred in economic theory has not been a result of ideological warfare. It has not resulted from divergent political beliefs or aims. It has responded almost entirely to the force of events; brute experience proved far more potent than the strongest of political or ideological preferences.[71]

Friedman was exaggerating. For although the 'brute experience' of the failure of Keynesian demand-led economic policies proved important in persuading governments in Britain to change tack, the fact that the IEA had predicted such a failure, and had worked out a coherent, intellectually satisfying alternative, meant that when the time came for that change of tack in the mid-1970s, there was really only one alternative and, by implication, one philosophical position to adopt – that of the IEA.

6

The Failure of Edward Heath's Government and the Founding of the Centre for Policy Studies

*

Given their growing influence within the Conservative Party during the 1960s, Edward Heath's victory in the election of 1970 was welcomed by the IEA as his government seemed to hold out, for the first time in post-war British history, the prospect of a significant degree of economic liberalism. Arthur Seldon even voted Conservative for the first time. As well as those Conservative politicians and younger activists who learnt their economic liberalism from the IEA, other Conservatives had also been developing their own critique of the Keynesian consensus, and putting their own alternatives forward within the official Party hierarchy. The most important group of Conservatives working within the Party for their own brand of economic liberalism gathered around the Conservative Party Public Sector Research Unit (CPSRU), set up in 1967 by Mark Schreiber and David Howell, the old Etonian ex-head of the Conservative Political Centre. Their patron within the Party was Ernest Marples, and David Howell was also very close to Edward Heath during the period of opposition. Although Howell was a consumer of the IEA's work from the late 1950s onwards, he drew on his own sources of inspiration to develop policies which would give flesh and blood to the vague notions of wider individual ownership and greater personal enterprise expressed by the Party leadership. Howell and Schreiber gathered most of their ideas during the course of several trips to America, and in particular from the work of Louis Kelso, who in his 1958 book *The Capitalist Manifesto* had recommended the mass ownership of industry and enterprise as the best alternative to the Keynesian state.[1] Howell and Schreiber advocated the adoption of business methods and practices in Government, and arranged a conference at Surridge Park in September 1969 to try and bring the businessmen and politicians together. The CPSRU produced several pamphlets on their proposed reorganization of Whitehall and the public sector. David Howell's *A New Style of Government*, published in May 1970, was probably the most significant of these, advocating the reduction of government and bureaucracy; a 'key instrument' in this drive for public economy was to be the 'process of transferring functions and activities [of Government] back to the private sector or running them down altogether'. To describe this process, which the IEA authors had called 'denationalization', Howell first used the word 'privatization' in a footnote – although he still thought the word 'hideously clumsy. Something better must be invented.'[2]

A practical example of 'privatization' was offered in the CPSRU pamphlet *Dial* ENTERPRISE *1971 – The Case for a Private Enterprise Telephone Service* published by the Conservative Political Centre in 1968, by David Alexander, who had moved from Swinton College to work for the CPSRU. Alexander drew largely on the IEA pamphlet by Michael Cane, *Telephones – Public or Private?*, to argue that the telephone system be allowed to attract private capital for profit, by removing it from the public sector. He also drew on the work of Russell Lewis, who in an article in the *Daily Telegraph* of 4 October 1968 had used the case of the German car-makers Volkswagen, which had been transferred to the private sector in 1960 by the sale of 3,600,000 shares to 1½ million individual investors, to argue that if the Volkswagen technique 'allied with tax concessions to lower income groups, were used to return nationalised industries to the private sector, this would have the advantages both of helping the creation of a Capital-owning democracy and of creating a vested interest in favour of denationalization'.[3] These were, of course, the first seeds of a concept which was to become known as 'privatization' and was to be the principal policy flagship of Mrs Thatcher's second government.

The IEA and the economic liberals within the Conservative ranks also received a certain amount of encouragement from the Party leader Edward Heath, who had told the Party Conference in the expectation of an election in the near future: 'We will remove the shackles of government from industry. We will banish the regulation and control of business activities. We will withdraw the Government from holdings in private firms. We will begin to reintroduce private ownership into nationalised industries.'

Hearing this sort of rhetoric, it was no surprise that Arthur Seldon looked forward to the prospect of Heath's Government breaking

Labour's hold on the 'Working Class, and destroy[ing] Socialism for all time'.[4]

Unfortunately, these turned out to be ludicrously high expectations. Despite the work of the IEA and other similarly inclined MPs and activists within the Conservative Party, many of the Party's leading politicians remained ideologically wedded to the politics of Keynesian demand-management and the efficacy of a large role for Government in the economy – the politics of the post-war consensus. Of no-one was this more true than Edward Heath; the limits of his radicalism lay in what his latest biographer, John Campbell, has described as a certain brand of 'technocratic pragmatism'. Despite his occasional genuflections towards economic liberalism, such as his abolition of RPM in 1964, Heath was essentially a 'pragmatic politician', a politician's politician.

> He had a clear vision of the sort of country he wanted Britain to become – much clearer than Wilson's. He had immense idealism and sincerity. But his political purposes were so broadly benevolent that they were in a curious way unpolitical. He simply wanted people to have the opportunity of leading richer and fuller lives. He had very little idea of how they were to be enabled to do so, except that British industry needed to become more efficient and the economy more competitive; that was the Tory way. But he had no interest in political philosophy or economic theory; that, he believed, was what the Labour Party suffered from. He thought essentially that making Britain prosperous and successful was a matter of practical common sense and political will, vigorously applied. Despite the best of intentions and all their differences of personality, this intellectual vacuum at the heart of Heath's politics was in the last analysis little different from the opportunist trickiness he so despised in Wilson. It was to lead him, despite himself, into inconsistency in trying to oppose the Labour Government . . . and to a fatal inconsistency of purpose when he eventually achieved power himself in 1970.[5]

This ambiguity of purpose and lack of clear ideological interest was fatally on display at Selsdon Park, where the Shadow Cabinet gathered for a conference in January 1970, on what was thought to be the eve of a general election. It was meant to be just a weekend get-together of the Shadow Cabinet, but due to a chapter of accidents and hastily prepared press releases, the attendant journalists concocted a story that the conference was in fact a planning session for a full-blooded assault on the twin issues of crime and immigration, and thus, by extension, the nationalized sector of industry and the economy as well. The newspapers interpreted this as a 'swing to the Right', and Wilson quickly jumped on the bandwagon and dubbed the new Heathite 'right-wing' Tory 'Selsdon Man'. In fact, the proceedings of the conference were extremely anodyne and discursive, as the minutes indicate, but the description of 'Selsdon Man' in the press proved immediately popular with the public, much to Wilson's horror and Heath's surprise. 'Selsdon Man' gave Heath's vague policy proposals a coherence that they had previously lacked, and which they did not deserve. 'Selsdon Man' thus rebounded on the Labour leader: 'at a stroke Wilson had succeeded, as Heath and all his advisers had constantly failed to do, in sharpening the Tories' image and opening up the appearance of a clear political choice between Labour and Conservative'. However, as John Campbell observes, although 'Selsdon Man' might have helped Heath in the short term, it also rebounded on him too – in the long run:

> For in 1970 he *was* 'Selsdon Man'. As with the glamorously dynamic image that was briefly foisted on him in 1965 he went along with it, smiling nervously, content after all his trials to ride the wave wherever it took him. He allowed himself to be identified with ideas and attitudes which were not really his own. He thus encouraged expectations among right-wing Conservatives (including a new generation which entered Parliament for the first time on his coat-tails in 1970, typified by Norman Tebbit) which he was bound to disappoint . . . It was a fatal error for Heath to allow himself to be thought to have more radical intentions than in fact he had.[6]

The story of Heath's ill-fated premiership will not be retold in full here, but it was obvious from the start that those expectations entertained by economic liberals at the IEA and within the new Government were to be quickly disappointed.[7] After an early commitment to abandoning the 'lame ducks' of industry to the financial disciplines of the market-place, the Government was soon taking the bulk of Rolls-Royce into public ownership, whereas the only two State businesses that the Government managed to privatize were the pubs in Carlisle, a legacy from the First World War, and the travel agents Thomas Cook. Jock Bruce-Gardyne, one of the economic liberal Conservative MPs wrote an obituary of the Government, appropriately entitled *Whatever Happened to the Quiet Revolution?*, in which he dated Heath's U-turn from economic liberal back to Keynesian interventionist to the summer of 1971, only a year into office: 'the July 19 1971 "mini-budget" marked a turning-point in the sense that the curbing of unemployment had overtaken the curbing of inflation as the primary objective of economic policy'.[8] By the end of that year the Chancellor, Anthony Barber, was announcing public spending of £600 million on specific programmes, followed by that anathema of the economic liberals, prices and incomes legislation. Nicholas Ridley has claimed that he resigned from the Department of Trade and Industry in April 1972 as a mark of protest. Even before he failed to meet the challenge laid down by the miners in 1973–4, Heath had earned the undying enmity of most economic liberals, who, perhaps unfairly, felt betrayed. Bruce-Gardyne analyzed the failure of Heath's premiership thus:

> There is nothing to inhibit governments from embarking on a change of course as soon as they assume office; indeed, the sooner they do so, the better. What is required of them – and what has been so signally missing in recent years – is a willingness then to wait for results: to recognise that it will be two years before they can begin to see the consequences of the economic changes – and that unless they are prepared to grit their teeth that long they might just as well not embark on a strategy in the first place.[9]

The biggest disappointment for the IEA came with the performance of those politicians who had seemed to be most interested in their ideas during the period of opposition, namely Keith Joseph, Margaret Thatcher and Geoffrey Howe, respectively Secretary of State for Social Services, Secretary of State for Education and Solicitor-General (and Minister for Trade and Consumer Affairs, 1972–4) in Heath's

Government. Joseph's innate political, as distinct from intellectual, caution was in evidence even before he entered the new Government in an exchange of letters with Arthur Seldon. Seldon sent Joseph a copy of a report on welfare that he had compiled for the Australian Government, and added the following note:

> May I also now hope, without knowing the result of the Election, that the Conservatives will take a little more courage in their hands and come out more clearly in favour of a growing private sector of medicine, and with proposals to help everyone – including the 'poor' – to pay for it. The Conservatives will then be seen to have more respect for the common man than the Socialists who speak for him on paper, but scorn him in practice.

To which Joseph replied rather defensively:

> I shall read [the Report] with great interest.
>
> But do please try to understand the degree of malicious distortion with which any proposals of the sort contained in your last paragraph would be treated by our opponents. We could only move in that direction if we had really well-worked out policies to do so and had been plugging them consistently – and been cross-examined on them successfully – for 3 or 4 years.
>
> You will say 'Hear, Hear'. But the first thing is to get the policies that some of us can put forward enthusiastically among our colleagues . . .[10]

The writing was on the wall even before Joseph moved into his new Department, where it quickly became apparent that he was not inclined to implement any of the radical proposals for restructuring the finances of the Welfare State with which he had been associated before the election. Indeed, quite the reverse happened as he proved adept at persuading the Treasury to release even more money to be spent on the administrative reorganization of the Health Service, aptly described by his biographer as a 'well-meaning disaster'.[11] It was evident that his civil servants were able to persuade their new Minister that the existing policies should be implemented, and much of Joseph's own agenda was quietly shelved. It was at this point in his career that Joseph earned the reputation of being rather too malleable in the hands of senior civil servants, by dint of his intellectual honesty and readiness to listen to all sides of an argument – and invariably, of course, the civil servants got the last word. Alfred Sherman, Joseph's intellectual mentor, despaired of Joseph's timidity in government, and liked to refer to him as 'a good man fallen amongst civil servants'.

Others despaired too. Seldon wrote to Joseph after a few months' observation of the new government, following a further meeting to discuss private health care. Seldon sent Joseph a further report, written for an Australian private insurance organization, and added:

> In view of our exchange last evening I send it with some sadness mingled with cynicism. For you my weakness is that I do not allow sufficiently for the politically possible (or administratively practicable?). . . . the weakness of Conservative politicians is that they under-estimate the importance of time – and the readiness of the people to accept Social reform. They are concerned too much with the Cross-men on the opposite benches, and too little with the latent aspirations of the people that they (mis)represent (with, or as Ted says without, respect I do not think the ballot box at all appropriate for discovering public opinion on individual services like health).
>
> But we shall not agree. And those of us who are anxious to see Socialism replaced sooner rather than later must hope that Conservative Ministers will compromise, if they must, only in Morley's sense, *pour mieux sauter*.[12]

Seldon carried on a vigorous correspondence with Joseph during 1971 and 1972, always trying to get Joseph to examine alternative methods of private funding for health care. Joseph refused to be drawn, pointing to the fact that there had been no commitment in the manifesto to such alternative funding, and always emphasizing the practical political difficulties of such schemes. For Seldon it was an increasingly frustrating and unrewarding correspondence, and in March 1972 he made his last, exasperated, plea for Joseph 'to at least consider the alternatives', rather than merely adding yet more layers to the existing bureaucratic structure of the NHS:

It would hardly do for a Minister of your integrity and intellectual insight to do nothing but make technocratic efforts to reduce the inefficiency of the NHS, which any Labour – or other Conservative – Minister could have been expected to do.

I think your advent to office aroused great expectations – for the reasons stated above and also because of the sort of speeches you made on general policy when out of office. The reactions to your activities are very different. Your best press is in papers like the *Guardian*, *Observer*, *New Society* and similar organs. You have given nothing to those who expected something different from you.[13]

This was Seldon's last letter of the 1970–4 Government to Joseph, and the Minister thereafter disappeared from sight as far as the economic liberals were concerned – until his famous reawakening in 1974. Mrs Thatcher also vanished without trace as, to a certain extent, did Geoffrey Howe. What is perhaps most surprising is that none of them raised any objections to Heath's change of policies in 1971 in Cabinet; but perhaps this was because of Heath's authoritarian style of government, which meant that several crucial decisions and issues never came to Cabinet. Howe was a great disappointment. In February 1972 Seldon sent him the galley proofs of a *Daily Telegraph* article which he had written urging the Heath Government to look again at the financing of the Welfare State. Howe's reply, legalistic and cautious in tone, reflected the essential conservatism of the Conservative government:

I fancy that the policies to which you refer . . . may fail to come through, not so much because of 'bureaucratic obstruction' but because of Ministerial assessment of the way in which the *political market* requires them to respond in light of the factors that you mentioned in your first two columns.

Opinion in favour of the policies you mentioned turn out to carry less weight than militant response (apparently very politically damaging) to even quite modest applications of those policies e.g. on school milk or student union finance . . .

> Thus there remains a very formidable [obstacle?] and I am not sure whose job it is to try and think out the way around this.

In a note at the bottom of Howe's letter, Arthur Seldon scribbled: 'Deep ponderings. Not convinced by these public schoolboys!'[14]

Concern about the Government's policies led Seldon to write to Heath in June 1971 offering him the opportunity to draw on the work of IEA economists, which drew the dusty reply that the Government already had enough sources of 'advice and research . . . both inside and outside the administration', and so did not need the help of the IEA.[15]

As none of the Ministers with whom the IEA was on friendly terms seemed to respond to the personal promptings of Seldon and Harris, in August 1971 the IEA 'went public' and published the first book to criticize Heath's Government from an economic liberal viewpoint. *Government and the Market Economy* (IEA, 1971) was written by Samuel Brittan, and most of the press hailed his book as the first critique of Heath's Government to show that it was singularly failing to live up to its early claims to be a market-orientated government.[16] The most interesting review came from Harold Lever, a Labour Minister and Chancellor of the Duchy of Lancaster with a wide-ranging economic brief in the Callaghan and Wilson Governments of 1974–9. He indicated how far certain sections of the Labour Party had come towards accepting Brittan's argument for what would soon be called a 'Social Market' economy:

> Though I would strongly dispute some of his [Brittan's] illustrative propositions such as the private generation of electricity or private buses, Mr. Brittan . . . makes out a case for a modern version of the market economy that is at once sensible and stimulating; not as a means of excusing the Government from pursuing socially desirable objectives but as in general the most effective mechanism for achieving them. This paper will be useful and thought-provoking for members of the Labour Party; but more urgently, it ought to be compulsory reading for the economic ministers in the present Government and their parliamentary supporters.[17]

The IEA returned to the attack in early 1975 when it published *British Economic Policy 1970–74; Two Views* (Hobart Paperback 7) by Ralph Harris and Brendon Sewill, Director of the Conservative Research Department from 1965 to 1970, and Special Adviser to Chancellor Barber from 1970 to 1974. Whilst Harris roundly condemned Heath for performing his U-turn, even Sewill admitted that the Government had been insufficiently concerned about inflation when coming into office, because the main points of the 1970 Manifesto had been established by 1965: 'This meant that by 1968 and 1969, when I proposed that price stability should be the main priority, the mould had set too hard for any fundamental change.'[18] Interestingly, Sewill was also a rare supporter of Heath's Government who admitted that the incoming government's programme had been 'one of economic liberalism'.[19]

Indeed, it was on the issue of 'inflation' that the IEA and the economic liberals attacked Heath most sharply. After the jobless total had reached the politically sensitive figure of one million in 1971, Heath reverted to a good old-fashioned Keynesian budgetary expansion, designed to spend the Government's way out of the encircling economic gloom – the 'Barber boom' of 1972–3. To the monetarist economists at the IEA and elsewhere this was criminally irresponsible, given the widely acknowledged link between the expansion of the money supply, public spending and inflation. Peter Jay, as has been noted, was one of those monetarists who predicted in *The Times* in 1973 that the 'Barber boom' had to go bust. Alan Walters was another. He had accepted a part-time job in the Cabinet Office as an economic adviser to the Central Policy Review Staff, and wrote later of his experience:

> I think I can say that I was utterly ineffective. In the second half of 1971, in pursuing an elusive goal of 'full employment', the Heath Government began a massive fiscal stimulus and tripling of the monetary growth rate. Virtually all economic advisers and commentators thought that there would be such an expansion of employment and real output that there would be a *reduction* in the rate of inflation. My view was quite the opposite. I forwarded to Mr Heath a memorandum entitled 'Inflation, Devaluation and More Inflation', where I predicted that by 1974 the inflation rate would be at least 10 and possibly as high as 15 per cent, that there would be a current deficit of as much as one

> billion sterling, and that he would be driven to reimpose prices and incomes controls. My advice was rejected and I was relieved of my part-time job. The Heath policy, pursued with increased vigour in 1972, came to grief in 1974 when the inflation rate reached 14.7 per cent, the current account deficit was more than 3.3 billion sterling, and prices and incomes controls had been reimposed. I published my memorandum in July 1972, so my Cassandra-like performance was on public record. In retrospect, it seems no big deal to have made and persisted with such predictions, yet the pressures to conform were considerable; but all the arguments made me even more convinced that I was correct.[20]

The document published as a pamphlet in 1972 was the celebrated 'Memorial to the Prime Minister', signed by Walters and a group of other economists, all of whom were associated with or had been published by the IEA; Brian Griffiths, Harry Johnson, the Chicago economist with a joint appointment at the LSE, David Laidler, one of the pioneers of the British study of monetary policy at Manchester University, S. H. Frankel of Oxford University, E. V. Morgan of Manchester University and Dr Malcolm Fisher of Cambridge University. They were joined by a brave and solitary MP, Richard Body, one of the IEA's earliest supporters. This group called themselves the 'economic radicals', and the 'Memorial to the Prime Minister' presented a direct challenge to Heath's Government on the central direction of economic policy – it also signalled the beginning of open rebellion against Heath's leadership of the Party, and provided the economic liberals with a rallying point. Their argument was quite simple, that the Government, through 'profligate' public spending, had increased the money supply to such an extent that inflation was rising to unacceptable levels. The main recommendation therefore, was that the 'rate of increase of the money supply' be 'diminished. We do not argue that the money stock should be reduced; indeed, we would like to see a steady and stable increase.'[21] The authors of the pamphlet, together with Dr J. B. Bracewell-Milnes, formerly Director of the Confederation of British Industry, and I. F. Pearce, Professor of Economic Theory at Southampton University, returned to the attack in 1974 with a second pamphlet, *Dear Prime Minister*, addressed to the new Labour Prime Minister, Harold Wilson. This second pamphlet was more apocalyptic in tone, arguing for immediate action on the money supply unless Britain was to plunge into the 'abyss of hyperinflation'. Peter Jay was writing along similar lines in *The Times*.

At the same time as the 'economic radicals' hoisted the flag of rebellion, unrest at Heath's disastrous economic policies began to spread on the Conservative back-benches. Nicholas Ridley, Jock Bruce-Gardyne and John Biffen were amongst the first dissenters, and founded the Economic Dining Club in 1972, a forum of twelve MPs (which included Enoch Powell) that met to discuss monetarism and what came to be called 'supply-side' economics. Ridley later recalled one confrontation they had with the Chancellor in 1972 (Ridley was Chairman of the Conservative Back-Bench Finance Committee at the time):

> Jock Bruce-Gardyne and I, both then officers of the Finance Committee, asked Alan Walters to help us prepare a paper on how to control the economy by using monetary policy. Our paper was scorned by the back-bench members of the Committee and when we took it to Anthony Barber, the Chancellor of the Exchequer, he scorned it even more. It was about the frostiest meeting I can remember. The officers of the Finance Committee and the Chancellor failed to agree about any one aspect of economic policy.[22]

The gulf between the two sides, economic liberals and Keynesians, was now as unbridgeable in the political arena as it had been in the intellectual arena for the previous thirty years. Lord Coleraine (Richard Law) expressed the sense of despair that the economic liberals felt about Edward Heath in a letter to Diana Spearman in 1973:

> Perhaps you will agree with me now that it would have been better for the Labour Party to have won the last election. Had they done so we would not, at this moment of time, be as far along the road to complete Socialism as we are today. In fact every Conservative Government we get goes twice as far towards the Socialist millennium as its Labour predecessor. As for Heath, I think his main difficulty is to decide whether he is President, Emperor or Pope ...

> Anyway I can't make up my mind whether things will be worse if Heath's policy succeeds, or if it fails. I think probably success would be the worse.[23]

The discontent with Heath – or 'the grocer' as he was now popularly known by his party opponents – over economic policy crystallized into outright opposition in the summer of 1973 with the founding of the Selsdon Group, the first of a plethora of distinct organizations founded on the fringes of the Conservative Party during the period 1973–5 to demand of the Conservative Party leadership a change of political direction, and to work actively for economic liberalism *within* the Party. It was the beginning of the end for the old politics of consensus and Keynesian economics. The name 'Selsdon Group' was, of course, an ironic reference to the conference at the Selsdon Park Hotel in January 1970 which had raised such false expectations amongst the economic liberals. The Selsdon Group was formed, as it proclaimed,

> to ensure that the case for the free market economy has the fullest hearing within the Conservative Party. The Group is for Conservatives who realise that economic freedom is the indispensable condition for political freedom. Its members reject the view that the 'Middle Ground' is where elections are won and lost; they believe the Party will be returned to Office when it adopts distinctive Conservative principles. It did so in 1970; it could do so again.

The 'Selsdon Declaration', adopted by the Selsdon Group at their first official meeting at the Selsdon Park Hotel in September 1973, was, in essence, a manifesto for what was to become Thatcherism:

> We believe that individual enterprise is the source of all progress in economics, the sciences and the arts, and that the task of politics is to create a framework within which the individual can flourish.
>
> We believe that every individual should be judged by his actions and not according to any arbitrary criteria of race, creed or colour.
>
> We believe that economic freedom is vital to political freedom because power is then diffused among many differ-

> ent enterprises instead of being concentrated on the State.
>
> We oppose the view that the State should have a monopoly in health, housing, education and welfare. We uphold the right of the individual to cater for his own preferences in the market, believing that State provision should supplement rather than replace private provision.
>
> We see the primary role as so to influence the Conservative Party that it embraces economic and social policies which extend the boundaries of personal choice.

The founders of the Selsdon Group included many of those who had been formative in establishing the doctrine of economic liberalism in the Party since the 1960s. The Patron was Lord Coleraine (Richard Law), whose *For Conservatives Only* was, to some extent, the book that best expressed their political and philosophical position. The MPs Nicholas Ridley, Richard Body, William Clark, Ronald Bell and Sir Frederick Corfield were the Vice-Presidents. The 'officers' of the Selsdon Group were mostly those younger Conservatives who had been heavily influenced by the IEA. David Alexander was the first Chairman, Stephen Eyres, of St Andrews and Swinton, was Deputy Chairman, Richard Henderson, of St Andrews, was the Treasurer, the Secretary was Anthony Vander Elst and the editorial director Philip Vander Elst. Dr Barry Bracewell-Milnes of the 'Economic Radicals' was on the Executive Committee, as was Paul Marland, who became an MP in 1979. Russell Lewis later became President of the Selsdon Group, and Alan Walters joined as a Vice-President. Philip Vander Elst, an Oxford graduate who had learnt his own economic liberalism from IEA pamphlets, outlined the aspirations of the Group in an article entitled 'Radical Toryism – The Libertarian Alternative' in *Political Quarterly* magazine in 1975. In this article, Vander Elst berated Heath's government for betraying the promises of 'Selsdon Man', and instead of Heath and Wilson's 'corporatism' he offered 'An alternative vision of Society', which offered a new principle of political action; 'that the State confines its role to laying down and policing minimum standards in health and education, while the actual services should in the main, or preferably entirely, be provided by competing private agencies.' He thus proposed widespread 'denationalization' and an assault on the 'Universalist' Welfare State. He ended thus:

> There will always be those in the ranks of the Conservative Party who will regard such a strategy as 'impossible' or 'politically unacceptable'. The types who manifest these reactions are, however, precisely those who for as long as one can remember have talked glowingly about the 'middle way' and Tory 'pragmatism'. Their counsels have reigned supreme for a long time and what has been the outcome? A country which has steadily become more Socialist despite the fact that Tory governments have held office for most of the past 40 years. That is not a record that anyone looking at the present condition can be proud of. We can only move forward by resolving to have done once and for all with the discredited policies and defeatist slogans of our corporatist past, and to face the future not with fear, but with a renewed and serene determination to win the battle for freedom.[24]

'Libertarianism' was very much an ideology of the younger economic liberals, and became the fashionable alternative to the Trotskyist 'Statism' of their contemporaries on the left – both preached 'power to the people', the libertarians' preferred mechanism being the widespread diffusion of shares and capital ownership. Amongst those who addressed the Selsdon Group in the mid-1970s were several of the intellectual mentors of the economic liberals and libertarians, including Hayek, Russell Lewis, Alan Walters, Ralph Harris, Samuel Brittan and Murray Rothbard. From the beginning, the Selsdon Group pursued a vigorous publishing programme and organized seminars and conferences on aspects of economic policy. It published a monthly newsletter, initially edited by David Alexander, which set the tone for its other publications. The first newsletter of February 1974 had articles by Alexander, Stephen Eyres, Philip Vander Elst, and a review of Hayek's *Law, Legislation and Liberty* by Sudha Shenoy, an Indian economist who wrote for the IEA. Most of those who were connected with the cause of economic liberalism, within or outside the party, addressed the group at one time or another. During March and April 1974, for instance, speakers included Antony Fisher of the IEA, Leon Brittan MP, Jock Bruce-Gardyne MP, Patrick Cosgrave, Allan Stewart of the CBI (later an MP), Alan Walters and James Bourlet, a lecturer in economics at the City of London Polytechnic Business School. John Biffen was guest of honour at the Group's annual dinner on 2 April.

The younger, ex-Swinton College tutors in the Selsdon Group used Swinton to run weekend courses on aspects of economic policy that would be of interest to them; on 22–4 March they ran a course on 'Prospects for Capitalism', at which the speakers included Brittan, Russell Lewis and Hayek himself, who was presented with an 1899 golden guinea on behalf of the group by Peter Clarke, another young 'activist' and very briefly chairman of the Selsdon Group during its first few weeks.[25]

The Selsdon Group ran an important publishing programme, divided into 'Selsdon Group Briefs' and 'Selsdon Group Policy Series'. The first publication, in March 1974, was *Wanted – A Policy for Wealth*, by David Alexander. He argued for the now familiar policies of reducing the size and scope of the State sector as a means of controlling inflation, and cutting taxation to restore incentives and enterprise. Alexander also called this alternative to Socialism a 'social market economy', which was becoming an increasingly popular label for the economic liberals when describing their alternative political vision. Other pamphlets included *An End to Whitehall Dole* by Jock Bruce-Gardyne, an attack on 'Regional Policy' as administered by Whitehall, *Killing the Goose: Taxes on Capital are Taxes on Capitalism* by Bracewell-Milnes and *They Voted No Aid to British Leyland*, by Richard Henderson and Nicholas Budgen. The Selsdon Group also published an important Report on Council Housing, compiled by Richard Henderson, which recommended the 'giving away' of council houses.[26] All these publications were available at Conservative Central Office bookshop, and were widely read by Conservatives. Many members of the Party were also attracted to an important 'Selsdon Group Seminar' on *Reducing the Public Sector* at St Ermin's Hotel, in June 1976, at which several Group members spoke, including Ridley, Richard Henderson and Russell Lewis, who had done much to propagate the idea of 'denationalization'. Concluding his speech, Lewis invited his audience to consider the popular 'revolution' that might flow from a policy of denationalization, anticipating the political tone of the 'privatization' programme of the mid-1980s:

> In fact denationalization is perfectly practicable, and there are many examples of it being carried out. These include coal mines in Germany and Queensland, Australia, railways in Belgium and shipping lines in the United States, Canada,

> Australia and France. The most encouraging example however is that of Volkswagen which was sold in 1960 to a million and a half shareholders. That is the example for Conservatives. Let them resolve to associate the demise of socialism with the growth of popular capitalism. Just as Henry VIII assured the success of the Reformation by selling the monasteries to the gentry, so the Conservative revolution of the future may be made safe by parcelling out State concerns among the people.[27]

The influence of the Selsdon Group is difficult to judge; however, it was important as the first grass-roots rebellion within the Conservative Party against the corporatist Keynesian policies reverted to by Heath after his U-turn of 1971. The Group was the first of a number of 'caucuses' and ginger-groups within and on the fringes of the Party to emerge during the period 1973–5. Indeed, in political terms this period bore more than a passing resemblance to the years 1942–4, when the same wing of the Conservative Party had first tried to organize itself to defend the principles of economic liberalism within the Party. Then, economic liberalism had been derided as a 'reactionary' doctrine; almost exactly thirty years later it was unashamedly touted as the 'radical alternative'. Furthermore, Harold Wilson's Government, which came to power in March 1974, after an initial outburst of radicalism guided by Tony Benn, was forced to retreat rapidly from its nationalization plans and large public-spending programme under the pressures of inflation and collapsing confidence in the currency; and by 1975 a retreat to what was virtually a monetarist position on the economy was in full swing. The Callaghan Government's capitulation to the IMF in 1976, and his speech to the Party Conference in September of the same year, merely rubber-stamped the analysis of Britain's economic plight offered by the IEA.[28] Indeed, by 1976, the Keynesian consensus had all but broken down, and, even in Cabinet, the IEA analysis had been accepted in preference to the alternative offered by the Labour Party's own left wing in the shape of Tony Benn's 'Alternative Strategy'.[29] The militancy of groups like the Selsdon Group reflected this shattering of the intellectual 'consensus' that had ruled British politics since the late 1940s, and which now buckled, as Hayek had predicted it would, under the weight of the brute experience of inflation, unemployment and the industrial disorder and strikes which accompanied inflation. Lord Blake, the historian of the Conservative Party, analyzed the circumstances in which the IEA's counter-revolution had come of age in an essay appropriately called 'A Changed Climate' which he wrote for a collection of essays entitled *The Conservative Opportunity*, in 1976. In Blake's view,

> The general point remains that the Conservatives embarked in 1970 on a new course which did not *at that time* – and this is a point of key importance – appear intellectually reputable. Lacking complete conviction in their own policies, constantly criticised by the 'opinion-formers', who still favoured a sort of Lab/Lib/Whitehall consensus, ministers under what they believed to be the pressure of circumstances made a volte-face.
>
> If the intellectual atmosphere is going to be the same at the next general election . . . there would be little prospect of Conservative success except in the event of a major economic crisis, some traumatic debacle such as the split in the Labour Party in 1931. *In fact, however, there are signs of one of those rare and profound changes in the intellectual climate which occur only once or twice in a hundred years, like the triumph of the entrepreneurial ethos in nineteenth-century England, or the rise of Voltairean scepticism in eighteenth-century France or the disappearance of Puritanism after 1660. There is a wind of change in Britain and much of the democratic world – and it comes from the right, not the left* . . .*
>
> The Trendy Lefties who were the apotheosis of the 1960s and early 1970s look like dinosaurs . . .
>
> Getting 'government off our backs', 'setting the people free', 'a property-owning democracy' – these are admirable Conservative objectives, but they will require hard work, determination and toughness if they are to be achieved. Yet there is no real alternative. The Conservative Party cannot seek the 'middle ground' as it did from 1950 to 1964. The World has changed. There is now no middle ground to seek. Nothing less will suffice than a major reversal of the trends which ever since 1945 Labour has promoted and

* Author's italics.

> Conservatives have accepted. There is no other way of reducing taxation and a Conservative Government which cannot achieve that might as well shut up shop.[30]

In support of Blake's thesis, two young Oxford Conservatives, John Patten and John Redwood (both future Cabinet Ministers in Mrs Thatcher's and John Major's Governments), sketched out the future course that such a reforming Conservative Government might take in essays on 'Housing and Society' (by Patten) and 'Managing the Economy' (by Redwood). The unusually feverish intellectual atmosphere that enveloped the Party in the wake of Heath's election defeat and the apparent failure of Keynesian economics was reflected not only in the formation of the Selsdon Group, but also in the founding of the Conservative Philosophy Group and the Salisbury Group. Both these Groups sought to bring some coherence to the ideological confusion that the failure of Heath's government provoked in the Party. The Conservative Philosophy Group (CPG) was started in 1973–4 by the Conservative MPs Hugh Fraser and Jonathan Aitken and the Cambridge academic John Casey, who, at Gonville and Caius, became the mentor to a rising generation of young Conservatives. The Group met initially at Fraser's house in Campden Hill Square, west London, and began life as a forum to involve academics and journalists in discussion of the Party's broad principles. The group met four or five times a year, when a paper was read by an academic or a politician, followed by an informal discussion. The paper was usually on a broad philosophical theme, such as Edward Norman on 'Christianity and the Bomb', which allowed the discussants to argue about general principles and ideas, rather than detailed policy proposals.* Amongst the first speakers at the CPG were Milton Friedman and Peter Bauer. The Group's proceedings were conducted in an informal manner, and the discussions were confidential. It did not seek to publish, or to put forward a coherent ideology of Conservatism, but it did provide a '"group" ethos of right-thinking academics' who provided substantial intellectual ballast

* Foremost amongst the academics at the CPG were Professor Roger Scruton, of Birkbeck College, London University, Anthony Quinton and Hugh Trevor-Roper from Oxford, Maurice Cowling from Cambridge, and Kenneth Minogue, Michael Oakeshott and William and Shirley Letwin from the LSE. Journalists who attended included Frank Johnson, Peregrine Worsthorne, John O'Sullivan, Ferdinand Mount, and, later, Charles Moore and Noel Malcolm.

to a Party which was entering one of its rare periods of intellectual introspection.[31] The 'Salisbury Group' was formed in 1976, similarly concerned with developing a broad philosophical position to exploit Blake's 'Conservative Opportunity'. The moving spirits behind the Salisbury Group (named after the late-Victorian Conservative Prime Minister the 2nd Marquess of Salisbury) were the present Marquess of Salisbury, Diana Spearman, Maurice Cowling, Michael Oakeshott, Peter Utley, William and Shirley Letwin and Charles Pickthorne, the son of the Conservative MP Sir Kenneth Pickthorne. The Salisbury Group published a series of pamphlets between 1978 and 1982, but otherwise met little; by the late 1970s it was little more than 'a moribund discussion group'.[32] It was only revitalized in the late 1970s with the arrival of Roger Scruton, who was introduced to the Group by Maurice Cowling; Scruton formed a close working relationship with Diana Spearman. This duo was largely responsible for launching the *Salisbury Review* magazine in 1982. To Scruton, the Salisbury Group, now firmly under his direction, became a tool for the elaboration of a Conservative social philosophy to complement the IEA's economic philosophy (the latter having, by 1982, become the dominant intellectual credo within the Party).[33] Scruton wrote the following 'Statement' for the first issue of the new magazine:

> The [Salisbury] Group has served as a forum for discussion; it has no official ties with the Conservative Party and no specific purpose other than that of giving voice to conservative instincts. Its members are, however, united in the view that there is more to conservatism than economic policy, and that the abiding Conservative vision can be given expression in a language suited to our changed and changing World.[34]

If this was a backhanded compliment to the IEA, the editors of the *Salisbury Review* quickly showed their independence of thought by publishing, in the first issue, John Casey's article on 'One Nation: The Politics of Race', in which he advocated the compulsory repatriation of immigrants. Thereafter, the *Salisbury Review* attracted more controversy than it merited – its influence on the Party was certainly less than is sometimes claimed. The group was chiefly interesting as a manifestation of the debate which would rage in the Conservative Party during the later 1970s and early 1980s about how far the doctrine of 'economic liberalism' had a role to play in a distinctly 'Conservative Philosophy'. It is ironic that the Group's most celebrated self-publicist, Roger Scruton, should have become, in the late 1980s, identified as a leading 'Thatcherite intellectual', when he was, with the Salisbury Group, a leading advocate of that traditional, authoritarian, hierarchical Conservatism that the IEA, the Selsdon Group and all the younger Conservatives were arguing was no longer relevant to the modern world. Scruton's book on *The Meaning of Conservatism*, published in 1980 was, if anything, a comprehensive rebuttal of Hayekian liberalism. He concluded that: 'In this book, I have argued for a view of legitimacy that places public before private, society before individual, privilege before right.'[35] If nothing else, the Salisbury Group at least demonstrated that the pivotal intellectual battle now ranged within the ranks of the *Conservatives*, rather than amongst the Socialists as it had from 1930 to 1970.

The Selsdon Group, the Conservative Philosophy Group and the Salisbury Group were all symptomatic of the Conservative Party's attempt to come to terms with the intellectual disintegration of the politics of the 'Middle Way' and to absorb the economic liberalism of the IEA into the mainstream of Conservative thinking. This was, of course, much easier to do in Opposition than in Government, and the Labour Party, by contrast, merely tried to ignore the intellectual confusion provoked by the economic crisis of 1974–6, and muddled through to electoral defeat in 1979.[36] On the fringes of the Conservative Party too, different organizations were founded to campaign for different aspects of the new agenda of economic liberalism. Chief amongst these was the National Association for Freedom, renamed the Freedom Association in 1979. The National Association For Freedom (NAFF) became the best known of the pressure-groups and ginger-groups of the Right during the 1970s by directly confronting the power of trade unions. The origins of NAFF are revealing, as it grew out of an initial conversation between representatives of two of the organizations which had been originally formed during the war, Aims of Industry and British United Industrialists, one charged with raising money from industry to put the case for free-market capitalism before the public, and the other to do the same within the Conservative Party. Norris McWhirter, one of the founders of NAFF, recalled later how the NAFF had come into being:

> In the dark days of 1975, with the IMF knocking at the door of 10 Downing Street, the IRA rampant in London, and 6¼ million fellow citizens inside [trade union] closed shops, two men met to suggest some new initiative. They were the late Colonel Juan Hobbs, Secretary of British United Industrialists, and Michael Ivens, Director of Aims of Industry. What was needed was some kind of association which would defend our rights and liberties.[37]

The man that Ivens and Hobbs sought out to lead such an 'association' was Viscount De L'Isle, VC, a distinguished soldier, who became the first Chairman of the NAFF. They were joined by the McWhirter brothers of *The Guinness Book of Records* fame, who had both been actively involved in Conservative politics since the 1950s. The death of Ross McWhirter at the hands of the IRA only a week before the launch of the NAFF on 2 December 1975 ensured that it was born in a blaze of publicity, which rarely let up thereafter. At its launch, De L'Isle 'spoke of there being four recognizable threats to freedom in Britain, a failure to see that the country was drifting towards drab collectivism; inflation; the growing machinery of Government; and the extra-Parliamentary powers of organized Labour'.[38] It was the latter 'threat to freedom' that the NAFF focused its efforts on, and the organization became famous for fighting the cause of workers against the closed shop, beginning with the case in 1976 of three British Rail employees who were sacked for not joining a union. The NAFF took their case to the European Court at Strasbourg and won. Their finest hour came with the celebrated Grunwick Dispute in 1977, when the NAFF gave considerable legal, financial and logistical support to the management of a film-reprocessing plant in London which would not accept the closed shop – the requirement that every worker belong to a union – in their factory. Grunwick was the scene of sometimes violent demonstrations on the picket line by militant trade unionists, but the NAFF, resorting to military-style tactics (and, indeed, using lorries from an Army barracks) managed to keep the plant open by smuggling film out of the plant under the cover of darkness. It was the first time that the power of the unions had been challenged at a practical level since the victory of the miners in 1972 and 1974, and the NAFF won a conclusive victory – it was also a portent of the industrial strife that was to characterize the Thatcher governments' attempt to repeat the success of Grunwick on a national scale against the miners in 1984–5. Intellectually, the power of the unions to enforce over-manning and low productivity in their own, short-term interests, had long been analyzed as a major obstacle to the fulfilment of a liberal counter-revolution, but the NAFF were Hayek's 'foot-soldiers' who actually went out and helped individual companies and individuals fight the unions.

The Grunwick dispute was of peculiar and long-term significance to the revival of economic liberalism: it represented the first concerted resistance to the power of organized labour to appear in Britain since the 1930s. The message of the NAFF was of the kind that would come to be known as staunchly 'Thatcherite' (Mrs Thatcher herself attended NAFF's inaugural subscription dinner in 1977), and in this sense the advent of 'Thatcherism' was, indeed, counter-revolutionary, in that groups like NAFF actively sought to reverse the tendency for trade-union power to increase ever more, an increase that had been sanctioned by the Keynesian system of demand management. That trade unions were able to enforce pay increases regardless of productivity ratios ensured, especially during the 1970s, that they were the only section of society to benefit from inflation; and so, *per se*, the fight against inflation became primarily a battle against trade union power. Although the Grunwick dispute was, ostensibly, only about one aspect of that power – the closed shop – the war effectively began at Grunwick. Nor is the martial metaphor chosen lightly, as the various organizations involved, such as NAFF and the Institute for the Study of Conflict, all used military-style tactics and were staffed by ex-army or, in a few cases, ex-intelligence personnel. For instance, John Gouriet, the first director and co-founder of NAFF, was an ex-army major, which perhaps accounted for NAFF's almost military approach to industrial conflicts 'in the field'. But then this was the sharp end of a counter-revolution which had now begun in earnest.

The NAFF attracted to its ranks several of those younger Conservatives who had learnt their free-market economics during the 1970s, mainly from the IEA, as well as the older generation of free-market Conservatives. Six Conservative MPs sat on the National Council of the NAFF – Ridley, Jill Knight, Rhodes Boyson, Winston Churchill, Stephen Hastings and Sir Frederic Bennett – as well as Peregrine Worsthorne, Ralph Harris, Michael Ivens, Teresa Gorman (Secretary of The Association of Self-Employed People and the most libertarian of future Conservative MPs) and Brian Crozier, Director of the Institute for the Study of Conflict (of which more later). A Director of NAFF was Robert Moss, a colleague of Crozier's at the Institute for the Study of Conflict and Director of The *Economist* Intelligence Unit and author, in 1976, of the important book *The Collapse of Democracy*. In 1976, the NAFF's magazine was started, initially entitled *Freedom Today*, and later called the *Free Nation*; it was edited by Stephen Eyres, of Swinton College and the Selsdon Group. Eyres was the only paid writer on the paper; the other principal contributors, all from the same background, were David Alexander, Russell Lewis, John O'Sullivan, Robert Moss, Brian Crozier and, rather more surprisingly, Edward Pearce, now of the *Guardian*.* Another frequent contributor was Ken Watkins, a Council Member of the NAFF, and Lecturer in Politics at Sheffield University. Like many, he was a former Communist who, as Chairman of the LSE Communist Club in the late 1940s, had been responsible for expelling Alfred Sherman from the Party. In the initial rush of enthusiasm for the NAFF it could count on up to fifteen part-time or full-time unpaid staff or assistants; men like Chris Tame, later founder of the Libertarian Alliance, Graham Mather, who was much involved in the legal actions over Grunwick, Nigel Morgan, an Irish Guards Officer who later worked for Alfred Sherman at the Centre for Policy Studies, and Gerald Hartup, one of the present-day staff of a much smaller Freedom Association. Another recruit to NAFF who attracted a lot of welcome publicity was Lady Morrison of Lambeth, Herbert Morrison's widow, who became a member of NAFF's governing council.[39]

NAFF was probably the most important of the 'libertarian' pressure groups formed in the mid-1970s. Especially during the Grunwick Dispute, it raised the question of restrictive practices and the closed shop to the top of the political agenda, and exposed to public scrutiny union practices which the union leaders would have preferred to have remained obscured from public view. Indeed, the NAFF was as much a 'consciousness-raising' exercise as anything else, and in this respect it was remarkably successful. By 1978, there were probably about twenty thousand members of NAFF, then a huge figure for a fringe political organization.[40] The NAFF also attracted other 'libertarians' to its

* Other contributors included Ridley, Norris McWhirter, Lord Blake, Teddy Taylor MP and Gerald Howarth, later also an MP.

ranks, including representatives of the 'Association of the Self-Employed People', run by Teresa Gorman and David Kelly, who wrote for the *Free Nation*. They had their own newspaper, called *Counter-attack*, and Teresa Gorman stood as a Libertarian candidate at Streatham in October 1974. Antony Fisher also set up his own newsletter in October 1974, *Yesterday, Today and Tomorrow*, edited by the ubiquitous Stephen Eyres, which dealt with much the same issues as NAFF. The NAFF was also closely linked, through Robert Moss and Brian Crozier, to the Institute for the Study of Conflict, founded in 1970 by Crozier. Crozier, again, a former left-winger, was a journalist who specialized in defence and counter-insurgency matters; he had made his name with *The Rebels*, a study of counter-insurgency methods published in 1964. In 1970 he founded the Institute for the Study of Conflict to analyze and report on the Communist threat of subversion and insurgency in Britain and throughout the world. The first Chairman of the Institute (ISC) was Leonard Schapiro, Professor of Government at the LSE; other members of the Council of the ISC included Max Beloff, S. E. Finer from Manchester University and Hugh Seton-Watson from London University. The Institute ran a series of 'Conflict Studies', as well as a range of 'Study Groups' on a variety of topics. A lot of the Institute's output covered overseas developments, but the ISC also specialized in looking at union subversion in Britain, thus, to a certain extent, complementing the work of the NAFF and even MI5. During the 1970s the ISC published a number of highly controversial documents on this subject, beginning with a 'Preliminary Survey' on 'Subversion in British Industry' by the new Conservative MP and former editor of the *Spectator*, Nigel Lawson. Lawson's survey was followed up by a full-scale ISC Report by a Study Group on 'Sources of Conflict in British Industry', published in February 1974, at the same time as Heath's Government was brought to its knees by the miners.* The Report claimed to be a comprehensive exposure of those politically motivated Trotskyist or Communist-linked trade unionists within the trade union movement, who, under cover of legitimate industrial action, sought to create a revolutionary situation. The ISC thus drew some grave conclusions about the threat to democracy in Britain:

* The Members of the Study Group were Ken Watkins, Brian Crozier, Professor A. J. M. Sykes of Strathclyde University, Professor A. R. Ilersic of Bedford College, University of London and Professor Raymond Thomas of the University of Bath.

> There can be no reasonable doubt that in several major British industries members of the Communist Party and other left-wing organizations exert substantial influence in provoking and exacerbating conflict . . . Any serious study of the available evidence does more than indicate that a deliberate effort of considerable magnitude is being staged to disrupt industry for political ends; *it shows that growing extremist organizations exist in some British Trade Unions capable of exerting influence wholly disproportionate to the numbers involved.* It also shows that the aims of the extremist organizations are incompatible with any normally-accepted concepts of democracy in Britain.[41]

Not surprisingly, given that this Report appeared at the time of the 1974 miners' strike, it attracted widespread publicity and the *Observer*, for instance, published Section 8 of the Report on 'Militant extremism and political subversion' in full. A similar Report by an ISC Study Group on 'Marxist and Radical Penetration' of higher education in Britain published in 1977 also commanded widespread press attention.* Mrs Thatcher took a great interest in the work of ISC, and Brian Crozier was introduced to her by Viscount De L'Isle and Norris McWhirter in 1976. Mrs Thatcher was impressed by Crozier's views on security and intelligence matters – a subject which she knew nothing about – and Crozier acted as an unofficial adviser to her on these subjects during the period 1976–9. She was also impressed by Robert Moss and he is widely credited with her 'Iron Lady' speech delivered at Kensington Town Hall in 1976, which first marked her out as an unusually implacable foe of Communism in an age of *détente*. Robert Conquest, the historian of Stalin's Russia, also contributed to several of her speeches on foreign affairs. The ISC gave Mrs Thatcher expert advice in a field of which she was largely ignorant – security and foreign affairs. Moss and Crozier were, like the NAFF, applying the broad principles of liberalism to specific, often controversial and occasionally hostile situations.[42]

The ISC, NAFF, Selsdon Group, Salisbury Group and eventually the Centre for Policy Studies were all symptomatic of the political

* The author of the Report was Professor Julius Gould, and other members of the Study Group were Caroline Cox, Kenneth Minogue from the LSE, Professor Antony Flew from Reading, Ken Watkins, Brian Crozier and Professor David Martin of the LSE.

realignment that took place in favour of economic liberalism during the mid-1970s. Their activities represented the end of the post-war consensus, not only on what had been regarded as the 'Right' of politics, but on the 'Left' as well. For one of the most interesting features of this realignment was the growing intellectual defection from Socialism and Marxism to the camp of economic liberalism as it became increasingly obvious that the 'liberty' and 'freedom' of the working class which many had fought to secure under Socialism was in fact a mirage, and that liberalism – and not Conservatism, as it was traditionally understood – offered a better path to those same goals of 'freedom' and 'liberty' which had proved so elusive under Socialism. Several of those involved in the work of the IEA (such as Arthur Seldon) and the NAFF (such as Brian Crozier) were just such intellectual converts. Brian Crozier, Australian by birth, took the philosophy of Marxism to be 'self-evident' during the 1930s when he moved to England, and the young Crozier became a member of the Left Book Club in 1937, a devotee of Harold Laski, and voted Labour at the 1945 general election. His political conversion happened while he was working on the foreign news desk of the *News Chronicle* when he read the 1947 memoirs of one of the first Communist dissidents, Victor Kravchenko, as well as George Orwell's *Animal Farm*. He later learnt his economic liberalism from Maurice Allais of the Mont Pèlerin Society.[43] Robert Conquest, Soviet Russia's most authoritative academic critic had also, briefly, been a member of the Communist Party. Harry Ferns, author of the IEA's original pamphlet on the founding of an independent university (which led to the establishment of Buckingham University) was also an ex-Communist. Caroline Cox, one of the foremost advocates of introducing a 'market' into education and an important member of the Centre for Policy Studies, was a former Fabian Socialist and Labour Party voter and supporter. These people developed their critique of Socialism from *within* the Socialist camp, and thus tended to be more zealous than the relatively apolitical Conservatives in their denunciation of their former Party allegiances. There is some truth to the claim that only good Socialists made good Thatcherites. The gradual trickle of defections to the 'free-market' camp turned into a flood in the mid-1970s, many of them ushered in that direction by the IEA or similar institutions – Brian Walden, Desmond Donnelly (rather earlier), Hugh Thomas (later Chairman of the Centre for Policy Studies), Bernard Levin of *The Times*, Reg Prentice, the former Labour

Cabinet Minister, the journalists Edward Pearce and Paul Johnson, the historian Max Beloff, and Lord Chalfont. Some of them published their own accounts of their intellectual journeys in a book called *Right Turn* (1978). Most of them laid the blame for their disenchantment with the Labour Party and Socialism on the unions and the intolerance and ideological dogmatism of the Marxists who now exerted considerable influence in the Labour Party and elsewhere. The most famous convert was probably Paul Johnson, as he had been at the heart of the Labour establishment for many years, most prominently as editor of the *New Statesman* from 1965 to 1970. In September 1977, his old paper published his own magisterial renunciation of his former faith in a series of articles which were called 'Farewell to the Labour Party', published in abbreviated form in the *Sunday Telegraph* on 11 September 1977. Johnson pinpointed the Labour Government's failure to pass its trade union reform proposals ('In Place of Strife') into legislation in 1969 as his own point of no return:

> In the meantime, the Unions had been given the 'closed shop' as part of the surrender. For me, this was the turning-point in my loyalty to the Party. For whatever the private reservations of certain Cabinet Ministers and back-benchers and some of them, I know, hate it as much as I do myself, they united without public dissent to legalise the Closed shop. It was what the Party now stood for; the right of union bureaucrats and bully-boys to coerce individuals into collective conformity, as a prelude to further erosions of human freedom ... It hands over the individual to the mercy of the Kangaroo court and the menace of the militant shop-floor mob.
>
> One reason why I joined the Labour Party was that I believed it stood by the helpless and persecuted, and by the angular non-conformist who – wrong-headedly perhaps – reserved the right to think for himself. Labour's closed shop legislation represented a historic shift in its doctrinal loyalties, from the beleaguered individual to the grinning triumph of the field-grey regiment. I, and others, found ourselves deceived. Where now was Bevan's 'imaginative tolerance'? ...
>
> For me personally, the issue is not primarily political but moral. As Labour has drifted into collectivism, I have come

> to appreciate, perhaps for the first time in my life, the overwhelming strength of my own attachment to the individual human spirit . . . the individual conscience is the most precious gift humanity possesses. A political creed which respects it – whatever evil it may otherwise do or stand for – is inherently healthy, for it contains within it a self-correcting mechanism. But in a system of belief where conscience is collectivised, there is no dependable barrier along the highway which ultimately may lead to Auschwitz and the Gulag.
>
> I do not intend to travel even one miserable inch along that fearful road.[44]

To Johnson and others, the prophecy of Hayek's *The Road to Serfdom* was rapidly coming to pass.

An equally spectacular retraction was made by the economist John (later Lord) Vaizey, who had served on the executive of the Fabian Society and who had served the Labour Party both locally and nationally since the late 1940s. In the early 1970s he got to know Mrs Thatcher whilst she was Secretary of State for Education, and by 1975 was one of her more trusted and intimate advisers. Although he was raised to the peerage in 1978 by Harold Wilson, he resigned the Labour Whip and took the Conservative Whip in 1979. On Mrs Thatcher's election as leader of the Conservative Party in 1975, Vaizey wrote her a letter of congratulation which expressed both the disenchantment of many like him and the hope that they saw in the liberal-Conservatives led by Mrs Thatcher:

> As one of your fans, I must say that I am extraordinarily glad for our country that you are now leader of a great party . . . You are not only the leader of the Tory Party, but you are the political leader of our nation, and I think that many people wish you to call attention to the fact that the nation is not divided by class or by sex or by race, but it is divided between the people who want to serve the nation by earning their own living, by giving voluntary services to the Community, and those who for purely selfish interests, in the trade unions or property developers, seek to make money for themselves and let the rest go to hell. It is divided between those who prudently wish to preserve their savings

> which they have seen, like myself, absolutely taken away by inflation and by penal taxation, and whose careful plans for their careers are utterly wrecked by the fact that things are changed overnight . . . You take with you my warmest and most deep congratulations, and the hope that after the crash which we are going to have this spring, the country will begin at last to pull itself together after a quarter of a century of absolutely catastrophic government by the Bill Piles of this age.[45]

During the period 1975 to 1979, Mrs Thatcher gently coaxed Vaizey towards a full declaration for the Conservative Party, writing to him in October 1978 that 'I realise that it will be difficult for you, but in a way the Labour Party has left *you* because it has changed so much from its former beliefs.'[46] In December 1980, Vaizey, awaiting a heart operation in St Thomas's Hospital which he did not expect to survive, went public with his conversion and wrote a long letter to *The Times* explaining his flight from the Labour Party to Mrs Thatcher's Conservatism, and his support for her policies as against any 'Social Democratic' alternative (as was then being proposed by the renegade Labour MPs Roy Jenkins, Shirley Williams, Bill Rodgers and David Owen). The letter, which he called his 'testament', is reproduced in full as Appendix IV as it is an unusually honest account of an intellectual conversion; it outlines why people such as Vaizey had to move over all the way to a 'Thatcherite' position, abandoning a 'Social Democratic' position altogether:

> There is no longer a set of social democratic ideas that will work. Keynesianism is intellectually dead. With Trade Unions no incomes policy can ever work. With our State industries productivity will always be abysmal. Nobody, not even Shirley Williams, has the faintest idea how to redistribute income; the tax and benefit system is far too complex and arbitrary to yield a simple progressive result free from major anomalies. Social democratic theory is just plain wrong.[47] *

* See Appendix IV for the letter in full.

Vaizey was inundated with letters from Mrs Thatcher's supporters thanking him for speaking out. The 'converts' were amongst the most committed ideologues of economic liberalism during the 1980s, as they campaigned for Thatcherism with all the messianic zeal with which they had formerly campaigned for Socialism or Communism. Temperamentally, they remained the same; they remained true believers, but merely changed the political doctrine in which they believed. 'They became crusaders against what had been the object of their passionate devotion.'[48] They became as skilled and articulate in their advocacy of Thatcherism as they had been in their advocacy of Socialism or Communism, and many of them went on to work for the 'think-tanks' of the Thatcherite counter-revolution. Moreover, they were, in the main, ideologues and *not* party politicians, which meant that they became the most devoted supporters of Mrs Thatcher's *idea* of economic liberalism, and so gave her the sort of unqualified intellectual support that she failed to find amongst her own Conservative backbenchers, pragmatic politicians who might have believed in economic liberalism, but only so far as it appeared to win them back their seats at the next elections. Vaizey, for instance, wrote Mrs Thatcher a stream of letters during her difficult first two years in power, offering her support and encouragement of a kind that she would not have found around her own Cabinet table. A typical reply from Mrs Thatcher was that of 10 March 1980:

> Thank you very much for your kind letter of February 26. I cannot tell you how much I appreciate your support and encouragement. It has done my morale no end of good. Yes, I shall continue to follow my instincts and not be put off by certain commentators who never seem to travel north of Watford except at Election time.[49]

The converts thus brought the passion and the intellectual vigour to economic liberalism, as well as the political and organizational skills to put the idea into practice, skills which they had often learnt on the other side of the political trenches. Of no-one was this more true than Alfred Sherman, the moving spirit of the Centre for Policy Studies.

The only problem with the 'Peasant's Revolt' against Heath was that it was just that – all peasants and no barons. Whilst the junior echelons of the Party organized themselves into ginger-groups, pressure-groups and debating societies, the leadership of the Party remained largely unaware – perhaps blissfully unaware – of the intellectual revolution that was taking place on the back-benches and amongst what amounted to a new cadre of Conservative activists. Even after Heath's election defeat in February 1974, the Shadow Cabinet, as it now became, showed little inclination to re-examine the Party's policies, let alone the whole intellectual basis on which those policies rested. Neither was this very surprising, as Harold Wilson's new Labour Government's majority rested on a knife-edge in a hung Parliament, and another election was expected within a few months. It was not surprising if the majority of the Shadow Cabinet were more preoccupied with the short term than with the long. 'The Tory instinct was not to go into another election campaign proclaiming doubts about the policies they had been following just a few months before.'[50]

The exception to this rule was Sir Keith Joseph, the great disappointment of the economic liberals in government. By 1973, when the 'economic radicals' and the Selsdon Group raised the standard of revolt against Heath's perceived reversion to Keynesian demand management, Sir Keith Joseph seemed to be a lost cause. However, Joseph had been 'shocked' out of his immersion in ministerial routine by two articles in the *Daily Telegraph* in August and September 1973 by a journalist who had helped him write articles and speeches in the late 1960s, Alfred Sherman. Sherman was a quintessential 'convert'; an East End Jew, educated at Hackney Downs Secondary School, the great forcing house of successful East End Jewry, he had embraced Socialism in the 1930s as the automatic political creed of his environment. (His father had been a Labour Councillor.) However, even then Sherman showed his disinclination to do anything by halves, and instead of merely joining the Labour Party he became a member of the Communist Party and went off to the Spanish Civil War as a machine-gunner. Sherman quoted Hegel half a century later to describe himself: 'men are so hungry for certainties that they will readily subordinate consciousness and conscience to it; men need great ideals to move them, and the passions created outlast the struggles they served.'[51]

He read economics at the LSE, and after the war undertook a tour of recently 'Communized' Yugoslavia as an interpreter for an NUS delegation. During the course of this tour he was paid for freelance articles by the *Observer*, being better informed than his NUS colleagues as he alone could speak Serbo-Croat, amongst a number of other languages. It was in Yugoslavia that he first questioned Communist orthodoxy after seeing the regime at work, and he quickly realized that the key principle of 'freedom' was being failed by Socialism in practice, and that 'freedom' for the masses was more likely to be found under economic liberalism. Like Popper in the Vienna of 1920s, he recognized that freedom was more important than equality, and that the attempt to realize equality under Communism had seriously endangered freedom. By the 1950s, Sherman was an avid and highly articulate exponent of the free market, which put him as much on the fringes of politics in Macmillan's Britain as Communism had put him on the edge of politics in Neville Chamberlain's Britain.

He worked as Foreign Editor for the *Jerusalem Post* briefly, and then as an economic adviser to Israel's Free Enterprise Party. In the early 1960s he returned to Britain, and was appointed Local Government Correspondent of the *Daily Telegraph*. It was through his work as a journalist that Sherman first met Sir Keith Joseph, who was then Minister of Housing. During Joseph's years of opposition, 1964–70, he chaired two conferences on local government which Sherman organized, and in 1968 Joseph showed Sherman a speech that he was intending to make and asked for his comments. Sherman proceeded to transform it in ten minutes, and Joseph, impressed with Sherman's ability to talk and think in headlines, used him as a speech- and article-writer from 1969 to 1970, when, in a series of articles for *The Times* and in speeches, Joseph began to articulate the new free-market brand of Conservatism, which he had already developed intellectually with the help of the IEA. Sherman was, as was the IEA, expecting great things of Joseph in Government, and was similarly disappointed. As Sherman wrote later: 'I had worked with Keith Joseph on speeches and articles in 1969–70, when he became a lion in opposition, but lost him to the Civil Servants when he returned to Office.'[52] However, as Sherman found out, all was not totally lost, as his two *Telegraph* articles of the summer of 1973 'spoilt [Joseph's] summer holiday', and prompted him to begin that process of re-thinking which led to his great denunciation of the Keynesian consensus.[53] The second article by Sherman was entitled 'The subsidised road to good intentions'; in it he challenged the 'fashionable view' that subsidized public transport reduced chaos on the roads. The first, 'Counting the cost of new towns' attacked the concept of social engineering that lay behind successive governments' development of New Towns:

> the social engineers destroyed older communities without producing new ones. Where the balance – social and demographic – which planners claim to be specially qualified to impose, is concerned, the new towns are patently worse than the natural produce. What was left of the extended family, resisting the assault on it by Welfare and 'housing', was sacrificed in the new towns. Characteristically, their creators and propagandists have not gone to live in them.[54]

This first article must have been particularly thought-provoking for Joseph, as he had been the minister responsible for much of the 'new housing' in the early 1960s. Both articles were characteristically trenchant and incisive critiques of the whole nature of *dirigiste* 'planning' and social engineering that Heath's Government – though it contained Mrs Thatcher and Joseph – still seemed to be blindly pursuing as the 1970s progressed.

In February 1974, even before the election, Joseph rang Sherman and invited him for a talk at his Mulberry Walk house in Chelsea. There began a series of long conversations, lasting into March and April, during which Sherman lambasted Heath's Government for deserting the promise of 'Selsdon Man', and in particular criticizing Heath's handling of monetary policy. Sherman had honed his critique of Heath's Government in the years that he spent watching it from the safety of the *Daily Telegraph*, and now all this was released in a verbal torrent. Sherman and Joseph were joined for some of these conversations by Alan Walters, who echoed Sherman's damning verdict on Heath's Government, and Walters convinced Joseph of the need for the tight control of the money supply if non-inflationary economic recovery were to be possible, much as he had argued in the 'Memorial to the Prime Minister'. Some of these conversations took place in Sherman's flat in Allen Street, off Kensington High Street, which was more convenient for Alan Walters who lived in Marloes Road, just around the corner from Sherman. At Joseph's house in Chelsea they were joined by Mrs Thatcher, who was as impressed as Joseph by the Sherman-Walters analysis; and David Howell also supported their critique. However, it was Joseph, not Mrs Thatcher, who resolved to argue the case for monetarism and the free-market as presented by Walters and Sherman within the Conservative Party.

Mrs Thatcher and Joseph were both attracted by Sherman's sheer intellectual brightness and his hunger for ideas. He could be a spell-binding talker, and his journalistic training meant that he could not only lay down complex principles and philosophical positions, but he could also translate those principles and philosophies into telling phrases and what we would now call 'sound-bites'. Nonetheless, Sherman and Joseph were also, as many people noted at the time, very different people:

> To Joseph, politics was a high-minded exercise in principle, ideally practised without descending to the distressing levels of personalities. Sherman, gnomic grin on his face, relished the level of personalities; he was deeply concerned with principles, too, but he liked to put a name to every bit of villainy he uncovered ... Then there was the contrast between the two men physically; the one slim and dapper and fairly obviously the product of an English public school; the other short and round, and looking like most Englishmen's idea of an alien.[55]

Sherman was the quintessential intellectual, a man who lived for ideas, and for those not interested in the role of ideas in the affairs of man – such as virtually all Conservative back-benchers – Sherman was thus of strictly limited appeal, for besides his intellectualism he had few social graces and little small talk. In an *Observer* profile of 21 August 1983 Sherman quoted Montesquieu to describe his own dilemma: 'A man of ideas usually has difficulty in a society. Few meet with his approval. He is bored with the majority of people whom he chooses to call bad company. Inevitably, they are made aware of his disapproval. Thus he creates so many enemies.' Furthermore, he could, on occasion, be arrogant and querulous; many people suspected that his chief pleasure in life was to *épater la bourgeoisie* – hence the stream of provocative and outspoken comments that would often shock guests around the lunch table at the CPS. He often seemed to specialize in being wilfully 'politically incorrect'. He managed to reserve his plainest speaking manner for the delicate subject of immigration, advocating an extremely restrictive policy that was always at odds with his libertarian views on economic matters. His views on immigration and, equally important, the way in which he expressed them put him beyond the pale even in such company as the Selsdon Group. He liked to think of himself as a 'man of ideas fallen among party politicians', and he did little to hide his disdain for the intelligence of the average Tory MP. A wise Conservative, like William Whitelaw, hid his intelligence behind a façade of bluff and humorous pragmatism. However, to those interested in ideas, there was no more stimulating companion than Alfred Sherman, and Sir Keith Joseph and Mrs Thatcher were both eager to learn from him in the 1970s. He had no greater admirer than Mrs Thatcher during that period, for, as she wrote to him after his contribution to her Party conference speech, 'Few people spark off ideas as well as you do . . .'[56]

Convinced by the Sherman-Walters analysis of where Heath's Government had gone wrong, Joseph pressed for a re-examination of economic policy within the Shadow Cabinet. However, two factors seem to have convinced him that he was not going to get the sort of thorough-going re-examination which he wanted. First, he was passed over for the job of Shadow Chancellor by Heath after the retirement from politics of Anthony Barber; Heath gave the job to Robert Carr. Instead, at his own request, Joseph was given responsibility for developing party policy, without a shadow departmental portfolio. Secondly, in the early summer of 1974, when Joseph finally persuaded Heath to hold a formal post-mortem inquest on his Government's economic policy, Heath rejected any criticism out of hand, thus slamming the door on any policy re-think *within* the Party. This Shadow Cabinet meeting was, by all accounts, a remarkable one. Both Alan Walters and Professor James Ball, the Principal of the London School of Business Studies, (present as the expert economic witnesses) agreed that the monetarist forecasts had been right, and the Government's pump-priming expansion of 1972–4 had been responsible for the subsequent inflation. Ball's verdict was particularly damning, as he was supposed to be Heath's main witness. John Ranelagh has related what happened next:

> Heath refused to accept Ball's view, and the meeting went on until close to midnight before Heath concluded as he had started. 'It's late, and it's time to sum up', he said. 'I think I can sum up the proceedings adequately. The main

> conclusion, I think, is that our policies were right, but that we didn't persist in them long enough'. He was absolutely refusing to concede that his economic policy had been wrong. Of the key players in the policy fight that was now to unfold, Sir Keith Joseph's eyebrows shot up; Angus Maude shook his head and looked down; Sir Geoffrey Howe looked astonished, and Margaret Thatcher sat without expression with her back to the wall, away from the centre table. Heath had lost his sense of objective reality. The division was forming between those who could not accept that the post-war consensus had got things wrong in a fundamental way, and those who were more convinced than ever that monetarist policies should be pursued.'[57]

It was these accumulated frustrations that led Sir Keith Joseph to devote his energies to the political development of the free-market approach *outside* the normal Party apparatus. However, there is considerable confusion as to who first suggested the idea of an Institute (which became the CPS) to undertake the policy re-think that Joseph thought was necessary. There is no doubt that in the direct aftermath of the February 1974 election Joseph called, as he had done in 1964, on the IEA to re-educate himself in market economics, and soon afterwards Joseph took Harris and Seldon out to dinner at Lockets', in Westminster, to tell them that he was going to set up his own 'think-tank', not as a rival to the IEA, but to do in political terms for the free-market what the IEA had so successfully done in the wider intellectual community. The suggestion has been made that it was Heath himself who proposed the idea of a separate office, working for Joseph himself, to undertake his new roving commission on Party policy. If so, Heath's intention must have been to give Joseph a chemistry set with which he would hopefully blow himself up. Whatever the truth, and there is no documentation to prove the case one way or another, the original aim of Joseph's new 'think-tank', as agreed with Heath, was to examine the use of market economics in European states, and particularly the successful application of the 'social market economy' to Germany. This was the way in which the CPS was sold to Heath, which showed considerable guile, as by appealing to Heath's passionate interest in Europe, Joseph ensured that Heath would at least not be obstructive to an institute which would naturally deflect funds away from the Conservative Party itself at a time when the Party was facing another election within months. The sanction of the Party leader was thus essential to an organization whose founder Chairman was Joseph and Deputy-Chairman was Mrs Thatcher, both prominent members of the Shadow Cabinet. Heath hoped to exercise some influence over the new enterprise by nominating his own Director (of three) to the CPS, Adam Ridley, an economic adviser in the Central Policy Review Staff (CPRS) from 1971–4, and special adviser to Heath himself on economics. Ridley testified to the fact that Heath had 'slight suspicions' of the CPS from the start, but by the time that the CPS really got into its stride, he was no longer Party leader anyway.[58] In fact, the CPS was to be essential to the intellectual revolution within the Party that Heath was so keen to resist.

Joseph's aim in founding the CPS in March 1974 (although the first formal board meeting was not until June of that year) was simple. As he told the author in 1991, 'My aim was to convert the Tory Party.'[59] As such, unlike the IEA, it was self-consciously a political institute, designed to 'articulate in political terms what the IEA had been thinking'.[60] The perception of Joseph and his co-founders was that many of the problems that Heath's Government had encountered during its supposedly 'free-market' phase in 1970–1 were essentially 'political' problems. The actual economic thinking had been right, but the political application of that thinking to the real economy had not been thought through. It was a job that the IEA could not do; but one which the CPS should. For a future Conservative government led by Joseph and Mrs Thatcher to put the ideas of the IEA into practice, they had to have a Party more effectively convinced of the need for economic liberalism, which it clearly was not in 1974. The CPS was thus vigorously committed to market economics from the outset, as a 'Draft Statement of Goals for the Centre' by Simon Webley made clear:

> The basic principle on which the centre operates is that to meet the needs and expectations of Society, wealth must be created by the efficient use of scarce resources. This can only be achieved by a vigorous, efficient and well motivated private sector, producing a surplus (profit), a proportion of which goes to sustain and develop 'welfare' services in their widest sense ... or in other words, – compassionate Capitalism.'[61]

One of Keith Joseph's first actions on conceiving of the CPS was to involve Alfred Sherman – he became the second Director of Studies in 1975 after Martin Wassall departed. Sherman was the moving spirit of the CPS from the beginning, and its effective head, although he was only paid a part-time salary and continued his work as a journalist. Sherman's own conception of the CPS was rather more grandiose than Joseph's. In a long memo written in 1983 when Sherman was being ousted from the CPS, he recalled that

> The original purpose of the Centre was to change the climate of opinion, in Party and Country, in order to pave the way for the implementation of policies we knew to be right. After Margaret Thatcher's election as leader this objective was modified to changing the climate of opinion in country and Party in order to expand the scope for Margaret Thatcher to propound, and ultimately to implement, those policies she knew to be right.
>
> The Centre – it was agreed – was to act as 'outsider', 'Skirmisher', 'trail-blazer', to moot new ideas and policies without committing the Party leadership in the hope that when sufficient headway had been made with public opinion and inside the Party, the leadership could move forward. *Our job was to question the unquestioned, think the unthinkable, blaze new trails.**

There was thus always a tension between the CPS's role as an organization active within Conservative Party politics and its wider role, as conceived by Sherman and others, of shaping and persuading public opinion in order to make the task of the economic liberal politicians easier in power, as they would thus be pushing against what might be at least a half-open door. Martin Wassall, one of the co-founders, was correct to point out that the CPS thus had a 'unique role', deriving 'from the fact that, while being close to the centre of power within the Conservative Party, it is at the same time financially and organizationally independent of the Party – thus permitting us to be both more radical and more public in the examination and promotion of Social Market policies'.[62] The tension between its role as forming opinion

* Author's italics.

within the Party and forming opinion outside the Party was one which was possible to sustain – just – whilst the Party was in opposition from 1974–9, but thereafter it was a tension that snapped abruptly once the Party got into power, leading to the removal of Sherman from the CPS in 1983. In 1976, on the second anniversary of its foundation, Sherman wrote a description of the CPS, in which he described it as a 'free-standing participant in the Conservative campaign of re-assessment and opinion-forming'. He added:

> From the moment of our conception, we took it for granted that the Party would be broadly in agreement with the direction we seek to take, indeed this is inherent in the concept of trail-blazer. Hence, there is no substance in the picture of the Centre presented here and there as a party within a party or private army. This Centre has its place in the Conservative scheme of things.[63]

This was, of course, optimistic in the extreme, written, probably, for public consumption, as the CPS was formed to fight the battle within the Party for economic liberalism, just as the IEA had fought the same battle in the wider intellectual community. The rivalry and resentment that the CPS was to encounter from certain sections of the Party was amply to confirm this.

In truth, as Sherman admitted later, the CPS never had a clear *raison d'être*, which was both its strength and its weakness. The CPS was much more driven by 'perceived or felt needs'.[64] Its greatest strength was its very flexibility, for during the years of Opposition (1974–9) it fulfilled a number of different roles both within the Party and beyond that could never have been filled by any other organization, be it the IEA or the Conservative Research Department. Neither could the CPS be described as a 'think-tank' in the way that that phrase is commonly understood. The staff of the CPS had done their thinking, they were already committed to the new economics of the market and monetarism. Their task was to change other peoples' minds. As Sherman later wrote, the CPS was set up with 'aspirations rather than a programme. Our task was to win over opinion-forming and policy-circles to an understanding of cause and effect in social affairs with practical reference to the role of the market and the counter-productive nature of much of the post-war intervention. We had no distinct idea of how we should do this. We began by speeches . . .'[65]

The first meeting of the CPS took place in Interview Room G at the House of Commons on 12 June 1974. Present were Sherman, Joseph, Mrs Thatcher, Nigel Vinson, Simon Webley and Julian Bower. Vinson was typical of the new breed of people that the CPS was to involve in politics. He was a successful self-made businessman, who had founded and built up Plastic Coating Ltd during the 1960s and 1970s, before selling out to BTR. In 1970 he became a Trustee of the IEA, and in 1974 was recommended to Keith Joseph as the man who should help set up the CPS. Vinson was the classic self-taught, free-market entrepreneur that the IEA and the CPS came to see as the potential source of Britain's industrial and economic regeneration. Vinson was responsible for all the practical details in setting up the CPS, most notably finding the CPS's first home at 8 Wilfred Street, near Westminster, which they moved into on 1 July 1974. Vinson was one of the CPS's first three Directors. Simon Webley also had considerable experience in the field of free-market economics. A former economics lecturer, he had written several pamphlets for Aims of Industry, where Michael Ivens had asked him to help set up the Foundation for Business Responsibilities. He had also set up the British North American Research Association in 1969 to study transatlantic economic questions. Sherman had met Webley through Aims of Industry, and asked him to help set up the CPS. Martin Wassall, who also played an important role in founding the CPS, had previously worked at the CBI. Although he was not present at the first meeting, Adam Ridley later attended Board Meetings of the CPS as Heath's appointee to the Board. At the first meeting on 12 June, the only matter that was definitely decided upon – in the absence of any better ideas – was that Sir Keith Joseph should make speeches.[66]

The CPS thus started life with Sherman writing Joseph's speeches in a cramped basement room at 8 Wilfred Street. Having been denied his opportunity to put the case for a rethink on economic policy to the Party by Heath, he determined to launch his own campaign, backed by the new resource of the CPS. Only ten days after the first meeting of the CPS in the House of Commons, he thus gave the most celebrated speech of his career, and one of the most important in post-war British history, at Upminster, attacking the post-war Keynesian consensus which he now blamed for the nation's post-war ills. It was exactly the message that Sherman and Walters had pressed upon

Joseph and Mrs Thatcher in the conversations of February–March 1974. Ostensibly, the speech was designed to introduce the CPS to the public, but he went on to draw broad comparisons between those foreign countries that practised more market-orientated economics and Britain;

> Compare our position today with that of our neighbours in north-west Europe – Germany, Sweden, Holland, France. They are no more talented than we are. Yet, compared with them, we have the lowest pay and the lowest production per head. We have the highest taxes and the lowest investment. We have the least prosperity, the most poor and lowest pensions. We have the largest nationalized sector and the worst labour troubles.

All this had been said many times before. It was the political dimension of the speech, however, that made it so forceful; for the first time a senior Conservative minister accepted that *both* political parties were responsible for Britain's decline relative to her neighbours, as *both* parties were responsible for those Keynesian, interventionist policies which had led to Britain's crisis of the mid-1970s, policies which Joseph was later to call 'well-intentioned statism'.[67] The speech began with a standard political attack on Mr Benn, the Secretary of State for Industry in Wilson's new Government, but Joseph went on to claim that the reason that Benn was able to contemplate a further programme of nationalization was because the path had been prepared for him by 'thirty years of Socialistic fashions . . . The path to Benn is paved with thirty years of interventions; thirty years of good intentions; thirty years of disappointments.' The enemy that Joseph was identifying was not Conservatism or Socialism, but the concept of 'collectivism' which had been shared by both parties. As he went on in his most important passage:

> This is no time to be mealy-mouthed. Since the end of the Second World War we have had altogether too much Socialism. There is no point in my trying to evade what everybody knows. For half of that thirty years Conservative Governments, for understandable reasons, did not consider it practicable to reverse the vast bulk of the accumulating detritus of Socialism which on each occasion they found

> when they returned to office. So we tried to build on its uncertain foundations instead. Socialist measures and socialist attitudes have been very pervasive.
>
> I must take my share of the blame for following too many of the fashions.[68]

It was thus Joseph who opened the debate about economic liberalism vs. collectivism within the Conservative Party with this speech. His famous *mea culpa* signalled one of those rare moments in political history when a senior Party spokesman acknowledged that *Party* policy in the past had been wrong. Those economic liberals who had been familiar with Joseph's argument since the mid-1960s immediately saw the great significance of the speech, and William Rees-Mogg and Peter Jay, for instance, at *The Times*, cleared several features from the paper to reproduce the speech almost in full. For all those in the IEA, Aims of Industry, the National Association of Freedom, the Selsdon Group, the Society of Individualists and all those others who had been warning of the dangers of collectivism from *whatever* political party, this was the speech which they had been waiting to hear for many years. So many requests were received by Joseph for copies of this speech that it was published, together with his other speeches of this period, by the CPS in 1975 in a book appropriately entitled *Reversing the Trend*. In the foreword to this book he wrote that: 'About twenty years ago I joined the Conservative Party, and later was adopted as Conservative candidate for the then safe seat of Leeds North-East. In 1959 I was given my first ministerial post. But it was only in 1974 that I was converted to Conservatism. (I had thought that I was a Conservative but I now see that I was not really one at all.)'[69]

Joseph's new brand of Conservatism was, in essence, economic liberalism. Joseph's conversion to what the Fabians had first identified as the politics of the 'New Right' was the breakthrough that the economic liberals had been waiting for, as they now had a very prominent politician to present their case in public. Sherman, who was largely responsible for the Upminster speech, could scarcely have expected a more sensational start to the work of the Centre for Policy Studies than the publicity and controversy provoked by Joseph's speech; just as the IEA had drawn up the battlelines between the anti-Keynesians and the Keynesians in the wider intellectual community, so the CPS now prepared to do the same within the Conservative Party.

7
'The Heroic Age' I
The Years of Opposition, 1974–1979

*

The years when the Conservative Party was in Opposition, 1974–9, and the first term of Mrs Thatcher's Government are often referred to as the 'Heroic Age' by those who worked with her during that period, especially the economic liberals in the Centre for Policy Studies. By the time of Mrs Thatcher's election to the leadership of the Conservative Party in 1975, most of the theoretical framework for what would be called the 'Thatcherite Revolution' had already been laid down; what remained to be done was to work out the specific policies that a Thatcher administration would pursue to, in Keith Joseph's phrase, 'reverse the trend' of collectivism and advance towards a free-market political economy. However, the economic liberals not only had to develop a political programme, they also had to fight the battle of ideas within the Conservative Party. Mrs Thatcher, as her biographers have pointed out, kept a relatively low profile during the years of opposition, showing considerable political astuteness in nudging the Party, rather than attempting to frog-march it, in the direction that she wanted to go.

This created a vital role for the CPS, the IEA and, after 1978, the Adam Smith Institute, as well as those other 'ginger-groups' referred to in the last chapter, in formulating the policies that were to form the core of her first term of office. The economic liberals within the higher echelons of the Party leadership such as Howe, Joseph and Ridley were to make an important contribution, but much of the essential policy thinking was done at the CPS, which also recruited many of the personnel – 'the Thatcherites' – who were to play crucial roles in the first, radical phase of Thatcherism from 1979 to 1981. This Chapter will thus focus on the work of the 'think-tanks', particularly the CPS, during this period, whilst placing their contributions within the wider context of the intellectual revival of economic liberalism within the Party at the same time.

In one sense, the work of the IEA was really over by the late 1970s, as it had laid down the broad principles of economic liberalism and had built up an intellectual consensus behind them. The task of the Centre for Policy Studies during the period 1974 to 1979 was to translate these economic principles into practical policy proposals, and to win acceptance for those policies within the Conservative Party, much of which was still wedded to the old consensus politics. The replacement of Edward Heath by Mrs Thatcher as Party leader in 1975 made little difference to this process, as the Party rejected Heath not because of his ideological position, but quite simply because he was an electoral failure, having lost three out of four elections. Few MPs knew what Mrs Thatcher stood for in 1975, let alone what the CPS was; they merely wanted a new leader who could promise them fresh electoral success. Naturally, the two election defeats of 1974 focused attention on the Party's policies as well as the leadership, and, as Sir Keith Joseph was the first to acknowledge, electoral failure as much as national economic failure made the Conservative Party in the mid-1970s unusually receptive to new ideas, as indeed it had been in the first few years after the 1945 defeat and the 1964 defeat. He explained his own reasoning, which many MPs would have shared with him, in a letter to the *Economist* in September 1974, in reply to an article calling him a 'follower' of Milton Friedman:

> Your reference to me as a 'follower' of Milton Friedman and to him as the source of my criticism though incidental at first sight provides a key to your misunderstanding. For it would suggest that I owe my changed views to conversion by Milton Friedman.
>
> You are in a position to know better. Though I have the highest regard for Professor Friedman and now broadly agree with his views, the evolution of my views owes little to him. On the contrary, it stems primarily – as you should know – from critical re-examination of local orthodoxies in the light of our own bitter experiences in the early 1970s. Then, albeit with misgivings deriving from earlier experience, we followed policies broadly in line with those you then advocated and still advocate. We expanded demand by deficit financing and tried to suppress inflation by administrative measures unsemantically called 'incomes policy'.

> By early this year, we had an historically high rate of inflation, an enfeebled economy, the worst relations with the trade unions movement in decades, and a lost election with the greatest fall in our share of the vote since 1929. Surely this was sufficient incentive to rethink – we are practical people who judge ideas and policies by results.[1]

It is arguable that the most important political contribution which the CPS made was in the production of the series of speeches delivered by Sir Keith Joseph in the first two years of its existence, from the Upminster Speech of June 1974 to the Stockton Lecture of 1976, entitled 'Monetarism Is Not Enough'. It had been agreed at the first CPS meeting in 1974 that the most urgent task was to articulate the need for an economic counter-revolution within a party political context, and the easiest weapon to hand was the high profile of Sir Keith Joseph himself. Most of the drafts for Joseph's speeches were written by Alfred Sherman, who was in his element translating complex economic and political propositions into pithy, catchy phrases and idioms which caught the headlines. In all his speeches, Joseph set out the reasons for Britain's economic problems, such as inflation, and then sketched in a programme of how a future Conservative government would tackle those problems in power.

The Upminster speech was followed in September by a speech at Preston, 'Inflation is caused by governments'. This was even more controversial, as the Party was only a few weeks away from the October election and some attempts were made to persuade Joseph not to give the speech, on the grounds that it would upset Party unity. However, Joseph went ahead, and once again laid equal blame on all post-war governments, 'led by well-intentioned and intelligent people advised by conscientious officials and economists', for the deficit financing and public borrowing which had led to the rising rate of inflation. For the first time, the speech laid out a specifically monetarist counter-inflationary policy, arguing that a stable money growth 'gradually brought closer into line with the growth of our production' was the essential prerequisite for tackling all the other ills of the British economy:

> If I had to give a personal guess about the total time horizon of a successful anti-inflation policy, I would say three or

> four years. A healthy economy – and more still an economy that needs to recover health – requires a reasonable time scale. Fine-tuning, quarterly budgets, short-term adjustments have not worked and will not work. We have the most frequent budgets in Western Europe – and the least successful economy. The time has surely come to turn for advice to economists, critical but constructive, who proved painfully right in their forebodings.[2]

The Preston speech was very important, as it dragged the concept of 'monetarism' to the centre of the political stage and made it a political issue; henceforth, 'monetarism' was no longer an apolitical, technical economic term. From 1974 on, 'monetarism' was used as a blanket term of abuse – or praise – for those espousing the policies of people like Joseph, and it quickly lost most of its very specific and limited original meaning.

Several themes echoed through all of Joseph's speeches during these years. The most important was that the fabled 'middle ground' of consensus politics, from which both political parties had supposedly garnered millions of votes since 1945, had all but disappeared; there was now no alternative between monetarism leading to economic liberalism and the sort of siege economy of nationalization and import controls advocated by Tony Benn, called, in the Labour Cabinet, the 'Alternative Economic Strategy'. This was Sherman's favourite theme, that the Conservatives now had no choice but to turn in Joseph's direction. In June 1975, at a time when there was much talk of 'National Coalitions' and 'Governments of National Safety' to rescue Britain from its dire financial position (usually led, in the popular imagination, by the septuagenarian Harold Macmillan), Sherman wrote a memo for Joseph, 'Coalition Escapism', arguing against any such coalition with 'moderates' of other parties:

> Talk of coalitions and PR is a form of escapism. It is an attempt to find instant solutions for our problems without digging into the causes. It ignores political history, economic theory and experience.
>
> 1. 'The Middle' – both parties have in fact set the tone of politics and policy for the past thirty odd years. They

> cannot deny paternity for their child. This is at the root of our problems.
>
> 2. . . . The Socialists who promised that the mixed economy of 1945–51 was more or less their 'final demand' now set out to benefit from its failure . . . and counsel 'more of the same' as the only cure for ills brought on by their medicine. Conservatives cannot stand on the unworkable wish-wash inherited from Butler and Macmillan. They must offer something workable.[3]

Instead, Joseph argued for a new consensus, a new 'common ground', of people who shared his belief that the country had 'gone astray', and could only be saved by some comparatively drastic economic surgery. This was the appeal of the CPS. Not for nothing was the second of his volume of speeches published by the CPS called *Stranded on the Middle Ground?*

As his overall political and economic position began to be caricatured in the press as 'monetarist', so Joseph also went to some lengths in a number of his speeches to reiterate the point he had made at Preston in September 1974 – that getting the money supply right was merely a prerequisite for a market economy to operate efficiently, thus taking Hayek's side in his debate with Friedman on the issue of the role of monetary policy in an overall economic policy. As Joseph told his audience at Preston: 'The monetarist thesis has been caricatured as implying that if we get the flow of money spending right, everything will be right. This is not – repeat not – my belief. What I believe is that if we get the money supply wrong – too high or too low – nothing will come right. Monetary control is a pre-essential for everything else we need and want to do.'[4] In his Stockton Lecture, of 1976, entitled 'Monetarism Is Not Enough', he clarified this point:

> I will try to restate this view in even broader terms: monetary stability provides a framework within which the individual can best serve his own – and therefore, if the laws and taxes are appropriately designed, the nation's – interests . . . If we desire a monetary framework within which steady growth and high levels of employment can be achieved, we have no alternative but to maintain a stable money supply, eschewing the use of demand creation as a short cut to growth and full

> employment. And to achieve this we must educate public opinion in the need for it.

In other words, the priority in economic decision making now had to be the control of inflation via control of the money supply rather than the maintenance of full employment through demand management; it was the same message that Callaghan delivered to the Labour Party Conference only a few months after Joseph delivered his Stockton Lecture. The new 'common ground' that the CPS was seeking to build was forming quicker than anyone had foreseen. Joseph ended his speech thus:

> Monetarism is not enough. This is not intended as a counsel of despair, but a warning note. Government's intention to contract the money supply is welcome and potentially beneficial to all. But it is not enough unless there is also the essential reduction of the state sector and the essential encouragement of enterprise. We are over-governed, over-spent, over-taxed, over-borrowed and over-manned. If we shirk the cure, the after-effects of continued over-taxation will be worse than anything we have endured hitherto. Our ability to distinguish between economic reality and economic make-believe will decline further. We shall experience accelerated worsening of job prospects, the growing flight of those with professional skills, talent and ability to other countries, and an increase in the shabbiness and squalor of everyday lives.
>
> That is why, by itself, the strict and unflinching control of money supply, though essential, is not enough. We must also have substantial cuts in tax and public spending and bold incentives and encouragements to the wealth creators, without whose renewed efforts we shall all grow poorer.[5]

The Stockton Lecture was also remarkable for its complex but frank critique of Keynesian economics, drawing on the work of William Hutt, Hayek, Robbins, Sir Arnold Plant and Theodore Gregory in the 'economic calculation' debate of the 1930s. Joseph also attacked the implementation of what he called 'pseudo-Keynesian' economics from

1945 onwards. It was only now, in 1976, that the economic objections to Keynesianism voiced by the founder-members of the Mont Pèlerin Society in the 1930s found their way into the political mainstream; there was surely no better vindication of Hayek's conviction that the long-term intellectual campaign that he had conceived of in 1947 would be successful in the end. Equally, Joseph's speeches surely bore out the force of Keynes's argument that politicians were, after all, slaves to those 'defunct economists' whom he had described at the end of *The General Theory* in 1936. 'Monetarism Is Not Enough' was the most cogent yet wide-ranging political critique of Keynesianism compressed into one political speech, and possibly the CPS's single most important contribution to the political debate of the 1970s. Sherman could feel justifiably proud of his handiwork.

The other major theme of Sir Keith Joseph's speeches and of much of the rest of the output of the CPS in the mid-1970s was the place of market economics in Conservative thinking. If the IEA had already won over many of the 'opinion-formers' in the country, such as journalists, academics, politicians and the like, a large part of the Conservative Party remained highly suspicious of the doctrine of economic liberalism on the grounds that the Conservative Party had always been a pragmatic, organic party, in the tradition of Burke, and had always eschewed embracing ideologies or dogmas – a vice characteristic of their opponents, the Socialists. Furthermore, as we have seen, collectivist values were deeply entrenched in the Conservative Party, and its post-war leaders had often harked back to the Disraelian critique of Victorian Capitalism which the former Party leader had elucidated in the 1840s (most notably in *Coningsby* and *Sybil*) to justify the Conservative Party's post-war support for the 'middle way' of the Keynesian mixed economy. Many agreed with Macmillan, who had claimed that 'Toryism has always been a form of paternal Socialism',[6] or with Eden who had said in 1947 that 'We are not a Party of unbridled, brutal capitalism, and never have been . . . we are not the political children of the "*laissez-faire*" school. We opposed them decade after decade.'[7] The 'paternalist' tradition of the Conservative Party was very strong, and still dominated the Party in the mid-1970s. In his T. S. Eliot Memorial Lectures 'The Politics of Imperfection' the philosopher Anthony Quinton traced a continuous tradition of Conservative thought stretching from Clarendon, Burke and Coleridge to Disraeli, Salisbury and Oakeshott, arguing that the tradition was based upon three essential principles, traditionalism, organicism and political scepticism, 'The belief that political wisdom . . . is not to be found in the theoretical speculations of isolated thinkers but in the historically accumulated social experiences of the community as a whole'.[8] Clearly, the revolution in economic policy envisaged by Joseph and the CPS was going to sit uneasily within such a tradition, just as Quinton had pinpointed the Conservative distrust of intellectuals, such as Hayek and Friedman.

W. H. Greenleaf has demonstrated that the Conservatives in fact owed their success to a 'twin inheritance', the one Tory, as described above by Quinton, and the other neo-liberal. Conservative writers as far back as Henry Mallock, writing in the late-nineteenth century, had analyzed the tension between these two apparently antithetical philosophical traditions within the Party. In fact, despite the rhetoric of Disraeli and the 'Tory Democrats' – exemplified in their rallying cry of 'One Nation' – the Party had always been essentially 'Peelite' in economic policy, dating their embrace of economic liberalism back to the free-trade policies of the 'Liberal-Tories' Huskisson and Peel in the 1820s. As Greenleaf concludes, 'A range of contrasting positions is possible therefore, each of them equally at home in the Conservative tradition and available according to personal predilection or the demands of circumstances.'[9] Joseph and the CPS writers sought to link the reinvigorated market economics of the 1970s with this older Tory tradition of 'liberal-Conservatism', thus legitimizing it as a vital strand of Conservative thought. Lord Coleraine had done this in *For Conservatives Only*, and Lord Blake, the historian of the Conservative Party, also located the economic policy of the 'New Right' firmly in the Conservative tradition in a talk he gave to the Conservative Philosophy Group in January 1976, arguing that economic liberalism was easily compatible with the four traditions that he identified in Conservative thinking, namely a belief in the limited role of government, a belief in the national (as opposed to sectional) interest, a belief in opportunity rather than equality, and a conception of the Conservative Party as the natural Party of Government.[10] Naturally, the 'New Right's' belief in a reduction of the role of the State in the economy dovetailed with the traditional Conservative scepticism of government 'planning' and 'rationalistic' attempts at imposing an ideological blueprint on the country. The economic liberals were seeking to release the individual energies and talents of the people which had been kept in check by the post-war era of over-intrusive and claustrophobic government. In a 1980 CPS pamphlet Nigel Lawson argued just this, that:

> The distinctive feature of the new Conservatism is its rejection of these false trails [of post-war social democracy, 'with its profound faith in the efficacy of government action'] and its return to the mainstream. Old lessons have to be painfully relearned. The old consensus is in the process of being re-established. To the extent that new Conservatives turn to new sages – such as Hayek and Friedman – that is partly because what those writers are doing is avowedly reinterpreting the traditional political and economic wisdom of Hume, Burke and Adam Smith in terms of the conditions of today; and partly because, as specialists in economics (although Hayek in particular is a great deal more than that) they are of particular interest in an age in which, for better or worse, economic policy has achieved a centrality in the political debate which it never enjoyed in, say, the golden age of Disraeli and Gladstone . . . The essential point is that what we are witnessing is the reversion to an older tradition in the light of the failure of what might be termed the new enlightenment. This is important politically, not in the sense of some kind of appeal to ancestor-worship or to the legitimacy of scriptural authority; it is important because these traditions are, even today, more deeply rooted in the hearts and minds of ordinary people than is the conventional wisdom of the recent past.[11]

Ralph Harris echoed Lawson's words in a speech he gave to a fringe meeting at the Conservative Party Conference in October 1980, urging Conservatives to 'fight the battle of ideas', and to align themselves squarely behind the 'free society'.[12] The best work of synthesis, marrying the Hayekian concepts of economic liberalism and a 'free society' to traditional Conservatism, was done by Tibor Szamuely, a Hungarian by birth who became involved with the younger generation of economic liberals at Swinton College in the 1960s. In 1968 he had argued that the primary contemporary purpose of the Party was to offer 'an intellectually based and firmly stated alternative to every ideological tenet of the "progressive" Socialist Creed'.[13] David Willetts, Director of

Studies at the CPS from 1987 to 1992, developed this argument at length in his book *Modern Conservatism*.[14]

For the sake of argument and for the rest of the book, I shall identify those Conservative politicians, like Powell, Joseph and Mrs Thatcher, who emphasized the role of the market in the defence of Conservative principles as 'liberal-Conservatives', as that epithet most accurately describes a philosophy which had more in common with the original liberal-Conservatives – Peel, Huskisson and Canning – than the party of Macmillan, Boyle and Eden. It is also a more accurate description than the other nomenclature of the late 1970s, such as 'right-wing' or 'dry'. Eventually, of course, the blanket term 'Thatcherism' was used to describe the 'liberal-Conservatives'.

In his own early speeches, Joseph tried to sweeten the pill for those Tory paternalists who found his brand of economic liberalism hard to swallow by referring to the free-market economy as the 'Social Market economy', that variant of economic liberalism developed in post-war Germany, the *Soziale Marktwirtschaft*, by the founder-members of the Mont Pèlerin society, Röpke, Walter Eucken and Ludwig Erhard. The 'Social Market Economy', a proven success in post-war Germany, was somewhat softer on the ear than the sharper cadences of 'the free market', and could even be thought of as 'caring capitalism', or 'compassionate capitalism', in order to distinguish economic liberalism (as developed by its post-war exponents such as Hayek) from the unbridled *laissez-faire* of Dickensian England, with which most Britons still associated the 'free market'. In a speech to Conservatives at Oxford in 1975, Joseph was quite explicit on this point:

> A market government needs to be an active one. But its activity will be designed to make the best use for all the people of the potential enterprise within a humane framework of laws and services.
>
> The government will need to ensure that there is genuine competition: there will need to be an effective policy to watch for and break up monopolies, to enforce sensible company law, to safeguard the interests of small business, to legislate against eventualities such as pollution, noise, etc. Government will need to be active to seek to secure equality of opportunity for all, and to seek to limit concentration of

power. The range and quality of public services are the province of government.

So certainly I am very far indeed from *laissez-faire* . . .[15]

One of the first pamphlets that the CPS published was *Why Britain Needs a Social Market Economy*, by Martin Wassall and Nigel Vinson, in 1975. The pamphlet defined the Social Market Economy as that of a 'socially responsible market economy, for a market economy is perfectly compatible with the promotion of a more compassionate society. Indeed, by encouraging the energies and initiative of the creative and sturdier members of our society, the resources available for helping the aged, the sick and the disabled are substantially enlarged.'[16] Soon afterwards, the CPS published a talk given by the historian Hugh Thomas, *History, Capitalism and Freedom*, in which he argued, like Lord Blake, that market economics was an integral part of the Conservative anti-collectivist tradition.[17] However, Joseph was later persuaded to cease using the term 'social market' by Shirley and William Letwin of the LSE, amongst Joseph's closest intellectual advisers, on the grounds that an appeal to the 'Social Market' only diluted the understanding of market economics and the need for a return to the primacy of the role of the market in economic affairs. Thereafter, Joseph would talk more of 'Capitalism' and 'the market', whilst always preserving the distinction between economic liberalism, the 'enterprise culture' and market economics as opposed to unfettered *laissez-faire*.

Despite the best efforts of Joseph and the CPS, there were many in the Conservative Party who remained wedded to an essentially collectivist, 'One Nation' conception of the Party, and regarded the politics of Joseph, Mrs Thatcher and the CPS as nothing less than an attempted hijacking of the Party by ideologues and dogmatists. Sir Ian Gilmour was the intellectual champion of this wing of the Party; his book, *Inside Right*, published in 1977, rejected the claims of ideas, more specifically the idea of monetarism and of economic liberalism, upon the Party. Many Shadow Cabinet Ministers, such as Peter Walker, Norman St John Stevas, Francis Pym and James Prior agreed with him; they regarded 'Thatcherism' as an aberration, from which the Party would, in time, recover. Edward Heath became, during the years of Mrs Thatcher's premiership, the most outspoken exponent of this view.[18] The internal debate that the CPS provoked within the Party was, of course, one of its aims, and led to the divisions and battles between 'Wets' and 'Drys' beloved of journalists in the early 1980s. It was a battle for the 'soul' of the Party that the CPS never completely won, despite the superficial successes of the 1980s, and which came back to haunt Mrs Thatcher every time the political situation looked particularly bleak, as in 1981, 1986 and particularly, and finally, in 1990. Even when a Minister in Mrs Thatcher's Government, Sir Ian Gilmour was still making explicit attacks on the whole enterprise of economic liberalism, safe in the knowledge that his views were widely shared within the Party. He told a Cambridge Union audience in February 1980 that 'Conservative political thought is wholly opposed to the so-called night-watchman state . . . In the Conservative view, therefore, economic liberalism, *à la* Professor Hayek, because of its starkness and its failure to create a sense of community, is not a safeguard of political freedom, but a threat to it.'[19] To the very end, there were many Conservatives who agreed with Gilmour, and they eventually had their victory in 1990.

One of Gilmour's leading disciples was Chris Patten, an ex-Balliol man who had strayed into the Conservative Party with an obscure reputation as an 'intellectual' and had become head of the Conservative Research Department during the opposition years. The CPS and the CRD conducted what amounted to guerilla warfare against each other for much of that time, reflecting the ideological divisions within the Party between the old, 'paternalist' Conservatism and the new 'free-market' version. Beneath the civilities of Conservative Party politics at the higher levels, the CRD tried to neutralize the work of the CPS, and the CPS tried to work around the CRD. In many ways the CPS and CRD were rival organizations, competing for funds and patronage, yet Martin Wassall, responding to yet another plea from the Party leadership for closer co-operation between the two bodies, analyzed a quite legitimate rivalry in a memo of October 1975 for Sir Keith Joseph:

> 1. Our roles are quite different. CPS's main function, as you rightly say, is to explain the merits and mechanism of a free enterprise/market system through a number of ways and channels. In this role we must feel free to air for debate a range of radical ideas with which the CRD would not wish to be associated. Not being of the Party, CPS can play a very useful role in 'shocking' public opinion by forcing

> increasing attention on policy changes which are as yet outside the spectrum of accepted policy options.
>
> 2. Whenever I come into contact with CRD I always gain the impression that its staff are somewhat disconcerted by the existence of CPS. First, the CPS confuses them because we do not fit into their perceptions of a tidy Party institutional structure. Secondly, they half-suspect the CPS of being a bunch of potentially dangerous radicals more versed in theory than experienced in the hard grind of practical politics which means winning votes ... CRD clearly believes it can do its job more effectively without the added distraction of a group of radicals who are more likely to make CRD's life difficult than make useful contributions.[20]

The natural rivalry between the CPS and the CRD, which acted principally as a research and reference organization for the Parliamentary Party, was, however, exacerbated by the scarcely concealed contempt that Sherman held for the CRD in general and Patten in particular; it was a contempt which was heartily reciprocated by Patten. In one of several vitriolic memos by Sherman on the subject of the relationship between the CPS and the CRD, he offered the following assessment of the CRD:

> ... the CRD has taken young men whose adolescence had already been extended by the transition direct from public school to Oxbridge, given them too great a sense of their own wisdom and importance, allowed then to draw their views at second hand from the *Guardian*, *Times* and *Observer* and pass them off as wisdom ... almost all precious and arrogant.

There was some justification in Sherman's claim that soon after the second 1974 election, when the CPS had been engaged in re-educating the Party, Patten had launched an 'offensive' against the CPS:

> He began to tell his familiars in the Press and Party that we were a dangerous brand of right-wing fanatics out to

> overthrow Heath, undermine the CRD, and turn the Party into a small southern minority.
>
> . . . Patten was wholly Heathite and believes that the sum of political wisdom is to bribe the public with its own money.[21]

To Sherman, the CRD was staffed by well-born time-servers and careerists, happy to trim and compromise to advance their career in the Party and win a seat; precisely those who had steered the country to disaster from the 'middle ground'. The CRD was, indeed, fond of leaking information to their 'familiars' in the Press, mainly to the *Economist* via Mark Schreiber, in order to discredit the liberal-Conservatives and the CPS in particular. The most damaging of these leaks was of Nicholas Ridley's internal Party report on a future Conservative Government's strategy for fighting the public sector unions, which appeared in the *Economist* on 27 May 1978. That same month, the Press, led by *The Times*, publicized the battle between Sherman, the CPS and the Party establishment for the first time, calling Sherman 'a particular focus of . . . hostility' within the Party.[22] Another paper published a demand by a Conservative MP for the CPS to be closed down.[23] It was through this rather circuitous route that Sherman first came to public prominence as Joseph's and Mrs Thatcher's sinister *éminence grise*. So dismissive of the CPS was Patten that he managed to write an entire chapter for a study of *Conservative Party Politics*, published in 1980, on 'Policy Making in Opposition' without once mentioning the CPS.[24] There was thus some truth in Sherman's and Thatcher's perception of the CRD as 'pink'. One CRD official has since written that

> within the Party bureaucracy it was felt essential to hold on to the respect of the media by indicating privately to journalists that the new leader was an aberration on the part of the MPs who elected her, that she would soon be out and Willie Whitelaw would replace her. In pursuit of these objectives, the Research Department acted as an unofficial custodian of the Heath/Whitelaw flame . . . Because of this resistance, CRD, traditionally the Party's think-tank, gave way in

> important respects to the independent Thatcherite Centre for Policy Studies . . .[25]

The personal antipathy between Sherman and Patten reflected the wider philosophical and political differences between the CRD and the CPS, which in their turn reflected the ideological conflict between the two wings of the Party, the 'Thatcherite' economic liberals of the CPS and the 'Tory paternalists'. To a certain extent the CPS won the intellectual argument, but Sherman was right to doubt how many Conservative MPs really – to use his own word – 'internalized' the new politics of economic liberalism, even by the time of Mrs Thatcher's third Government.

If the most obvious – and controversial – job of the CPS was to fight the 'war of ideas' for economic liberalism within the Party, another equally important role that the CPS played was as a recruiting-centre for those who might not have been 'Conservatives' in the strictest sense, but who wanted to work for the revival of a free market in Britain. Just as Alfred Sherman was the principal architect of Joseph's intellectual assault on the Party in his capacity as Joseph's main speech-writer, so he was also very active in attracting to the CPS those who would not normally have had much to do with politics – let alone Conservative Party politics – but who had skills which would be useful to Mrs Thatcher and Keith Joseph in government. From the start, a number of those 'political activists' who had worked at Swinton College, for the IEA, the Selsdon Group or for the National Association for Freedom helped at the CPS, either with research or on administrative tasks. Thus Nigel Morgan, who had been active in NAFF, became Sherman's assistant in 1979; John O'Sullivan and Frank Johnson helped out with press releases and relations with the media generally, especially before the Preston Speech; Chris Tame worked occasionally for the CPS, and the historian Lord Beloff, who had been closely involved in the founding of Buckingham University with the IEA, became a Director of the CPS in the early 1980s. Jock Bruce-Gardyne, who had been instrumental in founding the Selsdon Group, worked at the CPS for 2½ days a week from 1974 to 1979 after he lost his parliamentary seat in 1974. However, all these people were, to varying degrees, already staunch supporters of the 'New Right' and 'liberal-Conservatism', and might have been expected to become associated in some way with the CPS. More importantly, Sherman recruited a whole new cross-section of people, with a wide-ranging selection of skills and expertise, into the politics of the New Right; those who came to be known as the 'Thatcherites'.

Most, like Sherman, were not Conservatives by birth, or even inclination – they were essentially 'apolitical' in the sense that like Sherman they believed in the importance of ideas and convictions rather than party politics, and in particular the idea of economic liberalism as a solution to Britain's economic impasse of the mid-1970s. Sherman was also astute in wooing those, like himself, who had become disenchanted with the Left, and who became economic liberals in the mid-1970s out of ideological disillusion with Marxism and Socialism – their motives were discussed in the last chapter. Prominent amongst these was the historian of the Spanish Civil War, Hugh Thomas, who had started out as a 'Fabian' Socialist but who, like many others, felt that the Labour Party was betraying its original philosophical attachments to freedom by the early 1970s.[26] He was also co-author of a famous tract against *The Establishment* in the 1950s; he thus shared Sherman's and many in the CPS's distaste for the old, complacent, 'Liberal' establishment which they felt had presided with supreme indifference over Britain's precipitate decline since 1945. He had, possibly, much in common with Kingsley Amis, the novelist, who also ended up writing a pamphlet for the CPS and sitting on one of its Study Groups.[27] Thus did the 'Angry Young Men' of the 1950s become the Thatcherites of the 1980s. In the autumn of 1977 he delivered a CPS lecture at the Conservative Party Conference. In June 1977, Sherman wrote the following description of Thomas for the benefit of Mrs Thatcher, who wanted to meet him:

> Hugh Thomas is an outstanding member of the younger generation of British men of letters (he is in his forties) and a recent adherent to the Conservative Party. He would add considerable distinction to a Conservative platform . . . For many years, he was a Fabian and member of the Labour Party from which he eventually resigned. He voted Conservative in the Oct. 1974 general election and two years later joined the Conservative Party . . .[28]

Thomas's expertise lay in the field of foreign affairs, and he subsequently became one of Mrs Thatcher's few trusted advisers on foreign affairs during her premiership. He became Chairman of the CPS in 1979, and in 1981 was ennobled by Mrs Thatcher. Sherman was to bitterly regret his enthusiastic endorsement of Thomas, as his clash with Thomas concerning his own work at the CPS from 1979 to 1983 eventually led to his unceremonial ejection from the CPS in 1983. Another 'convert' who was attracted to Thatcherism by the CPS was David Young, later Lord Young of Graffham. He was a self-made businessman, who, like many Thatcherites, had voted Labour last in 1964, inspired by Wilson's promise of technocratic planning. He grew disillusioned with Wilson's government and voted for what he thought were the free-market economics of Heath in 1970. Once again, he was disappointed and nearly emigrated to America in the early 1970s. He was not a Conservative in the sense that he had any formal links with the Party, but was nevertheless very impressed by Sir Keith Joseph's speeches of 1974–5 and their emphasis on wealth creation. He sought Joseph out at the CPS and put his time at Joseph's disposal. Young helped out at the CPS and was also appointed by Joseph to serve on one of the Party's policy committees. In 1979 Young followed Sir Keith Joseph to the Department of Industry as a Special Adviser, before moving to become Chairman of the Manpower Services Commission and later a Minister in his own right. Young was in many ways typical of the people attracted to the CPS. He was a non-political businessman, who had – initially, at least – no ambition for a full-time political career, but believed in a business culture – or what came to be known as an 'enterprise culture' – and that economic liberalism as preached by Joseph and Mrs Thatcher offered a practical solution to Britain's economic difficulties.[29]

Two of the most important people recruited by the CPS came from backgrounds very similar to David Young's – John Hoskyns and Norman Strauss, who after 1979 became the CPS's two most important people in Mrs Thatcher's Government. Sherman met Hoskyns through a mutual acquaintance called Terry Price, whom Sherman used to meet at a discussion club called the Romney Street Group, founded in 1917 by the dramatic critic of *Punch*, Joseph Thorp. Price was a former top scientific civil servant who had gone into industry where he had met Hoskyns. They found that they both shared the same gloomy prognosis for British industry and had both independently tried to analyze Britain's problems using the computerized modelling methods used in industry. Hoskyns had been educated at Winchester before serving in the army from 1945 to 1957. He left to enter the computer business and in 1964 set up his own Hoskyns Group, which he eventually sold in 1975. In the computer industry he learnt the most modern techniques of systems analysis which led on to an interest in cybernetics, the study of mapping complex systems and of illustrating the interaction of causes and effects. Price lunched with Hoskyns once a week during the early 1970s, and so when Sherman invited Price to lunch at the CPS in the autumn of 1975, he brought Hoskyns with him. Sherman was immediately enthusiastic about their skills and analysis, and dashed off a memo to Joseph advising him that the CPS had been offered the prospect of 'help in the field of economic policy-formation from two really brilliant people who are keen to help'.[30] Hoskyns was a typical CPS person; he was 'apolitical' in the sense that he looked upon the economy as a 'technical problem'. Hoskyns had been in touch with the IEA since the 1960s, and admitted to becoming 'a self-taught economist through reading their publications'.[31] He was ready to place himself at the disposal of politicians of any hue, offering them technical expertise, and to this end he was in contact with Harold Lever, a Minister in James Callaghan's Cabinet, in 1976. As Hoskyns explained to Sherman in a letter after their first meeting in the autumn of 1975:

> while I am perhaps a little less concerned than Terry [Price], at this stage, about maintaining an apolitical stance, I am still reconnoitring the political world to see where my ideas may have some application. This naturally means talking to people in the political parties, the civil service and the unions ... I don't think there could possibly be any conflict of interest as any discussions would obviously be in confidence. But I thought it was important to make my own position clear. I am not a committed supporter of the Tory Party, but I find that their (or perhaps particularly the CPS) view of an organic socio-economic system rather than a mechanical one corresponds more closely with the real world.[32]

Sherman, however, was determined to capture the talents of Hoskyns and Price for the CPS, and introduced them to Joseph at a lunch on 5 November 1975 also attended by Norman Lamont, Patricia Hodgson (Chairman of the Bow Group), Norman Strauss, Simon Webley and

Frank Johnson. It was also the first time that Hoskyns had met Strauss. Joseph was very enthusiastic about the ideas of Hoskyns, Price and Strauss, particularly the systems analysis and rigorous scientific planning which seemed to offer a strategy to translate the ideas of Joseph and the CPS into a workable government programme. Joseph was particularly struck by Hoskyns's complex 'flow-charts', which quickly became his stock-in-trade at the CPS. Joseph recommended them both to Mrs Thatcher, and they met for the first time on 6 August 1976. Hoskyns had found the response of several groups of MPs whom he had talked to about his 'systems-analysis' distinctly disappointing, but in Joseph, Mrs Thatcher, and to a lesser degree Geoffrey Howe, Hoskyns, Price and Strauss found a group of politicians who were unusually receptive to new thinking and who were genuinely interested in translating ideas into action, and developing a coherent strategy to do so. Hoskyns's first and most important task in this respect was to develop a future government's strategic plan for office, which became the 'Stepping-Stones' project, of which more later. Strauss, like Hoskyns, came from an apolitical industrial background and was recruited by Sherman to apply certain skills learnt in his career as a marketing expert for Unilever. Strauss first met Joseph through Samuel Brittan, with whom he had attended Kilburn Grammar School. Joseph asked Strauss to do some work on 'profits', which Sherman then picked up at the CPS. It was Sherman who linked up Hoskyns to Strauss and they thereafter acted very much as a team, Hoskyns the more dapper, military, systemic thinker and Strauss the creative, aggressive and 'fizzy' member of the duo. Joseph described Strauss in his letter of introduction to Mrs Thatcher as a person whose 'skills include the underlying psychological impact of words and phrases. He has offered to give us part of his leisure to help us on our vocabulary.'[33] Strauss approached his work for the CPS in an entirely technocratic, managerial spirit; he was not party political, but the Conservative Party became his political home because they were the only party interested in his ideas. One of Strauss's first jobs for the CPS was to prepare a document entitled 'The need for new data', dated 3 August 1976, which outlined the need of the Party to develop a new vocabulary and new 'image' to create the confidence in the electorate that it was actually going to implement the policies that it was promising in Opposition. He called the document very 'Un-British' in tone and spirit, but explained that the crisis situation of 1976 needed extreme remedies. The key word which he used in this document was 'conviction'; if the electorate was not convinced that Mrs Thatcher had the 'will' to implement her policies, then there was no point in voting for the somewhat extreme policies that she was suggesting. The tone of the document anticipated much of the language and style of Mrs Thatcher's governments, and he correctly analyzed how the CPS acted as a catalyst for change within the Conservative Party. In a recording of a lunch conversation he had with Sherman at which he first outlined his views, Strauss expanded on this theme:

> The other big hang up that prevents anything happening in British society is the British disease, which is not so much the fact that our people are ineffective in their jobs if given freedom, but rather that they don't give themselves freedom. Culturally they prevent themselves from entering into any situation where conflict rises to a noticeable level. It is only conflict that can ensure issues are discussed, that people are challenged and that change occurs. Without conflict freedom is inextricably diminished in time. Now ironically the Tory Party and Tories are the least conflicting personalities when it comes to new ideas or making one's presence felt or disagreeing vehemently with another person's point of view. 'It is just not done old chap.' 'People don't do such things.' Frankly, market growth, political growth, seeking out the right ideas is no respecter of correct behaviour. Now this stance again can be radically altered, if not removed, by the presence of catalysts and change agents in policy groups.[34]

The CPS acted as the 'change agent' for the Conservative Party, much as Sir Keith Joseph himself acted as the 'change agent' for Mrs Thatcher, attracting a lot of the antagonism and animosity which might have been directed towards her during the years of opposition when she was still uncertain about her own position within the Conservative Party.

Journalists were also attracted to the CPS, where Sherman, himself a professional journalist, utilized their skills to put over the message of economic liberalism to both the public and the Party. Gerald Frost, a friend of Frank Johnson and John O'Sullivan, had been inspired by the teachings of Popper and Hayek whilst at the University of Sussex, having formerly voted Labour. Frost had worked for the Press Association and the *Daily Express*, and in 1974 became Sherman's assistant at the CPS, with a specific brief to collate the CPS's own set of unemployment figures. He left in 1981 to join the Institute of European Defence and Strategic Studies. He returned to the CPS as Director in 1992.

Frost and O'Sullivan both wrote occasional speeches and articles for Joseph as well. Another *Daily Telegraph* journalist, T. E . Utley, also helped at the CPS with seminars and speeches. The only paid staff at the CPS during the 1970s were Sherman, Frost and three secretaries. Another journalist who was recruited by Sherman was Christopher Monckton, the grandson of Walter Monckton, Churchill's Minister of Labour in his 1951–5 government. He was a leader-writer on the *Yorkshire Post* until 1977, when he went to work at the Press Office in Conservative Central Office. He met Sherman in Central Office one day in 1979, when Sherman asked him to take the minutes at the CPS's study group meetings. Later Monckton sat on some of these study groups himself, and wrote a rents-into-mortgages paper for Hoskyns which brought him to the attention of Downing Street. He later served in the Downing Street Policy Unit from 1982 to 1986. On the economic side, Alan Walters was, naturally, in touch with Sherman and Joseph, although from 1976 he was in America working at the World Bank and at Johns Hopkins University. It was the CPS, however, that was instrumental in engineering his return to Britain in 1980 as personal economic adviser to Mrs Thatcher. One of Walters's students at the LSE, Patrick Minford, came to the attention of Joseph and Sherman through a series of articles that he had written for the *Guardian* in 1976–7. In 1977 he met Joseph and in 1978 was introduced to Mrs Thatcher at a dinner attended by most of the leading 'liberal-Conservative' Shadow Cabinet ministers. Minford had done his Ph.D. under Walters on Rational Expectations, and in 1976 he took up a Professorship at Liverpool University where he conducted his own rational expectation research programme, and, after Walters, became the most celebrated source of economic advice to Downing Street during the 1980s. He also attended meetings at the CPS, and contributed to IEA and CPS publications.[35]

Another typical CPS recruit was Dr Elizabeth Cottrell, the daughter of a Welsh coal-miner. Her father was a Labour voter, albeit a very patriotic and nationalistic one, and she was brought up in a solidly Labour background. Like other 'Thatcherites', she had always been 'passionately concerned with the class from which she sprang', but felt that Socialism had 'deprived' the working class, rather than enriched it, and was thus also attracted to the speeches and writings of Sir Keith Joseph in 1974–5. She wrote to the CPS volunteering her services in 1980, and within a few days had been commissioned by Sherman to write a CPS report on the steel industry, utilizing her academic skills as a specialist in industrial economics.[36] She also administered the study groups for the CPS. Sherman recognized the value of 'converts' to the CPS and the cause of economic liberalism as many of them were from working-class backgrounds, thereby mitigating the charge often made against the Conservative Party that it solely represented narrow and selfish class interests. Sherman advised Mrs Thatcher to speak over the heads of her own Party to reach this new constituency, and was always trying to gather such people into the CPS to create the new 'middle-ground' that Joseph had talked of in his 1974–5 speeches. He wrote to Mrs Thatcher that:

> You personally, David Howell, Norman Fowler, Keith Joseph, Rhodes Boyson, Ray Whitney are among those who could speak to Labour 'defectors' and 'freedom fighters' . . . I cannot stress too much that it is precisely the former Labour men whom we need to carry forward the fight for change. They are political animals, they have the fire, the ideals, the knowledge of what they are fighting against. They carry conviction . . .[37]

The CPS also drew on a number of intellectuals and academics who helped with speeches and the seminars and discussion groups that the CPS ran. Prominent amongst these academics were Shirley and William Letwin. Shirley Letwin had been taught at the LSE and Chicago by, amongst others, Hayek and Friedman and had returned to teach part-time at the LSE in the Department of Philosophy; William was a political philosopher, also at the LSE. They were regulars at the IEA, and in 1975 Ralph Harris asked the Letwins to see Joseph to help formulate a philosophical framework for the new economics, and to develop the moral arguments for capitalism and market economics. They helped to write passages for Joseph's speeches, and Shirley

Letwin became a Director of the CPS in 1979. Peter Bauer, the economist from the LSE, also attended lunches and occasionally contributed to the work of the CPS, as did Professor Kenneth Minogue of the LSE, who lectured at the student seminar weekends that the CPS ran for university students. Tim Congdon, an economist in the City and formerly economics correspondent of *The Times*, also became an important CPS writer, publishing *Monetarism: An Essay in Definition* (CPS, 1978) and *Against Import Controls* (CPS, 1981). Congdon became the most widely respected independent monetarist economist. Again, few of these people would have felt at ease in the Conservative Party, but the CPS gave them a usefulness and a role in politics that only the CPS, committed to an ideology rather than a party, could provide.

Many of the CPS recruits, with their varying professional skills, were introduced directly to Mrs Thatcher and Sir Keith Joseph who later used them in some capacity in Government; David Young as a Minister, or Norman Strauss and John Hoskyns in the Downing Street Policy Unit. Sherman and the CPS were important to Mrs Thatcher in another way, however, as they helped to instil in her a sense of purpose and a sense of ideological rigour and the belief that she had to win the battle of ideas as much as anything else. A few days after her first election victory she wrote to Alfred Sherman that

> We are over the first hurdle; now for the real battle. In that I hope you will play as important a part as you have done over the past few years. You have been a constant inspiration to Keith and myself through difficult times. Your creative mind has been responsible for many skirmishing victories in the great battle of ideas, which I am convinced we are on the way to winning . . .
>
> None of us will forget that 'There is one thing stronger than armies and that is an idea whose time has come.'[38]

Everyone who worked with Mrs Thatcher at this time, before 1979, testified to how willing she was to learn. Norman Strauss said that 'Where she knew she had to learn, she was a very good pupil', and Sherman recalled that 'she was a very good listener'.[39] Mrs Thatcher was particularly keen to learn from Sherman and fully appreciated his skills as a dialectician and as a speech-writer. For his help in preparing her Party Conference speech in 1977, she wrote to thank him 'very much indeed, not only for what you did at Blackpool last week, but for all the assistance you have given over the last year or two. There is no way in which I can thank you adequately but I hope you know how much your work is appreciated by myself and everyone in my office.'[40] Sherman, for his part, regarded her with a tenacious loyalty during the period of opposition, bombarding her with a stream of memoranda on a bewildering variety of topics, from 'Britain's Ethnic Problems' in 1977 to the problems of the Labour Party in Wales in 1979.[41] When Mrs Thatcher moved to Downing Street in 1979 and the question of access became paramount in any 'adviser's' relationship with the Prime Minister, there were only very few for whom she would try to make time and to whom she would strive to listen , and they were, in the early years, John Hoskyns, Hugh Thomas, Ralph Harris, Alfred Sherman and Alan Walters. So the CPS and IEA were both well represented.

For Sherman's part, he felt that Mrs Thatcher had 'beliefs, not ideas', and that the 'CPS articulated her instincts'. The CPS expressed her deepest instincts and moral convictions in political terms. Contrary to her popular image, she was regarded in the CPS as a supremely cautious politician; Ronnie Millar, her long-serving speech-writer, used to call her 'Cautious Margaret'. Joseph was the intellectual adventurer – almost an intellectual dilettante – whilst Mrs Thatcher was the steely politician, who needed to be thoroughly convinced of an idea before embracing it. She was interested in ideas but was not of a reflective, enquiring temperament; the CPS did her reflecting and enquiring for her. Strauss later wrote of her: 'Mrs Thatcher says: "I am a great believer in taking things by steps. Once you show you can achieve one step you set a new target. I don't believe in being airy-fairy. I believe in what's practicable and achievable." This gets to the core of why the Prime Minister is not a systems thinker; she is an incremental pragmatist with convictions.'[42]

The CPS thus played a key role in not only articulating a political programme of economic liberalism, but in recruiting those men and women from varying – but mostly non-Tory – backgrounds who would work out the relevant policies and put them into operation in government. In terms of policy input into the Conservative Shadow Cabinet as it prepared for Government the CPS also played a vital role, although it might have seemed somewhat marginal at the time. On economic policy, the Party produced two documents in opposition, *The Right Approach* in 1976 and *The Right Approach to the Economy* in 1977. The latter was very much a compromise between the old 'Tory-Paternalist' wing of the Party and the 'liberal Conservatives', and was thus signed by not only the economic liberals Howe, Keith Joseph and David Howell but also by James Prior. This document broadly endorsed the new consensus on economic thinking which had developed in the mid-1970s, and promised to make the defeat of inflation a priority. The Conservative Party 'policy group' on the economy had no direct CPS input, but was staffed by several politicians and economists who had been associated with either the IEA, or the CPS, including Geoffrey Howe, Peter Cropper (who had drafted the Longbow Manifesto with Diana Spearman in 1967), David Howell, John Nott, Nigel Lawson and Adam Ridley. All in all, the Conservative Party was running ninety-six 'policy groups' by the time of the 1979 election to develop policy over a wide range of issues; it was thus with some justification that MPs could claim that Mrs Thatcher's government of 1979 was the best prepared in the Party's history. However, the only two 'policy groups' which mattered in the long run were the Economic Reconstruction Group, which drafted *The Right Approach to The Economy* and Nicholas Ridley's policy group on the nationalized industries, which first went into the practical mechanics of 'denationalization' as well as the possible confrontations which would arise with the unions if such policies were pursued. However, before any steps could be made towards a freer, more liberal economy most MPs and commentators agreed that there was a large stumbling block that stood in the way of any reform at all – the trade unions.

As Hayek had argued in his original paper to the 1947 Mont Pèlerin Society, the major obstacle to the practical implementation of the economic liberal reforms that his fellow Mont Pèlerin members wanted to see was the strong trade union movement in Britain. Indeed, as we have seen, the principal criticism by the Mont Pèlerins of Keynes was that he had invented his whole system of economics merely to sidestep the main issue of the ability of trade unions to exert a constant upwards pressure on wages, regardless of productivity or profit. This had become the burning issue of the 1970s, and, having been humbled by the miners in 1972 and 1974, the official Conservative Party policy-making machinery shied away from the issue of trade union reform, wary of antagonizing a trade union movement which many saw as all-powerful and unappeasable. The Party thus said very little on this issue, and the policy documents virtually skirted over it. Although the Party formally supported the management during the Grunwick dispute, few had appreciated the significance of it. The CPS, however, did, and it was on the issue of trade union power – and how to curb it – that the CPS now began to take up a position far in advance of the rest of the Conservative Party, and genuinely to think the unthinkable.

To the CPS, by the mid-1970s, the reform of the trade unions had become the sine qua non of everything else that they were trying to achieve. In *Monetarism Is Not Enough*, Joseph had argued that the control of the money supply to stabilize prices was merely the starting-point for everything else that the economic liberals wanted to do to recreate the market economy, and foremost amongst these tasks was the reform of trade union law, for without a decrease in the power of union 'barons' to dictate wages and conditions at arbitrary and *political* levels, the country could never enjoy the fruits of a market economy. Indeed, in many ways this was precisely the problem that Keynes had been grappling with forty years earlier. However, just as most of the Conservative Party, like Keynes, hesitated to attack the power of trade unions and sought to find easier ways around the problem, Sherman recognized that by the mid–late 1970s the trade unions, by their constant striking and blatant sectional self-interest, had made themselves uniquely unpopular, and had almost exhausted the public sympathy which they had enjoyed since the 1930s. Encouraged by the efforts of NAFF at Grunwick, Sherman recognized that the time was now ripe for a counter-attack against the unions. He outlined his views in a number of memos to Mrs Thatcher in 1978 and 1979. In December 1978 he wrote:

> Our approach to the country's labour problems and trade union reforms will succeed to the extent that it wins over the public to a frankly Hobbesian approach . . . we have reached a stage where trade union activity makes almost everybody, including most Trade-Unionists, worse off than they would otherwise be. Everyone stands to be more struck against than striking ('strike' is used here as a portmanteau word for strike, strike-threat, go-slow, restrictive practices, overmanning, non-cooperation, bad service, union-backed pilfering). Therefore, almost everyone has the incentive to accept reform.

WHY NOW?

The question arises why the unions do so much more perceived harm than they formerly did.

The reasons include:

The number of trade-unionists has quadrupled since the second world war. The public services, which affect people more directly, have been unionised.

The closed shop gives the politically committed and militants more power over the rank-and-file.

Inflation (caused basically by government under Keynesian illusions, though the Unions have helped press government into inflationary measures) makes strikers of us all. In a period of stable prices, many unions and their members will accept the status quo. In a period of inflation, no one can afford to be left behind; once they have tasted blood, even artificial blood, their appetite grows.

The balance of bargaining power has shifted as a result of several factors. First, governments have competed in 'getting on with the unions' i.e. making unrequited concessions. Second, the unintended results of the 1960 NI Act, which subsidises strikes (an unforeseen novelty here which exists nowhere in the world) lowers the cost of striking . . .

Thirdly, the climate of opinion has favoured Unions owing to the spread of Marxist and other forms of Socialist thought, while management has been demoralised by circumstances and by the lack of a cause or set of ideas to maintain their fighting spirit.

Fourthly, members of favoured unions can expect government rescue if they bankrupt their firm or industry. . . . Lastly, the law-enforcement authorities rarely enforce laws against violence and intimidation used by unions.

> SELF-DEFEATING POWERS
>
> The result is that trade-union action, which in this country is almost entirely negative ... has succeeded in turning against trade unions themselves ...
>
> Hence we shall be in an archetypal Hobbesian situation, in which we can tell the people, in effect, your life is increasingly nasty and brutish ... because each of you has at his disposal greater means of harming your fellows than of defending himself. It is in all your interests, therefore, to give up some of these powers if all others can be obliged to do so. Hence trade-union reform is not union-bashing, but in the interests of trade-Unionists.[43]

This was Sherman's crucial insight, that not only was trade-union reform a necessity, but that by 1978 such reform would also be popular with many trade unionists, to say nothing of the electorate in general. The Conservative Party still wanted to avoid the union issue out of fear that it would be a vote-loser, but the CPS argued that precisely the reverse was now true, that union reform could be electorally popular. As Sherman wrote in another 'Highly Confidential' memo to Mrs Thatcher in 1978:

> The public mood *vis à vis* the Unions has changed. The Unions' moral ascendancy has been eroded, they are no longer seen as valiant fighters for the underdog but as selfish and often ruthless operators ... What counts is that 'do something about the Unions' is again thinkable.
>
> We must put forward the principle that for a return to free responsible collective bargaining – which is essential to democracy and economic efficiency – we must first restore the balance of bargaining power. We must urge this as something in the Union's own interests ...[44]

Mrs Thatcher listened to Sherman and the CPS's views on the unions because they spoke with the added conviction of having been trade unionists or Socialists themselves. Chief amongst these was the remarkable and quietly spoken Sir Leonard Neal, who became Mrs Thatcher's most trusted independent adviser on trade union reform in the late 1970s and early 1980s. Like Mrs Thatcher, he came from a staunchly Methodist background, and like many at the CPS he came from a working-class family (in London), and was brought up during the depression of the 1930s; he was unemployed at the age of sixteen. He trained as a Methodist Minister at Richmond College, but abandoned his studies to join the 'True Church' – the trade union movement. He worked as a labourer and joined the TGWU, and in 1945 became a full-time official with the Union. In 1952 he went up to Trinity College, Cambridge, to take a degree at the age of thirty-nine, and got a 2:1; he was the first man to graduate from within the union movement. In the early 1960s he left the TGWU to work as the company negotiator for Esso at Fawley Oil Refinery, where he developed the idea of 'productivity bargaining', as opposed to negotiating automatic annual wage increases. His disillusion with trade unionism had already set in by that time, and his feelings of disenchantment were only strengthened by his work for the British Railways Board as their union negotiator during the late 1960s. Neal was one of Barbara Castle's advisers when she drafted her ill-fated attempt to reform the unions in 1969, 'In Place of Strife'. Neal then chaired the Commission for Industrial Relations from 1971 to 1974. He was thus well known in the world of industrial relations when Sir Keith Joseph grabbed his arm at a House of Commons drinks party in 1974 and asked him to advise the CPS, in an informal way, on trade union reform. Neal 'was apolitical' but admired what Joseph and Mrs Thatcher were trying to do, and of course, for Neal 'only if you worked closely in the unions [did] you realise how many defects the unions had.'[45] Neal started chairing meetings on Thursday nights at the CPS to discuss trade union reform, and chaired the first CPS 'Study Group' on trade union reform, popularly known as TURC. The most important members of TURC when it was at its most productive in the early 1980s were Neal, Lionel Bloch, a solicitor, Dr Paul McCormick, an academic from Nuffield College, Oxford, John Hoskyns, Graham Mather, Alfred Sherman, Gerald Frost, Ray Whitney MP and Robert Flack, a QC. TURC was the most important 'Study Group' that the CPS set up, and through the quiet but insistent conduit of Neal, it became the 'Study Group' that wielded the most influence with Mrs Thatcher and Joseph. TURC was prepared to offer the sort of radical advice that the official party apparatus dared not even contemplate, advice that the CPS was eager to give because the CPS had fewer hang-ups about dealing with the unions than the rather more fresh-faced, guilt-ridden public-schoolboys across Westminster at Conservative Central Office.

The collective wisdom of the CPS on the trade union problem was incorporated into a celebrated document that Strauss and Hoskyns produced for Sir Keith Joseph entitled 'Stepping Stones'. 'Stepping Stones' arose out of a particularly unproductive lunch that Hoskyns had with Joseph in 1976, after which he complained to Joseph that the CPS, in its constant speculations about what reforms they wanted to see implemented, was 'trying to build a tower-block without foundations'.[46] Joseph accepted this criticism, and invited Hoskyns, with Strauss, to write a paper on the strategy that would be needed by an incoming government to implement the ambitious economic reforms that Joseph wanted to see. No specific mention was made of trade unions at that point, but it became central to the whole document, which argued, as had Sherman, that the unions occupied a unique position in that they were capable of blocking all reform that the CPS wanted to implement, and so trade union reform itself had to be the highest priority; moreover, Hoskyns advocated making a virtue of tackling the unions as they were quickly reaching the nadir of their popularity – a point confirmed by the public reaction to the 'Winter of Discontent' of 1978–9 which took place only two years after 'Stepping Stones' was written. 'Stepping Stones' listed what it called four 'turnaround' policies designed to 'turn the economy around before it reaches the point where lasting recovery might be impossible': currency stabilization (requiring 'sustained monetary discipline, balanced budgets, public sector wage restraint'), a shift of personal tax from income to expenditure, the deregulation of the private sector (creating the 'enterprise culture') and using North Sea oil tax revenue to 'cut the borrowing requirements of the public sector, to keep interest rates low, encourage investment'. The first three of these aims were largely conditional on a reduction in union powers, as they cut directly at the vested interests of the old 'trade union barons'. The document was long, but set out in a way that demonstrated how all the issues which the prospective Conservative Government would have to deal with were inter-related, and how success on one 'Stepping Stone' would give the stability needed to move on to the next. It set out a long-term strategy for a government, much as private sector management had always used, and as such represented a new approach to government for politicians. Sir Keith Joseph's biographer has written that 'Mrs Thatcher was impatient of much of the paper that crossed her desk from the Party's hundred and one planning groups . . . but her eyes lit up when the draft of "Stepping Stones" was shown to her.'[47] The 'summary' of 'Stepping Stones' outlined the strategic thinking behind the document, and the central role that trade union reform would play in such a strategy:

'Stepping Stones'

SUMMARY

1. THE SIZE OF THE JOB

1.1 The task of the next Tory Government – national recovery – will be of a different order from that facing any other post-war government. Recovery requires a sea-change in Britain's political economy.

1.2 A Tory landslide is not enough, if it only reflects the electorate's material dissatisfaction since 1974. A landslide is needed, but it must represent an explicit rejection of socialism and the Labour–trades unions axis; and the demand for something morally and economically better.

1.3 The Tory Party's pre-election strategy must ensure that the preparation of policy includes plans for the removal of political obstacles to its implementation.

1.4 There is one major obstacle – the negative role of the trades unions. Unless a satisfying and creative role can be developed, national recovery will be virtually impossible.

1.5 To compete with Labour in seeking peaceful co-existence with an unchanged union movement will ensure continued economic decline, masked initially by North Sea oil. It may also make failure to win Office more, rather than less, likely for the Tories. There is nothing to gain (except just possibly, Office without authority), and everything to lose by such a 'low risk' approach.

1.6 Skilfully handled, however, the rising tide of public feeling could transform the unions from Labour's secret weapon into its major electoral liability, and the fear of union–Tory conflict could be laid to rest.[48]

Mrs Thatcher might have been impressed by 'Stepping Stones', but Hoskyns and Strauss still had to win over a very sceptical Shadow

Cabinet to their ideas. 'Stepping Stones' was circulated at the end of 1977, and during 1978 the two CPS men tried to persuade the Shadow Cabinet to accept it, but with little success. James Prior, the Shadow Minister for Employment and one of the most prominent Conservative collectivists, would not accept it, and another important Shadow Minister, Sir Ian Gilmour, stonewalled. Finally, in March 1979, at the height of the 'Winter of Discontent', the Shadow Cabinet came round to accepting the 'Stepping Stones' policy. Hoskyns and Strauss recall that John Biffen was the decisive figure in bringing the Shadow Cabinet around, as he had previously supported Prior and now 'crossed the floor' and supported Hoskyns and Strauss, although Biffen had no recollection of this when interviewed in 1991. Hoskyns and Strauss thus immediately got down to drawing up the necessary trade union legislation with Prior's 'Policy Group' on trade unions, legislation which would later emerge as Prior's first Employment Act. As it was, when the Conservatives came to power, the CPS's TURC was dismayed by the lack of radicalism and sense of urgency that Prior showed at the Department of Employment in the field of trade union reform, and it was in this policy area that the CPS thus worked to exert a great deal of influence during the first few years of Mrs Thatcher's administration. The work of the CPS on trade union reform was absolutely crucial to the Conservative Party's success at the 1979 election, as well as to the strategy pursued in government from 1979 to 1983. The CPS had made trade union reform a virtue out of necessity, and proved that the Conservative Party no longer needed to regard reform of trade union privileges as an electoral embarrassment.

If the CPS was successful in forcing trade union reform to the top of the Conservative Party's agenda, it was less successful in persuading the Party of the need to deal with another critical obstacle to economic reform – the Civil Service. The CPS, particularly Sherman, Hoskyns and Strauss, viewed the Civil Service as the most powerful vested interest in the country which stood to lose most from the economic reforms – particularly the cuts in government expenditure and denationalization – that the CPS wanted to see. The Civil Service, with a larger stake than most other sections of the community in the status quo, would thus try to blunt, or side-track, *any* radical reforms that the economic liberals wanted to carry out in government. It was an analysis that the CPS shared with the Left; Tony Benn and other Socialists had come to a similar conclusion about the capacity of the

Civil Service to muffle a government's programme of radical reforms after the Labour Party's experience in office from 1964 to 1970. It was also an analysis that seemed to be confirmed by the contents of Richard Crossman's Cabinet diaries, published in the mid-1970s. Sherman and Strauss also had a particular contempt for the quality of civil servants, viewing most of them as second-rate, unimaginative careerists who cared more for the minutiae of departmental procedure than the implementation of government policy. In a lecture at the LSE in 1984, Sherman told his audience that:

> The Civil Service is consensual rather than dialectical, conduct-oriented rather than achievement-oriented. It is incrementalist and sits ill with overviews, re-thinks, radical change. The career structure tends to generate commitment among senior ranks to the status quo. Civil Servants lead cloistered lives. They go from prep school to public school to university to Civil Service, facing few of the hazards of life; competition; the prospect of failure and its penalties; war; conflict; they enjoy job security, certain pensions, steady promotion prospects. The nature of human life, with its drastic self-generated changes, which call for equally drastic adjustments, is antithetic to their thinking, which rarely leaves room for discontinuities, which are an essential element of the human condition.[49]

He was much cruder than this in private, and reserved particular contempt, like many 'Thatcherites', for the Foreign Office. Sherman had also watched Sir Keith Joseph's performance in Government in 1970–4, and had concluded that he had simply been eaten alive by his civil servants. To bypass the Civil Service, Sherman thus recommended a 'Territorial Army of Advisers' of proven ideological conviction to advise Ministers in government. In July 1977, Sherman wrote a memo, in conjunction with Arthur Seldon, arguing that a recruitment drive for such an 'Army' of special advisers should start well before the election, so that they could move directly into Whitehall on the morrow of the election victory, to cover all Whitehall departments; Sherman warned that 'unless this is done the Civil Servants will make hay at our expense.'[50] However, on this issue, Sherman, Hoskyns and Strauss made little headway, as they could not get Joseph or Mrs

Thatcher to take a great interest in the subject; Joseph, in particular, had enormous respect for the Civil Service. To the CPS, this was to become *the* greatest problem facing the Government after its first few years of office. For their part, civil servants tended to view the CPS much as the CRD did, as wild-eyed revolutionaries who were best kept at arm's length. In an interview with the *Independent* in 1987, Sir Kenneth Clucas, a Permanent Secretary at the DTI until 1982, criticized the Thatcher governments' intellectual sources: 'The ideas they get from the Centre for Policy Studies and such like, have no intellectual rigour; some of the ideas may be quite good but some of them are just appalling, and generally speaking they are not of the quality that one needs for this process of policy-making.'[51] The CPS's disdain for the Civil Service was, in many instances, heartily reciprocated.

To strengthen its work on policy formulation and to expand it across a broader range of issues, in 1978–9 the CPS set up a number of other 'study groups' as well as TURC. By 1983 there were sixteen of these groups. Some, such as the 'Culture and Enterprise Group', chaired by Peter Utley, set up to discuss cultural and social resistance to 'the enterprise society' and consisting of Kingsley Amis, Elizabeth Jane Howard and Gerald Frost were rather more enjoyable than productive. But several of the study groups, which normally met about once a month at Wilfred Street, did develop coherent and important ideas and policies. Chief amongst these were TURC, the Nationalized Industries Study Group, the Soviet Relations Group (chaired by Lord Thomas), the Education Group (chaired by Caroline Cox), the Personal Capital Formation Group (chaired by Nigel Vinson), the Health Group (chaired by the surgeon George Bunton) as well as 'the Argonauts', a group formed specifically to create a link between the Government and industry during the 1980 steel strike. There were also, at one time or another, study groups on Defence, Energy, Communications, Crime and Juvenile Delinquency, Transport, Urban Land and Housing, Housing and Local Government, De-Regulation and Law. Most of these study groups were at their most productive in the early 1980s, and the work of some of them will thus be examined in the next chapter. Most groups consisted of about ten members and Nigel Morgan of the CPS usually took minutes. Many of the groups once again drew people from various walks of life into the activities of the CPS, people who would normally have had little to do with politics. Professor R. V.

Jones, chair of the Defence Study Group, was typical of those who only got involved through the CPS; the Soviet Relations Study Group, chaired by Hugh Thomas, consisted, by 1983, of Professor Leonard Schapiro, Dr George Urban, Professor Hugh Seton-Watson, Dr Iain Elliot, Dr Anthony Polonsky, Andrew Acland and Hoskyns as well as Malcolm Mackintosh from the Cabinet Office. Some study groups had an impressively active and well informed membership, whilst others merely limped along and produced little – productivity usually depended on the individual Chairs of the groups.

The 'study groups' provided the CPS with most of its publishing programme, which it embarked upon in 1976 to draw the attention of the wider public to the CPS's political and economic arguments. Apart from Joseph's collected speeches, the first CPS pamphlet, by Samuel Brittan, *Second Thoughts on Full Employment*, was published in June 1976, followed by Hugh Thomas's *History, Capitalism and Freedom*. Several MPs wrote for the CPS, including John Biffen and Jock Bruce-Gardyne, and Mrs Thatcher could usually be prevailed upon to write a foreword, thus increasing the attraction for aspiring Conservative Ministers of writing for the CPS. Some study groups produced only one or two pamphlets, but these were of some significance. *What We Ought to Do about the Soviet Threat*, published in 1983, a product of the Soviet Relations Study Group, was of some importance in maintaining a hard line against the Soviet Union, whilst the two Education pamphlets written by Antony Flew, *Power to the People* (1983) and *Education, Race and Revolution* (1984) also had a considerable impact. Some of the early CPS pamphlets were comparatively simplistic and badly presented by comparison with the IEA's productions, but by the mid-1980s the CPS's publishing programme was at least as good as the IEA's.

As part of Sherman's much cherished ambition to push back the boundaries of what was 'sayable' and what was 'thinkable' in politics, the CPS also set out on a concerted campaign to bring the message of economic liberalism and the free market to the next generation of opinion-formers and intellectuals – students. Foremost in this campaign to take the message to the universities, where, during the 1970s, students would rarely have heard or been exposed to anything other than 'left-wing' or collectivist arguments, was Joseph's own 'Campus Campaign'. Joseph toured the universities speaking in either overflowing or half-empty halls (depending on the effectiveness of the boycott organized by the student Socialist bodies) during the years 1975 to 1978. He made 150 speeches at universities and polytechnics during those years, usually to a largely hostile audience. The CPS did not draft any speeches for him, as he tended to extemporize from a prepared text, but the CPS was regularly called upon to answer small queries and points of historical or economic detail arising from questions asked by the students. Joseph's main theme was the moral and philosophical justification for capitalism. David Willetts, later Director of the CPS, was one of those in the audience at Oxford in 1975 when Joseph came to speak. Talking at the annual meeting of the CPS in 1987 in front of Mrs Thatcher, Willetts recalled that the main achievement of the CPS had been to establish

> the intellectual force of Conservatism, and above all that is thanks to Sir Keith Joseph.
>
> I remember when I was an undergraduate at Oxford ... going to a packed lecture hall to hear Sir Keith Joseph talk about free markets, about monetarism and about the perils of corporatism. Such ideas were in the air, but they were not understood and they were not accepted. They were the sort of things that a rather respectable parent would warn his son against; the sort of thing that an ambitious tutor would be worried about if his students started flirting with. Sir Keith's courageous visits to most of our Universities during the second half of the 1970s changed all that ...[52]

This was, perhaps, a pardonable exaggeration, but the 'Campus Campaign' did attract a good deal of publicity and interest. It was also one of the few things that Joseph really enjoyed doing; his biographer related how his 'face lit up' when asked about these speeches. 'The most fulfilment in his career, he said, had come with the speeches to students. It was "self-inflicted misery", of course but "it was *lovely*. (Of course it was horrible at the same time). Very large audiences – almost to a girl or boy convinced Statists if not socialists".'[53] To complement Joseph's own 'Campus Campaign' the CPS also ran about ten 'Student Weekend Seminars' from 1977 to 1979, mainly organized by Gerald Frost. Frost argued that the 'justification for giving such a high priority to students is that if successful we shall influence – both directly and through the missionary work of those who go away sympathetic to our view-point – a future generation of journalists, civil servants, academics, industrial and business leaders – at a stage of their lives when they are particularly amenable to intellectual argument and have not already arrived at fixed political beliefs.'[54] Amongst other speakers at these student weekends were T. E. Utley, Dr Eamonn Butler (later of the Adam Smith Institute), Jeremy Shearmur (Popper's research assistant at the LSE and later Director of Studies at the CPS), Peter Lilley (on 'The Delusion of Incomes Policy'), William Letwin (on the 'Ethics of Profit'), John O'Sullivan, Ian Gow, Reg Prentice, Jock Bruce-Gardyne, Hugh Thomas, Martin Wassall, John Blundell and even, on one occasion, Sir James Goldsmith, who was one of the CPS's most important early backers. The weekends were normally well attended, but stopped when the Conservatives got into power in 1979. Perhaps just as useful as the 'Student Seminars' were the regular lunches and dinners at Wilfred Street, at which Conservative MPs and other interested parties were exposed to the economic and political arguments of the CPS over wine (of a famously variable quality) and food. The CPS was run on a shoestring budget – by 1981, it had an income of only £120,000 a year and could usually afford to pay only a handful of staff – but the sheer enthusiasm of those who worked for the CPS, most of whom were unpaid, made up for the cramped working conditions (a constant source of complaint for Sherman) and the relative paucity of financial support.

Although the CPS made the most important contribution to the revival of economic liberalism within and outside the Conservative Party during the mid and late 1970s, other 'think-tanks' and similar organizations were also making their own contributions at the same time. The work of the National Association for Freedom has already been referred to; and the IEA also remained highly active, publishing a stream of pamphlets and paperbacks laying down the broad principles of what the CPS were arguing for within the Conservative Party, including monetarism, trade union reform and educational reforms. The IEA also expanded its domestic activities by founding the Social Affairs Unit in December 1980, under the directorship of a sociology lecturer (and gourmet) from Nottingham University, Dr Digby Anderson. Anderson had become disillusioned with the largely Marxist domination of academic sociology during the 1960s and 1970s, and had thus edited a book, *The Ignorance of Social Intervention*, challenging the prevailing wisdom on the subject. His research brought him into contact first with Michael Ivens of Aims of Industry, and then with Arthur Seldon. Seldon persuaded him to found his own 'think-tank' to continue his work in this field, and after a few years at 2 Lord North Street the Social Affairs Unit (SAU) moved to its own premises. Seldon and Anderson conceived of the SAU as doing for sociology and social policy what the IEA had done for economics, fighting an intellectual counter-revolution against the prevailing collectivist, interventionist orthodoxies which permeated most of contemporary social policy. In fact, the SAU proved to be a good deal more catholic in its analysis of ideas than that, but, nonetheless, the SAU soon earned the reputation, as *The Times* put if, of 'driving its coach and horses through the liberal consensus, scattering intellectual picket lines as it goes. It is equally famous for raising questions which strike most people most of the time as too dangerous or too difficult to think about.'[55] Like the IEA, the SAU was entirely apolitical, but saw itself as being provocative in challenging well established ideas in such areas as the Welfare State and health policy. During the 1980s the SAU published numerous well argued and academically respectable pamphlets and books across the whole range of social policy, from health issues, education and diet to 'consumer' questions and environmental issues. The SAU had a noticeable effect on the education debate during the 1980s with such pamphlets as *The Pied Pipers of Education* (SAU, 1981), written jointly by Antony Flew, John Marks, Caroline Cox and others, whilst its 1988 pamphlet on *Who Teaches the Teachers?*, by Anthony O'Hear had a significant influence on the debate about teacher-training that was going on at the time. *The Wayward Curriculum* (SAU, 1986), for instance, drew attention to the number of subjects of dubious academic validity which were finding their way on to the school curriculum, such as 'Peace Studies', 'Women's Studies' and 'Political Education'. The exact influence of the SAU is difficult to determine, as it is impossible exactly to trace its influence on the implementation of government policy, but there is no doubt that the SAU was an important voice in the 1980s calling for a re-examination of numerous post-war orthodoxies on a number of social policy issues, and analyzing where the market could be applied to improve social and welfare provision.[56]

Of more long-term importance for the practical implementation of economic liberalism in the 1980s was the emergence in the late 1970s of the Adam Smith Institute (ASI). The ASI was originally founded in 1976, on the bicentennial of the publication of Adam Smith's *The Wealth of Nations*. The ASI was started by three graduates of St Andrews University, Dr Madsen Pirie, Dr Eamonn Butler and his brother Dr Stuart Butler, reflecting the importance of St Andrews University as a centre of the intellectual development of economic liberalism during the 1960s and 1970s. All three were at St Andrews in the early 1970s, where they were very active, together with several later 'Thatcherite' MPs, in the University Conservative Association. At the 1971 Conservative Party Conference the young St Andrews Conservative delegation, as a protest against Heath's U-turn, produced a mock 'front-page' of a *Daily Telegraph* of June 1981, predicting the triumph of various free-market ideas. The mock '*Daily Telegraph*' reported on the floating pound, a rise in shares for 'Telecom' which had replaced the GPO and the sale of the last council house to its tenants. They not only got the price of the paper exactly right after inflation (15p), but also reported on the forthcoming serialization of a book about the success of 'one-time film star' Ronald Reagan in the previous November's Presidential Election. There was a temptation not to take these young free-market radicals too seriously, but even in 1971 they showed that they were already thinking 'the unthinkable'.

After leaving St Andrews Pirie and the Butlers worked in America for several years at Hillsdale College and for the Republican Study Committee founded by Dr Edwin Feulner Jr as a 'think-tank' for the Republican Party on Capitol Hill.[57] Feulner, who had studied at the LSE under Peter Bauer and who had worked part-time for Ralph Harris at the IEA in 1965, was one of the founding fathers, and later President, of the Heritage Foundation, the 'free-market' think-tank set up in Washington in 1973 to do for American politics what the CPS did for British politics.[58] The proximity of the founding dates of the CPS and Heritage – only one year apart – reflect the closely interwoven intellectual and political development of economic liberalism in Britain and the United States, as Hayek and Friedman's influence was just as pervasive on the 'New Right' in America as it was in Britain. Indeed, Heritage and the American Enterprise Institute (AEI), founded in 1943 (for largely the same reasons that Aims of Industry, the Society of Individualists and the Progress Trust were founded in Britain at exactly the same time) often worked closely with their British counterparts, although Heritage and AEI worked on an altogether different scale, employing hundreds, rather than a mere handful, of staff.[59] Just as Pirie and the Butlers worked for Feulner in the 1970s, so Stuart Butler, after founding the ASI in London, went to work as a policy analyst at the Heritage Foundation in 1981 and is now Vice-President for Domestic Policy Studies. John O'Sullivan, who shared a flat with Butler in London from 1977–9, spent four years at Heritage from 1979–83. After returning to London to work in Mrs Thatcher's Policy Unit from 1987 until late 1988, he later went on to be editor of the most influential organ of American Conservatism, the *National Review*, founded by William F. Buckley, Jr in 1955. The links between the British and American neo-liberal movements of the post-war era were thus close, guided as both movements were by the same economists and publicists of the Mont Pèlerin Society.[60] Henry Hazlitt, for instance, whose book review did so much to help the IEA in its early days, did his best to help similar fledgling organizations and journals such as the *Freeman*, in America.

In America, the Butlers, and particularly Pirie, became increasingly interested in the School of 'Public Choice Theory', developed by the Mont Pèlerin Nobel Laureate James Buchanan, which sought to apply the principles of market economics and techniques to the analysis of political behaviour.[61] 'Public Choice Theory' was concerned to design political institutions to 'maximise individual freedom for libertarian reasons. Most importantly, these institutions must impose constraints on the scope for spending allocation (and hence taxation needs) by politicians, and minimise the monopoly of the public sector.'[62] The Heritage Foundation developed its own application of this philosophy by making relatively specific policy proposals which would be applicable in practice to a given set of political and institutional circumstances. It was this strategy, which worked well in America, that the founders of ASI imported back into Britain when they returned from the United States in the mid-1970s. Pirie described the ASI as 'the creative counterpart of the Public Choice critique', and called the ASI analysis of policy-making 'Micropolitics', the title of a book on the subject that he wrote in 1988.[63] Pirie advocated a more detailed, pragmatic, and flexible approach to policy making if economic liberal policies were to be successfully applied and the ASI thus set out to provide the detailed analysis of how a policy could be implemented in practice. Pirie saw the failures of the Heath and Nixon administrations of the early 1970s as failures of 'policy engineering', not of intellectual nerve. He argued that although the IEA had played an outstanding role in publicizing and articulating the *ideas* of economic liberalism, a 'micropolitical' approach was needed to translate these ideas into usable policy proposals. Pirie's favourite metaphor was that of the scientist and the engineer, as the ASI acted as 'policy engineers', complementing the 'pure scientists' at the IEA. Whereas the IEA, or even the CPS, might establish the theoretical case for denationalizing British Steel, the ASI would provide the detailed, step-by-step proposals to show how this could be done in practice. For Pirie ideas were not enough:

> The successes achieved by the new-style policies [i.e. economic liberalism] allowed for the rise of the attractive but erroneous view that the work of lonely scholars, their acolytes and their advocates had finally paid off and brought results in its train. That these results had not come in the earlier administrations which attempted them was put down to a wrong climate or wrong personnel. In fact, it was wrong policies. It was the policy engineers, coming in the wake of the pure scientists of politics and economic theory, who made the machines which made events. The ideas had been sufficient to win the intellectual battle, but this was not enough. Men and women with spanners in their hands and grease on their fingers had first to devise the ways in which the ideas of pure theory could be turned into technical devices to alter reality. The idea at the core of micropolitics is that creative ingenuity is needed to apply to the practical world of interest group politics the concepts of free market theory.[64]

Whereas the IEA had provided the general theory and principles, and the CPS had won a party political constituency for those principles, the ASI found a niche for itself as the 'policy engineers' to develop practical policy proposals which could translate those principles into practice when the Conservative Government came to power. The *raisons d'être* of these three 'think-tanks' did, indeed, directly map the contours of the process of putting ideas into action. Hayek had always realized the need for such a progression from 'ideas' to 'practice' and the work of the ASI represented the final stage of that process whereby ideas came to be translated into practical policy proposals, to be implemented by a political party pledged to acting on those ideas. The ASI also represented the first of a 'second generation' of 'think-tanks' which owed their intellectual and practical inspiration to the IEA, founded twenty years before the ASI. At first the ASI acted as little more than a student-exchange organization, arranging courses for Hillsdale College students at Oxford and Cambridge summer schools. Eamonn Butler and John Blundell also organized specialist conferences and the St James Society Seminars, held twice yearly at the St James Hotel, London, on subjects such as 'The Idea of Competition' (with Hayek and Dr Rhodes Boyson), 'Competition in Politics' (with John O'Sullivan, Kenneth Minogue and Brian Walden) and 'Competition in Ideas' (with Professor Julius Gould and T. E. Utley). In January 1979, however, the ASI published its first policy pamphlet *The Trojan Horse*, by John Burton, on the role of trade union power in politics. The success of this pamphlet was helped by two articles based on it in successive issues of the *Daily Telegraph*, and thereafter the ASI published a steady stream of papers looking at how to apply market ideas to a number of areas which had not been covered by the other think-tanks. In July, 1979, the ASI published *Quango, Quango, Quango* by the Conservative MP Philip Holland, which proposed the closure of a thousand of the wasteful quasi-autonomous national governmental organizations that had proliferated under the previous Labour administration. The incoming Conservative Government eventually eliminated over six hundred of them. In October 1979 the ASI published, in conjunction with the National Federation of Self-Employed and Small Businesses, a pamphlet on the increasing powers of entry and inspection to homes and businesses enjoyed by the government in *An Inspector at the Door*. All these gained considerable press coverage, even in the *Sun*. Indeed, the ASI was always publicity-conscious, and became famous in political circles for its ability to grab the headlines by the clever and provocative packaging of its ideas. The ASI was also fortunate in being able to draw on the writing talents of many of the younger 'liberal-conservatives' who used the ASI to air their free-market ideas, such as the MPs John Moore and Michael Portillo. The ASI was also particularly well connected to the younger generation of St Andrews MPs, such as Christopher Chope, Michael Forsyth, Michael Fallon and Robert Jones, who either wrote for the ASI or contributed to some of its projects. Indeed, the St Andrews connection remained very important to the ASI – even its design format embraced the colours of St Andrews: light blue, white and dark blue. From the start the ASI was a 'low cost, low budget' operation, and for the first ten years neither the perennially bow-tied Pirie, President of the ASI, or Eamonn Butler, Director, drew salaries from the Institute. Sir James Goldsmith, however, was one of the early funders of the ASI, as he had been of the CPS, and did a good deal to promote the cause of the ASI in his short-lived *Now!* magazine. Clive Sinclair, the inventor, also funded the Institute from 1981 and from the early 1980s the ASI began to attract regular business sponsorship in the same way as the IEA. The ASI was 'apolitical' in the sense that it was not the creation of leading members of the Conservative Party like the CPS, and so was in no way beholden to the Party, but it acted with individual ministers and MPs to get certain policies implemented. This became an advantage when the Conservatives moved into government in 1979, as they could publish ideas and radical proposals as a bona-fide independent free-market institute, whilst the CPS gradually submerged under the difficulties of defining its relationship to the Party in government.

The general election of 3 May 1979 thus brought to power a Conservative Government with not only a clear ideological purpose, at least as far as Mrs Thatcher and the small, but key, number of ministers who supported her in Cabinet were concerned, but also the will and practical policies to implement the ideology. The CPS had given the Prime Minister, through 'Stepping Stones' and *Monetarism Is Not Enough*, a clear, pragmatic strategy to carry through an effective economic reform of the country over a period of five-ten years. In this sense, the Conservative Government that came to power in 1979 could claim to be the best prepared for office in British history, and much of this was down to what Sherman liked to call the 'para-politicians' of the CPS. More importantly, perhaps, the IEA and the CPS, as well as, to a lesser extent, such groups as the Selsdon Group, Aims of Industry and the National Association For Freedom had helped to change the intellectual climate in which politics was debated, thus making Mrs Thatcher's comparatively radical policy platform of 1979 politically possible. This was particularly true of the trade union issue. The IEA, just as much as the force of circumstances, had made 'monetarism' almost a commonly accepted working concept by the mid-1970s, but it took, perhaps, even greater courage and foresight to argue that the trade unions were finally vulnerable to a concerted attack even before the 'Winter of Discontent' of 1979 which helped Mrs Thatcher to power. Added to that the Adam Smith Institute was already, by

1979, shaping the detailed policy proposals which would help the new government put its ideas into practice.

The 1979 election victory was thus the culmination of nearly forty years of intellectual and political work since the 'Colloque Walter Lippmann' had assembled in Paris in 1938, and the first meeting of the Mont Pèlerin Society in 1947. Unusually in British politics, the 1979 election victory signalled the victory of an idea – the idea of economic liberalism. James Callaghan, the outgoing Labour Prime Minister, was aware of this as much as anyone else. Bernard Donoughue, the head of the Downing Street Policy Unit from 1974 to 1979, has written of a car journey he took with Callaghan towards the end of the 1979 campaign:

> As we drove round Parliament Square toward Whitehall and Downing Street, I drew Mr. Callaghan's attention to a recent improvement in the opinion polls, remarking that, with a little luck, and a few policy initiatives here and there, we might just squeak through. He turned to me and said quietly: 'I should not be too sure. You know there are times, perhaps once every thirty years, when there is a sea-change in politics. It then does not matter what the public wants and what it approves of. I suspect there is now such a sea-change – and it is for Mrs Thatcher.'[65]

On this occasion, the Prime Minister was more astute than his adviser, and even if it can be argued that this 'sea-change' was the result of the self-destruction, or 'implosion', of the Keynesian post-war economic system, there is no doubt that the economic liberals – the IEA, the CPS, the Society of Individualists, the Selsdon Group, NAFF et al – not only predicted the implosion with depressing accuracy, but, much more importantly, they were also around to pick up the pieces.

8

'The Heroic Age' II

Triumph and Despair, 1979–1983

*

Mrs Thatcher's election victory in 1979 meant that, for the first time since the 1930s, a British government, on election, was committed to those policies of economic liberalism that the Mont Pèlerin Society and the IEA – amongst others – had been advocating since the 1940s. More specifically, Mrs Thatcher was the first prime minister to accept the full implications of Hubert Henderson's memo written as far back as 1930* that the real solution to Britain's economic difficulties, which had hardly altered in the intervening fifty years, was to 'face up to the disagreeable reactionary necessity of cutting costs (including wages) in industry and cutting expenditure in public affairs'. The economic liberals had accused the Keynesians of running away 'under cover of complex sophistication, from the plain moral of the situation', and in Mrs Thatcher they finally found a political figure willing to 'face up' to those 'disagreeable necessities', albeit, perhaps, half a century too late. The election of 1979 signalled the *political* end to the Keynesian era of demand management and full employment – which had quickly become a euphemism for over-manning – and the beginning of an attempt to implement those policies of industrial and economic adjustment that Henderson et al. had urged on the government in 1929–30. 'Thatcherism' was certainly not a novel idea; but the failure, since 1930, of successive British governments to address the structural flaws in the economy ensured that Mrs Thatcher's aim of dismantling the detritus of fifty years of collectivist economic policies would only be achieved at what turned out to be an almost impossibly high cost.

However, although the economic liberals had every reason to be pleased with the election of Mrs Thatcher, beneath the superficial appearance of Cabinet unity and Party loyalty her first Government quickly turned out to be the most divided and unhappy in modern

* See page 39 for the full quotation.

British political history. Although she ensured that economic liberals occupied the key economic and industrial posts, the new Cabinet was dominated by the traditional Conservative collectivists who had looked askance at the work of the IEA and the CPS. Thus, although Geoffrey Howe and John Biffen went to the Treasury, and Sir Keith Joseph, with his special adviser from the CPS David Young, went to the Department of Industry, and other economic liberals like John Nott went to the Department of Trade, the Cabinet was predominantly made up of those, like James Prior at the Department of Employment, who had little sympathy with a radical programme of economic reform, let alone economic liberalism as a workable philosophy – the 'Wets', as they quickly came to be known. To many of her supporters, like Nicholas Ridley, it always seemed perverse that the Prime Minister should have shared her Cabinet table with so many who were opposed to her, whatever the arguments in favour of 'balance' and carrying all sections of the party with her. As Ridley later recalled, 'To me, and to my friends, it was always inexplicable why she appointed to her first Cabinet so many people who didn't share her ambitions or believe in her analysis of the nature of the cancer eating into the heart of Britain. I confess to being bitterly disappointed at finding myself dealing with the problems of Latin America and the Caribbean from the Foreign Office, where she sent me in 1979, while the Cabinet was packed with supporters of the old consensus, Heathite policies.'[1] The composition of the Cabinet ensured that Mrs Thatcher's first Government was as preoccupied with internal strife within the Cabinet as with the battle against the Labour Party. It was perhaps fortuitous that Labour proved to be more interested in its own self-immolation and fissures than in exposing the Conservatives' divisions; Labour's own identity crisis eventually brought about the creation of the Social Democratic Party in 1981. It was thus only after the 1983 election that Mrs Thatcher really consolidated her position in the Cabinet and commanded a clear majority for her reforms, buoyed by her landslide 1983 election victory. The debates and disputes within government about the speed and character of Mrs Thatcher's economic reforms from 1979 to 1983 might have made for an uneasy atmosphere in Cabinet, but it provided a vital job for the CPS, which, after all, had been founded to fight those very intellectual battles which dominated the 1979–83 Government.

Although the economic liberals might have won the wider argument about the crisis of Keynesianism which helped to shape the intellectual environment in which Mrs Thatcher came to power, they were still in a minority when it came to taking those 'disagreeable' political decisions which were needed to bring about the return of a free-market economy in Britain. Within a year of the 1979 election, by which time the magazine *Marxism Today* had invented the term 'Thatcherism' to describe the politics of the free economy and the strong State, the Cabinet was irrevocably split over the nature and pace of Mrs Thatcher's economic reforms. With the economic liberals almost completely isolated in Cabinet, the economic liberals in the 'think-tanks' – particularly the CPS – assumed a role of critical importance to the Prime Minister as sources of that advice and support which she failed to get from the rest of her Cabinet. This was particularly true of the crucial year of 1981, when the fate of the entire 'Thatcherite' enterprise hung in the balance. Once Mrs Thatcher had won the Falklands War in 1982, and the economy had begun to recover in 1983, allowing her to choose a Cabinet which better reflected her own political beliefs, so the importance of the 'para-politicians' from the CPS and elsewhere declined swiftly. Indeed, the departure of Sherman from the CPS in 1983 effectively brought the 'Heroic Age' to an end and the role of the CPS changed significantly; it became much more a creature of government than a quasi-autonomous fount of radical thinking.

The intellectual counter-revolution had not been won, then, by 1979: it was only after 1983 that the ideas of Thatcherism became, as Sherman had predicted, the new 'centre ground' of politics. I will deal in this chapter with that final phase of the counter-revolution, the first Thatcher administration; the battle in the Cabinet between the 'Wets' and the 'Drys' has often been chronicled, and I will confine myself to the activities of the 'para-politicians' from the 'think-tanks', who not only made a considerable contribution to the first Thatcher administration but who also prepared the policies that were to mark the high tide of Thatcherism from 1983 to 1988. Furthermore, by 1983 the documentary evidence needed to assess the contribution of the 'think-tanks' begins to dry up, and the oral evidence becomes confusing if not downright contradictory. Nor is this very surprising, as it is perhaps natural for as many people as possible to claim paternity for many of the successful economic reforms of the middle years of Mrs Thatcher's premiership. In 1989, for example, the ASI published a booklet entitled *The First Hundred*, which purported to show a hundred of the ASI's ideas that had been 'taken up by government' during the 1980s. It is, of course, impossible to judge such claims without any access to government papers in order to analyze the decision-making processes that lay behind any individual piece of legislation. As the ASI acknowledged in the introduction to the booklet, by the mid-1980s the ASI was only one of a 'chorus' of voices advocating market-led economic reforms, for, as the economic liberal revolution reached full flood, the sources of legislative proposals and legislative ideas became almost too many to count.[2] The 'Poll Tax' is a case in point. The ASI were happy to claim the Community Charge as one of their ideas, deriving from the work of the St Andrews University academic Douglas Mason (and in particular his pamphlet *Revising the Rating System*, published in April 1985) at a time when the Poll Tax was widely touted as the 'flagship' of Mrs Thatcher's third administration. However, careful research has shown that in fact the Government's own internal enquiry into a replacement for the rates had begun under the guidance of William Waldegrave six months before the publication of Mason's pamphlet. As Michael Crick has written, 'by the time these [ASI] documents came out, however, the Thatcher government was well down the road to the poll tax. Nobody involved in government work on the tax in 1984 and 1985 believes that the ASI had any influence at all. "Never heard of him", says one of the leading officials of Douglas Mason, though others were vaguely aware of his ideas.'[3] One of those who was certainly not aware of Douglas Mason's work was the Minister responsible for the implementation of much of the legislation, Nicholas Ridley, who had certainly 'never heard of him'.[4] Once the Poll Tax turned out to be Mrs Thatcher's most unpopular and miscalculated piece of legislation, the ASI went curiously quiet on the subject. As Crick has observed, 'the more any think-tank is thought to influence government policy the more it will be listened to and will win financial support.'[5] Naturally, every 'think-tank' thus has a vested interest in inflating its own reputation as an originator of ideas which were taken up by the legislators; and they have often proved quick to drop such claims of intellectual paternity if the legislation proved to be unworkable or unpopular. But then it is an old adage that 'success has a thousand fathers, and failure is an orphan'. Given, therefore, that the most I would be able to do in attempting to trace the exact influence of economic-liberal 'think-tanks' from 1979 onwards would be to speculate intelligently, I will forgo the pleasure of speculating at all, and, instead, in the spirit of Hayek's second cousin, Ludwig Wittgenstein, confine myself to an account of the work of the 'think-tanks' based on a degree of documentary evidence only, for 'what we cannot speak about we must pass over in silence.'[6] The following study does not, therefore, claim to be exhaustive, but does, nonetheless, highlight the main contributions of the 'think-tanks' to the application of economic liberalism in government during the early 1980s.

Ironically, it was the CPS which had stood to lose most by the election of Mrs Thatcher, as there were some in the new government who felt that it had fulfilled its role and should be closed down. In part, this was undoubtedly true, if one accepted Sir Keith Joseph's original conception of the CPS as an organization designed to convert the Conservative Party to a programme of economic liberalism which it could use in government. To that end Sir Keith Joseph and David Young, amongst others, felt that it had served its purpose.[7] Furthermore, as Minister and Special Adviser at the Department of Industry, Joseph and Young both felt unable to discuss departmental policy or problems at the CPS with their customary frankness because of the official restrictions on how much of their work they were allowed to discuss with 'outsiders'. Joseph, the founder and main beneficiary of the CPS, was the most rigid in this respect; he was completely loyal to his departmental civil servants, and on entering government completely cut himself off from the CPS, much to the dismay of Sherman. As Keith Joseph's biographer has written, 'The Sherman-Joseph axis was irredeemably fractured . . . Joseph had not made any determined effort to get [Sherman] a job in government, beyond arranging for him to have an interview with Sir Peter Carey, who asked Sherman what he would do with the Department of Industry. "Abolish it" said Sherman. It was not a fruitful interview.'[8] Sherman came to feel that, as in 1970–4, once installed at the Department of Industry Joseph was 'captured' by his civil servants and was thus not sufficiently radical in tackling Britain's industrial problems, but Sherman's concern for Joseph's fate at the hands of the Whitehall mandarins was naturally coloured by the fact that, by turning his back on the CPS in government, Joseph had cut the CPS off from their principal consumer and intellectual champion in the new Cabinet.[9]

However, despite the opinion of Joseph and Young that the CPS had no further role to play, the CPS did survive, mainly to accommodate the unusual skills of Sherman in as controlled and safe an environment as was possible, for it was clear that with his talent for tactless outspokenness he could emphatically not be a special adviser in government. Hugh Thomas was brought in to replace Joseph as Chairman of the CPS, partly to keep a watchful eye on Sherman. Theirs was a relationship which quickly deteriorated and by 1981 Thomas and Sherman were involved in a bitter and acrimonious dispute which led to Sherman's departure from his post. Their differences were partly personal, but also political, for they came to represent the two contrasting views of what the CPS *should* do in government.

To a certain extent, in 1979 the CPS found it had to reinvent itself, and it did this by exploiting its contacts in government to the full, even without the aid of Keith Joseph. The CPS failed to get its 'territorial army' of advisers into government, and only nine 'special' advisers were appointed throughout Whitehall after the election victory. Of these, only John Hoskyns and Norman Strauss in the Downing Street Policy Unit, Stuart Sexton at the Department of Education and Science and David Young at the Department of Industry had any close connections with the CPS, and Young followed the example of his Minister in largely ignoring the CPS in Government. The Treasury special advisers were Peter Cropper, Adam Ridley and George Cardona, none of whom had come up via the CPS. On the face of it, the permanent Civil Service thus seemed to have quashed any grand schemes the CPS might have entertained about effectively subverting the policy advice of the existing bureaucracy, and to a certain extent this was true. However, what they lacked in numbers the CPS made up for in quality: John Hoskyns, the head of the Policy Unit, and Professor Alan Walters, special economic adviser to the Prime Minister from January 1981, proved to be the two advisers most influential on the Prime Minister herself. Walters's appointment was made specifically at the suggestion of Sherman himself who quickly formed a low opinion of Terry Burns, who, as special adviser at the Treasury, was supposed to champion the cause of monetarism in the new government. In a memo to Mrs Thatcher of 24 April 1980, Sherman argued forcefully that she needed independent economic advice in Downing Street

> a) To cut through the miasma of unreconstructed Keynesianism, intellectual evasiveness, wishful thinking and sheer muddle which pervades the Treasury and associated milieux.

b) To provide a clear and coherent picture of the economic situation as a basis for high-policy making.

c) To present this understanding starkly and forcefully at relevant fora, *e.g.* Ministerial and parliamentary Committees, financial and political journalists, academics, and other opinion-formers.

According to Sherman, Burns (now Permanent Secretary of the Treasury) lacked all these 'qualities and aptitudes. As a result he has turned out inadequate and ineffective. He lacks intellectual power, let alone brilliance. He is not a forceful personality, nor a fighter. So he has lacked impact and tended to be assimilated cosily by the Treasury, enjoying the Status . . . It follows that we need someone better. The man who comes to mind is Alan Walters. He has brain-power, clarity, forcefulness and courage, and can find, or hack, his way through politico-bureaucratic thickets.'[10] Walters, who had struck up a useful working relationship with Mrs Thatcher in the early 1970s, thus returned from Washington in January 1981 to take up his new post at Downing Street. His salary (£50,000) was half-paid by the CPS, out of funds donated by British United Industrialists. Hoskyns, Walters and, to a lesser extent, Strauss formed the main link between the CPS and the Government.[11] Another important link was Sherman himself. Although Joseph might have severed his connections with Sherman and the CPS, Sherman was very much *persona grata* at 10 Downing Street, where he was still used as a speech-writer and as one of the few – together with Hoskyns, Walters, Hugh Thomas and Ralph Harris – who enjoyed easy access to the Prime Minister. From 1979 to 1983 Sherman supplied Mrs Thatcher with a steady flow of pithy, provocative memos on virtually every subject under the sun.[12] It is impossible to assess how much influence any of these individual memos had on the Prime Ministerial mind, but the fact that Sherman's output was not discouraged is testimony to the interest that Mrs Thatcher still took in his views. Hoskyns, Strauss, Walters and Sherman thus formed a central core of 'Prime Ministerial' advisers, who ensured, collectively, that the CPS exercised considerable influence on the Government until the summer of 1982, when this quartet split up.

To a certain extent Hoskyns, Strauss, Walters and Sherman acted together, co-ordinating their activities through the CPS and the Downing Street Policy Unit to exert pressure on the Government to follow the strategy outlined in 'Stepping Stones', and to keep to its promise of radical economic reform. Above all, Hoskyns and Strauss always tried to persuade the Government, and Mrs Thatcher in particular, to think 'strategically', and to keep to the long-term aim of economic reform over a period of ten years. In a Policy Unit paper of 10 June 1980 Hoskyns outlined the strategy: 'The Government is committed to reducing inflation to around 5 per cent by 1984. This involves a transitional phase of 4 years in which monetary growth decelerates, to a state of stability from which economic recovery can start. There is no alternative to that plan . . .'[13]

The CPS critique of Mrs Thatcher's administration was co-ordinated in a group known as the 'First Eleven', which met occasionally at the CPS to 'shadow' government policy. The group met for the first time on 28 August 1980 and consisted, initially, of Hoskyns, Strauss, Sherman, R. V. Jones, Hugh Thomas, Terry Price, Max Beloff, John Kelly, a New Zealand-born academic, Jan Hildreth (ex-Director-General of the Institute of Directors) and Christopher Monckton. Nigel Morgan took the minutes. At the first meeting Sherman, who was elected Chairman of the First Eleven, 'pointed out that [they] had the ear of the Prime Minister'.[14] The First Eleven produced no official papers or reports, but acted as a useful forum at which the CPS contingent in government could discuss their ideas with CPS colleagues. The most important policy recommendations from the CPS came through John Hoskyns's 'Strategy Reports' from the Policy Unit, which he submitted to Mrs Thatcher several times a year, together with Sherman's own independent memos to the Prime Minister, which usually complemented Hoskyns's work.

The consistent theme of both Hoskyns and Sherman in the first couple of years of the new Government was that economic reforms were not being implemented quickly enough or targeted at the right sections of the economy. At a time, 1980–1, when Mrs Thatcher faced a barrage of criticism from much of her own party – to say nothing of almost the entire media and the opposition parties – for being too dogmatic and severe in her implementation of 'monetarist doctrine', the Policy Unit, in a critique that would later become familiar in some circles, argued the exact opposite, that the Government's problems lay in not pursuing *all* their proposed economic views vigorously enough. In his third Policy Unit 'Strategy Report' of 18 December 1980, Hoskyns warned bluntly that

> In summary, the Government has barely started to address the strategic problems facing it . . . Our failure has been under-kill, not (as our critics suggest) over-kill. This all stems from the massive under-estimate of the size of the problem, which has persisted from 1978 in Opposition, right through into Office. The main result has been the lopsided Keynesian squeeze on the private sector . . . In short, we have been brutal to our friends – employers, small businesses, the private sector; and gentle with the real problems – trade unions, nationalised industries, lame ducks, public services pay.[15]

Sherman reiterated Hoskyns's gloomy message that the Government's concentration on the 'monetary squeeze' of 1980–1 – a period of very high interest rates – was, as *Monetarism Is Not Enough* had warned in 1976, simply not enough. In a memo for Mrs Thatcher entitled *Monetarism Is Not Enough. High Government spending is generating an inflationary recession which threatens to erode the Prime Minister's political base*, Sherman argued that

> unless there is radical change in policy, attempts to stem inflationary pressures by means of 'monetary targets' will intensify our endemic inflationary recession . . . Our monetary policies will only work if they are in tandem with measures to restore the private wealth-producing sector at the expense of the State and subsidised sectors. So long as the State sector is not actually cut back, monetary squeeze will simply buckle the productive base on which all else rests. As it is squeezed, the private sector is left with no alternative but to call for reflationary policies in order to survive in the short term . . .
>
> To sum up; so long as inflation is being generated by the public sector, to try to abate it by squeezing the private sector is both unworkable and unfair.[16]

The CPS argument was that 'monetarism', far from failing, was not even being tried. It is impossible, of course, to assess precisely the impact of this consistent critique of the Government's economic performance on Mrs Thatcher, but there is no doubt that, eventually, in the autumn of 1980, her Government started to execute a quiet change of policy by lowering interest rates a full two per cent on 14 November 1980, only a few weeks after the Prime Minister's celebrated announcement to the Conservative Party Conference that 'the Lady was not for turning'. The CPS thesis was backed up by Walters when he arrived in Downing Street at the turn of the year. He immediately recognized that monetary policy was far too tight, while public spending (the PSBR) was far too big. It was a diagnosis borne out by the Swiss economist Jurg Niehans, who was commissioned by Sherman to write an independent report on the British economy. The report cost the CPS £7,500, half of which came from British United Industrialists. The Niehans Report was extremely important, as it confirmed Walters's and the CPS's critique of the Government's monetarist policies; it was the subject of two seminars hosted by the CPS in January and February 1981, which were attended by most of the Ministers and special economic advisers who were closely involved in the Government's economic policy making, including all three of Geoffrey Howe's special advisers at the Treasury.

This was the background to the famous 1981 budget, which most of Mrs Thatcher's supporters saw as the turning-point of her, until then, embattled premiership. The main proposal of the Budget, presented by the Chancellor, Sir Geoffrey Howe, on 10 March, was the proposal to reduce the PSBR by 2.5 per cent of GDP, from £13.5 billion to £10.5 billion. As one of Mrs Thatcher's biographers has observed, 'All Keynesian economic orthodoxy demanded that at a time of recession the Government's role was to increase spending. Howe was doing exactly the opposite; increasing taxation and cutting spending.'[17] It was undoubtedly a radical budget, following through the suggestions of Hoskyns, Sherman and Walters, and shifting the burden of the Government's anti-inflationary policy from the monetary to the fiscal side. The exact paternity of the budget has been vigorously disputed. It has often been seen as a budget 'made in No. 10' by Walters, Mrs Thatcher and the Policy Unit against the will of a stubborn Treasury. Walters, in his own account of the budget, has claimed that *he* 'proposed the biggest budgetary squeeze in peacetime history' and 'After much fierce debate, Mrs Thatcher became convinced and, with characteristic courage, adopted this fiscal squeeze'.[18] Sir Geoffrey Howe, however, has directly contradicted Walters's account and has claimed that 'those budget judgements were, in fact, fashioned by the

Chancellor of the Exchequer with the help of other Treasury Ministers, and on the strength of Treasury advice'.[19] Whatever the truth of the matter – and all will not be revealed until the official papers are released – there can be no doubt that the CPS, through the co-ordinated action of Walters, Hoskyns and Sherman (as well as, indirectly, Niehans) exerted considerable and effective pressure on the Prime Minister to take the decision to modify the government's economic strategy in 1980–1, culminating in the 1981 Budget. It was a change in policy that undoubtedly saved the Government at the next election; for what all those involved in the 1981 budget *have* agreed on is that the budget laid the foundations of the economic boom of the mid-1980s. The participation of the CPS in the economic policy making of the first two years of Mrs Thatcher's Government constituted the most important contribution of the CPS to her Governments, and clearly justified the role of semi-independent, 'political' advisers like Walters, Sherman and Hoskyns.

The other subject on which the CPS did its best to maintain sustained and co-ordinated pressure on the Government was trade union reform. Having been instrumental in impressing the importance of trade union reform upon the Conservative leaders in opposition, the CPS, especially Sherman and Hoskyns, played a vital part in keeping up the pressure on the new administration to translate their ideas for trade union reform into law at a time when many ministers would still have preferred to let the matter rest. The CPS's activities in this field came to be focused on three separate bodies; the Downing Street Policy Unit, the Trade Union Reform Study Group (TURC), chaired by Sir Leonard Neal, and the 'Argonauts'. The Argonauts was a loose association of employers' organizations and trade associations formed by Sherman in the early months of 1980 to co-ordinate strategy between the employers and the CPS and the Government in the face of the 1980 steel strike. Michael Ivens of Aims of Industry was also instrumental in founding the Argonauts, and by 1983 the group included the Director of the Institute of Directors, Nicholas De Jongh of the Engineering Employers Federation, the Director General of the General Council of British Shipping, Anthony Fraser of the Society of Motor Manufacturers and Traders (most of whom represented 'steel consuming' industries), as well as Hoskyns, Walters, Ferdinand Mount (Hoskyns's successor at the Downing Street Policy Unit), Ray Whitney MP and Lord Cayzer of the CPS. It is doubtful whether the Argonauts played any substantial role in the steel strike itself – the first major test of resolve for Mrs Thatcher's Government on the trade union issue – but by July 1981 Sherman was able to report to the CPS Board of Directors that 'the most successful Study Groups had been TURC and the Argonauts. The latter were a group which met for lunch once a month and had been concentrating recently on problems of employment. Both these groups were valued by the staff at No. 10. There had been a definite change of attitude from the CBI on employment questions and their attitude was now more in line with Centre Thinking.'[20]

Hoskyns himself constantly reiterated the need for action on the trade union front in his Policy Unit papers to the Prime Minister, but it was the TURC which studied the issues in detail and put forward the concrete policy proposals on behalf of the CPS. TURC carried considerable clout in Whitehall because it was well known that Mrs Thatcher listened with unusual attention to Sir Leonard Neal and because the CPS, through Hoskyns and Strauss, had already acquired a reputation for expertise on trade union matters before the Conservative Party took office in 1979. It was with little irony that TURC came to be known as the 'Shadow Ministry of Employment' at the CPS, because the new Minister for Employment was Jim Prior, the archetypal consensual, collectivist Conservative politician who quickly proved himself to be the most effective and articulate opponent of Mrs Thatcher within government. Prior wanted to move cautiously on trade union reform, as he did on all the other economic reforms dear to the radical hearts at the CPS. The extent of the gulf between the CPS and Prior may be glimpsed from the following note from Hoskyns to Sherman of 4 November 1981 entitled *Alfred's Suggestion for Increased Press Contact*; Hoskyns wrote that

> When I had dinner with Alfred on 21 July, he suggested that Alan and I begin to cultivate reasonably friendly journalists in order to counter the very dangerous influence Jim Prior is now having – or at least trying to exert – on economic policy.
>
> . . . Alfred felt that it was time the general theme began to get about 'Jim Prior causes unemployment'. And this is indeed the truth . . .
>
> Our line should be that Jim Prior is absolutely sincere,

> believes that he is a lone Churchillian figure warning the Government of the great danger to which it is blind, but is actually profoundly mistaken and is in fact advocating a re-run of past blunders.[21]

From the moment that Prior moved into the Department of Employment, TURC entered into a written and verbal dialogue with the new Minister that was sometimes constructive, but more often merely tetchy. Prior was obliged to see Neal on several occasions because of Neal's standing with the Prime Minister – which he made use of on a number of occasions – and Neal later recalled that he and Prior did not get on at all well, and were often 'quite rude to each other'.[22] At the 1980 CPS annual meeting – an occasion at which Mrs Thatcher was always present – Neal gave full vent to his feelings about Prior and got an enormous roar of approval from the audience. Mrs Thatcher specifically drew Neal aside to congratulate him on his short speech.

Relations between TURC and Prior began amicably enough, as Prior's officials listened to their arguments and read their submissions, and even seemed to use some of their ideas. The Chairman of TURC was thus able to report to the Study Group in October 1980 that 'A good response had been received to the Committee's submission on *Picketing*, published on 12 September. It was encouraging to see several of the Committee's suggestions incorporated in the Sec. of State's *Code on Picketing*. A copy of the submission had been sent to Mr Prior and had been acknowledged with thanks . . .'[23] The principal document on trade union reform produced by the CPS, *Liberties and Liabilities: The Case for Trade Union Reform* (CPS, 1980) was also an important contribution to the debate, but Prior's response was, perhaps, predictable, and boded ill for the future as far as the CPS was concerned. Prior wrote to Hugh Thomas to thank him for a copy of *Liberties and Liabilities*, but added that 'As you predicted in your letter, I did not entirely agree with all the points made in the report nor do I accept all its conclusions . . .'[24] When Prior's proposed legislation was actually published in early January 1980, TURC was dismayed by the extent of Prior's caution and the slowness with which he proposed to tackle the trade union question. TURC then entered into a long and detailed correspondence with Prior to try and get him to strengthen the bill on various important points, such as the closed shop and trade union immunities. However, Prior proved obdurate in introducing his own, more accommodating legislation, and as a last resort Neal wrote to Mrs Thatcher in May 1980 to try and make her understand how deficient her own Secretary of State for Employment's legislation really was. The letter deserves to be quoted at length:

> I apologise for writing what will have to be a lengthy letter . . . I am doing so because now that the Employment Bill has passed its final stage in the Commons I wish to place on record my deep misgivings about the Bill and my fears about its likely consequences. These feelings are entirely shared by the Study group on industrial relations which I chair at the Centre and on whose behalf I write . . . Although our group includes members well-versed in politics, economics, law (both academic and practising), of administration and industrial relations, we feel that our views could scarcely have received less consideration.
>
> It has also become apparent that our basic philosophy and objections are very different from Mr Prior's. He speaks of the Bill's purpose as 'improving labour relations'. Whatever this may mean, it is not necessarily the same as the Government's stated objective of redressing the imbalance of bargaining power between unions and management, which, in common with the authors of the Conservative election manifesto, we regard as the proper objective of any legislation in this field. In short, we do not think the Bill is aiming at the main target . . .
>
> We feel that a great opportunity is being wasted to make a permanent and substantial improvement in a field that is central to our economic welfare. We are all most dismayed that the current approach is not only ineffectual, but liable to do more harm than good. Whatever its small achievements, they are outweighed by the natural tendency for people to conclude that the use of law in trade union matters is either counter-productive or at best divisive with very little pay-off. This will discredit the law.[25]

This was a damning indictment of Prior's 'softly, softly' approach to the unions and TURC was equally discouraged by Prior's 'Green Paper on Trade Union Immunities', published in 1981, Paul

McCormick describing it as a document which was 'obviously not intended to be a basis for legislation within the present Parliament and as one behind which the government intended to conceal its unwillingness to take action to strengthen the laws with regard to Trade Union immunities . . .'[26] These reservations about Prior's Green Paper were also communicated to Mrs Thatcher. As Neal had complained, Prior had stuck to his guns and despite his letter of protest to Mrs Thatcher of May 1980, Prior's Employment Bill became law in July 1980, going only some way towards the full reform of trade unions that the CPS wanted to see; outlawing secondary picketing, for instance, but failing to abolish the 'Closed Shop'. The CPS might have been relatively ineffective in beefing up Prior's legislation, but Neal, Hoskyns and TURC *were* successful in persuading Mrs Thatcher that trade union reform should not stop with Prior's first Bill, and that much more was needed. In September 1981 Prior was duly removed and sent to Northern Ireland; legend has it that it was Sherman's throwaway line to this effect at a CPS lunch in 1981 with Mrs Thatcher present which might have first planted the seed for this particular ministerial reshuffle in her mind. The new Secretary of State for Employment was Norman Tebbit, who, like Neal, was an ex-trade union official himself. Tebbit needed no encouragement on the issue of trade union reform, and his own legislation owed little to the suggestions of TURC or any other outside body.[27] The importance of TURC thus declined at the moment of its most decisive victory.

The impact that the CPS had on macro-economic policy and trade union policy, the two key elements of Mrs Thatcher's programme of radical reform, was vital and substantial, and was not matched by their influence on any other aspect of the Government's work. Nonetheless, other CPS 'study groups' did have isolated successes through their involvement in the work of several government departments. The success of the study groups tended to reflect not so much the efficacy or workability of their policy proposals, but more the personality of the ministers involved and their receptiveness to the involvement of outside groups like the CPS. One of the more successful groups was the 'Personal Capital Formation Group' chaired by Nigel Vinson. This group came up with three proposals which later became Government policy – Personal Pensions, Personal Equity Plans (originally called 'Personal Savings Pool') and the Enterprise Allowance Scheme. The latter scheme was Vinson's, 'to legitimize moonlighting', and he put the scheme personally to Prior while he was Minister for Employment.[28] In March 1983, when the Government finally introduced the enterprise allowance scheme Prior sent Vinson a letter of congratulations: 'It has taken a long while to persuade the Treasury to make the enterprise allowance a national scheme – the wheels of Government grind slowly. It was an idea that you hatched in my office and I am delighted that it has come to something.'[29]

The CPS's pension scheme was contained in the pamphlet *Personal and Portable Pensions for All* (CPS, 1981) and was used by Norman Fowler when he was Minister of Health and Social Security. Personal Equity Plans (PEPs) were eventually introduced by Nigel Lawson in 1987, although, again, it is impossible to ascribe the introduction of PEPs solely to the work of the CPS. The 'Nationalized Industries Study Group' was also important, chaired by Simon Webley, and including John Redwood (who went to the Policy Unit at Downing Street in 1983), Robin Harris (a special adviser at the Treasury), Denis Thatcher, Michael Ivens, Christopher Bailey, John Oakley, Dr Elizabeth Cottrell, Alfred Sherman and Graham Mather (then at the Institute of Directors), John Hatch and Michael Grylls MP. The aims of the Group, as agreed at its first meeting on 18 February 1980, were to

> a) Make practical suggestions for the more efficient working of state owned enterprises.
> b) To examine ways in which nationalised industries or parts of them can be split up.[30]

The Nationalized Industries Study Group was especially important in applying its efforts to finding a workable solution to the problem of breaking up the nationalized telecommunications industry. At a meeting of the Group at the Institute of Directors in November 1981, Webley announced that Patrick Jenkin (who had succeeded Joseph as Secretary of State for Industry)

> had made a request for help from the Group on future privatization of telecommunications.
>
> Three main constraints had been identified to further privatization:
>
> 1) the problem of monopoly

2) the problem of technology
3) the problem of infrastructure.

It is intended to set up a small telecommunications group drawn from the Nationalized Industry Study Group . . .[31]

The Study Group's report on British Telecom, *Switching Direction*, was subsequently published in 1982, and proved to be very important to the Government as it tackled several of the practical issues raised by Jenkin. Dr Cottrell invented the regulatory authority, OFTEL, originally called TRA (Telecommunications Regulating Authority), which would regulate the newly 'privatized' telecommunications industry. Jenkin much appreciated the CPS's work in this field, as did the Ministers who were eventually responsible for the actual privatization of BT in 1984. John Moore, then the rising young star of the Conservative economic liberals before his Ministerial career expired at the Department of Health, addressed the Study Group in February 1985, and told them that 'the sale of British Telecom had proved to be a great success. The marketing campaign which accompanied the flotation won people's attention to such an extent that, in my view, it had transformed the ground rules for further privatization measures.'[32]

John Redwood, an economist from Oxford, was invited to join the CPS by Sherman to work on the Study Group in 1980 after he wrote a book on the nationalized industries in early 1980. By 1983, after his work for the CPS Study Group, he had become an acknowledged expert on privatization (he was invited to join Norman Lamont at the Department of Energy with a brief to explore how to deregulate the gas industry), and in August 1983 became the new head of the Policy Unit in Downing Street specifically to develop the privatization programme. He did this in tandem with John Moore, a Minister at the Treasury and effectively the first unofficial 'Minister for Privatization'.[33] The Nationalized Industries Study Group produced reports on British Leyland, which were used by Sir Keith Joseph at the Department of Industry; and Sherman also commissioned Dr Cottrell to write a report on the steel industry, composed on the word-processor in David Hart's Chester Street home, which was read and commented upon by Ian Macgregor, the head of British Steel.

The only other Study Group which seems to have exerted much influence was the Education Study Group chaired by Caroline (later Baroness) Cox. It included several of those who had been involved in

'New Right' groups such as Dr John Marks (co-author with Cox of the celebrated pamphlet *Rape of Reason*), Dr Digby Anderson, Professor R.V. Jones, Patricia Morgan, Marjorie and Arthur Seldon, Oliver Letwin, son of William and Shirley Letwin, and Professor Arthur Pollard. The Education Study Group put forward several proposals on such themes as accountability, parent choice and school standards, many of which found their way into government legislation – eventually – towards the end of the 1980s. A 'ginger-group' of the 'Education Study Group', the Hillgate Group, consisting of Cox, Marks, Roger Scruton and Jessica Douglas-Home, produced an important report which was received sympathetically by the Prime Minister, and much of the document found its way into the 1987 Conservative Party election manifesto.

At the same time as the CPS helped to shape the central strategy of the government, the Adam Smith Institute pursued its own programme of publishing policy proposals at the 'micro-political' level, to complement the CPS's more strategic, wide-ranging work in government. The ASI thus dealt with the nuts and bolts of the Thatcher Government's reforms, especially when it came to formulating practical proposals to introduce a free market in areas such as local government and the nationalized industries. Very little thinking had been done about the practical implications of 'privatization' by the Conservative Party itself or by the civil servants in Whitehall. The ASI's ideas for contracting out local services were published in 1980 and attracted wide publicity. James Goldsmith's *Now!* magazine devoted an article to the ASI's concept of contracting out, which Mrs Thatcher instructed be sent out to all Conservative Councillors – so thousands of photocopies were sent to all corners of the United Kingdom.[34] Southend pioneered 'contracting out', followed by Ealing, and the 1988 Local Government Bill made it compulsory. The ASI also applied its 'micro-political', free-market approach to contracting out in the Health Service and local government. Through the publication of a pamphlet on *The Establishment of Freeports in the UK*, the ASI was also responsible for the introduction of freeports by the Chancellor of the Exchequer in 1983.

None of these areas of involvement were very glamorous or high-profile, but the replacement of local government monopolies with private monopolies was the sort of practical, micro-economic reform that was essential if the government's hopes of restoring a more genuinely free-market economy were to have any chance of success. Much of the work of the ASI was published in the bulky *OMEGA File*, edited by Eamonn Butler, Madsen Pirie and Peter Young which, in nineteen chapters, outlined the application of market-led reforms to every aspect of government policy, from Defence and Housing Policy to Communications Policy and Taxation Policy. The 'OMEGA' project, designed as a blueprint for Mrs Thatcher's second term of government was based, like much of the rest of the ASI's work, on an American model, in this case the Heritage Foundation's *Mandate for Leadership*, published in 1980 as a blueprint for the incoming government of Ronald Reagan. At the end of 1981, Heritage published a book called *The First Year*, cataloguing the impact that their policy proposals had had on the Reagan Administration.[35] The ASI were to follow in similar vein with *The First Hundred*. Each policy area in the OMEGA project was covered by a Committee of some four to eight people, many of whom had inside and often first-hand experience of the policy areas that their committee was covering. The purpose of the OMEGA projects' work was to make their policy proposals as easy to implement and practicable as possible. As Eamonn Butler explained, as distinct from the more aggressive approach of Alfred Sherman and others at the CPS, the ASI tried to develop a more flexible, pragmatic approach to problems of policy implementation, trying to work with civil servants and others rather than dismissing anyone who made objections to their ideas as obstructionist and hostile. It was a gradualist, 'Fabian approach'.[36] Many of those who worked on the OMEGA project committees were familiar names from the history of 'think-tanks' and economic liberalism – Richard Body, Brian Crozier, Baroness Cox, Professor Antony Flew, Michael Ivens, Russell Lewis and Linda Whetstone, for instance – but the OMEGA project also provided some up-and-coming young Conservative MPs and prospective MPs with an opportunity to develop their 'Thatcherite' credentials through work on privatization and other programmes with the OMEGA report.[37]* Many of these rising politicians, having honed their economic and policy skills in the OMEGA project, went on to achieve quick promotion under Mrs Thatcher, none more so than Portillo.[38] The ASI's particular expertise lay in the field of privatization, and by the mid-1980s the Institute had established itself as the single most important

* Such MPs and future MPs included, most notably, Michael Portillo (who was elected MP for Southgate in 1984), Robert Jones, Michael Fallon and Teresa Gorman.

source of ideas and policy proposals concerning privatization in Britain, holding yearly international conferences on privatization in London. Indeed, with the collapse of Communism in Eastern Europe in 1989, the ASI quickly extended its activities into the countries of the former 'Eastern bloc', advising the new Polish, Hungarian and Czech governments on the practical details of privatization within a few months of the breaching of the Berlin Wall. The ASI's *Manual on Privatization* was earnestly studied by a new generation of enthusiastic free-marketeers, born in previously Communist Eastern Europe, who now attempted to import 'Thatcherism' – as purveyed by the ASI – to their own newly 'liberated' countries.

Indeed, the internationalization of the work of the British 'think-tanks' was one of the most extraordinary features of economic liberalism as it developed in the 1980s. Once again, much of the internationalization of the work of the economic liberals owed its impetus to Antony Fisher, the founding father of the first British free-market institute. On the strength of his reputation with the IEA, he was invited in 1975 to become Co-Director of the Fraser Institute in Vancouver, Canada, founded by the Canadian businessman Pat Boyle in 1974. Fisher let the young director of the Fraser Institute, Dr Michael Walker, get on with the intellectual output of the Institute (just as he had given free rein to Seldon and Harris at the IEA) while he himself concentrated on the fund-raising side. The Fraser Institute proved to be an outstandingly successful enterprise, and on the strength of this North American success Fisher went on to set up a similar free-market institute in New York in 1977, originally called the International Center for Economic Policy Studies (ICEPS). The incorporation documents for the ICEPS were signed by the prominent attorney Bill Casey, later Director of the Central Intelligence Agency. The ICEPS was later renamed the Manhattan Institute for Policy Research, and under the directorship of William Hammet the Manhattan Institute became probably Fisher's greatest success after the IEA. It also concentrated on lengthy, academic publishing which had a notable impact on public policy debates during the late 1970s at a time of the renewed interest in economic liberalism in the United States which paralleled the British experience of the second half of the 1970s. In 1977, Fisher moved to San Francisco with his second wife Dorian, whom he had met through the Mont Pèlerin Society, and founded the Pacific Institute for Public Policy in 1979. Fisher and Friedman, the primary entrepreneurial and intellectual figures of the economic liberal movement, lived in the same apartment block in San Francisco during the 1980s. In the late 1970s Fisher also became involved in developing the Centre for Independent Studies (CIS) in Australia, directed by Greg Lindsay, which became an important contributor of free-market ideas to Australian politics during the 1980s. In 1981, to co-ordinate and establish a central focus for these institutes that Fisher found himself starting up all over the world, he created the Atlas Economic Research Foundation which in 1987 joined up with the Institute of Humane Studies (IHS) (founded by the Mont Pèlerin member F. A. Harper in 1961) to provide a central institutional structure for what quickly became an ever-expanding number of international free-market 'think-tanks' or research institutes, all basically modelled on the original concept of the IEA. John Blundell, who had worked with the CPS, ASI and the IEA, was President of both the Atlas Foundation and IHS (heading a full-time staff of over twenty) from 1987 to 1990; the mission of ATLAS, as he succinctly put it, 'is to litter the world with free-market think-tanks'.[39]

During the 1980s the original group of the IEA, the Fraser Institute, the Manhattan Institute, the Pacific Institute and the CIS had grown to an organization of over sixty think-tanks by 1990. On a final count in 1991, Atlas claimed that it had 'helped to create, supported with grants or advised in some way' no less than seventy-eight institutes, most notably thirty-one in Latin America; and it also claimed to have had a healthy and developing relationship with eighty-eight other institutes, spread over fifty-one countries. Fisher and the Atlas Foundation were particularly keen to promote the work of free-market institutes in areas of the world where the fight for economic liberalism was still at the stage it had been in North America and Britain during the 1940s, and so concentrated principally on Latin and South America and the Eastern Bloc countries of Europe. Not all of the institutes founded and advised by Atlas flourished – some closed down fairly soon after opening due to lack of funds or other reasons – but the growth of the ATLAS network during the 1980s was still phenomenal by any standards. When the Berlin Wall came down in 1989, there was an army of committed, international economic liberals reared in the Hayekian tradition, armed with clipboards and portable phones, waiting to move into Eastern Europe and the disintegrating Soviet Union to convert their ailing economies to the virtues of capitalism.

Almost all the Eastern bloc countries availed themselves of the help on offer from the ATLAS Foundation Institutes at some time during the late 1980s and early 1990s. From 1983, the IHS and ATLAS ran yearly workshops at its own base at George Mason University in Virginia, or around the world at conferences in Venezuela, Moscow, Brazil, New Zealand, Sydney, Guatemala and Jamaica. The 'Liberty and Society' seminars run by the IHS, and the 'International Workshops' run by ATLAS became increasingly international in character, with a strong Eastern European and Russian representation, schooling the future economic liberal thinkers and politicians of the twenty-first century. Fisher used the local and international gatherings of the Mont Pèlerin Society to find personnel, fund-raisers and donors for many of the ATLAS institutes. By the early 1980s, MPS meetings had mushroomed: over five hundred people attended, including many representatives or Directors of the ATLAS institutes. They compared notes and learnt from each other's experiences and mistakes. It is, of course, too early to assess the impact of the ATLAS foundation and the work of the IHS and related economic liberal think-tanks worldwide, but it is already certain that economic liberalism now enjoys an institutional, as well as intellectual, coherence that would have been unthinkable when the MPS was founded in 1947. It is indeed tempting to see the ATLAS Foundations and the IHS as the Comintern of the economic liberals, except, of course, that the economic liberals would never accept any government funding! In a very rare moment of self-congratulation, Fisher recalled to Oliver Smedley in 1984 that whereas the first working capital of the IEA amounted to some £500 for its first year, 'Today, on a world-wide basis, the twenty-one Institutes in fourteen countries probably have an aggregate income running at $5 million, which at an exchange rate of 1.40 equals some £3,600,000.'[40]

It had been a long and extraordinary road from Fisher's initial meeting with Hayek at the LSE some forty years before.

However, at the same time as the economic liberals in Britain enjoyed both a measure of domestic success and international acclaim, they also began to come up against the political limitations of their power in Whitehall. Although the CPS enjoyed considerable success in the fields of economic policy and, eventually, trade union reform, their failure in other areas of policy making hardly boded well for the future of the 'Thatcherite' revolution. Although, for instance, the Education

Study Group might have had some impact on the central issue of vouchers – which the IEA had been campaigning for since the mid-1960s – the Education Group failed to convince even as unashamed an economic radical as Sir Keith Joseph whilst he was Secretary of State for Education from 1981 to 1986. The 'voucher' had become the shibboleth of the Thatcherite radicals, and its rejection by their favourite minister was a crushing blow for the CPS and the IEA. It was ironic that it took Sir Keith Joseph to demonstrate the limits of their influence.[41] The frustrations of the Education Reform Study Group were echoed by the members of the Health Study Group, which produced a good deal of detailed, lucid work to little avail. The minutes of the Health Study Group are a record of frustration and impotence, as the distinguished members of the group found themselves battling against the brick wall of what they perceived to be an obdurate and blinkered bureaucracy. Dr George Buxton, the Chairman of the Study Group, produced a report called *Health 2000*, which made little impact on government. Arthur Seldon echoed the feelings of many in the group when he wrote a letter to Sir Keith Joseph explaining his resignation from the Study Group in September 1981:

> You may remember that when, in my room here about three years ago, I asked whether my time on it would be wasted, you said, reflectively, that it would not. I have now spent many hours talking, discussing, listening – and, of course, editing and writing the *Litmus Papers*, and all to no avail. The talk about what may be done in the second term does not impress me at all. Carlisle and Jenkin [the Health Ministers] run two gargantuan departments that not only embrace vast waste, but are also responsible for unnecessarily high taxation, oppressive bureaucracies, bolstering public sector trade unions hegemony, social injustice (the articulate get more than the poor), invasion of the family, the thwarting or frustration of macro-economic policy . . . And all that Carlisle and Jenkin have done is to administer, possibly slightly better, two vast social machines . . .[42]

Given his own feelings, Seldon would not have been surprised by Patrick Jenkin's letter to George Bunton explaining his own dilatoriness in taking up any of the CPS's ideas. Writing from the DHSS in

August 1981, he assured Bunton that he had read various CPS authors on the application of free-market economics to the Health Service, but still

> felt bound to say that I have not, as yet, ever reached a convincing, coherent and wholly satisfactory exposition of the philosophy of a free-market in health. Actually, I do not believe one exists, for the imperfections in any such market are bound to be of such a nature as to call into question the existence of a market at all . . .
>
> The success of the Black Books, on changing public attitudes in education, was, at least in part, due to the exposition by Max Beloff and others of a very clear, coherent philosophy on education . . .
>
> My officials will, I know, strive manfully to produce something in response to the remit which I have given them. I will certainly give them every encouragement to think boldly and imaginatively. But, please, I believe we have got to formulate a more rigorous, a more coherent, and a more convincing philosophy, if we are going to end up by doing more than just tinkering.
>
> I do not want to go down in history as a tinkerer! I am, I fully recognise, not cast in the mould myself of a bold and innovative thinker but more in the mould of the man who takes the good ideas of others, and casts them into practical form for practical implementation. I am bound to tell you George, I am groping![43]

From the point of view of the CPS, Jenkin flattered himself with the description of himself as a 'tinkerer'. As far as the CPS was concerned, Patrick Jenkin's successors were little better, and they failed to get the fundamental reforms across the whole breadth of the 'Welfare State' which they had been seeking before 1979. The CPS criticisms of Conservative Health and Social Security Ministers chimed with their criticisms of Conservative Ministers of Education; the failure to interest Health Ministers in a thorough-going free market in health seemed to echo the rejection of the voucher scheme by the DES. The experience of the CPS with Ministers in the larger Whitehall ministries quickly led to the development of a basic critique of the way Britain was governed, and, specifically, led to the targeting of the Civil Service as the major obstacle to the next round of Thatcherite reform. John Hoskyns, in particular, came round to this view little more than a year after he first moved into Downing Street. The dilemmas of Patrick Jenkin seemed to illustrate the impotence of ministers in the hands of an uncooperative and ideologically entrenched bureaucracy, trying to preserve the status quo. Unlike Joseph, who always kept his own counsel on the quality of his civil servants' advice, Jenkin explained to a meeting of the Health Study Group on 5 November 1979 that no new policy proposals ever came from his own DHSS officials; 'My civil servants tend to see things in the light of recent patterns.' That is why Jenkin looked to the CPS, as the 'Generation of New Ideas must come from people outside the DHSS. I am looking to the people around this table – a heavy responsibility.'[44] The 'people round the table' – the Health Study Group – were more than willing to shoulder this responsibility, only, as we have seen, to find their ideas either ignored by ministers or – as in the case of vouchers – ruthlessly picked to pieces by extremely hostile civil servants. John Hoskyns, surveying the minutes of the Health Study Group, wrote on 18 December 1980, that:

> It seems impossible for a minister to live and work in a hostile environment for a sustained period of time. Eventually he has to come to terms, leading to surrender of his position – as with PJ.
>
> I remain convinced that will not change the narrow assumptions of the civil servants. They are playing a game with PJ. They are definitely Enemy Number One.[45]

Hoskyns's analysis of the Civil Service as the major obstacle to further reform hardened into a CPS orthodoxy by the end of 1981. In June 1981, Hoskyns asked Sherman for a CPS paper on Civil Service Reform, and wrote that 'I think it was a full year after the election before I came fully to share Norman's [Strauss's] view that the Civil Service was a bigger problem than the Trade Union movement.'[46]

Norman Strauss, Hoskyns's colleague in the Policy Unit, had indeed become the CPS's most trenchant critic of the Civil Service. As a professional businessman, he was appalled by what he regarded as the amateurish, complacent and conservative culture of the Civil Service.

On 2 June 1981, he wrote a Policy Unit Paper on Civil Service Reform, arguing that to allow further radical economic and political reform, the Civil Service had to be reformed first. The paper was written for Mrs Thatcher and argued that:

> The top civil servants emphatically do *not* have the competence to do anything except run what they have inherited, the system which made them – 'the fish is shaped by the sea it swims in' (Karl Popper, I think). Their lifetime in the Civil Service, and the qualities of obedience, caution, don't make trouble, observe precedent, which got them to the top are the *definitive disqualifications* for being able to reform the systems and handle a period of turbulent national change. The one thing you *don't* want to reform the Civil Service is a civil servant . . . Indeed, you were specifically warned about this in 1977.
>
> . . . Both the Civil Servants and politicians seem to lack professional competence in *numeracy* and (quite different) *systemic* thinking and (quite different again) *systematic* thinking. Treasury meetings on Budget design, E Committee discussions on BL would horrify any modern business executive for their sheer lack of structure, discipline, rigour and instinctive feel for numbers.

Neither was Strauss much kinder about Mrs Thatcher's Cabinet colleagues, writing that many of her colleagues were, indeed

> so free of all jargon, that, after being in high office for two years, they still don't understand the difference between transition and Stable State, or the true implications of a decelerating money GDP . . . In other words, despite being members of what purports to be a team of twenty-three people charged with changing Britain's history, they are absolute amateurs – and it shows.[47]

In Hoskyns's analogy, the 'Stepping Stones' Report of 1977 had envisaged a Thatcher Government taking five years to 'put the fire out' that was then raging in the British economy, after which it would need another five years to enable Britain to catch up with the rest of the world.[48] In April 1982, a few days after the start of the Falklands Crisis, John Hoskyns presented the Prime Minister with an update of 'Stepping Stones', called the Westwell Report, subtitled 'A Programme of Action for winning the Next Election and Governing Effectively Thereafter'. This document reflected much of the thinking of the CPS at the time, and Douglas Hague, Norman Strauss, David Wolfson as well as Cecil Parkinson, Norman Lamont and David Howell were all consulted by Hoskyns in the process of drafting the Report. The Report referred to the long-term strategic plan of 'Stepping-Stones', of the 'full 5-year stabilization phase, to create a stable base on which a second 5-year rebuilding phase would be possible. A successful first 5 years could only get us to the "end of the beginning".'[49] The CPS stated that radical trade union reform had been essential to the period of 'Stabilization' – up to, say, 1983–4 – and that Civil Service reform was now the *sine qua non* of the next five years' 'rebuilding' phase, as the existing bureaucracy stood in the way of the application of supply-side reforms and the implementation of policies designed to create an 'enterprise culture'. The 'Westwell Report' could have left Mrs Thatcher in no doubt as to the importance which the CPS attached to the reform of the Civil Service, as the Report concluded, in a section called *Making It Happen*, that

> The Civil Service is a much more formidable obstacle to national recovery than the trade unions. It is difficult for 90 Ministers and a handful of advisers to shape history, in the face of three or four thousand senior civil servants who see it as their job to defend the status quo against assaults from Left or Right. Few officials accept our view that the so-called 'centre' has itself slipped to the Left and that this is the key to Britain's malaise. Civil Servants cannot accept this because they are *part of that malaise*. They do not understand, therefore, that we must move the whole spectrum of politics back to the Right, so that the *political* Centre ground at last coincides with the beliefs and values of the great mass of ordinary voters . . .

In paragraph 8.5.3, the Westwell Report therefore argued that

> The self-fulfilling conviction that the 'Market doesn't work any longer' pervades Whitehall, the public services, national-

> ised industries, the Manpower Services Commission, and much of the Conservative Party in Parliament. The Policy Unit believes that we will need a powerful cadre of *market-orientated* special advisers for the second term, as part of the long struggle to undo the damage done by a brain-washed corporatist establishment over the past 30 years. Independent-minded colleagues may argue that they can prevail against the suffocating conventional wisdom of Whitehall without such assistance, but we believe that it is almost impossible to do this in practice, without daily contact with kindred spirits.[50]

The 'Westwell Report' thesis was thus that only with immediate *institutional* reform could one proceed to further radical *economic* reform. Unfortunately for the CPS, Mrs Thatcher herself was not particularly interested in this argument, and the Civil Service, in the portly shape of Sir Robert Armstrong, the Cabinet Secretary, seems to have easily overcome any scruples she may have had over rejecting the Hoskyns-Strauss thesis.[51] Strauss was on only a two-year 'lease' from his company, Unilever, so he was bound to leave the Policy Unit in 1982 anyway, but in one of his last interviews he took the opportunity to present his paper on civil service reform to Mrs Thatcher in a 1½-hour meeting, during which it became obvious that the Prime Minister was not persuaded by the urgent need for the institutional/constitutional reforms urged on her by the Westwell Report. Strauss resigned soon afterwards, followed by Hoskyns in May 1982, who, like Strauss, felt that in trying to get measures to reform the Welfare State on the agenda, and in trying to stress the vital importance of Civil Service reform, he was already 'banging his head against a brick wall'.[52] With Hoskyns and Strauss gone, the influence of the CPS almost vanished overnight, especially as by this time Sherman himself was in an increasingly precarious position.

Despite the success of the Policy Unit and the CPS in influencing the Government's economic policy and speeding up its trade union reforms, Strauss, Hoskyns and, eventually, Sherman, left the corridors of power with an overwhelming sense of disillusionment. Although Mrs Thatcher might have *appeared* to be radical, at the vital moment she had failed to grasp the nettle of institutional reform that might have foreshadowed a *real* return to economic liberalism; as it turned out, the levels of public spending (in real terms) in 1990, when Mrs Thatcher left office, had hardly changed from the year when she had entered Downing Street in 1979. Measured by this important yardstick, 'Thatcherism' had thus made very little impact at all. Above all, Hoskyns, Strauss and Sherman realized that for all her other qualities, Mrs Thatcher was not a 'strategic' thinker, and, especially after the Falklands War of 1982, she ceased to listen to advice and did not appreciate the strategic implications of long-term planning as outlined in documents like the 'Westwell Report'. In a letter to Sherman in December 1980, Hoskyns was already bemoaning the failure of the Prime Minister to follow the 'Stepping Stones' approach, resorting instead to instinctive, piecemeal reform. Accompanying his third Policy Unit strategy paper, Hoskyns wrote that

> The Government's real problem is that Margaret herself cannot or will not operate in a 'strategic leadership role'. As a result there is no shared understanding and commitment; no really free (and heretical) intellectual debate about how to 'turn defeat into victory'; no machinery or managerial method for implementing the conclusions reached by that debate. Result? Confusion, recriminations and scapegoats, refusal to face reality and take tough decisions; and so drift, low morale, and gradual erosion of loyalty. It is sad, unnecessary – and fatal.[53]

It was an analysis that Sherman agreed with. Once they had left the Policy Unit, both Strauss and Hoskyns expressed their criticism of the Civil Service and the institutional inertia of Whitehall in a series of lectures and newspaper articles, but it cannot be said that their contributions had much effect.[54] By their own criteria, therefore, the CPS fell some way short of their ambition of implementing a full programme of economic liberal reforms, leaving many of the CPS staff bitter and disappointed. Even some of Mrs Thatcher's most loyal ministerial colleagues later came to realize the strength of the CPS's 1981–2 critique of the Government, for by turning her attention to 'Welfare State' and public sector reforms only in 1987, and rushing several ill-considered measures into the 1987 election manifesto, she therefore wasted several years of precious opportunity during which time the budgets of the Departments of Health, Social Security and Education and Science had ballooned out of control. Nicholas Ridley wrote in 1991 that 'In retrospect, I believe she should have started on reform much sooner. The 1983 to 1987 Parliament has often been described as a wasted opportunity; that was the time when a serious effort to effect reform should have been made.' As a result, 'Margaret Thatcher's government did not, in fact, succeed in controlling, let alone cutting, expenditure on the public services. The spending grew strongly in real terms. She got the worst of all worlds. She got the obloquy of "cuts" and she had to spend much more on the services as well.' The figures speak for themselves. The *real* increase (after inflation) on each programme between 1979–80 and 1990–1 was as follows:

Health – 37 per cent
Social Security – 35 per cent
Education and Science – 16 per cent[55]

As the CPS had argued prior to the 1981 budget, the Government could not implement an authentic 'monetarist' policy without deep cuts in public spending, and the lack of public service and institutional reform meant that those public spending reductions were never achieved. This was the failure of strategic thinking, which led, in part, to the renewed inflationary pressures of the late 1980s.

The failure of the CPS to exert any influence on what they saw as the central issues of government policy after 1982 was mirrored by the decline in influence and importance of the CPS itself. Not only did Strauss and Hoskyns leave the Policy Unit in 1982, but Walters left Downing Street to return to America after the 1983 election and, lastly, Sherman was forced out of the CPS later that year. To a certain extent Sherman brought his departure from the CPS upon himself, as he tried to combine the roles of confidential 'insider' with that of outspoken, public critic by continuing to publish in newspapers the criticisms of government economic policy that he was making in his confidential memoranda to the Prime Minister, most notably in an article called *Stop-Go Monetarism* in the *Observer* in November 1982. In this article, he argued that the contemporary 'Monetary' squeeze was little more than a Keynesian-Butskellite 'stop' in the manner of the old 'stop-go' cycle, because it was unaccompanied by any other economic, supply-side reforms that a real economic-liberal programme of reform should have embraced. It was essentially the argument of

Monetarism Is Not Enough.[56] This was little different from what he argued in his memos to Downing Street, but, as was pointed out to him forcefully on a number of occasions by Downing Street staff, what he could not do was criticize the Government *publicly*, if he was to retain any integrity and credibility as a private adviser. Sherman was well known to be close to Mrs Thatcher, and thus his public words carried an authority which was bound to be used against the Government by the Opposition. Sherman (and, by implication, the CPS) could not both cultivate his intellectual independence and be a close and confidential adviser. In the words of David Wolfson, Mrs Thatcher's Chief-of-Staff, such a position was 'untenable'.[57] In the last analysis, the CPS was so closely associated with Mrs Thatcher that it had to be either with her totally, or divorced from her. Sherman's own personal position thus reflected the difficult position of the CPS as a whole, arising out of the unique circumstances which had shaped its birth in 1974.

In the end, the decision was taken to end the CPS's intellectual independence of government, and to bring it totally under the Government's control. In a letter of October 1983, Hugh Thomas wrote to Sherman to outline the CPS's 'New Terms of Reference':

> 1. The CPS is a Centre of Research. It is at the disposal of the Prime Minister and other Ministers. It will do what is asked of it by those Ministers and will also make submissions to them on the initiative of either the Chairman or the Director of Studies.
>
> 2. The Centre, though independent, will maintain friendly relations with the Conservative Party, at all levels of organisation . . .
>
> 8. The Centre shall not seek publicity unless the Chairman [Thomas] and Director of Studies require it to promote specific policies . . .[58]

No more 'thinking the unthinkable', 'questioning the unquestioned' or 'trail-blazing' here, and Sherman, probably rightly, saw such 'terms of reference' as effectively curtailing the intellectual vitality and courage which had been such an important contribution to the Conservative Party in the past. As Sherman himself argued in a memo to Thomas in the autumn of 1983, protesting about the proposed changes to the CPS

> The whole point of the Centre lay in its commitment to ideas and policies without committing the party leadership ... It is precisely because the Centre and I did not commit the Party leaders that we were able to move the frontiers of debate and policy search within which the Conservative leaders are bound to operate ... The whole *raison d'être* of the Centre is threatened equally by turning it either into a research organisation – meritorious though such organisations may intrinsically be – or, as Elizabeth Cottrell proclaims, 'I see the Centre's role as being to support the Prime Minister and her administration, to be seen to be supportive'. If this is our main objective, then we commit the Prime Minister. This is surely the Party's job. If the Centre can do only the Party's job, it becomes redundant ...[59]

However, this was not the Party leadership's view, and, initially under the guise of a 'sabbatical' year, it was Sherman who was made redundant. The departure of Sherman, apart from anything else, resolved a scuffle which had been souring relations at the CPS for more than a year, as by 1983 Thomas and Sherman were scarcely on speaking terms.[60]

The 'coup' against Sherman, was, indeed, expertly handled, and must have ultimately received the Prime Ministerial sanction, although Mrs Thatcher had originally wanted Sherman to stay on at the CPS. Who persuaded her otherwise is a mystery; Hugh Thomas was the only person involved in the history of the CPS who refused to speak to me, so his motives and his tactics remain unknown. Doubtless Sherman had exasperated Thomas by his often scathing and personal attacks on some of Mrs Thatcher's colleagues and Party officials, usually in embarrassingly public circumstances, but this is no more than he had been doing for several years – and by all accounts it was the Prime Minister who enjoyed his remarks the most when they were reported back to her.

Perhaps Sherman's real crime was that he continued to 'think the unthinkable', even when his political masters no longer wanted to hear any criticisms of their own performances. Symptomatic of the CPS's new 'supportive' role for the Government was the fate of the Trade Union Reform Committee, the most important and radical of the CPS Study Groups, which had done so much to shape the Party's trade union policy since its inception in 1978. In March 1984 TURC published a CPS pamphlet on *The Right to Strike in Essential Services*, questioning the 'natural' right of the ambulance service and the fire brigade to strike and proposing other mechanisms by which they could register disapproval of their terms of employment. This document did not find favour in Downing Street, partly because it hit the headlines at a delicate time for the Government. Soon afterwards, TURC was gently wound up by Hugh Thomas, Neal and Bloch being left in no doubt that their sort of radical thinking was no longer what was required.[61] Most of those associated with Sherman's tenure at the CPS, such as Nigel Morgan and Dr Elizabeth Cottrell, left soon afterwards; Strauss and Hoskyns had already left. Jeremy Shearmur, previously Karl Popper's research assistant at the LSE and briefly the Director of Studies in 1985–6, was told by Thomas that 'Mrs Thatcher did not want Study Groups anymore, so as to avoid any political embarrassment', and 'Study Groups' were, thereafter, wound up or 'not encouraged' – Shearmur was specifically told that no new ones were to be started. The moment when radical thinking became a 'political embarrassment' signalled the end of the intellectual counter-revolution that had animated Thatcherism in the first place. The ideological movement that had been inspired by Hayek's *Road to Serfdom* of 1944 effectively lost its momentum in the mid-1980s, at a time when the political implementation of economic liberalism seemed to be in full flood. The contribution of the CPS's 'para-politicians' was terminated, and the intellectual sclerosis which set in after 1982–3 meant that 'Thatcherism' lost its consistency as an ideology. Thereafter, the lopsided economic reforms of the mid-1980s combined with Nigel Lawson's apostasy at the Treasury to undermine a lot of what had been achieved in the 1979–83 government.

The moment when radical thinking had become a 'political embarrassment' was also, surely, the moment to close down the CPS itself, but in fact it continued to be active, albeit in a much more subdued and cautious manner. In the opinion of Christopher Monckton, who worked both for the CPS and the Downing Street Policy Unit, the CPS 'died when Sherman left', a verdict which most people involved in Conservative politics would agree with.[62] Sherman himself viewed

Lord Thomas's CPS with contempt and bitterness, as he saw Thomas turning it into a 'sinecure for sycophants' and 'ceasing to challenge accepted ideas'.[63] Sherman accused Thomas of 'selling indulgences', of using the CPS to promote people's political careers rather than challenging convention; as he told Mrs Thatcher, 'the moment the CPS became a job, or a step up the ladder, rather than a vocation, which it had been when I set it up with KJ and drew collaborators around me, it ceased to question the status quo, and could no longer act as a lever.'[64]

The final rift between Sherman and the Conservative Party came in 1987, when he, a Jew, tried to bring the French Fascist leader Jean Marie Le Pen to the Conservative Party Conference to address a fringe meeting. This was 'political embarrassment' on a grand scale, and the Tory press went for Sherman with thinly disguised delight. Particularly wounding was an article by Bruce Anderson, commissioned by Peregrine Worsthorne, in the *Sunday Telegraph* of 27 September 1987, which accused Sherman of being 'ego-maniacal, spiteful, obsessive, prone to temper tantrums which would disgrace a three-year old' and much else besides. It was almost ten years to the month since the CPS, largely under Sherman's guidance, had produced the 'Stepping Stones' Report which had inspired the success of the Conservative Government which now sought effectively to end Sherman's career. It was a sad end to a uniquely fruitful partnership.

Epilogue

FOR THE TOMB OF ECONOMIC MAN

The Economic Man,
He went a crooked mile;
He made a crooked sixpence
By economic guile.
He bought a crooked cat,
Which caught a crooked mouse.
And they all lived together
In an Economic House

The house has fallen in
On Economic Man
It seems the present tenant's
Totalitarian.
The Fascist cat pursues
A Communistic mouse,
And they all fight together
In the new Collective House.

But Sociologic Man,
Inheriting the Mass
Will serve the commonwelfare
With social consciousness.
Co-operative cats
Will fraternize with mice,
And we'll all romp together
In a social paradise.

Morris Bishop,
New Yorker, 12 September 1942

The election victories of Mrs Thatcher's Governments in 1983 and 1987 seemed to assure the ideological hegemony of economic liberalism. For, even without the Falklands War to boost its poll ratings in the 1983 election, the Conservative Party was still returned to office with a majority of over one hundred seats. In the modern era, the 1987 victory completed a hat-trick of wins rivalled only by Lord Liverpool's electoral successes between 1812 and 1827 – and Lord Liverpool was, appropriately enough, the first British Prime Minister to preside over a legislative programme based on the political economy of economic liberalism. So, in many ways, the wheel had come full circle. Much of Mrs Thatcher's 1987 victory was based on those policies which had been developed by the 'think-tanks' before the 1983 election, namely the policies of further trade union reform, and, most spectacularly, the privatization programme which dominated the domestic political scene from 1984 to 1987.

Furthermore, most of the economic liberal agenda that the Conservative Party espoused during the 1980s was duly adopted by the Labour Party in the wake of their 1987 election defeat, out of a recognition that a Party proposing the old economic solutions of Keynesian public spending and nationalization (as Labour had done in 1983 and 1987) could no longer appeal to the broad mass of the newly affluent electorate. Indeed, by the 1992 election it became very hard to tell the two main political parties apart on economic policy. Thus the years 1987 to 1992 saw the process of 1945 to 1951 happening in reverse; the Labour Party were forced to discard most of their old Keynesian ideology to make themselves 'electable', just as the Conservatives had discarded much of their old free-market economic and industrial policy in the immediate post-war years to make themselves 'electable'. The result of the Conservative shift in policy in the 1940s was the politics of consensual 'Butskellism'; whilst by 1992 the Labour Party was promising to do little more than manage the new economic liberal 'political economy' more effectively than the Conservatives. Furthermore, both consensuses had been created as much out of failure and disappointment as optimism and success. The 'Butskellite' consensus owed as much to Labour's retreat from further nationalization and state planning after the economic body-blows it suffered in 1947 (such as the Convertibility Crisis) as it did to the Conservative Party's attempts to steal some of Labour's clothes for electoral gain. And so the new economic liberal consensus has been fashioned in the same way, the legacy of the retreat from full-blooded 'Thatcherism' skilfully conducted by John Major in the early 1990s as much as the Labour Party's attempts to steal the Conservative's clothes by reversing a lot of their policies on industrial and economic policy in the run up to the 1992 election. The 1992 election defeat only hastened this process in the Labour Party. Since then, John Smith dismantled the block vote at Labour Party Conferences, thus symbolically ending Labour's historic self-identification as a class-based party, whilst his successor Tony Blair has specifically pledged the Party to the politics of the market economy and has, at the time of writing, even committed the Party to the slaughter of its favourite ideological sacred cow, clause IV. The fact that he looks as if he will probably get away with this is an indication of how far Labour has come and how close the present generation of 'modernisers' are to achieving their aim of converting the Labour Party into a modern European Social Democratic Party, along the lines of Germany's SPD. Just as the SPD abandoned its own commitments to old-style class politics at its famous Bad Godesberg conference in 1959, so the Labour Party has now travelled most of the way down that particular road as well. Thus, just as Britain eventually adopted a broadly 'Social Market' approach to its own economy in order to try and emulate German economic success, so Britain is now finally coming to terms with the political consequences of those hard-fought economic lessons and evolving a German-style party political system to run its much-changed economic environment. The new ideological axis around which both of the major parties revolve is that of the efficacy of the market economy – the only disputes arise as to the extent of 'regulation' which might be desirable within that market economy. John Major and Tony Blair preside over this new consensus, both of them not so much idealists as ideas-less. In their dual commitment to the priority of controlling inflation, low direct taxation, keeping government control of industry to the minimum and taking Britain into what they hope will turn out to be a non-federal Europe, they both accept the main tenets of economic liberalism as it has evolved since the 1960s, albeit espousing a more politically sensitive brand of liberalism than the CPS or the IEA might have countenanced during the 1970s and 1980s. Just as 'Butskellism' was symbolic of the political limitations of the ideology of collectivism as much as anything else, so the political economy of 'Major Blair' is equally symbolic of the political limitations of the ideology of economic liberalism.

These political limitations were evident, as we have seen, from the early 1980s onwards. Whilst to her many detractors Mrs Thatcher always seemed to be a wild-eyed, hand-bagging revolutionary, to her advisers she was a cautious, insecure pragmatist, who eventually paid the price of not capitalizing on her electoral success early or boldly enough. As we have seen, by the end of her first term of office most of the economic liberals in or from the 'think-tanks' had already resigned out of frustration or given way to a new generation. By the end of 1983, Walters, Hoskyns, Strauss, Sherman and Neal had all left the CPS and government service, and both Seldon and Harris retired from the IEA in the mid-1980s. Particularly with the departure – enforced or otherwise – of the CPS quintet, it is clear that the ideological cutting-edge went out of the Thatcher administrations. To Sherman, Hoskyns and Strauss, the big failure of the Thatcher administrations in the early 1980s to tackle the public-sector bureaucracies – especially the Civil Service – meant that, in the end, the economic liberals could never achieve that fundamental shift in power from the State to the individual that had been at the core of the economic liberal agenda since the 1940s. To the economic liberals, therefore, the Thatcherite revolution was, at best, only a partial success. But then, just as no gentleman could ever be a hero to his valet, perhaps it was equally true that Mrs Thatcher could never be a heroine to her intellectual chaperons.

After 1983 the Thatcher governments succumbed to the twin vices of arrogance and uncertainty. The Prime Minister herself became less and less keen to listen to advice, particularly critical advice, flushed with the elixir of political success. To many of her advisers, the turning-point was the Falklands War, after which the Prime Minister developed a degree of self-confidence that was, eventually, her undoing. Worst of all, she suddenly discovered 'principles', which were usually somebody else's and which only added to her inflexibility. After that, the warnings of Sherman, Strauss and Hoskyns, amongst others, went unheeded. Furthermore, the Government's economic policy was beset by uncertainty, as Nigel Lawson became an apostate at the Treasury, quickly abandoning the tight monetary policy and floating exchange rates of the early years of Thatcherism in favour of a return to what Sir Keith Joseph had memorably called 'monetary incontinence'. Lawson pursued the grail of *de jure* fixed exchange rates and 'shadowed' the Deutschmark from 1985 onwards, eventually forcing the Government into the destructive embrace of the European Monetary System from 1990 to 1992. The tensions between Downing Street and the Treasury over the conduct of economic policy making eventually led to the ruin of both Lawson and Mrs Thatcher, but it is a mark of the intellectual complacency of the late Thatcher years that although the intellectual refuseniks such as Sherman and Tim Congdon began to warn of the dangers of the Lawson boom as early as 1986, by then no-one was interested any longer in those who continued to 'think the unthinkable'. Even as early as the mid-1980s, with Thatcherism apparently in full flood, government by ideological conviction had given way to government by political expediency.

As with politics, so with the 'think-tanks'. The importance of the 'think-tanks' to the revival of economic liberalism has demonstrated the inflexibility of Party research organizations, and their congenital inability to develop new ideas or even to 'think' at all: bodies like the Conservative Research Department contributed almost nothing to the break-through of economic liberalism in the Conservative Party. The record of the universities has been almost as disappointing, for outside individual departments such as the economics departments at the LSE and Liverpool University, or the Manchester University Inflation Workshop, there was little coherent or sustained contribution to the growth of economic liberal ideas in the post-war decades. The IEA, the CPS and the ASI thus filled the policy and ideological vacuums left by the traditional sources of political and economic thinking. The revival of economic liberalism was almost entirely based on the individual intellectual and entrepreneurial initiatives of such men as Hayek, Fisher, Harris, Seldon, Walters, Sherman, Pirie and Eamonn Butler, as well as individual MPs who took an interest, such as Geoffrey Howe, Enoch Powell and John Biffen. Most Conservative and Labour MPs learnt more about economic liberalism from the journalism of Samuel Brittan and Peter Jay than they did from their own Party 'research' organizations or from the universities.

Yet for all their undoubted achievements, the think-tanks, as we have seen, also fell victim to the intellectual sclerosis that gripped the Thatcher administrations from the mid-1980s onwards. Under its new Director of Studies, David Willetts, from 1987 to 1992 the Centre for Policy Studies found a comfortable niche as a public defender of the

Government's record on social policy, but it could hardly be said to have continued the Sherman tradition of 'thinking the unthinkable'. At the IEA, the new General Director Graham Mather endured an uncomfortable tenure as he fought a guerilla war with the 'old guard' about the appropriate role that the IEA should play in the new, post-Thatcherite era of politics. He was eventually forced to resign in 1992. The general intellectual disorientation that beset the Conservative Party from 1987 onwards was reflected in the work of the 'think-tanks'; critics and admirers alike suggested that they had become too cosy with the new Major Administration and were thus sacrificing intellectual integrity and independence for political gain – the charge against Mather at the IEA.

We will not be able to discern the exact nature of the influence of the 'para-politicians' of the 'think-tanks' on the conduct of British government during the 1980s until the official files are opened in thirty years' time, but I hope that the present study will at least have described their most prominent contributions to Thatcherism, even if it is at present impossible to compare the quality of that contribution to the input of, for instance, the Civil Service.

Whether, as is often alleged, the economic liberals 'hijacked' the Conservative Party in the mid-1970s is another matter. As we have seen, they argued, strenuously, that economic liberalism lay within the mainstream of Conservative thinking, and yet there can be little doubt that economic liberalism as an ideology in its own right never captured the hearts, let alone the minds, of more than a small minority of Conservative MPs, even during the heyday of Thatcherism in the mid-1980s. It would, perhaps, be more true to say that the economic liberals succeeded in convincing a section of the leadership of the Party in the mid-1970s that they should embrace economic liberalism as an alternative to a failed status quo; and then provided not only practical policy proposals but also, just as importantly, the personnel to implement a political programme of economic liberalism. This was the primary contribution of the 'think-tanks' to Thatcherism. Very few of the economic liberals were Conservative in the sense that they had sought a career in Conservative Party politics – many of them had never even voted Conservative – but they saw certain members of the Party, particularly Mrs Thatcher and Sir Keith Joseph, as the best political exponents of their ideas. That certain Conservatives objected to the undue influence that the small number of economic liberals came to exercise over the Party was more a reflection of the intellectual and political paralysis afflicting the 'Wets' than an indication of any underhand or entryist tactics on the part of the economic liberals. Most Conservatives, blessed with that peculiarly English combination of arrogance and ignorance, refused to take the economic liberals, or Margaret Thatcher for that matter, very seriously, until it was too late for their protestations to have much effect. The truth is that once the social democratic centre had collapsed, by the mid-1970s, the bulk of the Conservative Party, like the Labour Party, had little to offer in its stead; while the economic liberals most definitely *did*. The Conservative Party was 'hijacked' by the economic liberals – but only in the sense that once they had been smuggled on board past some very supine customs officials they were welcomed into the cockpit with open arms.

If imitation is the sincerest form of flattery, the founding of a crop of left-orientated think-tanks since the mid-1980s demonstrates that the Left has realized that it can learn from, and should seek to emulate the success of the IEA, the CPS and the ASI. Indeed, with the election of Tony Blair as the new leader of the Labour Party in the summer of 1994 it is possible to see the same ferment of ideas that gripped the Conservatives in the mid-1970s. All these new think-tanks are firmly on the 'modernising' wing of Labour politics, and, like their free-market forebears, they have all allocated themselves certain specific roles in the evolution of Labour's post-Bad Godesberg political revolution. The organization most closely identified with the Party itself in this process is the Institute for Public Policy Research, set up by the businessman Clive Hollick in conjunction with Neil Kinnock's office in 1988. Under the directorship of James Cornford the IPPR has become the most powerful modernising force within the Labour Party establishment, at least as far as policy is concerned. One of its officers, David Milliband, is now head of policy development in Tony Blair's private office. The IPPR is to the modern Labour Party what the CPS was to the Conservatives in the 1970s. A revitalised Fabian Society has led the way in campaigning for structural reforms within the Labour Party itself, publishing a celebrated series of 'Southern Discomfort' pamphlets arguing for different policies to attract back to Labour's ranks all those disaffected 'middle class' and 'upper working-class' supporters who went over to Thatcherism in the late 1970s and have stayed there ever since. Whilst the IPPR consciously modelled itself on the CPS, so Demos, founded in March 1993, owes much of its inspiration to the working methods of the IEA, and in particular the work of Arthur Seldon. Set up by Martin Jacques, the former editor of *Marxism Today* and inventor of the term Thatcherism, and Geoff Mulgan, the former research assistant to the Shadow Chancellor Gordon Brown, Demos seeks to map out the post-Thatcherite agenda in much the same way as the IEA shifted the parameters of political thinking in the 1960s and 1970s. The Social Market Foundation was founded in 1989 with funding from David Sainsbury as the intellectual legacy of the defunct Social Democratic Party and in particular the 'Owenite' faction of the SDP. Its director, Daniel Finkelstein, is a former adviser to Lord Owen.

What all these new (or, in the case of the Fabians, revivalist) think-tanks have in common is that they share a basic acceptance of the intellectual ground won by the IEA and the CPS – the role of the market in political and economic thinking is now axiomatic. This is the achievement of the IEA and CPS. But the new generation of think-tanks are now moving beyond the free-market and exploring new ways and methods of going about their Popperian 'piecemeal engineering' without recourse to the kinds of statism that was implicit in the old Socialism and in the more centralizing moments of Thatcherism. They are also strictly post-modernist in the sense that they are not seeking to uncover or even proselytize for a 'big idea' – such as the market. Rather they are involved in a much more pragmatic evolution of ideas and policies to deal with the *consequences* of market economics, drawing their inspiration from a much wider range of disciplines than in the past. Indeed, this is, to a certain extent, their *raison d'être*; economic liberalism is seen as reductionist, offering only one of many explanations for individual motivation and aspiration. Under the impact of economic liberalism in the 1980s, the old meta-narratives of society – Church, Monarchy, even conservatism and socialism – have broken down, creating fragmentation and diversity in their place. Market economics alone cannot be used as a tool of analysis to address the problems of the more complex society which it has helped to bring about. Just as the IEA's brand of economic liberalism owed much of its intellectual stimulus to the past, to Adam Smith *et al*, so the new political thinking owes much of its own inspiration to similarly old traditions, echoes of which can be found in Blair's appeals to a search for 'Community'. Even now, it is possible to see the emergence of the broad contours of this new thinking. The Social Market Foundation published two pamphlets in the summer of 1994, by John Gray and David Willetts, the former director of the CPS, which showed two Conservatives grappling with these very issues and while not discarding economic liberalism, arguing that it has to be complemented by other ideas and policies – values, even – if the market is to fulfill its real potential. This is the new ground of politics, recognising the achievements and the limitations of economic liberalism. Already, the wheel of ideas has taken another turn.

One of the lessons to ponder from the record of the work of the economic liberals since the Second World War is the way in which new ideological agendas can be surpassed by events. All new ideas are conceived in reaction to the status quo; but that status quo rarely remains stable for very long. The big black-hole in the ideological re-think that consumed the Conservatives in the 1960s and the 1970s was Europe. The IEA did publish two impressive papers on the subject (James Meade's *UK, Commonwealth and Common Market*, 1962 and Russel Lewis's *Rome or Brussels?*, 1972) but on the whole these were the exceptions which proved the rule. For far too long, Europe was the issue that dared not speak its name. Indeed, the subject of Europe was almost wholly ignored by the economic liberals until the *political* consequences of further European integration had become so pressing that they threatened to jeopardize all that the economic liberals thought that the Thatcher administrations had achieved during the 1980s. Only then, for example, did Ralph Harris found the Bruges Group, to continue the fight for economic liberalism in a European context that the IEA had fought in a domestic context. But by then it was too late. Considering that the drive towards a federal Europe did indeed endanger almost everything that the economic liberals had achieved, Europe proved to be a remarkable blind spot. It is ironic that at the very moment when Geoffrey Howe was finally breaking free from Britain's fixed exchange rate regime in 1979, Britain's European partners were embarking on the creation of the European Exchange Rate System, thereafter a slow fuse under the Thatcher governments of the 1980s, eventually detonating in 1990. Nothing that the economic liberal intellectuals and propagandists wrote or said in the 1950s, 1960s or 1970s prepared the Conservative governments for the complexities of dealing with the European issue in the 1980s. This was their failure. They might have had the 'big idea' – the free market – of the 1970s, but as far as the art of government was concerned this proved to be of increasingly marginal relevance as the 1980s progressed.

Bertrand de Jouvenel, the French writer and founder-member of the Mont Pèlerin Society, noted the same shortfall between ideology and the circumstances in which that ideology is applied in his critique of Attlee's government, *Problems of Socialist England*, written in 1947. De Jouvenel argued that by pursuing the Keynesian and Beveridgian policies of 'keeping permanently in being the conditions of extreme activity which have hitherto always been flowed by depression', a fatal 'paradox' had thus arisen:

> the paradox of the situation is that not unemployment but shortage of manpower, not the danger of slump but of under production, are the characteristics of England in the after-war period. With the result that the approach for today's problems is by way of a doctrine which was forged to meet an entirely different situation. Events have outstripped minds . . .[1]

Or, in Samuel Brittan's words, 'the Keynesian approach received most support when it was no longer needed and ultimately deleterious.' Like the 'Butskellite' governments before them, the Thatcher Governments similarly failed to adapt themselves intellectually to the circumstances in which they had to operate. Nothing that the economic liberals had written prepared the politicians for the European maelstrom of the late 1980s. Much as Keynesianism might have been useful doctrine in the 1930s, when it was largely rejected by governments, so economic liberalism would have been of enormous benefit to the country if used by governments in the 1950s, when the British economy was still strong enough to adapt and survive in a competitive international environment. As it was, economic liberalism as applied in the 1980s effectively wiped out a large part of Britain's manufacturing industry and, at the end of a decade of economic experiment and dislocation, left as many people unemployed as there were in the 1930s. Perhaps it is true that 'every age accepts the doctrines evolved to deal with a previous one and neglects the message most relevant to its own time',[2] in which case the intellectual triumph of economic liberalism in the 1980s demonstrated both the importance and the danger inherent in strong ideas, especially in the hands of politicians. To paraphrase Churchill, maybe it would have been better to 'see ideology less proud and industry more content'.

In a wider perspective, economic liberalism might have already been on the wane as the new hegemonic ideology in Britain by the late 1980s, but in 1989 the 'World-wide Liberal Revolution' (to use a chapter-title from Francis Fukuyama's *The End of History*) seemed to reach its apotheosis with the collapse of the Communist regimes in Eastern Europe, and eventually the implosion of the Soviet Union itself. It was a phenomenon that, once again, owed much to the ideological battle waged by the economic liberals in those countries, some operating from think-tanks supported by Antony Fisher's Atlas Foundation. It was at this point that Fukuyama, an American State Department official, delivered a lecture on 'The End of History' at, appropriately enough, the University of Chicago, home of Hayek, Friedman, Frank Knight, Stigler and many others, and central to the work of post-war liberalism. Fukuyama's lecture was published as an article in the *National Interest* in the summer of 1989, and later expanded into a book, *The End of History and the Last Man*. Fukuyama argued that a similar ideological transformation to that described in this book had been going on all over the world, and that the intellectual triumph of economic liberalism, or liberal democracy as he called it, was now complete. Deploying graphs and figures, Fukuyama purported to describe the irreversible triumph of liberal democracy which effectively spelt the end of history as an ideological progression; with one or two stubborn exceptions, mainly in south Asia, Socialism and Communism had been vanquished. In the original article, to use his own words, he argued that:

> a remarkable consensus concerning the legitimacy of liberal democracy as a system of government had emerged throughout the world over the past few years, as it conquered rival ideologies like hereditary monarchy, fascism and most recently Communism . . . while earlier forms of governments were characterised by grave defects and irrationalities that led to their eventual collapse, liberal democracy was arguably free from such fundamental internal contradictions. This was not to say that today's stable democracies, like the United States, France or Switzerland, were not without injustice or serious social problems. But these prob-

> lems were ones of incomplete implementation of the twin principles of liberty and equality on which modern democracy is founded, rather than flaws in the principles themselves. While some present-day countries might fail to achieve stable liberal democracy, and others might lapse back into other, more primitive forms of rule like theocracy or military dictatorship, the ideal of liberal democracy could not be improved on.[3]

Such ideological triumphalism is by no means new, however. Fukuyama's thesis bore a striking resemblance to two other books written to commemorate similar moments of ideological triumphalism in the past, Macaulay's *History of England* and Daniel Bell's *The End of Ideology*. *The History of England* was written to record the success of the first liberal revolution in England and the rise of material progress; the second book, *The End of Ideology*, was written by an American political scientist to celebrate the triumph of the Keynesian 'middle-way'. Both authors, like Fukuyama, assumed that the dominant ideologies of their age were *idées fixes*, as they seemed to be to their respective authors at the time. But both Macaulay and Bell were, in fact, writing at the cusp of a wave, at the very moment when the ideological tide was already turning. Thus Macaulay's first two volumes of his *History of England* were published in 1848, the year that Marx published *The Communist Manifesto*, foreshadowing the collectivist revolutions that were to become the orthodoxy only two generations later, whilst Daniel Bell was writing his book in 1960, only five years after the IEA had started its assault on the Keynesian settlement that Bell was describing which was to lead to the replacement of Keynesianism by economic liberalism as the new intellectual orthodoxy within the next generation.

Fukuyama's thesis stands at the same relationship to economic liberalism as Bell's did to Keynesianism and Macaulay's did to Victorian liberalism, for the intellectual revolution described in this book demonstrates how, over the course of forty or fifty years, intellectual orthodoxies are there to be challenged and overthrown. The Hayekian revolution in economic and political thinking from the 1920s to the 1980s reached the peak of its intellectual and political success in the late 1980s, before so much of what had been achieved became tarnished by the deepest recession since the 'Great Depression'. Fukuyama's book merely supplied the hubris which accompanies all such intellectual revolutions. John Kenneth Galbraith, the oldest of old Keynesians, provided a very different picture of the triumph of economic liberalism in his most recent work, published in 1992, *The Culture of Contentment*, in which he described the inherent instabilities in modern capitalist systems where up to forty per cent of the population have become so marginalized that they no longer participate in the democratic process, far less benefit from the growth in Society's wealth that the economic liberal revolutions of the 1980s brought in their wake. Perhaps Galbraith's work stands in the same relation to our own time as Hayek's *Road to Serfdom* did to the 1940s. Far from it being the 'End of History', we are now at the point where the counter-revolution against economic liberalism will start, and the Hayekian campaign of intellectual persuasion provides the modern model of how to effect the next intellectual counter-revolution. But that is up to the 'academic scribblers' of the present generation, whose 'frenzy' will be distilled by the 'madmen in authority' of the next generation.

Appendix I

Mont Pèlerin Conference Participants

Mont Pèlerin Conference.
1st - 10th April 1947.

List of Participants.

Prof.M.Allais,Ecole Nationale Supérieure des Mines, 218,Boulevard St.Germain, PARIS 7e

Prof.C.Antoni, Istituto Nazionale per le Relazioni Culturali con l'Estero, Piazza Firenze 27,ROME

Prof.K.Brandt, Food Research Institute, Stanford University, CALIFORNIA, U.S.A.

Prof.H.Barth, Université de Zurich, Heilighüsli 18, ZURICH.

Mr.J.Davenport, Fortune Magazine, 350 Fifth Ave.NEW YORK.

Prof.S.Dennison, Gonville & Caius College, CAMBRIDGE

Prof.A.Director, The Law School, University of Chicago, CHICAGO 37, ILLINOIS, U.S.A.

Prof.W.Eucken, Goethestrasse 10, FREIBURG i.Br.

Dr.E.Eyck, Chilswell House, Boars Hill, nr.OXFORD

Prof.M.Friedman, Dept.of Economics,University of Chicago, CHICAGO 37, ILLINOIS, U.S.A.

H.D.Gideonse, President, Brooklyn College, Bedford Ave, & Avenue H., BROOKLYN 10, N.Y., U.S.A.

Prof.F.D.Graham,Princeton University, 214,Western ay PRINCETON, New Jersey, U.S.A.

Prof.F.A.Harper, The Foundation for Economic Education, IRVINGTON-on-HUDSON, N.Y., U.S.A.

Prof.F.A.Hayek, The London School of Economics & Political Science, Houghton St. Aldwych, LONDON, W.C.2.

Mr.H.Hazlitt, Newsweek, Newsweek-Bldg, Broadway & 42nd St., New York 18, N.Y.,U.S.A.

Dr.T.J.B.Hoff, Roald Amundsensgate, 1, OSLO.

Dr.A.Hunold, Bünishof, Feldmeilen, ZURICH.

Mr.B.de Jouvenel, CHEXBRES, Vaud

-2-

Prof.C.Iversen, Ny Toldsbotgade 49, COPENHAGEN

Prof.J.Jewkes, Dept.of Economics, The University of Manchester, MANCHESTER.

Prof.F.H.Knight, University of Chicago, CHICAGO 37, Illinois, U.S.A.

Prof.F.Machlup, University of Buffalo, N.Y., U.S.A.

+Mr.L.B.Miller, Director of Bureau of Governmental Research, 153 E.Elisabeth, DETROIT 1, Michigan, U.S.A.

+Prof.L.v.Mises, 777 West End Ave, New York 25, U.S.A.

Mr.Felix Morley, 1 Wetherill Rd., Washington 16, D.C. U.S.A.

+Prof.M.Polanyi, The University of Manchester, Dept. of Chemistry, MANCHESTER.

Dr.K.R.Popper, The London School of Economics, LONDON, W.C.2.

-Prof.W.E.Rappard, Institut Universitaire des Hautes Etudes Internationales, 132 rue de Lausanne, GENEVE.

Mr.L.E.Read, President, The Foundation for Economic Education, IRVINGTON-on-HUDSON, N.Y., U.S.A.

Prof.L.Robbins, The London School of Economics & Pol. Science, Houghton St., Aldwych, LONDON,W.C.2.

-Prof.W.Röpke, Institut Universitaire des Hautes Etudes Internationales, 45 Ave.de Champel, GENEVE.

Prof.G.J.Stigler, Brown University,PROVIDENCE R.I. U.S.A.

rProf.H.Tingsten,Dagens Nyheter, STOCKHOLM.

Prof.F.Trevoux, 10 Rue Duquesne, LYON.

Mr.V.O.Watts, The Foundation of Economic Education, IRVINGTON-on-HUDSON, New York, U.S.A.

Miss C.V.Wedgwood, Time & Tide, 32 Bloomsbury St., LONDON, W.C.1.

-3-

<u>List of Observers.</u>

Mr.H.C.Cornuelle, The Foundation for Economic Education,
IRVINGTON-on-HUDSON, N.Y., U.S.A.

Mr.H. de Lovinfosse, Château Roos, WAASMUNSTER, Belgique

Mr.G.Révay, The Readers' Digest, 216 Bd.Saint Germain,
PARIS.

Appendix II

Mont Pèlerin Conference Proceedings

Mont Pèlerin Conference
April 1st - 10th 1947.

PROCEEDINGS

Tuesday, April 1st.

Morning. Chair: Rappard
Report on aims and organisation of Conference by Hayek, Discussion of programme and time table. Allais, Dennison, Friedman, Hayek, Hunold elected as Standing Committee, Hayek and Hunold to act as Conference Secretaries.

Afternoon & Evening. Chair: Rappard
"Free" Enterprise or Competitive Order
Discussion opened by Hayek, Director & Eucken.
Speakers: Iversen, Eucken, Miller, Mises, Robbins, Polanyi, Friedman, Hazlitt, Rappard, Jouvenel, Gideonse, Tingsten.

Wednesday, April 2nd

Morning. Chair: Robbins
Modern Historiography & Political Education
Discussion opened by Wedgwood & Antoni.
Speakers: Eyck, Tingsten, Hayek, Popper, Mises, Rappard, Roepke, Barth Knight.

Afternoon & Evening. Chair: Iversen
The Future of Germany
Speakers: Eucken, Brandt, Robbins, Friedman, Rappard, Graham, Stigler.

Thursday, April 3rd

Morning & Evening. Chair: Allais
The Problems & Chances of European Federation
Discussion opened by Jouvenel
Speakers: Lovinfosse, Iversen, Morley, Rappard, Knight, Popper, Polanyi, Trevoux, Mises, Hayek, Machlup, Graham

The afternoon was occupied by an excursion to Chateau de Coppet.

--2-

Friday April 4th	Morning. Chair: Eucken Liberalism & Christianity Discussion opened by Knight Speakers: Hoff, Davenport, Allais, Hayek, Polanyi, Popper, Gideonse, Roepke, Brandt, Jouvenel, Graham, Morley.
	Afternoon. Chair: Antoni General Discussion of aims and purposes of a permanent organisation. Speakers: Hayek, Hazlitt, Robbins, Knight, Stigler, Machlup, Jewkes, Graham, Hoff, Jouvenel, Friedman, Popper, Polanyi, Dennison. Committee appointed to draft statement of aims consisting of Eucken, Gideonse, Hayek, Hazlitt, Iversen, Jewkes.
Saturday, Apl. 5th & Sunday Apl. 6th	Excursion to Schwyz and Einsiedeln.
Monday April 7th.	Afternoon. Chair: Hoff Contra-Cyclical Measures, Full Employment & Monetary Reform. Opened by Stigler Speakers: Graham, Hazlitt, Robbins, Director, Roepke, Allais, Knight, Jouvenel, & Friedman
	Evening Discussion of Draft Statement of Aims
Tuesday April 8th	Morning. Chair: Graham Wage Policy & Trade Unions Opened by Machlup Speakers: Allais, Lovinfosse, Graham, Dennison, Polanyi, Iversen, Knight, Rappard, Watts, Brandt, Jouvenel, Davenport, Jewkes.
	Evening. Chair: Mises Taxation, Poverty & Income Distribution Opened by Friedman Speakers: Jewkes, Miller, Polanyi, Dennison, Rappard, Allais, Jouvenel, Hayek, Knight, Brandt, Popper, Watts.

-3-

Wednesday April 9th	Morning. Chair: Read Agricultural Policy Opened by Brandt Speakers: Director, Roepke, Miller, Robbins, Hayek, Eucken, Rappard, Graham, Mises.
	Afternoon. Chair: Morley Discussion of Organisation of permanent body.
	Evening. Chair: Gideonse The Present Political Crisis Opened by Polanyi Speakers: Davenport, Jouvenel, Knight, Popper, Brandt, Watts, Wedgwood, Robbins.
Thursday April 10th	Morning. Chair: Hayek Discussion and adoption of "Memorandum of Association" of Mont Pèlerin Society.

Appendix III

Arthur Seldon

My qualifications – and disqualifications – for writing this piece should be stated simply to be judged by the reader.

I am an intellectual with ten years' experience of industry – and its commercial attitudes, salesmanship and profit-making that often offend intellectuals. For nearly ten years I have been an entrepreneur in intellectualism as editorial director of the Institute of Economic Affairs. And I have no party allegiance (although I usually vote Liberal) but a social philosophy that, if I must have a label, makes me a radical conservative, or a conservative radical.

The third qualification – or disqualification – explains much of what follows. My origins are working-class or *très très petit bourgeois* (my foster-father was a self-employed cobbler in a working-class area). I developed Labour politics as a youth, rejected them under the influence of an economic historian in the sixth form, reinforced by the teachings of and talks with Arnold Plant (to whom we all owe a debt we can never repay – so much for social cost/benefit analysis) and Lionel Robbins, spent my undergraduate years as an ardent Liberal in frustrating, futile protest against Hitler, Mussolini and Stalin, Hoare and Chamberlain, worked for the Liberal Party on and off till the middle 1950s. I have emerged with a passionate desire to raise the working man to dignity, independence and self-respect but with confirmed apprehension that his Labour leaders espouse or pursue policies that will deny him these urges, conditions and rewards of social progress, and a growing conviction that in the end he will achieve them, even if he has to reject his class allegiance.

Hence my radical conservatism. I would conserve – and refine and strengthen – the *conditio sine qua non* of what Walter Lippmann in a lucid interval called 'The Good Society': personal liberty (I would take risks with licence if the alternative is over-cautious repression), individual and corporate initiative, decentralised authority, and government limited to services that cannot be organised by spontaneous contract in the market. This is the classic formulation, of what I shall insist on describing as liberalism, by Adam Smith, Abraham Lincoln, John Maynard Keynes and the younger Robbins. But I would be radical about reforming the legal institutional framework in order to preserve these principles – the laws on property, contract, industrial organisation, sale and purchase of goods and services.

Hence also my love-hate relationship with Conservatives for not understanding or for failing to recreate conservatism. This is the dilemma that has both nurtured and soured the relationship between intellectuals and Conservatives in my adult life. Two denigratory half-truths have periodically been levelled at Conservatives (but not necessarily at conservatism): 'the stupid party'; 'you can't trust the Tories'. The first was valid sometimes, less often in recent years. The second has been true even in recent years, but not of some individual Conservative leaders.

The ambivalence of public opinion is paralleled by what seems ambivalence among intellectuals. Professor George Stigler has said 'the professional study of economics makes one politically conservative'. Professor F. A. Hayek added a post-script entitled 'Why I am not a Conservative' to his book *The Constitution of Liberty*. Professor J. R. (now Sir John) Hicks of All Souls College, Oxford, said in a wartime essay: 'Our economic system has developed out of the relatively free enterprise of the nineteenth century . . . What had not happened before was the association of free enterprise with a framework of ideas . . . which have fallen into such disrepute that . . . there are few to do them honour; yet they deserve to be honoured. Manchesterism was not a mere demand by the successful businessman to be allowed to prosecute his own interests in his own way without interference – the caricatures drawn alike by the young Disraeli, by Marx, and by Goebbels. It was a demand for an economic policy based on moral principles; although those principles are not in all respects the same as ours, and in any case the deductions we should draw from them are widely different, the thread which comes down from that old liberalism is still discernible. It is a noble heritage . . .'

But what is this 'conservatism' or 'liberalism' that intellectuals who reject, fear and resist centralised political authority both support and reject it? Professor Stigler defines a conservative in economic matters as 'a person who wishes most economic activity to be conducted by private enterprise, and who believes that abuses of private power will usually be checked, and incitements to efficiency and progress usually provided, by the forces of competition.' Professor Hayek rejects conservatism because the philosophy for which he stands – he describes himself as a liberal or an Old (i.e. pre-French Revolution) Whig – although sometimes described as conservatism, is different from conservatism as it has developed in practice – a negative resistance to change (which is laudable if change is undesirable) but not an alternative to current undesirable étatist tendencies which can prevent their continuance, so that is has 'invariably been the fate of conservatism to be dragged along a path not of its own choosing'. And what is, or should be, the conservative or liberal alternative? Sir John Hicks' statement of 'the moral principles of Manchesterism' will satisfy me: 'The first was Freedom: the right of the adult human being to be treated as an adult, to have the power to choose and the opportunity to bear responsibility for his own actions. The second was Equality or Fairness'. The second principle means not the egalitarianism of the present-day universalists who want equal social benefits for all, even in unequal circumstances, but the treatment of all citizens as equal before the law and objection to privilege – as in the levying of taxation on the few, because they are few, to benefit the many, or customs duties levied on the many to benefit the few in protected industries. Other liberals would put the content of liberalism differently; I want to emphasise that liberalism is not merely an economic system that yields commercial opulence, but a moral order.

And there's the rub. Conservatism in our day has too often appeared to be a negative opposition to change, a stubborn adherence to the status quo, with nothing to put in its place. Conservatives have not yet resolved the dilemma whether it stands for the established order because at least it works and because change may be bad, or whether it stands for a body of good principles which it will introduce in place of the bad principles it inherits from its opponents. Of course, there is a good case for continuity, for caution in replacing what is perhaps not so good but is at least known by something that may be better but is unknown. But that is no case for continuing what is being done even though it is thought bad. This is conservative conservatism; it preserves the institutional framework as well as the principles, good or bad. It has refused over a large part of society to change the legal and institutional framework and in so doing risks and further weakens the principles of liberty, decentralised initiative and limited government. This is what the Conservatives did in 1931 when they took over ideas on transport licensing, agricultural marketing, coal organisation, public boards and other forms of quasi-socialism left over from Labour. They were rather better when they followed Labour in 1951, although even Labour might have continued to dismantle the apparatus of wartime controls if they had stayed in office. But the Conservatives did nothing, or almost nothing to denationalise the state-controlled fuel, transport or welfare services introduced by Labour. The most disappointing case was that of Enoch Powell who taught the virtues of individual liberty and freedom of choice between alternatives in markets, yet did almost nothing to restore them when he was Minister of Health from 1960 to 1963. Perhaps he needed more time, or his colleagues were obstructive, or he wanted more evidence of public support for change. But the record stands.

This is the dilemma of Conservatives that mystifies antagonists or repels intellectuals. Are they no more than pragmatists without principles who run the state machine rather more cleverly and more subtly than Labour by better timing, more influential connections, more persuasive power ('leadership') or the divine right to rule? Quintin Hogg's book on conservatism came perilously close to arguing the superior virtue of political flexibility over fixed principle. Or do Conservatives stand for an identifiable philosophy that is different from Labour's? Do they propose to run the nationalised sector, now nearly half of the economy, rather better than Labour? Does all their raillery against 'socialism' mean no more than that they think, arrogantly and with no support from experience, that nationalisation is nauseous except when run by the right chaps in old school ties?

This is the impression created by Messrs Maudling on income policy and planning, Boyle (and Kathleen Ollerenshaw) on education, Boyd Carpenter (when in office) on social insurance, among the seniors and Raison, Howell, Watts, Spicer, and now Rhys-Williams among the juniors. And the outsider has some difficulty in reconciling their views with those of Powell, Joseph, Thatcher, Maude, Macmillan (the Younger), Howe, Biffen, Braine, Jenkin and others who offer a distinctive philosophy and distinctive principles. Conservatives speak with two voices: there is no doubt which must prevail if they are to regain the respect and encouragement, but never, never, never, the slavish subservience of intellectuals.

I have argued, like Tibor Szamuely, that the Conservatives should present a coherent structure of principles so that the electorate will not only have a choice between two systems of principles but also know what will guide the Conservatives in office. They are now offered a choice of men. That will not suffice. Conservatives will have to work their passage back to a position of trust that they partly forfeited during the thirteen years in which their praiseworthy but inadequate acts of commission were outnumbered by their failures in acts of omission. If a choice of men is not enough, I am not asking for a choice of measures, for no opposition can or should anticipate the acts it will have to perform in office. But there is a third choice that can be offered. Not men, for that is not enough; not measures, for that is too much; but method, principle philosophy.

Four years out of office should have given time for refinement of radical Conservative principles. They rest on a philosophy that Labour has ignored, rarely mentions, and in practice frustrates: the philosophy that sees the prime mover of social and economic vitality and advance in the individual and his family. This is not to erect self-interest, or selfishness, as the mainspring of human conduct. It is to recognise that, except in short bursts of war or emergency, men can work only for the people and the purposes they know, and understand, and love: their families, their friends, their personal, local, causes, clubs, churches, hospitals, schools. Edward Heath is the first Conservative Party leader in my life-time who has echoed this theme, and more distinctive and systematic repetition would cause the heart to beat faster and the spirit to lift.

The primacy of the individual and all that flows from it – the role of the family as the social unit, freedom for individual and corporate imitative, the essential morality of independent business enterprise, commerce, salesmanship and advertising in competition contrasted with the sickening mendacity and sanctimonious humbug of the politician who pretends to serve 'the public interest', the supremacy of the consumer in the economy, freedom for and encouragement of local, voluntary effort in welfare, social and cultural activities, the subjection of the official and the bureaucrat to the taxpayer and the recipient of social benefits, not least freedom from political influence in education, research, learning and scholarship – these are what intellectuals should, and I think overwhelmingly would, support.

And the last is not the least. It is incredible to me that intellectuals have supported social and economic policies that require central control or direction by the State, which must in time entail restriction of freedom in literature, the arts, and the sciences. Happily the recent reaction has come only a few years after the Government began to extend the power of the State in 1964. Whatever their individual views on the desirable form of society, intellectuals must increasingly yearn for freedom from political control of universities and colleges. Professor Edward Shils, no conservative or liberal (in the European sense) spoke in the first number of Minerva of the 'governmentalisation' of learning, and there is a growing reaction by intellectuals of all schools against the increasing control of British universities through the University Grants Committee. Little wonder that some are turning to the idea of establishing independent universities financed by a multiplicity of private sources. And businessmen will see that the money they have contributed to the foundation of universities in Sussex, Essex, Kent, Warwick, Aston, Bradford, Strathclyde . . . has established institutions that increase the power of the State to make mistakes and the power of politicians to play politics.

The experience of the Communist countries under their Stalins, and their efforts in recent years to restore liberty in Yugoslavia, Hungary, and now Czechoslovakia and even Russia itself, must be showing many intellectuals that where economic freedom is suppressed, there literary, artistic and cultural freedom cannot breathe. Even in the USA, which has been going down the wrong road back to statism for some years, there are signs of reaction against the State. Mr Robert Kennedy, regarded as a 'liberal' of the wrong (American) sort, made a remarkable speech last summer in favour of private enterprise. And in September, Mr Daniel P. Moynihan, Director of the Institute for Urban Studies at Harvard University, also a 'liberal' of the collectivist school, warned against the trend to political centralisation in Washington, and urged alliance with political 'conservatives' (i.e. liberals in the European sense) 'who recognise that unyielding rigidity is just as much a threat to the continuity of things as is an anarchic desire for change', and that 'we must begin getting private business involved in domestic programmes . . . what aerospace corporations have done for getting us to the moon, urban housing corporations can do for the slums. All that is necessary, is to enable enough men to make enough money out of doing so . . . The task of liberals is to make it politically worthwhile and possible for the (Washington) administration to disengage'.

And not only intellectuals will support a party that offers to restore freedom.

The emerging masses, even more than the suppressed middle classes, will want freedom to spend their rising incomes. Professor John Vaizey has recently pointed to 'the grave internal contradiction' in 'the ideology of equality' that it cannot at the same time concentrate what resources the State can command on the less gifted or fortunate in the name of equality and on the more gifted in the name of excellence. The dilemma of the egalitarian must be increasingly painful. Should he give his child the advantages he has inherited directly in wealth or indirectly in ability and so sacrifice his principles? Or should he share the State service that is no better than the State can supply for everyone and sacrifice his child? This is not only a conflict between public profession and private performance. A Wedgwood Benn can salve his conscience by the reflection that you do not have to practice to be a good preacher. The dilemma of the egalitarian is far more intractable. It is that, as long as incomes are unequal and the family is not abolished, parents will want to spend their money on something that benefits their family: there is not much sense in forcing them to spend it all on colour TV, cars, hair-dos and fun fairs; they will want better schooling, doctors and hospitals, houses and pensions: and these are freedoms that the State denies, but will sooner or later have to yield.

The yearning for intellectual freedom must be described by the name it has been given by political philosophy down the years since the eighteenth century: liberalism. It is a noble word that has been prostituted by étatists in North America, but I agree with Professor Milton Friedman that we should not let the devil get away with misleading labellings. 'Democratic' has been defiled in the communist 'democratic people's republics'; 'selectivity' is being made a new shield for progressive taxation; 'micro-Economic' is being naively applied to arbitrary, discriminatory, capricious government favours to individual industries or even firms. All these words should be rescued from captivity. They have been misappropriated because they describe ideas that their misappropriators sense express underlying understanding of what is good, true and civilised. Let the devil sing his own malevolent songs.

But the Conservatives are not the only party to whom intellectuals can turn. Some businessmen turned to Labour in the early 1960s for the wrong policies. But Labour could adopt the right policies for a host of reasons from cynical expediency to a belated recognition that the ordinary people in a western society want more freedom. As the defects, incompetence and dangers of State control spreading from economic to cultural life become more apparent, Labour could change its policies, as it might have done under Gaitskell, and the Social Democrats have done in Germany, away from State socialism to acceptance of competitive capitalism and private enterprise.

I should be more at home with some Labour men or Liberals than with some Conservatives. In politics, as elsewhere, competition is essential for good order, responsibility and sanity. If the Conservatives want the advice and encouragement of intellectuals they had better lose no more time in saying where they stand and giving an earnest of their intention to act on it when they return to office.

Appendix IV

John Vaizey's letter to The Times, *2 December 1980*

Sir, I left the Labour Party in 1978 after 33 years' membership. I had served the party in several humble capacities, and when Sir Harold Wilson recommended me for a peerage I took the Labour whip. I resigned it in 1978 and a year later, in May 1979, I took the Conservative whip.

Hitherto I have made no public statement about this. It is painful to break the habits of a lifetime. One's friends feel betrayed. Several whom I regularly see cut me dead. The feelings are as hard as those aroused by the Anglican defectors who became Catholics when Dr Newman did. They are friends whom I value and whom any country might be proud to have in political life – the late Tony Crosland and Richard Titmuss, Shirley Williams, David Northfield, Barbara Wootton, Olive Gibbs, Harold Lever, Bill Rodgers, Michael Barnes, Frank Field. Some are still my friends but clearly they feel betrayed. And for months I felt a traitor too. A decent silence seemed best.

I left for two reasons and I am prompted to break my silence by the remarkable letter from Councillor Frears of Leicestershire (December 1). More of us should speak up.

By 1978 there was scarcely a Labour policy that I could support and many seemed actively harmful. Scottish and Welsh devolution were unworkable, naked vote-catching based on no logical or constitutional principle. The slavish subservience to the trades union leadership handed the country's government over to a crew of self-satisfied bosses who could neither lead their membership nor agree on incomes policy. The Chancellor's economic policy was half-hearted monetarism that led uniquely to rising unemployment and a collapsing currency. The vaunted redistribution of income and wealth had made the poor poorer and the rich richer. The comprehensive reform had been so badly handled that in Inner London well over a quarter of the fifth formers were officially truanting every day and the pupils I received from them at the university were often barely literate. The gaols were full. The hospitals seemed to be run for the benefit of the Trotskyite porters. This was socialism at work.

Increasingly the Labour membership was swamped by bombastic polytechnic lecturers regurgitating inaccurately the half-baked ideas of sentimental Marxists that Tawney would not have let in to his lecture room. As serious analysis of social and economic affairs it was pathetic.

And this was socialism. Some Cabinet Ministers I knew just loved their cars, their drivers, office, and were openly cynical about what they were supposed to have been elected to support. To suppose that the average decent Labour party member could change this state of affairs was daft. In so far as the country was being governed at all it was being run by an ever-more powerful Civil Service and second-rate businessmen in the state monopolies, monopolies for the most part chaired by Labour party hacks. The Prime Minister shamelessly appointed his son-in-law to the Washington Embassy.

So, like lots of others, I left the Labour Party.

I knew and liked Margaret Thatcher. She is what the papers say she is. But she is much more – honest, a patriot and ready to listen. Increasingly I came to think she would restore honest government, reduce the overblown bureaucracy, strip the state industries of their bloated payrolls, save the currency and give us a foreign policy that decent people could respect. When she and Peter Carrington asked me for their support I gave it.

Of course it's tough. No government gets everything right. But by God she's trying. There is no longer a set of social democrat ideas that will work. Keynesianism is intellectually dead. With our trade unions no incomes policy can ever work. With our state industries productivity will always be abysmal. Nobody, not even Shirley Williams, has the faintest idea how to redistribute income: the tax and benefit system is far too complex and arbitrary to yield a simple progressive result free from major anomalies. Social democratic theory is just plain wrong. Torsten Husen, the great Swedish educator, apostle of the comprehensive reform, has just announced its failure as an egalitarian tool in Sweden. Is Shirley Williams going to nail her colours to that fallen mast ?

The only workable set of political principles in free Europe today is Tory pragmatism. And that's why I support the Government, apart from the fact that they seem to be a fairly honest lot.

Appendix V

The Reader's Digest *publishes an abridged version of Hayek's* The Road to Serfdom

The READER'S DIGEST
An article a day of enduring significance, in condensed permanent booklet form
April 1945

THE ROAD TO SERFDOM

A CONDENSATION FROM THE BOOK BY

Friedrich A. Hayek

"In *The Road to Serfdom*," writes Henry Hazlitt in the New York *Times*, "Friedrich A. Hayek has written one of the most important books of our generation. It restates for our time the issue between liberty and authority. It is an arresting call to all well-intentioned planners and socialists, to all those who are sincere democrats and liberals at heart, to stop, look and listen."

The author is an internationally known economist. An Austrian by birth, he was director of the Austrian Institute for Economic Research and lecturer in economics at the University of Vienna during the years of the rise of fascism in Central Europe. He has lived in England since 1931, when he became Professor of Economic Science at the University of London, and is now a British citizen.

Professor Hayek, with great power and rigor of reasoning, sounds a grim warning to Americans and Britons who look to the government to provide the way out of all our economic difficulties. He demonstrates that fascism and what the Germans correctly call National Socialism are the inevitable results of the increasing growth of state control and state power, of national "planning" and of socialism.

In a foreword to *The Road to Serfdom* John Chamberlain, book editor of *Harper's*, writes: "This book is a warning cry in a time of hesitation. It says to us: Stop, look and listen. Its logic is incontestable, and it should have the widest possible audience."

Reference Notes

All books cited are published in the United Kingdom unless otherwise stated.

INTRODUCTION

1. Andrew Gamble, *The Free Economy and the Strong State; the politics of Thatcherism* (Macmillan, 1988)
2. This article was reprinted in Maurice Cowling, *Mill and Liberalism* (2nd edn; Cambridge University Press, 1990), pp. xxxvi–xxxvii
3. Samuel Brittan, *The Role and Limits of Government; Essays in Political Economy* (Temple Smith, 1984), p. 50
4. John Gray, *Liberalism* (Oxford University Press, 1986), p. 50
5. Hayek, *Studies in Philosophy, Politics and Economics* (Routledge, 1967). Chapter 11 on 'The Principles of a Liberal Social Order', pp. 162–3. This is the best short exposition of Liberalism by Hayek, but see also his much more substantial *Constitution of Liberty* (University of Chicago Press, 1960). Samuel Brittan's *A Restatement of Economic Liberalism* (Macmillan, 1988) is also good on this issue.
6. Karl Popper, *Unended Quest* (Routledge and Kegan Paul, 1992), p. 36

CHAPTER ONE

1. Proceedings of *Le Colloque Walter Lippmann* published as *Le Compte-Rendu des séances du Colloque Walter Lippmann* in the possession of Professor Max Hartwell. I am indebted to Professor Hartwell for letting me see this document and for letting me read the draft of his *History of the Mont Pèlerin Society* on which much of my account of Le Colloque Walter Lippmann is based.
2. Walter Lippmann, *The Good Society* (George Allen, 1937)
3. ibid., p. 370
4. ibid., pp. 238–9
5. ibid., p. 388
6. *Compte-Rendu des séances du Colloque Walter Lippmann*
7. Röpke and Rustow, *A Note on the Urgent Necessity of Re-Orientations of Social Sciences*, MPS Papers
8. Röpke and Rustow, p. 8
9. A. V. Dicey, *Lectures on the Relation between Law and Public Opinion in England during the Nineteenth Century* (Macmillan, 1905)
10. W. H. Greenleaf, *The Rise of Collectivism* (Methuen, 1983). *The Ideological Heritage* (Methuen, 1983)
11. Greenleaf, *The Rise of Collectivism*, p. 15
12. *The Times*, 25 March 1935, quoted by Greenleaf p. 30
13. Greenleaf, pp. 30–31
14. Quoted by Greenleaf in *The Ideological Inheritance* p. 366; see also A. M. McBriar, *Fabian Socialism and English Politics 1884–1918* (Cambridge University Press, 1966)
15. Quoted by Greenleaf, *The Ideological Inheritance*, p. 380
16. ibid., p. 82
17. See John Turner, *Politics and the Great War* (Yale University Press, 1992), for an account of British political responses to the 1914–18 conflict
18. See Greenleaf, *The Rise of Collectivism*, p. 31, and Peacock and Wiseman, *The Growth of Public Expenditure in the U.K.* (George Allen and Unwin, 1967)
19. Greenleaf, *The Rise of Collectivism*, p. 109
20. Quoted by Greenleaf, *The Ideological Inheritance*, p. 81

21. See Dr. E. J. Bristow on 'The Liberty and Property Defence League and Individualism' in the *Historical Journal*, XVIII (1975)
22. See Greenleaf, *The Ideological Inheritance*, p. 272
23. N. Solden, *The Liberty and Property Defence League 1882–1914* in K. D. Brown (ed.), *Essays in Anti-Labour History* (Macmillan, 1974)
24. ibid., p. 208
25. See K. D. Brown, *The Anti-Socialist Union, 1908–1949*, Chapter 10 of *Essays in Anti-Labour History*
26. Harold Laski, *The Decline of Liberalism*, L. T. Hobhouse Memorial Trust Lecture, No. 10 (Oxford University Press, 1940)
27. John Baker-White, *True Blue* (Frederick Muller, 1970) p. 149
28. Jose Ortega y Gasset, *The Revolt of the Masses* (George Allen and Unwin, 1932); see also Christian Cepilecha, *The Historical Thought of Jose Ortega y Gasset* (Catholic University of America Press, 1958)
29. Edwin G. Dolan, *The Foundations of Modern Austrian Economics* (Sheed and Ward, I.H.S., 1976), p. x. See also Louis M. Spadaro (ed.) *New Directions in Austrian Economics*, for an account of the Austrian School
30. Ludwig von Mises, *Socialism* (Jonathan Cape, 1936) pp. 25–26
31. ibid., p. 122
32. ibid., p. 276
33. For von Mises's work in America, see George Nash, *The Conservative Intellectual Movement in America since 1945* (Basic Books, 1979)
34. Interview with Hayek by Gitta Sereny in *The Times*, 5 May 1985; see also Hayek's obituary in the *Independent* by Arthur Seldon, 25 March 1992
35. George Nash, p. 10
36. For a good description of the Russell/Wittgenstein relationship see Ray Monk *Ludwig Wittgenstein; The Duty of Genius* (Jonathan Cape, 1990)
37. Lionel Robbins, *Autobiography of an Economist* (Macmillan, 1971), p. 106
38. D.P. O'Brien, *Lionel Robbins* (Macmillan, 1988), p. 12. I am grateful to Simon Burgis for bringing my attention to this book.
39. Robbins, p. 108
40. Interview with Peter Cropper, June 1991
41. Robbins, p. 127
42. Robbins, p. 128
43. Robbins, p. 129
44. Hayek to Popper, 27 December 1943; Popper Papers, Box 305, Hoover Centre
45. See Kingsley Martin, *Harold Laski; A Life* (Gollancz, 1953)
46. See Harold Laski, *Parliamentary Government in England; A Commentary* (George Allen and Unwin, 1938).
47. Leo Abse (ed.), *My LSE* (Robson Books, 1977) p. 36
48. F. A. Hayek, Chapter 13 of *Studies in Philosophy, Politics and Economics* (Routledge, 1967), p. 196
49. Economica, February 1946
50. John Gray in Norman Barry (ed.) *The Road to Serfdom: Forty Years On* (IEA, 1984), p. 35. For the impact of Hayek on the LSE see also Alan Peacock, *LSE and Postwar Economic Policy* in *Atlantic Journal*, Vol. X, No.1, March 1982
51. Aubrey Jones in Leo Abse (ed.), *My LSE*
52. G. L. S. Shachle, in D. P. O'Brien and John Presley, *Pioneers of Modern Economics in Britain* (Macmillan, 1981)
53. Robbins to Law, 14 November 1946; Coleraine Papers
54. Hayek, Inaugural Lecture, 'The Trend of Economic Thinking' in *Economica*, 33, Vol. 13, 1933, p. 135
55. ibid., p. 136
56. ibid., p. 136
57. See Robert Skidelsky, *Politicians and the Slump; The Labour Governments of 1929–31* (Macmillan, 1967)
58. For the Work of the E.A.C and the 'Keynesian' arguments put to the Committee see Peter Clarke, *The Keynesian Revolution in the Making 1924–36* (Clarendon Press, 1988) and D. E. Moggridge *Keynes An Economist's Biography* (Routledge, 1992) pp. 497–511 and Skidelsky, *John Maynard Keynes, The Economist*

as Saviour 1920–37 (Macmillan, 1992), Chapter 11

59. D. E. Moggridge, quoted on p. 469
60. Robbins, *The Great Depression* (Macmillan, 1934) pp. 60–61 and 186
61. D. E. Moggridge, p. 501
62. Quoted by Peter Clarke, *The Treasury's Analytical Model of the British Economy between the Wars*, in Mary O. Furner and Barry Suple (ed.), *The State and Economic Knowledge* (Cambridge University Press), pp. 185–6
63. Robbins later repudiated *The Great Depression* in his autobiography as 'something which I would willingly see forgotten'. Robbins's whole relationship with Keynesianism in the post-war era is somewhat contradictory, but his most recent biographer has interpreted his later recantations as symptomatic of the criticism that dissenters from 'Keynesian' economics had to endure from the later 1930s onwards: 'There is no doubt that to some extent the attacks got through to Robbins. In particular he was acutely sensitive about the accusation that he was a "deflationist", and he came to insist that controlling inflation of aggregate expenditure was not the same thing as deflation. It is, however, worth making the point that, despite the elaborate contrition expressed in the *Autobiography*, Robbins in fact remained opposed to the vast majority of what were called "Keynesian" policies. In particular he was not happy about the . . . use of fiscal policy for fine tuning; he continued to oppose Beveridge's plans for permanent excess demand of the Labour Market . . . His surrender to "Keynesianism" . . . was strictly qualified.' (D. P. O'Brien, *Lionel Robbins*, Macmillan 1988, pp. 14–15.) We await Susan Howson's forthcoming biography of Robbins for a fuller account of his career and thinking.
64. Clarke, *The Treasury's Analytical Model*. . ., p. 191
65. Quoted by Clarke, ibid., p. 186
66. Quoted by Moggridge, p. 505. For Henderson's other arguments against Keynes and his work on the Economic Advisory Councils see Henderson, *The Inter-war Years and Other Papers* (Oxford University Press, 1955)
67. Moggridge, p. 506
68. See Robbins's account of his disagreements with the Committee in *Autobiography of an Economist*, p. 152
69. J. M. Keynes, *The General Theory of Employment, Interest and Money* (Macmillan, 1936) pp. 378–9
70. Frank Knight's review in *Canadian Journal of Economics and Political Science*, Feb 1937, pp. 100–23
71. Jacob Viner's review in *Quarterly Journal of Economics*, Vol. 51, 1936–37, pp. 146–7, quoted in Hazlitt, ed., *The Critics of Keynesian Economics* (Van Nostrand, 1960)
72. ibid., p. 366
73. Rueff in *The Quarterly Journal of Economics*, in Hazlitt (ed.), p. 261
74. Hayek, *The Constitution of Liberty* (Chicago University Press, 1960), p. 280
75. Quoted in Hazlitt, pp. 372–3
76. Hayek, *A Tiger by the Tail* (IEA, 1972) p. 100
77. Skidelsky, *J. M. Keynes: The Economist as Saviour* (Macmillan, 1992), p. 439
78. Keynes, *The General Theory* . . ., p. 383
79. Skidelsky, *J. M. Keynes: The Economist as Saviour*, p. 344
80. 'On Sticking to One's Last', in Presley and Dennison (ed.), *Robertson on Economic Policy* (St. Martin's Press, 1992), pp. 154–5
81. Dennison and Presley, p. 9. See Part One of this work for a description of the difference between Robertson and Keynes
82. W. H. Hutt, *Politically Impossible* (IEA, 1971), p. 66. To the Chicago School, Keynes, in developing an acceptable 'political economy' for a collectivist system, was performing the same task as Henry Simons, the doyen of the Chicago free-market school, had done for the political

economy of the free-market. As Aaron Director wrote in 1948, 'Just as Lord Keynes provided a respectable foundation for the adherents of collectivism, so Simons was providing a respectable foundation for the older faith of freedom and equality.' ('Prefatory Notice', in Henry Simons *Economic Policy for a Free Society*, University of Chicago Press, 1948, p. v)

83. Julien Benda, *La Trahison des Clercs* (Routledge, 1928), pp. 32 and 36
84. Keynes quote from D. E. Moggridge, p. 469
85. See, for instance, Arthur Marwick, 'Middle Opinion and Planning in the 1930s', *English Historical Review*, 1964
86. Henderson's letter to Roy Harrod, 2 April 1936; quoted in Clarke, *The Keynesian Revolution in the Making*, p. 308. Henderson's review of *The General Theory* . . . was in the *Spectator*, and his address to the Marshall Society is reproduced as 'Mr. Keynes's Theories' in Henderson, *The Inter-War Years and Other Papers* (Oxford/Clarendon Press, 1955)
87. For this debate, see, for example, T.W. Hutchinson, *Keynes vs. the Keynesians . . . ?* (IEA, 1977), and Alex Leijonhufund, *Keynes and the Classics* (IEA 1969)
88. D. P. O'Brien, *Lionel Robbins* (Macmillan, 1988) p. 65
89. Keynes, *Collected Writings* (Macmillan, 1973) Vol. 2, pp. 148
90. The exchange is in Keynes, *Collected Writings* (Macmillan, 1973), Vol. XIII, pp. 243–8. See also Skidelsky, *John Maynard Keynes*, pp. 454–9
91. ibid., p. 252
92. Hayek, *Tiger by the Tail*, complied by Sudha R. Shenoy (IEA, 1972), p. 100
93. *Hayek and the Great Planning Debate of the 1940s*, private draft, p. 5
94. See Hayek, *Studies in Philosophy, Politics and Economics* (Clarion, 1967), Chapter 11, for a short explanation of catallaxy
95. Simon Burgess, *The Attlee Governments in Perspective – Commitment and detachment in the writing of contemporary history*. Unpublished London University Ph.D., 1992
96. For a brief account of Robertson's career, see Chapter 6 by Presley on Robertson in O'Brien and Presley, *Pioneers of Modern Economics in Britain*; for his differences with Keynes, see D. E. Moggridge, pp. 597–603
97. John Vaizey, 'Emergence of a British Economist' in *Journal of International Social Science*, Vol. XXV, 1973, pp. 156–7
98. Interview with Friedman, September 1991
99. Rougier, *Les Mystiques Politiques* (Institut des Hautes Etudes Internationales, 1936), p. 121
100. Rougier, *Les Mystiques Economiques* (Institut des Hautes Etudes Internationales, 1936), p. 9

CHAPTER TWO

1. Robbins, *Autobiography of an Economist* (Macmillan, 1971), pp. 172–4. See also Alec Cairncross and Nita Watts, *The Economic Section, 1939–1961: A Study in Economic Advising* (Routledge, 1989)
2. Paul Addison, *The Road to 1945* (Cape, 1975). See also Angus Calder, *The People's War* (Cape, 1969)
3. Kevin Jefferys, *The Churchill coalition and wartime politics 1940–45* (Manchester University Press, 1991), p. 115
4. Paul Addison's sympathetic description of the New Jerusalemers has recently been challenged, most notably by Correlli Barnett's *The Audit of War; the Illusion and Reality of Britain as a Great Power* (Macmillan, 1986)
5. Laski, *The Decline of Liberalism* (Oxford University Press, 1940)
6. *Report on Social Insurance and Allied Services*, p. 6
7. Dr Harriet Jones, *The Conservative Party and the Welfare State, 1942–1955* (Unpublished Ph.D., University of London, 1992), p. 70
8. Jefferys, p. 116

9. Spencer Summers, MP for Northampton 1940–50; Buckinghamshire, Aylesbury 1950–1970
10. This and other quotations from the committee's Report taken from Harriet Jones, pp. 72–80
11. Harmut Kopsch, *The Approach of the Conservative Party to Social Policy during the Second World War* (Unpublished Ph.D., University of London, 1970), p. 109
12. Jefferys, p. 116
13. Jefferys, pp. 5–6
14. Jefferys, p. 171
15. Meade to Keynes, 8 January 1943; Keynes, *Collected Works*, Vol. 27, p. 314
16. Cairncross and Watts, pp. 85–6
17. Moggridge's summary of Henderson's views in Keynes, *Collected Works*, Vol. 27, p. 572
18. Keynes's memo of 27 March 1944 in Keynes, *Collected Works*, Vol. 27, pp. 372–375
19. Jefferys, p. 171; See also Jim Tomlinson, Employment Policy; *The Crucial Years, 1939–55* (Oxford University Press, 1987)
20. Peter Clarke, *The Keynesian Revolution in the Making*, p. 322
21. Jewkes's paper on *The White Paper on Employment Policy, 1944; A Defence* in the papers of the Institute of Economic Affairs
22. IEA Readings, No. 14 (1976)
23. See Dr Richard Cockett, *The Government, the Press and Politics 1937–1945* (Unpublished Ph.D., University of London, 1988), Chapter 5
24. Hartmut Kopsch, p. 70; see also Harriet Jones, pp. 79–80
25. John Benn in Deryck Abel's *Ernest Benn – Counsel for Liberty* (Benn, 1960), p. 10
26. ibid., p. 13
27. For the murky history of *Truth*, see Richard Cockett, 'Chamberlain, Ball and the secret control of *Truth*' (*Historical Journal*, 33, 1, 1990, pp. 131–42)
28. S. W. Alexander, unpublished autobiography (in the possession of his son), Chapter 6
29. The Manifesto is reproduced in full in Deryck Abel, pp. 111–12
30. See Greenleaf, Vol. II, *The Ideological Inheritance*, p. 295
31. *National Review*, July–December 1945, No. 751, p. 251; 'You have been warned'.
32. Interview with Alastair Forbes of BUI. See also Kind and Nugent (ed.) *Respectable Rebels: Middle Class Campaigns in Britain in the 1970s* (Hodder and Stoughton, 1978), pp. 77–8. In King and Nugent's book it is claimed that BUI was founded in 1959, but, as no records for BUI exist, this is impossible to prove; Alastair Forbes put its foundation date at 1943 or 1944
33. ibid.
34. See Martin Gilbert, *Road to Victory; Winston S. Churchill, 1941–45* (Heinemann, 1986), pp. 367–8
35. Quotations in Harriet Jones, p. 57
36. Quoted in Harriet Jones, p. 62
37. Kingsley Martin, *Harold Laski – A biographical memoir* (Gollancz, 1953) p. 161
38. Von Mises, *Bureaucracy* (Yale University Press, 1944) and *Omnipotent Government* (Yale University Press, 1944)
39. George Schwartz, *Why Planning?* (Signpost Press, 1944); F. W. Hirst, *Principles of Prosperity* (Hollis and Carter, 1944)
40. Colin Clark, 'Public Finance and Changes in the Value of Money', *Economic Journal*, Vol. 55, 1945. Jacques Rueff, *L'Ordre Social* (Paris, 1945)
41. Michael Oakeshott, *Rationalism in Politics* (*Cambridge Journal*, Vol. I, 1947). For an alternative view of the debate, see E. Lipson, *A Planned Economy or Free Enterprise* (A and C Black, 1944)
42. Hayek, *Road to Serfdom* (Routledge, 1944), p. v
43. Hayek to Routledge, 30 May 1943; Routledge, Kegan and Paul Papers (*hereafter:* RKPP)
44. Hayek to Routledge, 9 August 1943; RKPP
45. Hayek, p. v

46. Hayek to Routledge, 30 May 1943; RKPP
47. Hayek, p. v
48. Hayek to Routledge, 13 November 1943; RKPP
49. See Karl Popper, *Unended Quest; An Intellectual Autobiography* (Routledge, 1992), pp. 107–10, for an account of Popper's intellectual introduction to England in 1935–6
50. Hayek to Popper, 12 July 1943; Popper Archive, Hoover Centre (PA)
51. Popper to Hayek, 16 December 1943; PA
52. Popper to Hayek, 6 January 1944; PA
53. Popper to Hayek, 28 May 1944; PA
54. See Chapter 8 of Popper's autobiography, *Unended Quest*, for an account of his political odyssey in post-war Vienna
55. Popper to Hayek, 28 May 1944, PA
56. Karl Popper, *The Open Society and its Enemies*, Vol. I. (Routledge, 1945), p. viii
57. Hayek to Mr Ragg (of Routledge), 4 February 1944; RKPP
58. Popper to Mr Read (of Routledge), 28 March 1945; RKPP
59. Popper to Mr Read, 12 July 1944, RKPP
60. De Crespigny and Minogue (ed.), *Contemporary Political Philosophers* (Methuen, 1976), p. 149
61. Routledge to Hayek, 11 April 1944; RKPP
62. Popper to Hayek, 29 May 1944; PA
63. Hayek, *Road to Serfdom*, pp. 2–3
64. Hayek, *Studies in Politics, Philosophy and Economics* (Clarion, 1967), Chapter 5, p. 217
65. Hayek, *Road to Serfdom*, p. 31
66. *Political Quarterly*, Vol. XV, No. 3
67. *Observer*, 9 April 1944
68. Evan Durbin's review of *Road to Serfdom* in Durbin, *Problems of Economic Planning* (Routledge, Kegan and Paul, 1949), Chap. V
69. Keynes, *Collected Works*, Vol. 27, pp. 385–8, Keynes to Hayek, 28 June 1944
70. Quoted in Greenleaf, *The Ideological Inheritance*, p. 310
71. Moran, *The Struggle for Survival*, p. 276
72. Attlee to Assheton, 27 April 1944; Papers of Lord Clitheroe (Clith. Mss.)
73. Assheton memo to Sir Hubert Henderson, 26 May 1943; Clith. Mss.
74. Churchill's minute and speech in Clith. Mss.
75. Jefferys, *The Churchill Coalition and Wartime Politics*, p. 196
76. Correspondence in RKPP
77. Arthur Greenwood's speech of 19 June 1945, quoted in McCallum and Readman, *The British General Election of 1945* (Oxford University Press, 1947), p. 144
78. Interview with David Clarke, December 1991
79. Quoted by Simon Burgess, *The Attlee Governments in Perspective – Commitment and detachment in the writing of contemporary history* (Unpublished Ph.D., University of London, 1992), p. 8
80. Jefferys, p. 188
81. McCallum and Readman, p. 144
82. Interview with John Wood, June 1991
83. Hayek to Popper, 8 July 1944, PA
84. Harriet Jones, p. 100
85. A. J. P. Taylor, *Beaverbrook* (Hamish Hamilton, 1972), pp. 728–729
86. Clith. Mss.
87. See Harriet Jones's thesis for a detailed exploration of this theme
88. Richard Law, *Return from Utopia* (Faber and Faber, 1950), p. 9
89. Law to Diana Spearman, 10 October 1945; Coleraine Papers
90. For Hayek's input on the debate about the Welfare State during wartime Britain, see José Harris, 'Political ideas and the debate on State Welfare, 1940–45', in H. C. Smith (ed.), *War and Social Change* (Manchester University Press, 1987)

CHAPTER THREE

1. See James H. Gissurarson's essay on the publication of *The Road to Serfdom* in Norman Barry (ed.), *Hayek's Road to Serfdom Revisited* (IEA, 1984)

2. Interview with Hayek in *The Times*, 5 May 1985
3. Barry D. Karl, *Charles E. Merrian and the Study of Politics* (University of Chicago Press, 1974), p. 121. I am grateful to Simon Burgiss for this reference.
4. The paper is reproduced in full in Chapter 9, *Historians and the Future of Europe*, in Hayek, *Studies in Philosophy, Politics and Economics* (Clarion, 1967), p. 135
5. Röpke, *Plan for an International Periodical*; Mont Pèlerin Society Archive (MPSA), Box 1
6. Hunold's article in *World Liberalism*, Spring 1945; MPSA Box 1
7. Hayek's letter, 28 December 1946; MPSA, Box 2
8. Hayek's paper, 13 February 1947; MPSA, Box 14
9. Hayek's paper on 'The Prospect of Freedom'; MPSA, Box 14
10. Hayek's paper on 'The Intellectual and Socialism', August 1948; MPSA, Box 14
11. Jewkes, *Ordeal by Planning* (Macmillan, 1948), p. xi
12. ibid., p. 65
13. Robbins, *The Economic Problem in Peace and War* (Macmillan, 1947), p. 23. Sir Hubert Henderson, by then the Professor of Political Economy at Oxford University, delivered a similar message to the same audience on 9 May 1947 in his Rede Lecture, published as *The Uses and Abuses of Economic Planning* (Cambridge University Press, 1947). Henderson did not go as far as Robbins in his critique of planning, but nonetheless warned that 'the belief that our economic and industrial achievement under war conditions was phenomenal was largely illusory' (pp. 9–10). He concluded that planning was therefore not 'a magic talisman', by which Britain's economic difficulties could be 'charmed away' (p. 31).
14. Drusilla Scott, *Everyman Revisited: The Common Sense of Michael Polanyi* (Book Guild, 1985), p. 5. This is the best short introduction to Polanyi's work.
15. Polanyi's three pamphlets were *The Right and Duties of Science* (1945), *The Planning of Science* (1946) and *The Federation of Academic Freedom* (1949)
16. Taylor to Hunold, 18 December 1948; MPSA, Box 1
17. See Hayek's 'Opening Address to the Mont Pèlerin Society' in *Studies in Philosophy, Politics and Economics*, Chapter 10.
18. See Chapter 13 of *Studies in Philosophy, Politics and Economics*
19. See, for example, Hazlitt's *Economics in One Lesson* (Benn, 1947) and *The Failure of the New Economics; An analysis of the Keynesian fallacies* (D. Van Nostrand Company, 1959)
20. Samuel Brittan's *A Restatement of Economic Liberalism* (Social Market Foundation, 1990) contains a good brief account of the Social Market School. Josef Molsberger's paper on 'Germany's Social Market Economy; A Liberal Programme and its Political Course', delivered to the Mont Pèlerin Society, is also an excellent guide to the Social Market Economy.
21. B. de Jouvenel, *Problems of Socialist England* (Batchworth Press, 1949)
22. Rappard, 'Address at the opening meeting on Tuesday April 1st'; Milton Friedman Private Papers
23. Hayek's paper on '"Free" Enterprise and Competitive Order'; MPSA, Box 2
24. Information from Professor Max Hartwell's unpublished history of the Mont Pèlerin Society
25. Polanyi to Hunold, 19 April 1947; MPSA, Box 1
26. Jewkes to Hunold, 20 December 1947; MPSA, Box 1
27. Interview with Aaron Director, September 1991
28. The full document is reproduced in Antony Fisher, *Must History Repeat Itself?* (Churchill Press, 1974)
29. Brandt memo of 28 June 1949; MPSA, Box 1
30. Lord Grantchester to Hunold, 8 November 1954; MPSA
31. Hartwell, *History of the Mont Pèlerin Society*

32. ibid.,
33. The full list of speakers and papers at these two conferences is in MPSA, Box 27
34. Griffin to Hunold, 2 August 1949; MPSA, Box 2
35. Robbins to Hunold, 7 June 1950; MPSA, Box 2

CHAPTER FOUR

1. Interview with Milton Friedman, September 1991
2. Account by Fisher's daughter, Mrs Linda Whetstone; Fisher Private Papers (FPP)
3. Antony Fisher, *Must History Repeat Itself?* (Churchill Press, 1974), p. 103
4. Antony Fisher, *The Case for Freedom* (Runnymede Press, 1947), p. 9
5. Interview with Friedman, September 1991
6. Interview with Andrew Alexander, November 1991
7. Smedley to Fisher, 8 November 1982; Smedley Papers, in the possession of his son Charles Smedley (SP)
8. See King and Nugent (ed.), *Respectable Rebels* (Hodder and Stoughton, 1979), pp. 79–80, for an account of the political activities of Martell.
9. Greenleaf, *The Ideological Inheritance*, p. 180
10. Alan Peacock, *The Welfare Society* (Unservile State Group, 1961), p. 21
11. Andrew Gamble, 'Liberals and the Economy', Chapter 9 in Vernon Bogdanor (ed.), *Liberal Party Politics* (Clarendon Press, 1983), pp. 199–200. See also Alan Watkins, *The Liberal Dilemma* (MacGibbon and Kee, 1966)
12. Fisher to Smedley, 22 May 1956; FPP
13. Smedley to Fisher, 25 June 1956; FPP
14. Fisher to F. Gough, 7 June 1956; FPP
15. *Newsweek*, 25 July 1955
16. Fisher to Smedley, 8 December 1982; SP
17. Smedley to Fisher, 26 June 1956; FPP
18. Fisher to Harris, 7 June 1956; FPP
19. Arthur Seldon, *Capitalism* (Blackwell, 1990), p. 34
20. ibid., p. 35
21. Seldon writing in Norman Barry (ed.), Hayek's *Road to Serfdom Revisited*, p. xxiii
22. Interview with Seldon, July 1991. Seldon won considerable acclaim as an economist in his own right during his years at the IEA, and for a general appreciation of his work see the 'festschrift' produced in his honour, *The Unfinished Agenda* (IEA, 1986)
23. Obituary in the *Daily Telegraph*, 23 August 1991
24. Fisher to Smedley, 8 December 1982; FPP
25. Smedley to Fisher, 8 November 1982; SP
26. Seldon to Lord Balniel, 16 November 1967; IEA Archive
27. Seldon, *Capitalism*, p. 42
28. ibid., p. 42
29. Interview with Lord Grimond, November 1992
30. Seldon and Harris, 'The Tactics and Strategy of the Advance to a Free Society'; MPSA, Box 14
31. Pardoe to Seldon, 28 April 1971; IEA Papers
32. 'The Tactics and Strategy of the Advance to a Free Society', p. 11
33. Harris and Seldon, *'Not From Benevolence . . .'; Twenty Years of Economic Dissent* (IEA, Hobart Paperback, 1977)
34. ibid., p. ix
35. Fisher's own account of his conversation with Heath is in his *Must History Repeat Itself?*
36. Seldon, 'A Time now for Self-Help' in the *Daily Telegraph*, 8 October 1970
37. Harris to Hutt, 3 October 1975; IEA Papers
38. Hutt, *Politically Impossible?*, p. 71
39. Sudha R. Shenoy, *A Tiger by the Tail* (IEA, 1972) p. 119
40. For the best short history of, and guide to, monetarism, see Tim Congdon, *Monetarism: An Essay in Definition* (CPS, 1978); for a less

sympathetic and more journalistic account, see David Smith, *The Rise and Fall of Monetarism* (Penguin, 1987). For a lucid and scholarly explanation of monetarism, see Samuel Brittan, *How to end the Monetarist Controversy* (IEA, 1981); N. Crafts and Nicholas Woodward, *The British Economy since 1945* (Clarendon Press, 1991) gives a good academic account of the impact of monetarism; see also the works of Milton Friedman, most particularly *The Counter-Revolution in Monetary Theory* (IEA, 1970)

41. For a full account of the Radcliffe Committee, see Harris and Seldon, '*Not from Benevolence . . .*', Chapter 3
42. Friedman's own favourite account of his overall economic and political philosophy is to be found in the February 1973 issue of *Playboy* Magazine, 'Interview with Milton Friedman'.
43. Alan Walters, 'A Life Philosophy', in *The American Economist*, Vol. XXXIII, No. 2, 1989
44. ibid., pp. 21–22
45. Alan Walters, *Money in Boom and Slump* (IEA, 3rd edn, 1971), p. 5
46. Interview with Friedman, September 1991
47. Alan Walters, *Economists and the British Economy* (IEA Occasional Paper No. 54, 1977), p. 19
48. ibid., p. 31
49. Peacock to Seldon, 15 July 1975; IEA Archives
50. *Daily Telegraph*, 11 June 1978
51. Collard, *The New Right: a Critique* (Fabian Tract No. 387, 1968), pp. 1–5
52. Interview with Friedman, September 1991

CHAPTER FIVE

1. For a full account of the Churchill government's attempts to curb public expenditure, see Harriet Jones, *The Conservative Party and the Welfare State*, Chapters 3–7; for an account of the denationalization of Iron and Steel, see Dr Kathy Burk, *The First Privatisation* (Historian's Press, 1991)
2. David Willetts, *Modern Conservatism* (Penguin, 1992), pp. 41–42. For a similar interpretation of modern Conservatism, see Nigel Lawson, *The New Conservatism* (CPS, 1980), David Young, *The Enterprise Years* (Headline, 1990) and Nicholas Ridley, *My Style of Government – The Thatcher Years* (Hutchinson, 1991), Chapter One
3. Lord Harris (Ralph Harris), *The Challenge of a Radical Reactionary* (CPS, 1980), p. 7
4. Sir Keith Joseph's letter to *The Economist*, 28 September 1974
5. One Nation (CPC, 1950), p. 93
6. *Change is our Ally* (CPC, 1954)
7. Joseph interview with Anthony Seldon in *Contemporary Record*, Vol. I, 1987
8. Willetts, p. 38; see also Greenleaf, *The Ideological Inheritance*, pp. 311–16
9. See Alastair Horne's account of these resignations in *Macmillan – 1957–1986* (Macmillan, 1989), pp. 63–78 and Cosgrave, *The Lives of Enoch Powell* (Bodley Head, 1989). However, in a recent paper given to the Modern British Politics and Administration Seminar at the Institute of Historical Research, University of London, Dr John Turner has re-examined the circumstances of this celebrated event, and has concluded that the resignation of the Treasury team cannot be seen as a precursor for Thatcherite monetarism.
10. Interview with Enoch Powell, June 1991
11. Enoch Powell, *Freedom and Reality* (Paperprint, 1969). See also Greenleaf, *The Ideological Inheritance*, Chapter 9, for a discussion of Powell's thinking.
12. 'Manifesto for Freedom', p. 4; Coleraine Papers
13. ibid., p. 10
14. Law to John Jewkes, 7 April 1967; Coleraine Papers
15. Coleraine, *For Conservatives Only* (Tom Stacey, 1970), pp. 37–8

16. ibid., p. 77
17. See, for example, Powell's speeches in J. Wood (ed.), *A Nation Not Afraid; The thinking of Enoch Powell* (London, 1965); Enoch Powell, *Still to Decide* (Paperprint, 1972)
18. I am indebted to Dr John Campbell for pointing this out to me.
19. Morrison Halcrow, *Keith Joseph – A Single Mind* (Macmillan, 1989), p. 37
20. Joseph to Seldon, 6 November 1965; IEA Archives
21. Seldon to Joseph, 19 August 1970; IEA Archives
22. Interview with John Biffen, November 1991
23. 'Paying your Money and Taking your Choice', *Daily Telegraph*, 31 January 1964. See also Howe's other articles in the same paper, such as 'Key to a Healthier Service', 12 August 1969; 'A new approach to Welfare', 23 February 1966; 'Welfare spending gone astray', 21 April 1963.
24. Memo from 'J.C.' to Seldon and Harris, 31 October 1969; IEA Papers
25. Howe to Antony Fisher, 9 July 1987, FPP
26. Seldon to Howe, 24 October 1969 and Howe to Seldon, 28 October 1969; IEA Papers
27. Margaret Thatcher, *What's Wrong with Politics* (CPC, 1968)
28. Seldon to Thatcher, 1 April 1969; IEA papers
29. Thatcher to Harris, 10 January 1977; FPP
30. Thatcher to Harris, 18 May 1979; IEA Papers
31. Thatcher to Antony Fisher, 20 February 1980; FPP
32. Interview with Friedman, September 1991
33. John Ranelagh, *Thatcher's People* (Fontana, 1992), p. ix
34. Interview with John Wood, June 1991
35. Interview with Sir Adam Ridley, November 1991
36. ibid.
37. See J. H. Dunn, *The New Right in Britain* (Unpublished Ph.D., Reading University, 1985), for a fuller account of the Churchill Press.
38. ibid.
39. Seldon to Lord Balniel, 2 November 1967; IEA Papers
40. Seldon to Walden, 19 July 1967; IEA Papers
41. Seldon to John Pardoe, 23 August 1967; IEA Papers
42. *Hansard*, Vol. 774, Cmns 97–104
43. Seldon letter, 13 December 1968: IEA Archives
44. As reported in the *Grimsby Evening Telegraph*, 11 November 1969
45. Donnelly Memo, 'Some Just Talk; Others Act'; IEA Archives
46. Seldon to John Biffen, 24 September 1970; IEA Archives
47. John Blundell, 'How to Move a Nation; Could a chicken-farmer and two economists change British history?', in *Reason Magazine*, February 1987, p. 32
48. Fisher to Harris, 4 August 1976; IEA Archives
49. Interview with John O'Sullivan, September 1991
50. See Duff Hart-Davis, *The House the Berrys Built – Inside the Telegraph 1928–1986* (Hodder and Stoughton, 1990), pp. 248–9
51. Brittan to Seldon, 21 January, 1985; IEA Archives
52. See, for instance, 'Why Unemployment is still an enigma', *Financial Times*, 24 February 1972, and 'The Road to Industrial Serfdom', *Financial Times*
53. Brittan, *Second thoughts on Full Employment Policy* (CPS, 1976)
54. Interview with Peter Cropper, June 1991
55. See *The Times*, 27 November 1969, for Jay's article on the Federal Reserve Bank of St Louis
56. Jay's article 'The Boom that must go Bust' in *The Times*, 7 May 1975
57. The lecture is reproduced, together with other writings from this period, in *The Crisis for Western Political Economy and Other Essays* (André Deutsch, 1984)
58. Callaghan's speech, given on 28 September 1976, is quoted at length in Kenneth Harris's *Thatcher*

(Weidenfeld and Nicolson, 1988), p. 66
59. Interview with Lord Rees-Mogg, March 1992
60. See page 104
61. Interviews with John Marshall MP, June 1991, and Dr Eamonn Butler, October 1991
62. Madsen Pirie to Antony Fisher, 8 October 1975; FPP
63. Stephen Eyres's obituary in the *Daily Telegraph*, 28 February 1991
64. *Swinton Journal*, Summer 1968, pp. 6–7; Conservative Party Archives (CPA)
65. *Swinton Journal*, Spring 1970, p. 32; CPA
66. Ronald Butt, 'Is it politically possible to lay the ghost of Keynes?', in *The Times*, 8 January 1976
67. *New Society*, 5 July 1979
68. *New Statesman*, 4 July 1975
69. Sir Douglas Allen to Ralph Harris, 17 January 1977; IEA Archives. See also John Vaizey's review of *Not from Benevolence...* in the *Times Higher Educational Supplement*, 21 January 1977, as well as the reviews in the *Sunday Telegraph*, 9 January 1977, and *Economist*, 8 January 1977.
70. Crafts and Woodward (ed.), *The British Economy since 1945* (Clarendon Press, 1991), pp. 116–17 and Roy Jenkins, *A Life at the Centre* (Macmillan, 1991), Chapters 11–15
71. Milton Friedman, *Inflation and Unemployment* (IEA Occasional Paper, No. 51, 1977)

CHAPTER SIX

1. Interview with David Howell, March 1922; and see David Howell, *The New Capitalism* (CPS, 1986) p. 5; see also John Ramsden, *The Making of Conservative Party Policy* (Longman, 1980), pp. 256–8
2. David Howell, *A New Style of Government* (CPC, 1970), p. 8
3. David Alexander, *Dial ENTERPRISE 1971 – The Case for a Private Enterprise Telephone Service* (CPC, 1968), pp. 10–11
4. Seldon to Joseph, 19 August 1970; IEA Archives
5. John Campbell, *Edward Heath* (Hutchinson, 1993), p. 179
6. Campbell, *Heath*, pp. 245–6
7. The best account of Heath's government remains Martin Holmes, *Political Pressure and Economic Policy; British Government 1970–1974* (Butterworth, 1982)
8. Jock Bruce-Gardyne, *Whatever Happened to the Quiet Revolution? – The story of a brave experiment in Government* (Charles Knight and Co., 1974), p. 76
9. ibid., p. 169
10. Seldon to Joseph, 10 June 1970, and Joseph to Seldon, 12 June 1970; IEA Archives
11. Morrison Halcrow, *Keith Joseph – A Single Mind*, p. 49. See Chapter 7 of this book for Joseph's tenure at the Department of Social Services
12. Seldon to Joseph, 7 August 1970; IEA Archives
13. Seldon to Joseph, 7 February 1972; IEA Archives
14. Howe to Seldon, 7 February 1972; IEA Archives
15. Heath's Private Secretary to Seldon, 6 July 1971; IEA Archives
16. See in particular Peter Wilsner in the *Sunday Times*, 18 July 1971 and the *Daily Telegraph* leader of 19 July 1971
17. Harold Lever writing in the *Financial Times*, 22 July 1971
18. Harris and Sewill, *British Economic Policy 1970–74; Two views* (IEA, 1975), p. 31
19. ibid., p. 30
20. Alan Walters, 'A Life Philosophy' in the *American Economist*, Vol. XXXIII, Fall 1989, Number 2, p. 22
21. Economic Radicals, *Memorial to the Prime Minister*, IEA Library
22. Ridley, *My Style of Government*, p. 5
23. Law to Diana Spearman, 30 May 1973; Coleraine Papers
24. Philip Vander Elst, 'Radical Toryism – The Libertarian Alternative' in *Political Quarterly*, Jan-March 1975. See also Philip Vander Elst's article 'Libertarianism – an alternative' in the *Spectator* of July 1974

25. From the *Selsdon Newsletter*, Nos. 1 and 2; David Alexander Papers (DAP)
26. These and other pamphlets in the papers of David Alexander
27. Russell Lewis's speech to Selsdon Group Seminar, 16 June 1976; DAP
28. For the most recent history of the IMF crisis, see Kathleen Burk and Alec Cairncross, *Goodbye Great Britain* (Yale University Press, 1992)
29. For an exposition of the 'Alternative Strategy', see Tony Benn, *Against the Tide; Diaries, 1973–1976* (Hutchinson, 1989), particularly p. 725 and Chapter 5 in general, 'The death of Consensus'
30. Lord Blake and John Patten (ed.), *The Conservative Opportunity* (Macmillan, 1976), pp. 3 and 12
31. Interview with Shirley Letwin, March 1992
32. ibid.,
33. Interview with Professor Roger Scruton, March 1992
34. *Salisbury Review*, Autumn 1982, p. 2
35. Roger Scruton, *The Meaning of Conservatism* (Penguin, 1980), p. 189
36. See Martin Holmes, *The Labour Governments 1974–79* (Macmillan, 1985), for the best account of the Labour Party's trials and tribulations in power during this period.
37. Norris McWhirter, 'Lord De L'Isle and the founding of the Freedom Association' in *Freedom Today*, August 1991
38. Neil Nugent, 'The National Association for Freedom', Chapter 4 in King and Nugent (ed.), *Respectable Rebels*, p. 84
39. ibid., p. 77
40. ibid., p. 85
41. See Brian Crozier's memoir *Free Agent* (HarperCollins, 1993) for an account of his work for Mrs Thatcher and the details of the 'Shield' Committee that he set up to advise her on domestic subversion during the 1970s.
42. *Sources of Conflict in British Industry* (Institute for the study of Conflict, 1974), p. 26
43. Interview with Brian Crozier, March 1992
44. Paul Johnson, 'Farewell to the Labour Party', *Sunday Telegraph*, 11 September 1977; see also his *The Recovery of Freedom* (Basil Blackwell, 1979)
45. Vaizey to Mrs Thatcher, 27 October 1978; Thatcher File, Vaizey Papers
46. Mrs Thatcher to Vaizey, 27 October 1978; Thatcher File, Vaizey Papers
47. *The Times*, 3 December 1980
48. Sidney Blumenthal, *The Rise of the Counter-Establishment* (*Times* Books, 1986), p. 15. Blumenthal describes a similar intellectual process going on in America during the same period; Irving Kristol was, perhaps, the most important example of such intellectual converts.
49. Mrs Thatcher to Vaizey, 10 March 1980; Thatcher File, Vaizey Papers
50. Morrison Halcrow, *Keith Joseph*, p. 63
51. Sherman, 'Learning to grab ideas by the horns', *Guardian*, 12 September 1988
52. ibid.
53. Interview with Lord Joseph, June 1991
54. *Daily Telegraph*, 29 August and 10 August 1973 respectively
55. Morrison Halcrow, p. 62
56. Mrs Thatcher to Sherman, 20 October 1977; Sherman Personal Papers
57. Ranelagh, *Thatcher's People*, p. 127
58. Interview with Sir Adam Ridley, October 1991
59. Interview with Lord Joseph, June 1991
60. Interview with Lord Vinson, May 1991
61. Webley draft 'Statement of Aims' for CPS, 7 June 1974; Sherman Papers, ARCP/A80/1/2.
62. Memo by Webley, 6 May 1975
63. Sherman memo; Sherman Papers, AR CPS/A80/8/3
64. Sherman's notes on the CPS written for the author, Jan/Feb, 1992
65. Memo by Sherman, 16 May 1980; Sherman Papers AR CPS/LMPC/25

66. Minutes of 1st Meeting of the CPS Board, 12 June 1974; Sherman Papers AR CPS/A80/1/4
67. Interview with Sir Keith Joseph, *Contemporary Record*, Vol. I, No. 1, Spring 1987
68. Sir Keith Joseph, *Reversing the Trend* (CPS, 1975) p. 6
69. ibid., p. 4

CHAPTER SEVEN

1. Sir Keith Joseph letter to *The Economist*, 28 September 1974
2. This and other speeches in Sir Keith Joseph , *Reversing the Trend* (Barry Rose Publishers, 1975)
3. Sherman memo, 9 July 1970; Sherman Papers, AC2/B1–1–3a
4. Joseph, *Stranded on the Middle Ground?* (CPS, 1975); See particularly *The quest for common ground*, pp. 19–34
5. Sir Keith Joseph, *Monetarism Is Not Enough* (CPS, 1975), p. 19
6. Quoted in Anthony Sampson, *Macmillan* (Pelican, 1967), p. 36
7. Eden, *The New Conservatism* (CPC, 1955), pp. 11–12
8. Charles Lovell, *The Redefinition of Conservative Politics and Doctrine* (Macmillan, 1986), p. x
9. Greenleaf, *The Ideological Inheritance* (Methuen, 1983), pp. 193–4
10. Lord Blake, *Conservatism in an Age of Revolution* (Churchill Press, 1976), p. 22
11. Nigel Lawson, *The New Conservatism* (CPS, 1980), pp. 2–3
12. Lord Harris, *The Challenge of a Radical Reactionary* (CPS, 1980)
13. Tibor Szamuely, *Unique Conservative* (CPC, 1973), p. 26
14. David Willetts, *Modern Conservatism* (Penguin, 1992). See also the revealing discussion on this subject in Andrew Gamble's *The Free Economy and the Strong State*, Chapter 6. Philip Vander Elst discusses the same issue in 'Conservatives and Libertarians' in the *Salisbury Review*, September 1991, Vol. 10, No. 1; and for a more recent rehearsal of the arguments see John Gray, *A Conservative disposition; Individualism, the free market and the common life* (CPS, 1991)
15. Sir Keith Joseph 'Conservatives and the Market' in *Reversing the Trend*, p. 70
16. *Why Britain needs a Social Market Economy* (CPS, 1975)
17. Hugh Thomas, *History, Capitalism and Freedom* (CPS, 1976)
18. See Andrew Gamble, p. 151, and Hugo Young, *One of Us*
19. Sir Ian Gilmour's speech to the Cambridge Union, 7 February 1980
20. Memo by Martin Wassall, 23 October 1975; Simon Webley Papers
21. Memo, 11 June 1979; Sherman Papers, AR CPS/CMPC/6
22. *The Times* (leader), 29 May 1978
23. *Evening Standard*, 2 June 1978
24. Zig Layton-Henry (ed.), *Conservative Party Politics* (Macmillan 1980), Chapter One by Chris Patten
25. John Ranelagh, *Thatcher's People* (Fontana, 1991) p. x
26. See Thomas's essay of self-explanation in *Turn to the Right*
27. Kingsley Amis, *An Arts Policy?* (CPS, 1979)
28. Sherman memo to Mrs Thatcher, 2 June 1977; Sherman Papers, ARMT/M/1/2
29. Interview with Lord Young, November 1991; see also Lord Young, *The Enterprise Years*
30. Sherman memo to Joseph, 6 October 1975; Sherman Papers, File 1, Box 19
31. Interview with John Hoskyns, July 1991
32. Hoskyns to Sherman, 3 October 1975; Sherman Papers, File 1, Box 19
33. Joseph to Thatcher, 6 August 1976; Sherman Papers, File 1, Box 19
34. 'The Need for New Data', p. 4; Norman Strauss Papers
35. For instance, see *Is Monetarism Enough?* (IEA, 1980) and also Patrick Minford, *Unemployment, Cause and Cure* (Oxford, 1983)
36. Interview with Dr Elizabeth Cottrell, May 1991

37. Memo on the Labour Party; Sherman Papers, AR/M/MISC 7/1/16
38. Thatcher to Sherman, 11 May 1979; Sherman Papers
39. Interview with Norman Strauss, March 1992; Interview with Sherman, May 1991
40. Thatcher to Sherman, 20 October 1977; Sherman Personal Papers
41. These memos are in Box 6 of the Sherman Papers
42. *Daily Telegraph*, 3 August 1988
43. Sherman, 'Notes on Policy for the Unions and its presentation to Mrs T', 12 August 1978; Sherman Papers, AR MT/5/2/3
44. Sherman memo, 'Our exposed flank; free collective bargaining – October-November 1978', 11 December 1978; Sherman Papers AR MT/5/2/3
45. Interview with Sir Leonard Neal, July 1991. Interview with Sir John Hoskyns, July 1991
46. ibid.
47. Morrison Halcrow, *Keith Joseph*, p. 125
48. 'Stepping Stones'; Sherman Personal Papers
49. Lecture at the London School of Economics, 1 May 1984; Sherman Papers, AC 1322
50. Sherman memo to Joseph, 13 July 1977; Sherman Papers, Ac 89/B1–3–38
51. *Independent*, 17 November 1987
52. David Willetts's speech at the Annual General Meeting of the CPS on 9 April 1987; Sherman Papers, AR/M/MISC 9/4/1
53. Halcrow, p. 104
54. CPS memo on Student Seminar Weekend ; Sherman Papers
55. This quote is reproduced on all SAU publications
56. For examples of SAU's work on the Welfare Sate, see *Breaking the Spell of the Welfare State* (1981). For examples of SAU's work on lifestyle and health issues, see Digby Anderson, *A Diet of Reason* (1986) and *Health, Lifestyle and Environment; Countering the Panic* (1991). On racial issues, see Mervyn Hiskett, *Schooling for British Muslims* and J. G. Davies, *Asian Housing in Britain* (1985)
57. For an account of the work of the Republican Study Committee, see Edward Feulner Jr, *Conservatives Stalk the House* (Green Hill Publishers, 1983)
58. Interview with Edward Feulner, August 1991; for a survey of the American free-market (and other) think-tanks, see James A. Smith, *The Idea Brokers; Think-Tanks and the rise of the new Policy Elite* (The Free Press, 1991). Smith describes the founding and work of the Heritage Foundation on pp. 196–201
59. See Smith, pp. 175–80. For the overall intellectual development of economic liberalism in America since 1945, and its close similarity to the British experience, see George Nash, *The Conservative Intellectual Movement in America* (Basic Books, 1979)
60. See Nash, pp. 145–53, for William Buckley and the founding of the *National Review*
61. See IEA publications for an explanation of 'Public Choice Theory'; *The Economics of Politics* (IEA Readings 18, 1978), Gordon Tulloch, *The Vote Motive* (IEA, 1976) and James M. Buchanan *Constitutional Economics* (IEA/Blackwell, 1990)
62. Desmond King, *The New Right; Politics, Markets and Citizenship* (Macmillan, 1987), p. 12
63. Madsen Pirie, *Micropolitics; The Creation of Successful Policy* (Wildwood House, 1988)
64. Pirie, p. 267
65. Bernard Donoghue, *Prime Minister; The Conduct of Policy under Harold Wilson and James Callaghan* (Jonathan Cape, 1987), p. 190

CHAPTER EIGHT

1. Nicholas Ridley, *My Style of Government; The Thatcher Years* (Century Hutchinson, 1991), p. 25

2. See *The First Hundred* (ASI, 1989), p. 1
3. Michael Crick and Adrian Van Klaveren, 'Mrs Thatcher's Greatest Blunder', in *Contemporary Record*, Vol. 5, No. 3, Winter 1991, p. 407. The article is an excellent account of the origins of the Poll Tax
4. Interview with Nicholas Ridley, May 1991. See also the Government Green Paper proposing the Poll Tax legislation, *Paying for Local Government* (HMSO, 1986), which, in the foreword (p. viii), lists the real authors of the Poll Tax
5. Crick and Van Klaveren, p. 406
6. Ludwig Wittgenstein, *Tractatus Logico-Philosophicus* (Routledge and Kegan Paul, 1978), p. 74, Proposition Six
7. Interview with Lord Young, February 1992
8. Halcrow, *Keith Joseph*, p. 157
9. For Sherman's attitude towards Joseph in government, see Halcrow, p. 157 and especially Sherman's memo to Mrs Thatcher of 14 September 1980
10. Sherman memo on 'Need for Better Economic Advice', 24 April 1980; Sherman Papers, AR MT/M/3/9
11. See Alan Walters's *The Economic Adviser's Role* (CPS, 1981) for his own description of his new job
12. Many of these memos are in Box 8, Folder 3 of the Sherman Papers
13. Policy Unit Paper, 10 June 1980; Sherman Personal Papers
14. 'Report on first XI'; CPS Papers, in possession of Nigel Morgan (CPS)
15. Policy Unit, 'Government Strategy; Paper Number 3', 18 December 1980; Sherman Papers, File 4, Box 19
16. Sherman memo (Undated); Sherman Papers, ARMT/5/1/6
17. Kenneth Harris, *Thatcher* (Weidenfeld and Nicolson, 1988), p. 110. See pp. 109–11 for an account of the budget.
18. Alan Walters, 'My Life Philosophy' in *The American Economist*, Fall 1989, No. 2, p. 23
19. See Geoffrey Howe, 'The 364 Economists; Ten Years On' in *Fiscal Studies*, Vol. 12, No.4, November 1991, p. 98
20. Minutes of Meeting of Board of Directors of CPS, 14 July 1981; Simon Webley Papers
21. Hoskyns's note to Sherman, 4 November 1981; Sherman Papers, File 4, Box 19
22. Interview with Neal, July 1991
23. TURC Meeting, 20 October 1980; Lionel Bloch Papers (*hereafter*: Bloch Papers)
24. Prior to Thomas, 4 December 1980; Bloch Papers
25. Neal to Mrs Thatcher, 10 May 1980; Bloch Papers
26. TURC Meeting, 5 February 1981; Bloch Papers
27. Norman Tebbit, letter to the author, March 1992
28. Interview with Lord Vinson, June 1991
29. Prior to Vinson, 20 March 1983; in the possession of Lord Vinson
30. Minutes of Meeting of Nationalised Industry Study Group (NISG), 8 February 1980; Simon Webley Papers
31. Minutes of NISG, 4 November 1981; Webley Papers
32. John Moore speaking at NISG meeting on 6 February 1985; Webley Papers
33. Interview with John Redwood, March 1992; see also Cento Veljanovski, *Selling the State: Privatisation in Britain* (Weidenfeld and Nicolson, 1987) and Redwood and Hatch, *Controlling Public Industries* (Basil Blackwell, 1982)
34. Interview with Madsen Pirie, July 1991
35. Richard Howell (ed.), *The First Year* (Heritage Foundation, 1981)
36. Interview with Dr Butler, October 1991
37. For a full list of those involved in the OMEGA Project, see Butler, Pirie, Young (ed.), *The OMEGA File* (ASI, 1985)
38. For a profile of Portillo and his 'right-wing credentials' established on the OMEGA Project, see, for instance, *Sunday Times*, 6 May 1990

39. Interview with John Blundell, September 1991
40. Fisher to Smedley, 16 January 1984; Smedley Papers
41. For a CPS/IEA view of the rejection of the Vouchers Scheme, see Arthur Seldon, *The Riddle of the Voucher* (IEA, 1986)
42. Arthur Seldon to Sir Keith Joseph, 14 September 1981; IEA Papers
43. Jenkin to Dr Buxton, 4 August 1981; Health Study Group File, Box 11, Sherman Papers
44. Minutes of Health Study Group, 5 November 1979; Sherman Papers, Box 11, File 1
45. Hoskyns Minute for Health Study Group meeting of 18 December 1980; Sherman Papers, Box 11
46. Hoskyns to Sherman, 2 June 1981; Sherman Papers, File 4, Box 19
47. Norman Strauss, 'Reform of the Civil Service', 2 June 1981; Sherman Papers, File 4, Box 19
48. Interview with Sir John Hoskyns, July 1991
49. Westwell Report, p. 1; CPS Papers
50. Westwell Report, p. 74; CPS Papers
51. See Peter Hennessy, *Whitehall* (Secker and Warburg, 1989) pp. 638–43, for a discussion of the Hoskyns/Strauss analysis and the Whitehall response
52. Interview with Sir John Hoskyns, July 1991
53. Hoskyns to Sherman, 12 December 1980; Sherman Papers, File 4, Box 19
54. See, for instance, John Hoskyns 'Needed Now: A Tory National Plan' in *The Times*, 9 October 1984, and Norman Strauss, 'Civil Servants must catch up with modern times' in the *Daily Telegraph*, 4 August 1988
55. Quotations and figures from Nicholas Ridley, *My Style of Government*, pp. 84–5
56. See 'Stop-Go Monetarism', *Observer*, 21 November 1982; for other such articles by Sherman, see 'Keynes at crunch point', *Daily Telegraph*, 19 November 1980, and 'Confessions of a man of ideas fallen among party politicians', *Guardian*, 29 June 1981
57. Interview with David Wolfson, July 1991
58. Thomas to Sherman, 3 October 1983; Sherman Papers AR CPS/LMPC/148.2
59. Sherman Memo on 'Preconditions for Sherman to work at the centre', Autumn 1983; Sherman Papers, AR CPS/A 80/7/6
60. Sherman to David Wolfson, 17 August 1983; Sherman Papers AR/M/Misc 7/1/15
61. Interview with Lionel Bloch, August 1991
62. Interview with Christopher Monckton, March 1992
63. Interview with Sherman, May 1991
64. Interview with Sherman, June 1992

EPILOGUE

1. Bertrand de Jouvenel, *Problems of Socialist England* (Batchworth Press, 1949), p. 41
2. Samuel Brittan, 'Why unemployment is still an enigma', *Financial Times*, 24 February 1972
3. Francis Fukuyama, *The End of History and the Last Man* (Penguin, 1992), p. xi

Sources

A. PRIVATE PAPERS AND ARCHIVES

Lionel Bloch Papers (Bloch Papers)
—In the possession of Lionel Bloch
Lord Coleraine Papers (Coleraine Papers)
—In the possession of Lord Coleraine
Centre for Policy Studies Papers (CPS Papers)
—In the possession of Nigel Morgan
Lord Clitheroe Papers (Clith Mss.)
—In the possession of Lord Clitheroe
Conservative Party Archives (CPA)
—Bodleian Library, Oxford
Friedman Papers
—Hoover Institute, San Francisco, America
Institute of Economic Affairs Archive (IEA Archive)
— In the possession of Mrs Linda Whetstone
Mont Pèlerin Society Archives (MPSA)
—Hoover Institute
Karl Popper Archive (PA)
—Hoover Institute
Routledge and Kegan Paul Papers (RKPP)
—Reading University Archives
Sherman Papers (Sherman Papers)
—Royal Holloway College, University of London
Oliver Smedley Papers (SP)
—In the possession of Charles Smedley
Norman Strauss Papers
—In the possession of Norman Strauss
Simon Webley Papers
—In the possession of Simon Webley
Sir Antony Fisher Private Papers (FPP)
—In the possession of Mrs Linda Whetstone

B. INTERVIEWS

Andrew Alexander
David Alexander
Dr Digby Anderson
Nigel Ashford
John Barnes
Lord Bauer
Tony Benn MP
Lord Beloff
Rt Hon. John Biffen MP
Lionel Bloch
John Blundell
Dr. Eamonn Butler
Dr Stuart Butler
W. Glenn Campbell
Mrs Merrie Cave
David Clarke
Dr Elizabeth Cottrell
Baroness Cox
Peter Cropper
Brian Crozier
Professor Aaron Director
Timothy Evans
Ed Feulner Jr
Alastair Forbes
Professor Milton Friedman
Gerald Frost
Dr Edmund Golberger
Lord Grimond
Lord Harris of High Cross
Gerald Hartup
Professor Max Hartwell
Sir John Hoskyns
Lord Houghton of Sowerby
Lord Howe of Aberavon
Rt Hon. David Howell MP
Michael Ivens
Peter Jay
Lord Joseph
Dr Shirley Robin Letwin
Dr William Letwin
Russell Lewis
John Marshall MP
Graham Mather
Professor Patrick Minford
Christopher Monckton
Chris De Mooth
Nigel Morgan
Sir Leonard Neal

John O'Sullivan
Dr Madsen Pirie
Rt Hon. J. Enoch Powell
John Redwood MP
Lord Rees-Mogg
Sir Adam Ridley
Rt Hon. Nicholas Ridley MP
Arthur Seldon
Marjorie Seldon
Sir Alfred Sherman
Charles Smedley
Norman Strauss
Chris Tame
Philip Vander Elst
Lord Vinson
Professor Sir Alan Walters
Dr George Watson
Simon Webley
Linda Whetstone
David Willetts MP
David Wolfson
John B. Wood

Bibliography

This is not a comprehensive list, but only those publications which I found most useful. Other works are referred to in the footnotes and references. All titles cited were published in the United Kingdom, unless otherwise stated.

A. PRIMARY BOOKS AND PAMPHLETS

John Baker-White – *True Blue* (Muller, 1970)

Peter Bauer and Basil Yamey – *Markets, Market Control and Market Reform* (Weidenfeld and Nicolson, 1968)

Julien Benda – *The Great Betrayal* (Routledge, 1928)

Ernest Benn – *Confessions of a Capitalist* (Hutchinson, 1925)

Ernest Benn – *Account Rendered* (Benn, 1930)

Ernest Benn – *Happier Days; Recollections and Reflections* (Benn, 1949)

Robert Blake (ed.) – *The Conservative Opportunity* (Macmillan, 1976)

Robert Blake – *Conservatism in an Age of Revolution* (Churchill Press, 1976)

Lord Coleraine – *For Conservatives Only* (Tom Stacey Ltd, 1970)

Evan Durbin – *Problems of Economic Planning* (Routledge and Kegan Paul, 1949)

Milton Friedman – *Capitalism and Freedom* (University of Chicago Press, 1962)

Milton Friedman – *The Counter-Revolution in Monetary Theory* (IEA, 1970)

Milton Friedman – *Free to Choose* (Secker and Warburg, 1980)

Ian Gilmour – *Inside Right. Conservatism, Policies and People* (Hutchinson, 1977)

Ralph Harris and Brendan Sewill – *British Economic Policy, 1970–74: Two Views* (IEA, 1975)

F. A. Hayek – *Collectivist Economic Planning* (Routledge, 1935)

F. A. Hayek – *The Road to Serfdom* (Routledge, 1944)

F. A. Hayek – *Individualism and Economic Order* (Routledge and Kegan Paul, 1949)

F. A. Hayek – *The Constitution of Liberty* (Chicago University Press, 1960)

F. A. Hayek – *Studies in Philosophy, Politics and Economics* (Routledge, 1967)

F. A. Hayek – *A Tiger by the Tail* (IEA, 1972)

Henry Hazlitt – *Economics in One Lesson* (Ernest Benn Ltd, 1947)

Henry Hazlitt – *The Failure of the New Economics – An Analysis of the Keynesian Fallacies* (D. Van Nostrand Company Inc, 1959)

Henry Hazlitt (ed.) – *The Critics of Keynesian Economics* (Van Nostrand, 1960)
Hubert Henderson – *The Uses and Abuses of Economic Planning* (Cambridge University Press, 1947)
Hubert Henderson – *The Inter-War Years and Other Papers* (Oxford University Press, 1955)
F. W. Hirst – *Economic Freedom and Private Property* (Duckworth, 1935)
F. W. Hirst – *Liberty and Tyranny* (Duckworth, 1935)
F. W. Hirst – *Principles of Prosperity* (Hollis and Carter, 1944)
Graham Hutton – *All Capitalists Now* (IEA, 1960)
Graham Hutton – *We Too Can Prosper. The promise of productivity* (George Allen and Unwin, 1960)
Douglas Jay – *The Socialist Case* (Faber and Faber, 1937)
Peter Jay – *The Crisis for Western Political Economy and Other Essays* (André Deutsch, 1984)
John Jewkes – *Ordeal by Planning* (Macmillan, 1948)
John Jewkes – *Public and Private Enterprise* (Routledge, 1965)
John Jewkes – *The New Ordeal by Planning* (Macmillan, 1968)
Bertrand de Jouvenel – *Problems of Socialist England* (London, 1949)
J. M. Keynes – *A Treatise on Money* (Macmillan, 1930)
J. M. Keynes – *Essays in Persuasion* (Macmillan, 1931)
J. M. Keynes – *The General Theory of Employment, Interest and Money* (Macmillan, 1936)
J. M. Keynes – *The Collective Writings of John Maynard Keynes*, eds. D. E. Moggridge and Sir Austin Robinson (Macmillan, 1971–89); Vols. XIII, XXVII and XXXV are of especial interest
Harold Laski – *The Decline of Liberalism* (Oxford University Press, 1940)
Richard Law – *Return from Utopia* (Faber, 1950)
Walter Lippmann – *The Good Society* (George Allen, 1937)
E. Lipson – *A Planned Economy or Free Enterprise* (A and C Black, 1944)
K. Martin – *Harold Laski, A Biographical Memoir* (Gollancz, 1953)
R. B. McCallum and Alison Readman – *The British General Election of 1945* (Oxford University Press, 1947)
Patrick Minford – *Is Monetarism Enough ?* (IEA, 1980)
Patrick Minford – *Unemployment, Cause and Cure* (Oxford University Press, 1983)
Ludwig von Mises – *Socialism; An Economic and Sociological Analysis* (Jonathan Cape, 1936)
Ludwig von Mises – *Bureaucracy* (Yale University Press, 1944)
Ludwig von Mises – *Human Action – A Treatise on Economics* (William Hodge, 1949)
Ludwig von Mises – *Omnipotent Government* (Yale University Press, 1944)
H. G. Nicholas – *Washington Despatches (1941–45)* (Weidenfeld and Nicolson, 1981)

James Nisbitt – *A Case for Laissez-Faire* (P. S. King and Son, 1929)
James Nisbitt – *Britain's Economic Resources* (Oliver and Boyd, 1941)
James Nisbitt (ed.) – *Britain and Social Security; an Appraisal of the Beveridge Plan* (1943)
Michael Oakeshott – *Rationalism in politics and other essays* (Liberty Press, 1991)
Jose Ortega y Gasset – *The Revolt of the Masses* (George Allen and Unwin, 1932)
Alan Peacock and Jack Wiseman – *Education for Democrats: A Study of the financing of Education in a free Society* (IEA, 1964)
Alan Peacock and Jack Wiseman – *The Growth of Public Expenditure in the U.K.* (George Allen and Unwin, 1967)
Karl Popper – *The Open Society and Its Enemies* (2 vols; Routledge, 1952)
Karl Popper – *The Poverty of Historicism* (Routledge, 1957)
Karl Popper – *The Logic of Scientific Discovery* (Hutchinson, 1959)
Enoch Powell – *A Nation Not Afraid: The Thinking of Enoch Powell*, ed. J. Wood (London, 1965)
Enoch Powell – *Freedom and Reality* (Batsford, 1969)
Enoch Powell – *Still to Decide* (Batsford, 1972)
Leonard Read – *The Free Market and its Economy* (FEE, 1965)
Lionel Robbins – *The Great Depression* (Macmillan, 1934)
Lionel Robbins – *Economic Planning and International Order* (Macmillan, 1937)
Lionel Robbins – *Politics and Economics; Papers in Political Economy* (Macmillan, 1963)
Lionel Robbins – *Autobiography of an Economist* (Macmillan, 1971)
Lionel Robbins – *Liberty and Equality* (IEA, 1977)
Lionel Robbins – *An Essay on the Nature and Significance of Economic Science* (Macmillan, 1984)
Louise Rougier – *Les Mystiques economiques* (Paris: L'Institut Universitaire des Hautes Etudes Internationales, 1938)
Louise Rougier – *Les Mystiques politiques contemporaines et leurs incidences internationales* (Paris, 1937)
Jacques Rueff – *L'Ordre social* (Paris, 1949)
Jacques Rueff (ed.) – *Inflation et ordre monetaire international* (Publications de L'Institut Universitaire de Hautes Etudes Internationales, 1953)
Jacques Rueff – *L'Age de l'inflation* (Paris, 1963)
Wilhem Röpke – *'Civitas Humana': A Humane Order of Society* (William Hodge, 1948)
Wilhem Röpke – *Welfare, Freedom and Inflation* (Pall Mall Press, 1957)
Wilhem Röpke – *A Humane Economy: The Social Framework of The Free Economy* (Henry Regnery Company, Chicago, 1960)
George Schwartz – *Why Planning?* (The Signpost Press, 1944)
Arthur Seldon – *Capitalism* (Blackwell, 1990)

Hugh Thomas (ed.) – *The Establishment* (Anthony Blond, 1959)
Alan Walters – *Money in Boom and Slump* (IEA, 1969)
Alan Walters – *Economists and the British Economy* (IEA, 1978)

B. SECONDARY LITERATURE

Deryck Abel – *Ernest Benn; Counsel for Liberty* (Ernest Benn, 1960)
Leo Abse – *My LSE* (Falmer Press, 1977)
Paul Addison – *The Road to 1945* (Cape, 1975)
Norman Barry – *Hayek's Social and Economic Philosophy* (Macmillan, 1979)
Norman Barry (ed.) – *The Road to Serfdom: Forty Years On* (IEA, 1984)
Norman Barry – *On Classical Liberalism and Libertarianism* (Macmillan, 1986)
Norman Barry – *The New Right* (Croom Helm, 1987)
Vernon Bogdanor – *Liberal Party Politics* (Clarendon Press, 1983)
Nicholas Bosanquet – *After the New Right* (Heinemann, 1983)
Samuel Brittan – *A Restatement of Economic Liberalism* (Macmillan, 1988)
Samuel Brittan – *The Role and Limits of Government; Essays in Political Economy* (Temple Smith, 1984)
K. D. Brown (ed.) – *Essays in Anti-Labour History* (Macmillan, 1974)
Jock Bruce-Gardyne – *Whatever Happened to the Quiet Revolution?: The story of a brave experiment in government* (Charles Knight and Co., 1974)
Alec Cairncross and N. Watts – *The Economic Section, 1939–61: A Study in Economic Advising* (Routledge, 1989)
John Campbell – *Edward Heath* (Hutchinson, 1993)
Christian Ceplecha – *The Historical thought of Jose Ortega y Gasset* (Catholic University of America Press, 1958)
Peter Clarke – *The New Enlightenment: The Rebirth of Liberalism* (Macmillan, 1986)
Peter Clarke – *The Keynesian Revolution in the Making* (Clarendon Press, 1988)
Richard Cockett – *My Dear Max: The Correspondence of Lord Beaverbrook and Brendan Bracken* (The Historian's Press, 1990)
Patrick Cosgrave – *The Lives of Enoch Powell* (Bodley Head, 1989)
Stanley Dennison and John Presley – *Robertson on Economic Policy* (St. Martin's Press, 1992)
Bernard Donoghue – *Prime Minister; The Conduct of Policy under Harold Wilson and James Callaghan* (Cape, 1987)
Elizabeth Durbin – *New Jerusalemers: The Labour Party and The Economics of Democratic Socialism* (Routledge and Kegan Paul, 1985)
Walter Eltis and Robert Bacon – *Too Few Producers* (Macmillan, 1977)
Andrew Gamble – *The Conservative Nation* (Routledge and Kegan Paul, 1974)
Andrew Gamble – *The Free Economy and The Strong State: The Politics of Thatcherism* (Macmillan, 1988)

Martin Gilbert – *Winston S. Churchill: The Road to Victory, 1941–45* (Heinemann, 1986)
John Gray – *Liberalism* (Open University Press, 1980)
John Gray – *Hayek on Liberty* (Basil Blackwell, 1984)
W. H. Greenleaf – *The British Political Tradition Vol. I: The Rise of Collectivism; Vol. II : The Ideological Inheritance* (Methuen, 1983)
G. C. Harcourt (ed.) – *Keynes and his Contemporaries* (Macmillan, 1985)
José Harris – *William Beveridge, A Biography* (Clarendon Press, 1977)
José Harris – *Unemployment and Politics; A Study in English Social Policy, 1886–1914* (Clarendon, 1972)
José Harris – 'Political ideas and the debate on State Welfare, 1940–45', in H. L. Smith (ed.), *War and Social Change* (Manchester University Press, 1987)
Kenneth Harris – *Thatcher* (Weidenfeld and Nicolson, 1988)
Nigel Harris – *Competition and The Corporate Society. British Conservatives, The State and Industry, 1945–64* (Methuen, 1922)
Peter Hennessy – *Whitehall* (Secker and Warburg, 1989)
J. D. Hoffman – *The Conservative Party in Opposition 1945–51* (MacGibbon and Kee, 1964)
Martin Holmes – *Political Pressure and Economic Policy: British Government 1970–74* (Butterworth, 1982)
Martin Holmes – *The First Thatcher Governments, 1979–83* (Wheatsheaf, 1985)
Martin Holmes – *The Labour Governments, 1974–79; political aims and economic reality* (Macmillan, 1985)
Martin Holmes – *Thatcherism; Scope and Limits, 1983–1987* (Macmillan, 1987)
Susan Howson and D. E. Moggridge (eds) – *The Collected Papers of James Meade IV, The Cabinet Office Diary, 1944–46* (Unwin Hyman, 1990)
Susan Howson and D. E. Moggridge (eds) – *The Wartime Diaries of Lionel Robbins and James Meade, 1943–45* (Macmillan, 1990)
J. W. Hutchinson – *Keynes versus the Keynesians* (IEA, 1977)
Michael Ivens and Reginald Dunstan (eds) – *The Case for Capitalism* (Michael Joseph, 1967)
Kevin Jefferys – *The Churchill Coalition and Wartime Politics, 1940–45* (Manchester University Press, 1991)
Barry D. Karl – *Charles E. Merrian and The Study of Politics* (Chicago, 1974)
Dennis Kavanagh – *Thatcherism and British Politics: The End of Consensus?* (Oxford University Press, 1987)
Desmond King – *The New Right; Politics, Markets and Citizenship* (Macmillan, 1987)
Roger King and Neil Nugent (eds) – *Respectable Rebels: Middle Class Campaigns in Britain in the 1970s* (Hodder and Stoughton, 1979)

Christopher Knight – *The Making of Tory Education Policy in Post War Britain, 1950–1986* (Falmer, 1990)
Zig Layton-Henry (ed.) – *Conservative Party Politics* (Macmillan, 1980)
A. Leijonhufund – *Keynes and The Classics* (IEA, 1969)
Shirley Robin Letwin – *The Anatomy of Thatcherism* (Fontana Press, 1992)
A. M. McBriar – *Fabian Socialism and English Politics, 1884–1914* (Cambridge, 1966)
Keith Middlemas – *Power, Competition and the State, Vol. I: Britain in search of Balance, 1940–61* (Macmillan, 1986)
Kenneth Minogue and Anthony De Crespigny – *Contemporary Political Philosophers* (Methuen, 1976)
D. E. Moggridge – *Maynard Keynes; An Economist's Biography* (Routledge, 1992)
D. E. Moggridge – *Keynes* (Macmillan, 1980)
D. P. O'Brien – *Lionel Robbins* (Macmillan, 1988)
Madsen Pirie – *Micropolitics; The Creation of Successful Policy* (Wildwood House, 1988)
John Presley and D. P. O'Brien – *Pioneers of Modern Economics in Britain* (Macmillan, 1981)
John Presley – *Robertsonian Economics* (Macmillan, 1984)
John Ramsden – *The Making of Conservative Party Policy* (Longman, 1980)
Nicholas Ridley – *My Style of Government* (Hutchinson, 1991)
Roger Scruton – *The Meaning of Conservatism* (Penguin, 1980)
Anthony Seldon – *Churchill's Indian Summer. The Conservative Government, 1951–55* (Hodder and Stoughton, 1981)
Anthony Seldon and Stuart Ball (eds) – *The Conservative Party during the Twentieth Century* (Oxford University Press, 1994)
Arthur Seldon (ed.) – *Inflation; Causes, Consequences, Cures* (IEA, 1978)
Mary Senuholz (ed.) – *'On Freedom and Enterprise'. Essays in honour of Ludwig von Mises* (D. Van Nostrand Company)
Robert Skidelsky – *Politicians and the Slump* (Macmillan, 1967)
Robert Skidelsky – *John Maynard Keynes; Hopes Betrayed, 1883–1920* (Macmillan, 1983)
Robert Skidelsky – *John Maynard Keynes; The Economist as Saviour, 1920–1937* (Macmillan, 1992)
David Smith – *The Rise and Fall of Monetarism* (Penguin, 1987)
Erich Streissler (ed.) – *Roads to Freedom: Essays in honour of Friedrich A. Von Hayek* (Routledge and Kegan Paul, 1969)
Jim Tomlinson – *Employment Policy – The Crucial Years 1939–55* (Clarendon Press, 1987)
Cento Veljanovski – *Selling the State: Privatisation in Britain* (Weidenfeld and Nicolson, 1988)
David Willetts – *Modern Conservatism* (Penguin, 1992)

C. ARTICLES

T. Balogh – Review of *Road to Serfdom*, *Political Quarterly*, Vol. XV, No. 3, 1944

A. Booth – 'The "Keynesian Revolution" in Economic Policy-Making', *Economic History Review*, 2nd Ser, XXXVI, 1983

E. J. Bristow – 'The Liberty and Property Defence League and Individualism', *Historical Journal*, XVIII, 1975

Colin Clark – 'Public Finance and Changes in the Value of Money', *Economic Journal*, Vol. 55, 1945

Peter Clarke – 'The Treasury's analytical model of the British economy between the Wars', in Furner and Supple (eds), *The State and Economic Knowledge; the American and British Experiences* (Cambridge University Press, 1990)

Peter Clarke – 'Churchill's Economic Ideas, 1900–1930', in Blake and Louis (eds), *Churchill – A Major New Assessment of his Life in Peace and War* (Oxford University Press, 1993)

José Harris – 'Political thought and the Welfare State 1870–1914: An Intellectual Framework for British Social Policy', *Past and Present*, 135, 1992

F. A. Hayek – 'The London School of Economics', *Economica*, Feb. 1946

F. A. Hayek – 'The Trend of Economic Thinking', *Economica*, 33, Vol. 13

Kevin Jefferys – 'British Politics and Social Policy during the Second World War', *Historical Journal*, 30, 1, 1987

John Jewkes – 'Is British Industry Inefficient?', *The Manchester School*, Vol. XIV, Jan. 1946

G. C. Peden – 'Sir Richard Hopkins and the "Keynesian Revolution" in Employment Policy, 1929 – 45', *Economic History Review*, 2nd Ser, XXXVI, May 1983

G. C. Peden – 'The "Treasury View" on Public Works and Unemployment in the Interwar Period', *Economic History Review*, 2nd Ser, XXVII, May 1984

John Ramsden – 'A Party for Owners or a Party for Earners? How far did the Conservative Party Really Change after 1945?', *Transactions of the Royal Historical Society*, 5th Ser, 37, 1987

Philip Vander Elst – 'Libertarianism – An Alternative', *Spectator*, July 1974

Philip Vander Elst – 'Radical Toryism; the Libertarian Alternative', *Political Quarterly*, Jan.–March 1975

D. UNPUBLISHED DOCTORAL THESES AND MISCELLANY

S. W. Alexander – unpublished *Autobiography* (in the possession of Andrew Alexander)

Simon Burgess – *The Attlee Governments in Perspective – Commitment and detachment in the writing of contemporary history* (London University Ph.D., 1992)

J. H. Dunn – *The New Right in Britain* (Reading University Ph.D., 1985)

Max Hartwell – unpublished *History of the Mont Pèlerin Society*

Harriet Jones – *The Conservative Party and the Welfare State, 1942–1955* (London University Ph.D., 1992)

Hartmut Kopsch – *The Approach of the Conservative Party to Social Policy during the Second World War* (London University Ph.D., 1970)

John Raybould – *Hayek: A Tribute*, an audio-visual presentation produced for the Mont Pèlerin Society meeting in Vancouver, Canada, and organized by the Fraser Institute (videocassette published by the Adam Smith Institute and the Atlas Economic Research Foundation, 1993)

INDEX

(ASI = Adam Smith Institute, CPS = Centre for Policy Studies, CWP = Le Colloque Walter Lippmann, IEA = Institute of Economic Affairs, MPS = Mont Pèrelin Society, EAC = Economic Advisory Council, LSE = London School of Economics, NAFF = National Association for Freedom)

Index

s